D1599422

The Global Refuge

The Global Refuge

Huguenots in an Age of Empire

OWEN STANWOOD

OXFORD
UNIVERSITY PRESS

OXFORD
UNIVERSITY PRESS

Oxford University Press is a department of the University of Oxford. It furthers
the University's objective of excellence in research, scholarship, and education
by publishing worldwide. Oxford is a registered trade mark of Oxford University
Press in the UK and certain other countries.

Published in the United States of America by Oxford University Press
198 Madison Avenue, New York, NY 10016, United States of America.

© Oxford University Press 2020

CIP data is on file at the Library of Congress
ISBN 978-0-19-026474-1

1 3 5 7 9 8 6 4 2

Printed by Integrated Books International, United States of America

For JZ

CONTENTS

ACKNOWLEDGMENTS

This book exists because I wanted to go to Switzerland. In early 2010 Phil Benedict invited me to a swanky, weeklong conference at a former utopian colony overlooking a lake in the Swiss-Italian Alps. My charge was to talk about Huguenots and the Whig historical tradition—something I knew almost nothing about. But I longed to spend that week in the mountains, and the conference convinced me that the global story of the Huguenot Refuge was a tale worth telling. I am grateful to Phil for inviting me and then providing encouragement as I started this project, and to all of the participants at that conference for their inspiration. It ended up being the start of a long journey that took me around the world in search of the traces of refugees. It was difficult at times, but extremely rewarding, thanks to the many friends, acquaintances, and strangers who helped along the way.

Like the Huguenots who counted on states, churches, and companies for assistance, I also depended on institutions. The first and most important was the John Carter Brown Library, which offered me a fellowship where I read widely in political economy and developed what eventually became the argument of this book. The JCB has welcomed me back many times since and become my intellectual home, and I must thank Neil Safier and all the staff there for their support, as well as the fellows in the fall of 2011 for their inspiration. In particular, I got to know Alexandre Dubé, who has taught me more about the French Atlantic world than almost anyone. After leaving the JCB I set out for the United Kingdom, where a Newberry Library/British Academy grant and an Eccles Visiting Professorship at the British Library allowed me to complete much of the primary research for the book. These grants also got me close enough to continental Europe to make a number of research trips. I am grateful to many librarians and archivists around the continent, from Zurich to The Hague to Aix-en-Provence, who welcomed a clueless American into their reading rooms. Without their heroic efforts to preserve these materials, this book would not exist—nor would any historical scholarship. Finally, I must acknowledge all the old and new friends who kept me company on my travels, above all Karen O'Brien and James Jones in London, who opened their home to me so many times and made that city not just more affordable but also much more enjoyable.

Closer to home, I benefited greatly from the intellectual community at Boston College and in the greater New England area. The Morrissey College of Arts and Sciences and the Clough Center for Constitutional Studies at BC supported numerous research trips, including a phenomenal weeklong journey to South Africa, where Jaco Van Der Merwe showed me around the Western Cape Archives. My colleagues in the History Department always supported my endeavors, in particular Ginny Reinburg, Thomas Dodman, and Kevin Kenny. Nonetheless, it is above all my students who have made BC such an engaging place. I am especially grateful to my former and current doctoral students, several of whom served as research assistants for this project and all of whom asked tough questions and shared their perspectives—Jared Hardesty, Craig Gallagher, John Morton, Michael Bailey, and Daniel Crown. Marie Pellissier, who is now an early Americanist in her own right, also provided invaluable research assistance.

Slightly farther down the road, the School of Historical Studies at the Institute for Advanced Study gave me a fellowship at just the right time to start putting my thoughts on to the page. Spending a year at the institute was as close to being in Eden as a scholar could imagine. I am grateful to everyone there, but especially Jonathan Israel, for welcoming me, and to my fellow early modernist members, especially Adam Beaver, Nicole Reinhardt, and Marco Barducci, for their excellent camaraderie. In addition, I have to acknowledge all the creatures of the institute woods—deer, frogs, turtles of all sorts, groundhogs, and above all the great horned owls—for providing companionship as I wandered through the forest contemplating early modern religious history.

It takes far more than a village to write a global history, as I was constantly coming to the limits of my own historical knowledge. I called on numerous people for advice, and many others shared research tips, sources, and their own knowledge on the many people and places mentioned in this book. I am grateful to all my old friends and mentors who continue to support me, especially Tim Breen, Max Edelson, Alison Games, Karl Gunther, Evan Haefeli, Chris Hodson, Mark Peterson, Dan Richter, Brett Rushforth, Phil Stern, and Scott Sowerby. Beyond this old cadre I made many new friends while working on this project, especially at the many conferences, seminars, and lectures where I shared my work. Many of them shared their wisdom, in particular David Bell, Catherine Brekus, Jon Butler, Kate Carte, Leslie Choquette, Linda Colley, Brian Cowan, Natalie Zemon Davis, Allan Greer, François Furstenberg, Katharine Gerbner,

Jessica Harland-Jacobs, Lauric Henneton, Eric Hinderaker, Wim Klooster, Peter Mancall, Ben Marsh, Laura Mitchell, Andy Murphy, Elodie Peyrol, Jenny Hale Pulsipher, Dana Rabin, Mark Valeri, Michiel van Groesen, and Grant Tapsell. For a project like this I must also thank my language teachers: Wijnie de Groot and Frans Blom tried, and sort of succeeded, in teaching me early modern Dutch, while Silvia Calligaro immensely improved my French.

As I discovered in the mountains of Switzerland, the world of Huguenot history is vast, fascinating, and somewhat intimidating. I am grateful to other scholars of le Refuge for welcoming me into the camp. Many scholars influenced me with their scholarship and encouraged me in conversation and correspond-ence, including Mickaël Augeron, Phil Benedict, Hubert Bost, Paula Carlo, Pieter Coertzen, Hugues Daussy, Michael Green, Neil Kamil, Carolyn Chappell Lougee, Ray Mentzer, Ruth Whelan, and the late Myriam Yardeni. But two scholars really made this book possible. Susanne Lachenicht inspired me with her knowledge and erudition, provided extensive comments on my work, and encouraged me to move forward even at times when I was not sure of my own contributions. Bertrand Van Ruymbeke, the great historian of the Atlantic Refuge, became not just a reader and critic of my work but a collaborator and a friend. He has read most of the manuscript and offered innumerable suggestions, but more than that, he has convinced me that I am doing something worthwhile and important.

Finally, there is PEAG (the Providence Early American Group), my phenom-enal writing and drinking cohort—Ted Andrews, Charlotte Carrington-Farmer, Lin Fisher, and Adrian Weimer. These brave souls read the whole manuscript as well as drafts of many of its individual chapters, and did heroic labors in helping me hone my argument and, even more importantly, settle on a title. I could not ask for a more brilliant or supportive group of readers, whose complementary talents have made this book so much better.

I published portions of my research in a number of places—the American Historical Review; French Historical Studies; and in several edited volumes. I am grateful to the editors and anonymous readers at all those journals, especially Rob Schneider and Pat Griffin, for their counsel. In addition, Susan Ferber at Oxford University Press believed in this project from the outset and made exten-sive comments on the manuscript itself. I am grateful for her support, as well as the suggestions from a number of anonymous outside readers.

As the protagonists of this book surely knew, a long and uncertain journey is made much better by good traveling companions. My parents Leslie and Patricia Stanwood dragged me around Europe for the first time when I was four years old, giving me the curiosity about places, people, and travel that ultimately inspired this book about European travelers. Simon Stanwood-Halpin has grown up with this project, and has become not just a great conversationalist about history and other things, but also my companion on all sorts of adventures. Finally, Jennifer Zartarian willingly followed me around the world in search of Huguenots, from the Luberon Valley of Provence to dusty back roads in South Carolina. Having her along for the journey has made all the difference.

The Global Refuge

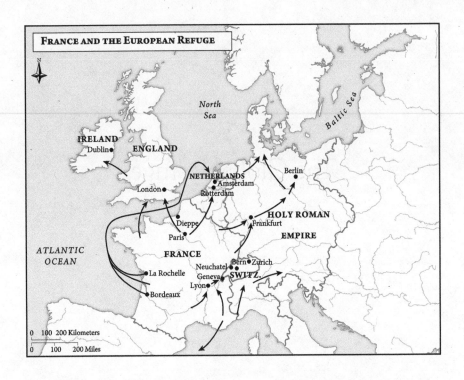

FRANCE AND THE EUROPEAN REFUGE

North Sea

Baltic Sea

IRELAND
• Dublin

ENGLAND

London •

ATLANTIC OCEAN

• Dieppe

Paris •

FRANCE

• La Rochelle

• Bordeaux

NETHERLANDS
• Amsterdam
• Rotterdam

• Berlin

HOLY ROMAN
Frankfurt •

EMPIRE

Neuchatel •
Geneva •   Bern • Zurich
Lyon •   SWITZ.

0 100 200 Kilometers
0 100   200 Miles

THE NORTH AMERICAN REFUGE

NEWFOUNDLAND
• Placentia

ACADIA
NOVA SCOTIA
• Halifax
★ Lunenberg

• Quebec
Montreal •

NEW
ENGLAND

Oxford ★ ★ Boston
New Paltz ★ ★ Providence
New Rochelle ★ Narragansett
PENNSYLVANIA • ★ New York
• Philadelphia

NEW FRANCE

VIRGINIA
★
Manakintown

NORTH
CAROLINA

SOUTH
CAROLINA ★
New Bordeaux ★   ★ Santee
Purrysburgh ★ ★ Orange Quarter
GEORGIA Savannah •

ATLANTIC OCEAN

LOUISIANA
Mobile • ★
New Orleans • Pensacola

• Saint Augustine

FLORIDA

NEW
SPAIN

Gulf of Mexico

British colonies
French colonies
Spanish colonies
★ Center of Huguenot Settlement

0 200 400 Kilometers
0   200   400 Miles

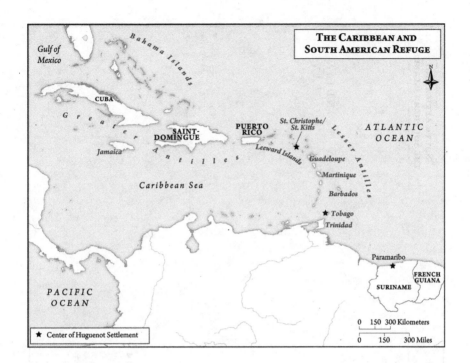

THE CARIBBEAN AND
SOUTH AMERICAN REFUGE

Gulf of
Mexico

Bahama Islands

CUBA

Greater

SAINT-
DOMINGUE

PUERTO
RICO

St. Christophe/
St. Kitts

ATLANTIC
OCEAN

Leeward Islands

Antilles

Jamaica

Guadeloupe

Lesser Antilles

Caribbean Sea

Martinique

Barbados

Tobago
Trinidad

Paramaribo

FRENCH
GUIANA

PACIFIC
OCEAN

SURINAME

N

0   150   300 Kilometers

0   150   300 Miles

★ Center of Huguenot Settlement

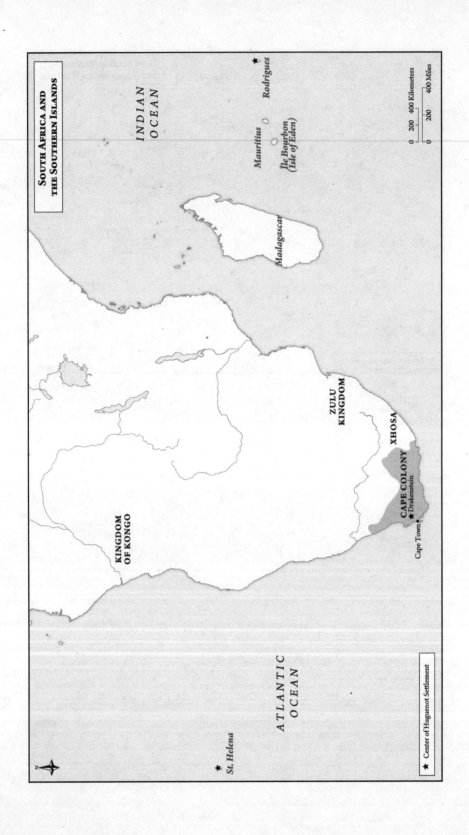

SOUTH AFRICA AND
THE SOUTHERN ISLANDS

INDIAN
OCEAN

Rodrigues

Mauritius

Île Bourbon
(Isle of Eden)

Madagascar

0   200   400 Kilometers
0   200   400 Miles

ATLANTIC
OCEAN

St. Helena

KINGDOM
OF KONGO

ZULU
KINGDOM

XHOSA

CAPE COLONY
Drakenstein

Cape Town

★ Center of Huguenot Settlement

N

Introduction

A Vine in the Wilderness

> But when they persecute you in this city, flee ye into another: for verily
> I say unto you, Ye shall not have gone over the cities of Israel, till the
> Son of man be come.
>
> Matt. 10:23

> Thou hast brought a vine out of Egypt: thou hast cast out the heathen,
> and planted it. Thou madst room for it, and didst cause it to take root,
> and it filled the land.
>
> Psalm 80:8–9

Élie Neau was just twelve years old when he signed on as a ship's hand and set out to the New World. Like many in his home province of Saintonge in southwestern France, Neau was a Protestant, and at least according to a letter he wrote some twenty years later, religion inspired him to leave his hometown of Moëze and sail off into the Atlantic in 1679. King Louis XIV was making life difficult for Neau's coreligionists—the people known as Huguenots—experimenting with new methods of forced conversion. The arrival of these troubles convinced Neau that he might be able to practice his faith more freely across the seas. He settled in the young French Caribbean colony of Saint-Domingue and spent a few years moving between Dutch and French islands before persecution came to the Caribbean as well. Still not yet twenty years old, Neau fled to Boston, a city in the English empire dominated by fellow Calvinists, where he became a merchant. Then in 1692, disaster hit. On a trading voyage from Boston to Jamaica, Neau's ship encountered French privateers. They took the mariner back to France, where authorities condemned him to labor in the king's galleys as a virtual slave, since they deemed him to be a "fugitive" who had "established himself in a foreign country without the king's permission." The prisoner could gain his freedom simply by converting to Catholicism, but Neau refused to take that step, and as a result he spent the better part of the next decade in the galleys and

The Global Refuge. Owen Stanwood, Oxford University Press (2020). © Oxford University Press.
DOI: 10.1093/oso/9780190264741.001.0001

dungeons of southern France, where he suffered alongside hundreds of other Huguenot prisoners who had also declined to convert.[1]

Unlike many of his fellow Huguenots, Neau eventually gained both his freedom and some degree of fame. In 1697 he returned to North America, this time settling in New York, and his story made him a minor celebrity in the Protestant world. According to his childhood pastor Jean Morin, who edited his letters from prison in a devotional tract aimed at French Protestants, Neau was a martyr, a simple man who had been willing to give up everything rather than abandon the true faith. Alongside other prisoners, he kept the light of French Protestantism shining in a country where it had nearly gone out. His story appealed, meanwhile, not just to his fellow Huguenots but to his North American neighbors as well. The Puritan Cotton Mather, for instance, presented Neau's tribulations to New England readers, casting the refugee as a fellow soldier against popish tyranny. Mather was in the midst of writing his own history of New England, which he portrayed as a promised land for Protestants, and he could not have failed to notice that even to non-English refugees like Neau, the "American strand" proved to be an attractive retreat, a bastion of the pure faith.[2]

Stories like Neau's have usually dominated Huguenot history. The persecuted Protestants of France often appear as singular Christian heroes, and this has been especially true of those who ventured from France to the Americas or the Cape Colony of southern Africa. These people were simply obeying Jesus Christ's instructions in the Gospel of Matthew, scattering across the world to avoid persecutors and preserve the true church. Many of their former friends and family members, after all, had not been able to resist the temptations and fell into idolatry. The late seventeenth-century wave of persecution had resulted in three-fourths of France's Protestants converting to Catholicism. Those who left, meanwhile, were God's true remnant, a global elect who had chosen Christ over the earthly rewards that came with converting to popery. As a nineteenth-century descendant of a refugee put it, his ancestors "were no instruments in the hands of ambitious Princes for the aggrandizement of their wealth and power." Instead, they crossed the seas "to escape persecution," to find "the transcendent sweets of religious and political liberty."[3]

Such stories are not entirely wrong. Huguenot refugees like Neau did make extraordinary sacrifices to practice their faith. Nonetheless, there was far more to the tale than meets the eye. There is an entirely different way to read Élie Neau's story, one that moves "ambitious Princes" and other state actors from the edges of the narrative to the center. Whatever his religious convictions, Neau deftly navigated the world of states and empires. He learned about his own strategic value as a teenage mariner during the 1680s, when he frequently crossed borders between French and Dutch island colonies, and once he was settled in Boston he knew enough to quickly seek naturalization as a subject of the English king. This move was necessary if Neau hoped to make a living as a merchant in the English empire, but it also saved him from his French captivity. It was King William III's ministers, negotiating with their counterparts in Versailles, who insisted that Neau regain his freedom, since he was a legal English subject. Once home in New York, Neau became even more entrenched in English institutions. He converted to Anglicanism and took a salary from the Society of the Propagation of the Gospel in Foreign Parts, the missionary wing of the Church of England. Under the Society's auspices, he dedicated much of his later life to the task of Christianizing New York's African slaves. The French Protestant hero and international merchant remade himself as an Anglican missionary, and it was access to institutional power—whether the English crown or the Church of England—that allowed Neau to prosper in a foreign world.[4]

Élie Neau's story was far from unique. Huguenot refugees like him abounded not just in England and its colonies, but throughout the world in the seventeenth and eighteenth centuries. One could find them in Virginia, where they attempted to make wine in the piedmont, or in South Carolina, where they experimented with silk. Several hundred settled near the Cape of Good Hope, where the Dutch East India Company had created a colony to replenish its ships to the Indies, and others ended up in the Dutch South American colony of Suriname, where they established a number of lucrative sugar plantations and defended the vulnerable colony from attacks by the French and other hostile neighbors. Some ran merchant houses that traded from London and Rotterdam to New York, Boston, and the Caribbean, following in Neau's footsteps. These refugees founded distinct communities—from Oxford in Massachusetts to New Bordeaux in South Carolina—and established French Calvinist churches all around the Atlantic. They also rose within key institutions in their adopted homelands. From merchant companies to the military to banks, churches, and missionary organizations, Huguenots seemed to be everywhere.

In fact, the Huguenots' path to prominence in a world of empires was not straightforward. There were many false starts along the way, and like other refugee groups they experienced a great deal of dislocation and discrimination. Nonetheless, the Huguenots persevered, and their story reveals much about the critical role of religious minority groups in the early modern European world. In order to win sympathy and support, the Huguenots had to define themselves as special people. They did this, for the most part, with the same language that Élie Neau's minister used when he spoke of the prisoner's steadfastness in the face of persecution. The refugees were special because they faced down the looming Catholic threat, one that in the late 1600s seemed to be gradually taking over the world. The Huguenots' status as godly martyrs bought them important credibility in Protestant circles from Berlin to London and beyond, as officials lined up to offer support to these "poor French Protestants" who had sacrificed everything for their faith. By the end of the 1680s the most prominent Huguenots had gained the patronage of some of the most powerful people in Europe, from the Elector of Brandenburg to the King of England, and the tens of thousands of refugees around Europe found plenty of their neighbors willing to give them aid. In post-Reformation Europe, where confessional allegiances and boundaries remained critical, being chosen people opened many doors. The refugees quickly emerged as leading symbols of what scholars have called the "Protestant International," a transnational union against the pretensions of the Sun King and global Catholicism.[5]

Still, the Huguenots needed more than just sympathy. If the seventeenth century remained an age of faith, it was also an age of statecraft. From the early seventeenth century onward European leaders embraced the study of political economy, the notion that princes should take control of national economies by controlling population and production and attempting to manage consumption. Most political economists believed people were the lifeblood of states, which made outmigration a national problem. Additionally, they obsessed over balance of trade, believing that a nation needed to send out more than it brought in from foreign competitors lest it lose out on its share of the world's wealth. Huguenot refugees absorbed this political economic language and learned to use it to promote themselves. They were chosen people, therefore, in economic as well as religious terms. For one thing, they were productive subjects, and if France's rivals could steal them away that meant more tax revenue and economic production for the host countries. Second, the Huguenots were not just ordinary people. They had a plethora of special talents, most especially in the creation of valued Mediterranean commodities like silk, wine, and olive oil. Northern Europeans had little experience or aptitude with these products, but they loved to consume them, and nothing proved more detrimental to their balance of trade. Huguenot refugee leaders made a persuasive argument that bringing in these newcomers would not just be an act of charity toward fellow godly people, but would benefit the national economies of whoever accepted them.

There was a final aspect of the Huguenots' self-promotion that made them even more valuable. If the late seventeenth century was an age of faith and an age of political economy, it was also an age of expansion and empire, when European states began in earnest to try and conquer the world. This push overseas was closely linked to the rise of states, since many political economists believed that colonial commodities could bring in needed raw materials and perhaps even jumpstart production in the metropole. There was a problem, however. If productive subjects went overseas, they sapped production at home. Huguenots provided a path for the English and the Dutch to develop their empires without losing people. The refugees, after all, came from another state altogether, and one that was a leading rival. Moreover, Huguenots were not only willing to travel to the ends of the earth; many of them had experience in overseas trade and navigation. Protestants had been disproportionately active in France's own overseas efforts since the sixteenth century. From the 1670s onward dozens of them lobbied for land and aid to go overseas, whether in league with the English or the Dutch, to create new refugee colonies around the world. While they proposed to do a great many things, they tended to come back to the holy trinity of political economists: silk, wine, and olive oil. This self-promotion opened more doors to the Huguenots, and hundreds of them boarded ships to the Americas, Africa, and the East, where they attempted to realize these diverse dreams.[6]

Telling the Huguenots' story requires a vast chronology and an even vaster geography. From its beginnings in France, the drama of persecution led to a century of tribulation, with refugees scattering around at least four continents. During the 1680s Louis XIV escalated his harassment of his kingdom's Protestants, ending with the outright revocation of the Edict of Nantes, which since 1598 had guaranteed limited rights to the Huguenots. The Revocation led to a mass exodus, as nearly 150,000 refugees were to flee France by land and sea over the course of a decade, finding shelter in neighboring Protestant states from Germany to England. These refugees changed Europe. They crowded the streets of port cities and drained charitable resources, even as they jumpstarted certain industries and transformed some regions. While many of these newcomers simply blended in to their host societies, the most prominent among them attempted quite explicitly to preserve their religion and culture by forming what they called "colonies" —distinct French Protestant communities that retained some degree of independence in preparation for a future return to the homeland. This colonial vision first appeared in Germany, but it became a prototype for Huguenot expansion, appearing around the continent as the Huguenots tried to find the best terms for their beleaguered coreligionists. Throughout this drama, the refugees tried to leverage both their status as sufferers for the faith with their productive capacities. They had lots of special skills and could develop certain industries, refugee leaders proclaimed, even as they brought blessings on the godly rulers who granted them refuge.[7]

It was not long before this colonization program went global. For one thing, suitable European retreats quickly filled up with refugees; even German princes like the elector of Brandenburg stopped welcoming as many new migrants by the late 1680s. But more than that, Huguenots were particularly susceptible to utopian propaganda about the possibilities of new worlds. French Protestants had been active traders, champions, and occasionally colonizers in both the West and East Indies back to the sixteenth century, and many of them lived in regions of France, like Saintonge or Normandy, that looked out on the Atlantic. Even before the Revocation occurred, some Huguenots were inquiring with English and Dutch authorities to try and find places to plant their own new settlements overseas, where they often tried to apply the same colonial logic that had worked in Europe itself. This movement only accelerated in the late 1680s, since officials in both host countries were running out of room for the refugees in Europe, but realized that the Huguenots could help them accomplish any number of treasured imperial goals, from making silk and wine to defending vulnerable frontiers.

These ambitions and interests combined to send thousands of Huguenots to the edges of empires. The number is difficult to recover due to the nature of the sources, but could have reached five to ten thousand, which would have been three to six percent of Europe's refugees. They tended to scatter in three regions of the world, where they formed a number of distinct communities. The oldest of these were in the Caribbean basin, Élie Neau's old stomping ground, where large numbers of Huguenots had been prominent in the French empire and where they founded communities on several Dutch, English, and Danish islands as well as on the neighboring Dutch mainland colony of Suriname. Others moved north to English North America, where refugee colonies emerged up and down the Atlantic seaboard, from New England and New York to Virginia and South Carolina. Finally, some refugees set their sights on the East Indies, settling in the Dutch colony at the Cape of Good Hope as well as smaller enclaves on St. Helena in the Atlantic and in the Mascarene Islands off the coast of Madagascar. By the eighteenth century the Huguenot diaspora spanned the globe, and some individual refugees had traveled to several continents in their search for refuge and advantage.[8]

Beyond the places that the Huguenots really settled, their empire aspired to move even farther. In fact, some of the colonies were no more than small placeholders in locales where refugee leaders hoped and expected that hundreds or even thousands of Huguenots would eventually settle. As a result, the number of refugees who actually lived or traveled in the Indies does not accurately reflect the pull of new worlds, since many more people considered moving to these distant retreats. The prototype of these aspirational colonies was auspiciously called the Isle of Eden. Envisioned by the gentleman Henri Duquesne during the late 1680s, Eden was only obliquely linked to a European state—in this case the Dutch. Duquesne meant it to be a semiindependent "republic" in the tropics, a place where refugees could live in peace and comfort. No one ever actually went to the Isle of Eden, which was more commonly known as Île Bourbon; but visions like this one traveled widely around the refuge, inspiring a number of settlements and capturing the Huguenot imagination.[9]

Wherever they were, these Huguenot overseas colonies combined religious vision with imperial geopolitics and economics. The refugees were willing to devote themselves to improving their British and Dutch overlords' empires, but they expected autonomy in return, and many of them tried, like Duquesne, to build new Edens in the Indies. They soon learned, however, that Eden and empire rarely went together. Tensions quickly emerged in nearly all of these settlements, pitting the refugees both against each other and, more often, against their foreign masters, who had little respect for Huguenot autonomy or independence in either politics or religious life. As a result, many of the ambitious colonies that dotted the shores of the Atlantic and Indian Oceans either never really got off the ground or faded quickly into irrelevance, their inhabitants returning to Europe or blending into English or Dutch communities in North America or southern Africa. "Everywhere they fled, everywhere they vanished," concluded one historian of early American Huguenots in a verdict that appeared to mark the end of the saga. Despite dreams of independence, the Huguenots rapidly assimilated and faded away. Demographic evidence would seem to confirm the story, as many second-generation refugees married outside their communities and stopped using French in their daily lives.[10]

Nonetheless, it is important not to overstate this disappearance. By the eighteenth century many Huguenots had indeed blended in, but they retained their global networks and sought to move the empires that they inhabited in particular directions. One of the primary purposes, even decades after the Revocation, was to act as ambassadors for international Protestantism, ensuring that the British empire in particular continued to promote the true faith. To this end, many former refugees became active, like Élie Neau, in the Society for the Propagation of the Gospel in Foreign Parts, while others advanced in the military or as merchants. Whatever their occupation, these Huguenots did not forget their coreligionists back in France, and continued to advocate for their interests. In fact, by the 1750s a new phase of Huguenot colonization began, and over the next two decades a number of colonies formed, from Nova Scotia to Florida, that drew on the same religious and political economic logic of the 1680s. Thus the history of Huguenot expansion and imperialism showed remarkable continuity in vision, from the Revocation to the very eve of the Age of Revolution.[11]

Those American and French revolutions, however, changed things in important ways, and brought this particular chapter of global Huguenot history to a close. After all the twists and turns of a century of turmoil, the refugees and their descendants had become creatures of the ancien régime, comfortable in a world of princes, kings, and ministers. When their patrons left, when a world of nation-states replaced the old world of empires, they found themselves marginalized, cut off from the networks of power they had learned to navigate so well. The Huguenots' story did not just end, of course. They maintained economic links across national borders, and they remade themselves as characters in a number of national histories—from the United States to Great Britain and South Africa. They would never again, however, be the imperial power players that they had been after the Revocation. The Huguenots' era of crisis in the century after the Revocation, ironically enough, had been their golden age.

———

No one has told the Huguenots' global story before. To be sure, they have never lacked scholars, from the seventeenth century to the present. The first historians of what later became known as *le Refuge* were the refugees themselves, who related dramatic tales of their escape from Babylon and their search for new worlds—stories that not surprisingly cast the Huguenots as religious heroes in the mold of Élie Neau. During the nineteenth century a new generation of historians, many of them descendants of the original refugees, adopted these perspectives with little skepticism, lauding the brave exploits of their forbears. These types of stories proved especially influential in the refugees' old imperial haunts, the United States and South Africa, where the Huguenots became heroes of religious freedom in rapidly changing societies that were dealing with the complicated legacies of their colonial pasts.[12]

As the nineteenth century turned into the twentieth, however, stories about the Huguenots lost their luster. A more critical generation of historians looked with skepticism on the exaggerated, hagiographic tales of the Huguenot past. No longer global heroes, the refugees became bit players in a variety of regional and national histories—interesting curiosities, perhaps, but not central actors. The fragmentation of history into national fields has done little to help illuminate the Huguenots' explicitly global story. French historians, for instance, have rarely cared much about people who left the kingdom, and while specialists on the places where the refugees ended up have been eager to integrate the Huguenots into local histories, they have rarely examined connections either back to France or with other parts of the Refuge. It is only by looking beyond any one nation's boundaries, however, by viewing connections across borders and even across oceans, that the Huguenots' larger significance becomes clear.[13]

The rush to abandon the hagiographic histories of the past has also served to obscure the Huguenots' global impact. To be sure, the refugees and their first historians were not critical scholars. They boasted of their people's numbers and accomplishments, seeking to cast themselves above all, like Élie Neau, as heroes and martyrs. In the end, that was exactly the point—other Protestants believed these stories about the Huguenots, about their religious heroism as well as their economic prowess. As a result, the refugees were able to insinuate themselves into a number of foreign states and especially into overseas empires, carving out critical roles for themselves in the world even as they remained a small and embattled minority. The key is not to reject stories of these Huguenot heroes but to demystify them, to place them in their larger, proper context. Religion, especially in the early modern era, could never be divorced from politics. The Huguenots themselves viewed the European conquest of the world as a divinely ordained event that would help them to save their own, true religion, connecting Europe's long Reformation to a burgeoning age of global expansion. They were not the first or the last religious minorities to view new worlds as theaters for their ambition, but their close relationship to a number of different states and institutions made them different. These children of the Reformation became agents of empire.[14]

The Huguenots forged a place in the world by advocating for a new kind of Protestant imperialism. Though French, they offered their bodies and their skills to other states. Their implicit, and sometimes explicit, argument was that they would make the world more Protestant and more productive, two goals that most assuredly went together. If bastions of global Protestantism like England and the Netherlands experienced economic growth, if they took more of the world's wealth from their popish rivals, especially France, that could only be good for the preservation and spread of true religion, including back in France itself. Material comfort and spiritual health were most assuredly linked, and Protestant people of all nations faced the same struggle. The task of the Huguenots was to promote themselves as leaders in that battle, as special people destined to direct the larger Protestant cause. Here they answered another biblical call, one expressed in the eightieth Psalm. Following God's example, the Huguenots left Egypt to plant a vine in the wilderness—in many cases a literal vine. If these vines made a lot of money for both the refugees and their sponsors, this was all the better. The refugees' promised land could also be a land of profit. By combining their status as persecuted Protestants with that of imperial subjects, the Huguenots globalized the Reformation and lent a sense of divine mission to European expansion. Their legacy would inspire future migrants and remain in popular memory long after the Huguenots themselves had faded into obscurity.

The Beginning of the End
of the World

The Huguenot Refuge emerged at a moment of apocalyptic anticipation and political intrigue. No one better exemplified this distinctive mix of politics and prophecy than the former minister of Sedan, Pierre Jurieu. In 1681 Jurieu took a new job at Rotterdam's Église Wallonne, or Walloon Church, and from that Dutch city, the main trade link between France and the Low Countries, Jurieu watched the world cave in for his fellow Huguenots. By 1686, he looked out on the ruins of his church, made illegal by Louis XIV's Edict of Fontainebleau, and welcomed thousands of refugees, who arrived in the port city on the mouth of the Rhine River by land and sea. Surveying the chaos, Jurieu could reach only one conclusion: the persecution corresponded to the last gasps of the "Antichristian Empire," foretold in scripture. Soon the people of God would rise again, toppling the Antichrist and paving the way for Jesus Christ's return to earth. In short, the Apocalypse was near, and the Huguenots would play a key role in the last great chapter of Christian history.[1]

Jurieu spelled out his theory in a book that became a bestseller throughout the Protestant world. The *Accomplissement des prophéties*—soon translated into English as *The Accomplishment of the Scripture Prophecies*—consisted largely of calculations about the confusing prophetic passages in Revelation, a mysterious book that Christian thinkers often considered the key to the end times. What made Jurieu's work distinct from the plethora of Protestant apocalyptic works was its connection to contemporary politics, and especially to the sufferings of his people, the French Protestants. Jurieu labeled the Huguenots as the "two witnesses in sackcloth" whose persecution would bring about the "the last trumpet blast and the thousand year reign of Jesus Christ and the church." His people were particular vessels of God's grace; they had kept the faith through the centuries of rule by an "Antichristian Empire," but their sufferings indicated that the end was near. The formula was not self-evident, Jurieu admitted, but he predicted the complete fall of Antichrist, embodied in the Catholic Church,

The Global Refuge. Owen Stanwood, Oxford University Press (2020). © Oxford University Press.
DOI: 10.1093/oso/9780190264741.001.0001

around the year 1710, by which time the French king would have embraced the true religion and the Huguenots could return home to live in peace and plenty. At some undefined point after that, by the end of the eighteenth century, Christ himself would take his temporal throne.[2]

Jurieu's prophecies captured the fear, hope, and uncertainty that accompanied the creation of a vast Huguenot diaspora that scattered across, and even beyond, Protestant Europe in the 1680s. To be sure, most of his fellow French Protestant intellectuals rejected Jurieu's apocalyptic speculations, thinking they smacked of an "enthusiasm" and militancy that went against the conservative grain of seventeenth-century French Calvinism. At the same time, Jurieu found many adherents in two different crowds. Ordinary French Protestants were enthusiastic partisans of the Rotterdam minister—not surprisingly, as he gave them hope for a happy ending after several decades of travails. In addition, his ideas appealed greatly to non-French Calvinists, especially English and Dutch thinkers who generally embraced millennial speculations more than their Huguenot counterparts. Jurieu's book quickly appeared in English and traveled to the ends of the Protestant world. Boston's minister and resident millennialist Increase Mather read the book in 1686, while a planter on the frontier of Virginia, William Byrd, asked his London correspondents to get him a copy of "Jurieu's Scripture Prophecies" in the summer of 1690. Not coincidentally, both men would eventually play roles in the drama that brought many of Jurieu's coreligionists from France into the English and Dutch empires.[3]

Like many prophecies, Jurieu's speculations combined historical interpretation with an almost utopian vision of a glorious future. The minister sought to help his fellow Huguenots and their neighbors to understand their place in time, and to explain why they faced such great suffering and what it meant in the longer span of Christian history. Most importantly, Jurieu's prophecies provided hope. The minister made a classic Calvinist argument that had been common since the days of the sixteenth-century martyrs. He identified suffering with godliness, and argued that the Huguenots' current troubles marked them as the people of God, as a special remnant of His elect. This was doubly true for those who managed to hold on to their faith amidst great persecution. God intended to use these people as a vanguard to create a new world—an Eden, a Canaan—on the ashes of the old Antichristian empire.[4]

At the same time, Jurieu understood the practical obstacles to building paradise on earth. While God would provide, He often worked through human agents, and so Jurieu and other Huguenots concocted a secular plan to help speed along Jesus's return and to ensure that the suffering people of God received food and shelter in the meantime. For one thing, Jurieu knew that if he could convince foreign leaders of the Huguenots' specialness, they would be far more likely to help out, providing land and charity to allow the refugees to survive. Other prominent Huguenots, even those who did not accept Jurieu's apocalypticism, shared this belief, and lobbied heavily to create an international Protestant movement with the Huguenots at its center.[5] By promoting themselves as the chosen people, in a biblical sense, the Huguenots could gain earthly comforts. Jurieu and his allies were fairly successful in these efforts. The Huguenots stood at the emotional center of European geopolitics in the late 1600s, and gained friends and patrons around Europe and beyond. But as many refugees learned, politics forced compromises, and pushed the Huguenots in directions that no one could have predicted. Most Protestants agreed that the refugees were special people, but the purpose of their particular mission became less clear after a decade of intrigue and struggle.

———

The persecution that created the Huguenot Refuge proceeded in fits and starts, reaching a crescendo during the 1680s. Pierre Jurieu dated its exact beginning to 1655, when "the Duke of Savoy set out to destroy the faithful of the Valleys of Piedmont," the French-speaking Vaudois Protestants who were close cousins to the Huguenots.[6] Another refugee, Jean Valat, placed the origins of the crisis far further back in "the first times of the Reformation," when "prisons, gallows, and stakes were the rewards for those who first embraced" the new religion.[7] The truth was far more complicated than either man admitted. The coming of the Reformation had caused great turmoil in sixteenth-century France, where the teachings of Jean Calvin and other reformers attracted many converts, especially in the kingdom's southern and western provinces. By 1562 religious divisions led to bloody civil war that lasted for much of the next three decades, dividing France and leaving lasting scars. After years of conflict, Henri IV calmed French religious tensions by issuing the Edict of Nantes in 1598. Life under the Edict was not a utopia for Protestants—it prohibited them from building new churches and forbade them from expanding beyond the zones of France they already inhabited. It did not prevent all conflict between Catholics and Protestants, as evidenced by the bloodshed of 1627–1628, when royal forces besieged and sacked the Protestant fortress town of La Rochelle, leading to a significant limitation of the liberties in the original Edict.[8]

Nonetheless, most of the seventeenth century was calm for individual French Protestants. Around 1660, there were nearly 800,000 of them living quietly in a variety of places around the kingdom—in port towns like La Rochelle, Bordeaux, or Dieppe; in small villages in the western provinces like Poitou or Guyenne; or especially in the vast swath of southern France that had become known as a hotbed of "heresy," stretching from the cities of Montpellier and Nîmes through the mountains and valleys of the Cévennes and Dauphiné to

Lyon. The Huguenots were a diverse group in terms of occupations and social position, incorporating merchants, lawyers, and gentlemen in the north and peasants in the Cévennes, but they were all united as members of a common church establishment, the Églises Reformées de France (Reformed Churches of France). In addition, the Huguenots shared a particular conception of themselves that combined the *French* and *Reformed* parts of their identity. On the one hand, the French Protestants conceived of their flock, like most Calvinists, as a group apart, a remnant of God's elect. At the same time, they had adapted to life as a minority within a Catholic kingdom. So while Huguenots argued with their Catholic neighbors, they usually did so respectfully; at least in public and in print, Protestants refrained from more extreme rhetoric such as labeling the pope as Antichrist. In addition to showing restraint in religious debates, French Protestants usually paid respect to their king and to principles of absolute monarchy—perhaps not surprisingly, since their own privileges came directly from the beneficence of Henri IV.[9]

If the Huguenots loved their king, however, it soon became clear that the feeling was not mutual. Louis XIV had never fully trusted the Huguenots, and after the Peace of Nijmegen ended a lengthy Franco-Dutch War in 1678, the king accelerated a legal and military campaign to enforce doctrinal uniformity in his kingdom. There were a number of factors behind Louis's gradual abandonment of France's experiment in partial toleration, but the most important seem to have been political as much as religious. As absolutists and centralizers, Louis and his ministers did not want to maintain a Protestant "state within a state" in their midst, and many believed that Huguenots, despite their protestations of loyalty, still retained the anti-monarchical doctrines that defined their cause in the late Wars of Religion, when thinkers like François Hotman came up with new theories to justify resistance to tyrannical rulers. Finally, Louis spent much of his reign in a battle with the pope for control over the French church, and he may have believed that by converting the Protestants he would cement his status as the "most Christian king." Whatever the causes, Huguenots were soon on the defensive. Authorities read the Edict of Nantes in the most restrictive way, demolishing churches that violated its terms, and steadily dismantled the legal structures that had existed to protect the Protestant minority. Royal officials used numerous means, including both bribes and threats, to encourage Huguenots to abjure their faith and embrace Catholicism.[10]

Despite the complicated roots of their troubles, individual Huguenots tended to interpret their persecution in religious terms, as an unprecedented test of their faith. This was especially true after 1681, when the strictures against Protestants took a frightening new form: the *dragonnade*. Several times over the previous decades the crown had experimented with stationing royal dragoons in places that had resisted royal authority. The troops lodged in the houses of ordinary

people, who by law had to house and feed them. In 1681 the intendant of
Poitou, a western province with one of the kingdom's largest concentration of
Huguenots, decided to use dragonnades as a means of conversion. The logic was
simple and cruel: the royal troops would eat Protestant families out of house and
home, destroy their possessions, and generally make their lives hell. There was a
simple way out: if the Protestants abjured their faith and turned to Catholicism,
the troops would leave and normal life would resume.

During the first half of the 1680s dragoons roamed Protestant regions of
western France with terrifying results. In the Poitevin town of Mougon, the
troops reached Jean and Elisabeth Migault's house in August 1681 and demanded
that they abjure their faith or pay for the troops' upkeep indefinitely. After Jean
fled, leaving his ailing wife alone with the troops, matters got worse. In an attempt to terrify Elisabeth into abandoning her faith, the soldiers built a large fire
in her room, feeding the flames with the family's furniture while they "swore and
blasphemed God's name in their ordinary way, saying that they would make her
burn if she did not want to convert." Elisabeth eventually escaped, but most of
the town's Protestants either converted or faced the loss of their estates.[11]

Four years later and several hundred miles to the southeast in Montauban,
Samuel de Pechels faced similar treatment. On August 26, 1685, the troops
arrived, and within days had taken nearly everything the family owned. As in
Migault's case, the troops especially targeted Pechels's wife, who was on the
verge of childbirth—seeking to use the Huguenots' family ties against them.
They refused to allow Madame de Pechels to sleep, and finally the family left
their house and lived on the street, eventually finding refuge with benevolent
neighbors.[12] The dragonnades pushed many people to the edge; "I implored
them a hundred times to kill me," reported one Protestant, "but they answered
We have no order to kill you, just to torment you until you convert."[13]

By 1685 the dragonnades had accomplished impressive results. Once word
of the terrors reached Protestant communities, most people converted en
masse. As Jean Migault reported with sorrow, most did so the day the troops
arrived at their houses, "without having suffered in the least."[14] Others relented
after realizing that keeping their faith would mean losing everything else; one
Protestant in the Norman seaport of Dieppe "was persuaded by his Catholic
friends to abjure in order to be rid of his cruel visitors. He did it, weeping
in the Archbishop's arms." Soon most of his neighbors rushed to follow his
example. "Within a few days there were few who had failed to sign," noted
the Norman gentleman Isaac Dumont de Bostaquet.[15] Even some of the most
steadfast eventually abjured—Bostaquet himself did so because he feared
what the dragoons would do to his female relations, while Jean Migault, to
his great shame, abandoned his faith after several weeks in a dark La Rochelle
dungeon, at the urging of a concerned daughter. "The horror of my sin became

so strongly apparent to me," Migault later wrote, "that I was near the point of despair for some time."[16]

By October the results were impressive enough that Louis's ministers convinced themselves that they had solved the kingdom's heretic problem. The Edict of Nantes, they declared, had become a dead letter. On October 25 from his royal palace in Fontainebleau, Louis revoked the "irrevocable" Edict and made Protestantism illegal in his realms. As the king noted, his efforts to dismantle the Protestant churches had been so successful that "the best and the biggest part of the said R.P.R. [the 'religion prétendue réformée' or 'so-called reformed religion,' as it appeared in official parlance] have embraced Catholicism." In official terms, the French Reformed churches ceased to exist, and their former adherents took the new label of "nouveaux Catholiques" or "nouveaux convertis," new converts to the dominant church.[17]

While conversion was the easiest and most common path for France's Protestants, there were two other options. The first was resistance, either through passive refusal to abjure or the more active resistance advocated by the lawyer and minister Claude Brousson in Languedoc, who instructed the faithful to return and worship on the sites of demolished temples and generally refuse to obey anti-Protestant laws. These acts of resistance tended not to accomplish much aside from creating martyrs. Resisters usually ended up in prison, as "slaves" on the king's galleys, or in Caribbean exile, while the most recalcitrant ended up suffering worse fates. Things were especially bad for those who "relapsed" into heresy, like one elderly man in Nérac who initially abjured but then recanted his abjuration before the priest, spitting out the consecrated host that the curé forced into the old man's mouth. "And with this he was condemned to the fire," Pierre Jurieu wrote, "to be burned alive. He went to this horrible torture with all the joy of the holy Martyrs."[18]

For those who did not desire a martyr's crown there was a third option: flight. When Jean Migault reached the port of La Rochelle in the fall of 1681 he found many of his neighbors who "having found foreign vessels, caught a glimpse of safety there and found it, some in Holland, others in England, Ireland, and some in Carolina, delivering themselves by these means from persecution."[19] While not as dangerous as open resistance, flight came with its own set of risks. First of all, many people, like Migault in 1681, did not have the connections or financial resources to make good on their ambitions to leave. This proved especially true for women and widowers with large families.[20] Moreover, royal officials placed severe restrictions on the movement of Protestants. In July 1682 the king reissued a 1669 law prohibiting his subjects from leaving the kingdom without permission, noting that "our subjects of the R.P.R." often had the design of "retiring in foreign countries." The law made it legally impossible for Protestants to sell their goods in order to remove overseas, since anyone found buying those goods, Protestant or Catholic alike, would have them confiscated with no compensation.[21] These strictures became even worse after the issuing of the Edict of Fontainebleau, which expressly forbade new converts from leaving France. By the end of 1685 no person could leave a French port in a foreign ship without the express written permission of local admiralty officials. Only by evading the authorities, and risking the lives of themselves and their friends and neighbors, could anyone hope to reach the Refuge.[22]

Nonetheless, tens of thousands of people successfully escaped detection and fled abroad during the 1680s. Most of them remained reticent about sharing their paths to safety, but surviving accounts reveal several regional patterns of flight.[23] Matters proved easiest for those in Normandy and other parts of France bordering the English Channel—and indeed, a disproportionate number of Norman and other northern Protestants fled their province for English or Dutch exile. Isaac Minet of Calais, for instance, simply sent word to a brother in Dover that he needed help fleeing the kingdom, and his family sent a boat to meet him on a deserted beach.[24] Many were less fortunate than Minet; coast guards ranged the Atlantic seaboard of France, and those who escaped could do so only after careful planning and usually in the dark of night. Jean Migault plotted his departure from La Rochelle for over a year and against great odds, since he had several small children in tow and his wife had died in childbirth. His friends warned him "that it was impossible at that time to leave" since "the port and the coasts were guarded so well." He managed to escape with his family on a Dutch ship in December 1687, but only with the help of several nervous Catholic and newly converted friends who sheltered the family at great personal risk.[25]

However difficult escape could be for northern and western Huguenots, it proved even worse for those who lived in the south. A gentleman originally from Dauphiné, known only by his surname Durand, was living on some of his properties in a Provençal village when persecution hit. He fled to the relative anonymity of Marseille, where he hid in the house of some friends while he waited for any ship that could take him out of the kingdom, as he "preferred to obey God rather than the King." Lying to a consul, he claimed he was a Catholic from Provence aiming to go on a pilgrimage to Rome, and he eventually made his way to the Italian city of Livorno, where he booked passage on an English merchant ship that took him to London by way of Cadiz.[26]

Many other southerners chose to escape by land, through the Rhône Valley and the Alps to Geneva, but it was a long road and full of perils. Jean Valat successfully made the journey in 1686, but faced frequent interrogations from officials and ordinary people who suspected him of being a Calvinist (the penalties for harboring fugitive Protestants were so heavy that few innkeepers would grant them lodging). He escaped by tapping into a network of foreigners, former Protestants, and sympathetic Catholics who worked to move fugitives

from Lyon to Geneva. Many of the prospective guides, however, were oppor-
tunistic scoundrels profiting on the refugees' plight. The first guide simply took
Valat's money and disappeared, while the second extorted payments from the
poor Protestants at each turn. The guides forced the party to march all night
and spend the day sleeping at a friend's house, where the guide told them that a
neighbor had learned the fugitives were there and promised to turn them into
authorities—unless they each paid him a sizable bribe. Valat understood that
"the guides would be able to cheat them on many pretexts and that in the end
they could be stripped of all that they had." Only on the third try did Valat finally
reach Geneva, exhausted and nearly broke, before "we found ourselves outside
the power of our enemies."[27]

In the end only a minority of France's Protestants found refuge in foreign
countries. Of around 750,000 Huguenots, nearly 600,000 chose to abandon their
faiths—though not all did so permanently. Still, the flood of around 150,000
people into Protestant lands wrought dramatic changes on European politics
and demography. If seventeenth-century Huguenots already viewed themselves as a remnant of the true church, those who had managed to find refuge
abroad were a remnant of that remnant, a cadre of souls who benefited from
the workings of God's Providence. The minister Jacques Fontaine expressed as
much when he later recounted the many narrow escapes on the path to exile.
We "had run more risks in fleeing our country, family, friends, and property,"
Fontaine noted, "than the greediest people take to gain them. We received the
sign of God's love for us by our love for Him, which we had shown."[28] Another
refugee celebrated those who left their "delicious gardens, agreeable countryside, rich farms, and great vineyards," in order to be "rejected and disdained
by the world," just as Jesus Christ promised of his true followers.[29] As Pierre
Jurieu noted, these circumstances mirrored all previous rounds of persecution: the weak succumbed to the persecutors, while God's chosen resisted and
prospered—either by embracing martyrdom or by finding liberty in new lands.
"These are the miracles," Jurieu noted, "but if they were frequent and ordinary,
they would no longer be miraculous."[30] Many of the refugees learned to wear
this special status on their sleeves. They were the survivors, the victims of persecution who God had led to liberty. But liberty, as they found, would not come
without significant trials and tribulations.

———

Long before significant numbers of refugees left France, word of their
sufferings circulated around the Protestant world. Benjamin Harris's *Imperial
Protestant Mercury*, a short-lived London newspaper dedicated to relating
popish outrages from around the continent, began detailing the sufferings

Figure 1.1 This 1696 Dutch woodcut illustrates the Huguenot migration out of France following the Revocation of the Edict of Nantes. "Het weg vlugten der Gereformeerde uyt Vrankryk" (The Escape of the Reformed Refugees from France) from Élie Benoist, *Historie der Gereformeerde Kerken van Vranykryk* (Amsterdam, 1696), Typ. 632.96.202, Houghton Library, Harvard University.

of the Huguenots in 1681, at the time of the first Poitevin dragonnades. The Huguenots fled their towns and cities in the face of unprecedented cruelty, Harris reported. Some had "the soles of their Feet burnt with flaming Brass, to force them to Abjure their Religion," and the Catholics tortured even Protestant children, who they forced "to put one of their Fingers into a small *hole*, and then drive a wedge upon it, with several other Barbarities which seem almost Incredible, had we not seen and *Examined* these poor Soules just upon their Landing, not being then Cured of some of the Wounds occasioned by their Tortures."[31] Harris was not the only English newsmaker obsessed with Huguenot suffering. In September 1683, for instance, a London newsletter told of an incident in Dauphiné, where a group of Protestants gathered to worship at a church that had been shuttered. A "detachmt of Dragoones" attacked the worshippers, killing two hundred of them on the spot and forcing more than a hundred others to a barn that they then set on fire, consuming the poor Protestants in the flames.[32]

These reports took on a particular meaning in light of recent events in English politics. In 1678 the kingdom had been rocked by revelations of a "popish plot" to assassinate King Charles II and re-establish the Catholic Church—a design supposedly spearheaded by English Catholic recusants but aided by foreign agents of Louis XIV and other Catholic rulers. The plot turned out to be a complete fabrication, but it turned the state upside down for a time, leading to a series of show trials and executions. The Huguenots played a leading role in the drama because their sufferings pointed to the natural cruelty of Catholic rulers. To make matters worse, the heir to the English throne, James, duke of York, was himself a Roman Catholic with close ties to France. Protestant propagandists like Benjamin Harris sent a clear message when they dwelt on Huguenot suffering. If we are not careful, they declared, we may soon experience similar persecution here in England.[33]

In continental Europe tales of the Huguenots had similar political implications. The Netherlands was still reeling from a destructive war that had culminated in Louis XIV's invasion in 1672, and the aftermath of the conflict had brought out stark political divisions between William of Orange, the stadholder and military commander, and the municipal authorities who dominated the Republic's legislature, the States General.[34] The arrival of Huguenots gave a boost to the Orangist cause, which opposed compromise with the French— and distressed the French ambassador in The Hague who was close to getting key concessions from his Dutch counterparts. By October 1685, he reported with alarm, hordes of refugees made their way from Sedan across the Dutch Republic, and their stories of mistreatment "strongly motivate everyone here" to the extent that he feared people would seek revenge on Dutch Catholics.[35] Perhaps nowhere did Huguenot sufferings raise more sympathy or alarm then in Geneva, an independent city-state on the French border that was a longtime center of Francophone Calvinism. Genevans watched helplessly in 1685 as dragoons destroyed churches in the neighboring Pays de Gex, while "every day an infinity of poor people of the religion arrive in Geneva who flee the horrible desolations that the dragoons have made on these poor churches." With French troops massed on the border, Genevan Protestants logically feared that the Sun King would do to Calvin's city what he had recently done to Strasbourg, re-establishing "popery" in the heartland of the Reformation.[36]

In general, European Protestants tended to see mirrors of themselves in the suffering Huguenots, who became symbols of the embattled global Protestant interest. Perhaps the most ideal expression of this sentiment appeared in a sermon from Boston, an ocean away from the dragonnades. In 1681 the Reverend Increase Mather dedicated a fast day sermon to the Protestants in France. He noted that the history of Christianity had always been a story of violent struggle between the godly and forces of evil, as "the Churches of God have been subject unto horrible slaughters for opposing Antichristian Superstitious Doctrines." As an apocalyptic scholar in his own right, moreover, Mather saw something special in this latest round of persecution. It certainly foretold great turmoil, along the lines of the predictions in the Book of Revelation. "A dying Beast will bite cruelly," Mather noted, "so is Antichrist, a dying beast." In making this prediction Mather spurred his listeners to action. They had to support the cause, especially by giving aid to the latest victims of persecution, the Huguenots. "If enquiry be made of those that are going from us, to other parts of the world, What are they doing in *New-England*," Mather hoped, "The Reply may be, They are Fasting, & praying for the persecuted people of God in the world. I say, if any ask of you, What are they doing in *New England*, they did no sooner hear of the persecuted Condition of the *Protestants in France*, but they set themselves, to Fast, Pray to the God of Heaven, for them."[37]

In the wake of news came the first waves of refugees—hundreds and then thousands of people traveling by sea and land to escape France. The coming of actual people tested the sentiments displayed in Mather's sermon. It was far easier to fast and pray than to provide food and shelter to strangers. The geography of the 1681 dragonnades meant that England received an early test of its resolve. The greatest persecutions took place in Poitou, near the Atlantic coast, where many refugees had trade and family connections to English ports like Plymouth, Dover, and Bristol. Those with means could easily sail across the channel to safety, and by September 1681 ships full of *"French* distrest *Protestants"* showed up in England.[38] These numbers increased when a group of Huguenots presented a memorial to Charles II attesting to the "great Hardships and Persecutions, which are brought unto them for the sake of their Religion." Some of the king's allies, led by the Bishop of London Henry Compton, convinced the king to grant the refugees aid, "looking upon them not only as distressed Strangers, but chiefly as Persecuted Protestants."[39]

The king did not act out of a deep commitment to liberty of conscience. Indeed, even as he welcomed the Huguenots, Charles was presiding over a frightening crackdown on Protestant dissenters in England and Scotland. In truth, opening the doors to the refugees fit into his larger strategy to encourage conformity to the Church of England. The Huguenot persecution had become a *cause célèbre* in a country primed for stories of popish cruelty, and proved especially popular among Whigs and dissenters like Increase Mather, who implicitly or explicitly compared Charles to his persecuting cousin across the Channel. By establishing himself as a patron of the Huguenots, Charles strengthened his antipopish bona fides. He also effectively prevented the flood of refugees from strengthening the Whig cause. Most Huguenot leaders sang the praises of the benevolent king and accepted his key condition, that refugees take communion in the Church of England if they wished to receive funds from his "Royal Bounty."

In 1681 even the ministers of the French and Dutch churches in London, both of which operated independent of the national church, effusively thanked Charles for his charity. They declared the king as a "Benefactor" and "Defender of the Faith," since he used his "Soveraign Power to that end which God has ordain'd it, which is to procure as much as possible, the happiness of all Men."[40]

Within several years of this declaration, persecution had become more severe and widespread around France, and London lost its status as a special refuge. In 1684 large numbers of southern French Protestants fled to Geneva, which soon became overwhelmed with new arrivals. Ministers in the city-state depended on a "bourse française" (founded a century earlier during a previous age of crisis) to deal with expenses for the new arrivals, most of whom then kept moving beyond the city's borders into Switzerland, which at that time began only a few miles east of Geneva's gates. Passing refugees clogged the roads to the larger, German-speaking cities of Bern, Zurich, and beyond. Each of these places did their best to provide aid and comfort to the travelers, but the sheer numbers overwhelmed local authorities. Geneva's fund for the refugees ran out in early November of 1685.[41] In the much smaller town of Vevey, meanwhile, 160 Dauphinois refugees arrived in September with only "the shirts on their backs" looking for aid and land.[42] Hospitals in the pays de Vaud, the Swiss Francophone territory east of Geneva, refashioned themselves to help ailing refugees, and most towns dedicated a share of alms-collection to their cause. But the numbers kept increasing. In Schaffhausen, a Protestant city on the German border, 530 refugees passed through in 1685, over 5,000 the following year, and a staggering 9,006 in 1687.[43]

Many of these travelers had no desire to stay in Switzerland. In fact, much of the flood materialized not just due to the Revocation of the Edict of Nantes, but after the subsequent passage of the Edict of Potsdam. On October 29, 1685, the elector of Brandenburg, Friedrich Wilhelm I, issued a declaration inviting France's distressed Protestants to settle in his territories. The Edict of Potsdam quickly vaulted the "Great Elector" into a role as leader of the Huguenot cause. His terms were far more generous than Charles II's had been four years earlier; he required no confessional test and guaranteed Huguenots land, tax relief, and a degree of self-governance. Friedrich Wilhelm's beneficence reflected self-interest as well as charity, however. Many of his lands still remained depopulated from the ravages of the Thirty Years' War, and he was especially keen to attract Calvinists like himself to his overwhelmingly Lutheran realm. In all, around 18,000 refugees heeded the Great Elector's call, with many of them heading to Berlin, where by the early 1700s Huguenots made up 15 percent of the population.[44] By early 1687 the elector had sent a representative to Geneva specifically to serve as an agent for new arrivals from France, even giving them money for transportation to their new German homes.[45]

Aside from the pull of Brandenburg, many of the French refugees in Switzerland headed northwest toward the Rhineland. Moving through Frankfurt—whose Reformed Church became an important way station for Huguenots—the travelers continued on to Rotterdam and the other cities of the Dutch Republic, where they joined masses of new arrivals who came in by sea. The Netherlands was a common refuge for persecuted peoples from around Europe, thanks to its relatively tolerant atmosphere, and the existence of dozens of Walloon Churches, formed a century earlier by French-speaking refugees from the Spanish Netherlands, provided spiritual comfort for many French newcomers. As early as September 1680 officials in the Walloon Churches noticed the large numbers of "persecuted brethren" arriving in the United Provinces, and formed a commission to lobby the States General to create a "general collection" to help the refugees.[46]

By 1685 a flood of new arrivals showed up in Dutch cities nearly every day. A French ambassador believed that only a month after the Revocation there were five thousand refugees in Rotterdam and twice that number in Amsterdam—an inflated number, perhaps, but one that reflected the sense of panic among French officials.[47] In Rotterdam, Isaac Dumont de Bostaquet claimed that the port city "had become almost French because so many inhabitants of Rouen and Dieppe had sought refuge there."[48] Records of the Walloon Church confirm this sentiment; by November 1685 the church was so crowded that the people could no longer take communion together, and the elders had to hire a new, part-time minister and add extra services to accommodate the "very notable increase in numbers."[49]

In The Hague, as in London and Berlin, a network of worthies came to espouse the Huguenot cause. As a gentleman, Bostaquet met many of them. Some were Huguenots themselves, like the Marquise de Sommelsdijck, a French Protestant lady of aristocratic birth who married a leading Dutch noble and served as a champion of the refugee cause. Some were British exiles, like Gibert Burnet, a Scottish bishop forced to leave for his political views, and the young philosopher John Locke.[50] Most powerful was the stadholder William, Prince of Orange, the champion of European resistance to France. William had personal reasons to support the Huguenots, since his ancestral principality in the Rhône Valley was a traditional center of French Protestantism. More than that, however, he spoke for the anti-French interest in Dutch and European politics, and the refugees perfectly symbolized why he found Louis XIV's ambitions so alarming. He was also, not surprisingly, a close ally of Friedrich Wilhelm. Bostaquet spoke for many when he sung the praises of "Our great Prince," who "combined the qualities of a hero with the zeal of true piety and love of his religion." The Norman nobleman arranged an audience with the prince and offered him his services, and he was not alone. By the end of 1685 ex-French soldiers abounded in The

Hague, where according to the French ambassador they "are at all moments in the antechamber of the Prince of Orange, where they seek employment."[51]

While officials from London to Berlin had good reasons to embrace the refugees, the newcomers also faced profound difficulties. These problems multiplied over the course of 1686 and 1687, when thousands of French Protestants continued to travel to cities and towns that were quickly running out of resources to aid them. In March 1687 over a thousand French Protestants landed in London over the course of less than a week, noted one newsletter writer, adding that witnesses from France reported "greate numbers get away & severall villages & Townes on the sea side are left destitute of People."[52] Several months later in Geneva a minister reported that three hundred new refugees arrived each week during the winter months, and that number had swelled to nearly 350 each day during August. This enlarged number included not just those from France itself but also Francophone Protestants from the valleys of Piedmont in Savoy, where at the Sun King's urging the Catholic duke Victor Amadeus II had implemented his own program of persecution.[53]

Aside from demographic pressures, the refugees caused political problems. Nowhere was this more apparent than in Geneva. An independent city-state, Geneva was surrounded on three sides by France and depended on its powerful neighbor for grain imports. When Geneva began filling up with refugees, the king gave firm orders to the Genevans that they could not give refuge to any "of my subjects of the so-called reformed religion" who had "left my States without my permission."[54]

The Sun King's demand put the Genevan council in a delicate position. They protested that they could not close their gates to travelers, being a "place of passage," but also insisted that they harbored no refugees within the town since they all soon left for Switzerland. After the Revocation of the Edict of Nantes, meanwhile, the town fathers acted to make this presumption a reality. They issued an edict declaring that all French refugees who had arrived in the past year had to leave the city, and then sent marshals door to door to ensure that all townspeople knew that they could no longer lodge any French newcomers.[55] At the urging of the Sun King's local representative, the *résident* Roland Dupré, they also expelled the handful of French ministers who had come to the city—even though the Edict of Fontainebleau allowed them the right of emigration—and stunningly, expelled a few local pastors who had simply ministered in French towns just across the border. In addition, the council promised not to allow any printed matter to circulate that criticized the Sun King, and they made good on their promise, confiscating a number of copies of an anti-French tract that had made the rounds of local bookstores.[56]

The city's leaders believed they could not risk displeasing the Sun King and their actions probably reflected the will of most of the inhabitants. Even officials of the local consistory urged the council to expel French ministers, noting that if the town fathers angered the king and lost control of the city, the consequences to the larger Reformed cause would be dire. The town did not have the defenses to win a battle against French troops, so the only way to preserve the town's "temporal and spiritual liberty" was to keep the king from attacking at all by sending the refugees packing to Switzerland. Nonetheless, there were those in the city who did not agree, to the point that the council spent much of its time in the last months of 1685 policing against seditious speech by those who, like one concerned citizen, predicted that "Geneva would perish like Sodom and Gomorrah because they cruelly chased out the French Ministers."[57] By the middle of 1686 the whole city was paralyzed by fear. Magistrates worried that they were about to lose their sovereignty, while ordinary people were "persuaded that His Majesty [Louis XIV] has resolved to reestablish the Catholic faith" in Geneva.[58]

If Geneva's geography made it distinct, a version of the same political dilemma appeared in England. In February 1685, just as persecution heated up across the Channel, Charles II died and his Catholic brother, James II, took the throne. As a Catholic ruling over a Protestant population, James was particularly sensitive to any slights of his adopted faith, and he depended on his French cousin for diplomatic and financial support. At the same time, he was developing his own program of religious toleration, one that would eventually lead him to issue a Declaration of Indulgence in 1687. His actions toward the French Protestants reflected this balancing act. On the one hand, the king actively suppressed anti-French propaganda. In 1686, for instance, he ordered the common hangman to burn copies of the minister Jean Claude's popular tract *An account of the persecutions and oppressions of the Protestants in France*, which he considered a libel against Louis XIV. At the same time, he continued to quietly support incoming refugees out of the remaining funds in the Royal Bounty, though the numbers of new arrivals fell in comparison to the Netherlands and Brandenburg. Apparently some refugees, like their English Protestant counterparts, worried that James II's supposed belief in toleration was just a ruse to get Protestants to lower their defenses. Daniel Brousson, for instance, soured on his resolution to go to England when he heard that the "papist" James II "governed the Kingdom with an absolute power" and decided on the Netherlands instead.[59]

In fact, refugees in England and elsewhere had greater problems than Catholic rulers and fearful magistrates. They also faced mistrust and occasional violence from ordinary people, who sometimes viewed the newcomers as competitors for jobs and resources. For one thing, it was difficult to distinguish French Protestants from French Catholics—a problem that would continue to plague Huguenots for some time. In 1681 one English newsletter reported on fears that French "papists" came to England "under the Notion of protestants to be ready to doe mischeife," and noted that authorities would do more to ensure that only the right kind of French found refuge in England.[60] These religious fears could easily meld with economic ones, as was the case with Jacques Fontaine, who settled and opened a shop in the English city of Taunton in 1686. By his own accounts, Fontaine's business did quite well, thanks to connections with French and Dutch merchants—so well, in fact, that he drove some of his English competitors to the brink of bankruptcy. They turned against him en masse, denouncing Fontaine as a "Jesuit in disguise" and a "French dog who took the bread out of the mouths of the English." Some English shopkeepers brought charges against Fontaine before the town's leaders, alleging unfair business practices and practicing several trades despite never being an apprentice.[61] While he eventually escaped punishment, Fontaine's ordeal showed the difficulties of working in a European labor market still dominated by guilds and chartered interest groups, not just in England but nearly everywhere the refugees settled. "In all the countries of the world," a Genevan correspondent warned the Huguenot doctor Elie Bouhéreau, "a stranger . . . ordinarily finds many difficulties in making himself known and established . . . especially where there are many people who work in the same trade."[62]

These political and economic issues forced many officials to tread cautiously, but it did not dampen their enthusiasm for welcoming refugees. It was important, however, to make sure that the refugees settled in the right areas, where they would not attract controversy or compete with local artisans and manufacturers. Both Dutch and English authorities actively recruited newcomers to towns that needed skilled artisans, and both looked with particular envy at the Lyonnais silk and textile workers, who they hoped would build up sectors of the economy traditionally dominated by the French and Italians. The French language gazettes in the Netherlands played a particular role in tempting refugees. In August 1681 the *Nouvelles extraordinaires de divers endroits*, more commonly known as the *Gazette de Leyde*, noted that the leaders of Middelburg "have made public that they will give great advantages to Merchants and artisans who want to settle in their city," while those in Amsterdam and Leiden wanted people active in "commerce and manufacturing." The decade witnessed a variety of refugee-led economic experiments around the Dutch Republic, most of which ended in disappointment but still mobilized the transportation of hundreds of skilled laborers.[63]

English authorities made similar efforts to use the refugees to develop particular sectors of the economy. In 1681, after Charles II's first brief in favor of the Huguenots, officials attempted to use French newcomers to develop linen manufacturing in Ipswich, a beleaguered East Anglian town with high unemployment that taxed the poor rolls, a design town leaders lauded as "in time very advantageous not only to our town, but also to the whole Kingdom." Fishermen, meanwhile, settled in the town of Rye in Sussex, while silk workers—the most desired of all—set up shop in Canterbury and the East London district of

Spitalfields.[64] Indeed, there was something of a competition for refugee labor in some parts of the kingdom, as evidenced in a missive from William Lloyd, the Bishop of St. Asaph in North Wales, who proposed planting a "small colony" of French people who could "teach our people Art & Industry," with a preference for "fishers or makers of french stuffs." For over a year the bishop continued in his project, even sending a representative to Switzerland to treat with a minister from Dauphiné who promised to settle "some husbandmen" and "stuff-makers" to one of the towns on Wales's north coast. Their settlement would be "most advantage[ous] to the Countrey," the bishop concluded, "which I believ[e] might be very much improved by a Plantation of these poor People." The Huguenots had gained reputations as "good immigrants," especially to economically depressed places like Ipswich or culturally marginal ones like Wales.[65]

As Jacques Fontaine and the prospective Welsh immigrants showed, Huguenots occupied a strange position in late seventeenth-century Europe. They had come to view themselves as a people apart, as particular vessels of God's providence, and some of their Protestant neighbors were inclined to agree—especially since espousing the Huguenot cause had particular political connotations in each part of the Protestant world. At the same time, the flood of newcomers aroused suspicions and fears, both from leaders and ordinary people. In order to weather the storm, the refugees would need to find ways to work within Protestant Europe's precarious political system, to demonstrate to leaders that the benefits of welcoming the refugees—whether spiritual, political, or economic—surpassed the dangers. In order to do this, the Huguenots needed to become more than just symbols of the Protestant cause; they needed to become lobbyists.

———

When Jean Migault finally arrived in Rotterdam after years of tribulations, one of his first stops was the city's famous Walloon Church, the center of refugee life in the bustling port. There he joined the legions of other new arrivals who had abjured their faith under pressure in France, "publicly confessing their sins before God and in the face of the Church." Additionally, the group of newcomers "heard for the first time the celebrated M. Jurieu," the church's pastor who had already gained a reputation as the foremost champion of the downtrodden Protestants of France.[66] From his perch in one of the most important institutions in French Protestantism, Jurieu served as a gatekeeper of the Refuge, and one of the key go-betweens linking ordinary refugees like Migault to the avenues of power occupied by the Bishop of London or the Prince of Orange. Jurieu was part of an informal institution that might be called the Huguenot senate. Alongside a network of pastors, military officers, and gentlemen stretching from London to

Geneva, Jurieu attempted to organize and mobilize the masses of new arrivals who crowded into northern and central European cities. His first task was to see to the refugees' physical survival, but the goals of the Huguenot senate were somewhat loftier. First, Jurieu and others had to convince the refugees themselves that they were special people, favored by God, with a particular role to play in European affairs. Next, he and his allies needed to make the same argument in the courts of Protestant Europe. So the Huguenot senate embarked on a massive public relations campaign on behalf of the refugees, one that endeavored above all to use the resources of state and private institutions to set up something of a Huguenot republic that united refugees around the continent.[67]

Ministers like Jurieu constituted the backbone of the Huguenot senate. In the Edict of Fontainebleau Louis XIV allowed all Reformed ministers to leave within fifteen days—as long as they left their goods and any children older than seven behind.[68] Of the 870 ministers active in France at the time of the Revocation, more than 75 percent chose exile over abjuration, meaning that the Refuge filled with clergy disconnected from their flocks. The largest number went to the Netherlands, which already possessed a wide network of Walloon churches.[69] Others looked for work in England, but linguistic challenges and the complications of ecclesiastical politics prevented most from finding steady employment. In fact, many young ministers ended up essentially becoming servants for English bishops. The bishop of St. Asaph, the same man who tried to settle Huguenots in North Wales, employed one refugee minister: "a truly good man," the bishop noted, whose lack of English made him "not so capable" in any regular ministerial job.[70]

The best of these ministers worked to rebuild some of the same ecclesiastical networks that had existed before the Revocation. Establishing a transnational Huguenot church was out of the question, but ministers and elders did the next best thing, fashioning informal correspondence links between churches to keep track of the floods of new arrivals and help ensure some modicum of doctrinal uniformity. Alongside the Walloon churches the most important center emerged at the Threadneedle Street Church in London, where the ministers not only dealt with the stunning numbers of new arrivals, but also served as a clearinghouse to relay information to French churches and communities around Britain and its empire.[71]

Aside from their important logistical role, Huguenot theologians and ministers created meaning for the Refuge. This proved true even for those who could not find established positions in any church, many of whom ended up working as teachers, tutors, editors, or printers. Indeed, the refugees formed the backbone of a pan-European "republic of letters," taking its name from the newspaper edited by the refugee-philosophe Pierre Bayle. But if Bayle is best remembered by posterity, it was others who took the lead in defining the refugee cause during the troubled first years of its existence. One of the first was Jean Claude, previously minister at Charenton, the temple outside Paris that served as a national church for Huguenots before the Revocation. He joined the Prince of Orange's entourage in The Hague, where he received "an infinity of visitors" in late 1685.[72] Claude was an elderly man, however, and his death in 1687 passed the mantle to others, most notably Pierre Jurieu. The heir to two famous ministerial families, the Jurieus and the du Moulins, Jurieu was a talented theologian who wrote in a lively and readable style. In 1686 he began publishing a series of "pastoral letters" urging those left behind in France to resist Catholicism.[73] Jurieu smuggled these printed letters into his former homeland, but in the meantime he also became famous among non-French Protestants for his scripture prophecies, which provided a theological justification to the most potent political movement within the Huguenot Refuge.

The minister's apocalyptic speculations did not differ in most respects from other seventeenth-century prophetic writings. Jurieu drew heavily from the standard Protestant interpretations of the book of Revelation, especially those of the mid-century English theologian Joseph Mede.[74] When it came to specific interpretations of the key passages of scripture, however, Jurieu hewed his own path, and his interpretations had important political implications. For example, he differed with Mede and other commentators by identifying the "great city" of Rev. 11:8, where the "two witnesses" met their doom, not as Rome but as France, the most powerful nation in the Antichristian empire. That new interpretation meant that the witnesses themselves could be none other than the suffering Huguenots, who had long struggled against the "Babylonian Empire." The prophecy continued by stating that the bodies of the witnesses would "lie in the street of the Great City" for three and a half days, after which time they would be resurrected and a "great earthquake" would mark the beginning of the fall of Babylon. Jurieu interpreted the three and a half days in the passage as years, meaning that the resurrection of the witnesses would happen in 1689, followed by a struggle that would turn the tide of the war. Moving on, he predicted that France would play a key role in the struggle and specifically foresaw that the French king (whether Louis XIV or his more tolerant son he did not specify) would convert to Protestantism, removing the most powerful kingdom from the popish cause.[75]

These prophecies called for political action. In particular, leaders of the places "where the flame of the Reformation has not dimmed" had the duty to offer "asylum and aid" to the refugees, and especially to "Pastors, who God preserves to relight the torch of pure doctrine." In addition, Jurieu believed that the bible prophesied a political union, described in scripture as the "people and kindred and tongues and nations" who were in truth "the chosen, the elect among the people, the faithful scattered around all the nations of Europe," whose task was to prevent "the total destruction of the Reformation in France." Jurieu called on these people to band together in the name of truth to beat back Louis XIV's universalist ambitions. Significantly, however, he imagined a broad coalition— one led by the Calvinist "elect" of all nations, but a union capacious enough to include kingdoms like England, a Protestant realm ruled by a Catholic, or even some Catholic states, like Spain or Austria, who understood that their "security" depended on defending the French Reformed against their enemies. In short, Jurieu gave a spiritual purpose to the League of Augsburg, an alliance against Louis XIV that would come together the same year that he published his book.[76]

Jurieu's prophecies did not appeal to all of the refugee intelligentsia. From Pierre Bayle to Jacques Basnage, many prominent ministers and thinkers decried Jurieu's theology as well as his politics, afraid that his embrace of militant action against the Sun King would undercut efforts to convince Louis to re-establish toleration. Nonetheless, there was no better intellectual manifesto for the creation of the Refuge. Jurieu convinced both ordinary refugees and potential patrons that the Huguenots were special people who deserved aid. His message was essentially optimistic, but it demanded action. He also made clear the larger goal: the return to a France that would be safe for Protestantism, the old Babylon transformed into a new Eden. This overall aim, the ability to return home, lay behind most of the refugees' intellectual and political efforts, even among those, like Bayle, who believed that conciliation with the Sun King would be more effective than militant resistance.[77]

Jurieu's philosophies provided a core political philosophy for the making of a continental Huguenot network. As chosen people, the refugees had to stick together—in coherent communities, if possible, but certainly through correspondence networks so that those in different countries could track the state of the larger Huguenot project. Since Jurieu and many others believed that return to France was not just a goal but a near certainty, the remaining French Protestants had to work hard to keep their language and liturgy intact. Only then could they easily transplant themselves when the king had a change of heart and invited them to return. Alongside Jurieu a cadre of people worked together to further this political goal, to see to the survival and prosperity of the church in exile. Many of these people were pastors like Jurieu, or elders of the important churches in the Netherlands, London, Switzerland, and a number of German states. As the gathering places for most refugees and in many cases the dispensers of financial assistance, the churches became important strategic centers. Beyond them, the Huguenot senate also depended on gentlemen with clout and connections, especially in European courts. The former Nîmes lawyer Henri de Mirmand was one such person; he forged connections in both Zurich and Berlin that allowed him to work with particular effectiveness for the refugees' interests. The last deputy general of the churches in France, Henri de Ruvigny, who eventually settled in England and Ireland, performed a similar role, connecting churches to state institutions.[78]

Despite their diverse interests and opinions, these Huguenot leaders collaborated to make the Refuge work as a transnational polity. They sought to create the kind of continental Protestant movement that Jurieu anticipated, while making sure that their own people played a special role in this new union. Through their efforts they managed to create something like a constitution for the Refuge. This emerged out of a number of delicate negotiations from 1685 to 1688, as refugee leaders implored their neighbors to grant them land and aid. The first manifestos appeared from Switzerland, where the lawyer-minister Claude Brousson took the lead in lobbying in capitals around Europe. The Huguenots used a religious message to gain adherents to their cause. In one characteristic petition, a group of "pastors, elders, and other Protestant Christians of France, refugees in Switzerland" implored potential patrons to form "a union and communion of saints," a Protestant coalition to resist Louis XIV. In addition, the petitioners asked that leaders "give our poor people retreats, and lands to cultivate wherever they are available." While they were very different kinds of documents, the petitions used identical language from Jurieu's prophecies and other more theoretical works.[79]

This transnational political network attempted to do something fairly novel in seventeenth-century Europe. During an era of state consolidation, the Huguenots hoped to create semiautonomous institutions that operated in tandem with local authorities, but also transcended particular borders. They wanted autonomy and the chance to preserve their own churches and legal privileges. All of this would be done, moreover, in the name of a Protestant cause that was larger than any one nation's interest. The building blocks of this new polity would be known as *colonies*, and refugee leaders like Mirmand and Brousson hoped to plant them around the continent, wherever they could find land and willing princes who would offer advantages to the newcomers.

―――

The development of a colonial program can best be examined from the vantage point of Switzerland. To be sure, many of the refugees took entirely different paths, by sea or land to England or the Netherlands, but the precarious nature of the Swiss Refuge—where massive numbers of refugees took one path through a land that did not have the resources to take care of them—made it a fertile place for colonial projectors. Beyond that, the leaders of the Swiss Refuge left behind numerous letters and memoirs that allow for a reconstruction of the tumultuous development of the Refuge from the time of the Revocation well into the 1690s. They portray a time of possibilities and troubles, as certain paths opened for the refugees only to close soon afterward, as the most appealing retreats seemed to move farther and farther afield, and as local authorities increasingly lost patience with their guests.[80]

The concept of a Huguenot colony first appeared in Friedrich Wilhelm I's Edict of Potsdam. Brandenburg's "Great Elector" offered advantageous terms to potential Huguenot migrants, including relief from taxation and essentially free land. He went a step further when he allowed the newcomers to create their own administrative and judicial bureaucracies and maintain their own autonomous churches. The elector declared that "in the cities where they have established their families," those of the "French nation" could choose someone who could settle differences among them, with no recourse to the local authorities unless the conflict involved a German. In short, the Huguenot colonies would exist as states within the state, nearly autonomous from the larger power structure. In contrast to the situation in England, where many Huguenots became "denizens" or naturalized subjects of the king, the Huguenots in Brandenburg remained a people apart, under the protection of the elector and the directors of the "French Commission" but responsible for their own affairs. The churches, meanwhile, could form consistories in the style of the old French churches, though the elector retained theoretical oversight in case of theological controversies.[81]

The possibilities of autonomous French communities perfectly suited the goals of Huguenot leaders like Jurieu and Mirmand. If the goal was a quick return to France, refugees had to retain as much of their language and liturgy as possible. Becoming a legal subject of a foreign prince might bring tempo-rary advantages but was not an essential strategy, since most refugees thought they would reclaim their old status as French subjects soon enough anyway. As a result, the various Huguenot spokespeople around the continent quickly adopted Friedrich Wilhelm's colonial vision as the ideal arrangement for refugee communities. They worked to move as many people to Brandenburg as pos-sible, where twenty-five "Huguenot colonies" formed before 1688, with twenty-three more coming into existence over the subsequent four decades. Despite the elector's desire for new Calvinist inhabitants, there was not unlimited space, and the numbers of newcomers only increased during the late 1680s. So Henri de Mirmand, himself an affiliate of the elector's Berlin court, worked alongside refugees pastors in Switzerland to find other European princes who would offer similar terms to refugees elsewhere in Europe.[82]

One internal memorandum offered something of an outline and justification of the colonial program. The "Mémoire pour le dessein des colonies" ["Memoir on the purpose of colonies"] provided a primer on how refugee leaders could convince princes to grant their people land and aid. The first step was to identify prospective homelands, places with sympathetic rulers and plenty of available land. Next, representatives of the Swiss Huguenot communities would need to visit these places and make sure that any available lands "would be good enough to live up to the work and hope of the refugees." Assuming the lands were suitable, the next step was to convince leaders to grant the newcomers enough advantages that the establishment would succeed. The *mémoire* suggested a secular argument: the newcomers would "augment the number of subjects" and bring in new tax revenues. They would also "be obliged to a much greater fidelity, obedience, and service by the recognition of the graces that had been granted to them." The Huguenots would be perfect subjects, while the "colonies will become eternal monuments to the charity that they [the princes] had shown toward the poor people." In short, it was in the interests of all rulers to assent to the creation of refugee colonies in their territories—not just as an act of charity but to strengthen the state.[83]

The need for new lands for colonies became especially dire in 1687 and 1688. The Great Elector died in April 1688, leaving the Huguenots without their leading champion. Although his son Friedrich also favored the refugees, opportunities were dwindling in Brandenburg itself, even as the numbers of new arrivals in Switzerland showed no signs of abating. The rolls of new arrivals in Zurich hinted at the depth of the problem: the calendar year 1687 saw over 9,000 refugees register in the city, 2,836 in the month of September alone. Numbers remained high through the middle of 1688, with an average of 370 each month, even in the winter.[84] To meet the crisis, Henri de Mirmand went on a tour of potential colonies in northern Europe with the minister Claude Bernard. Armed with letters of recommendation from Friedrich Wilhelm, they stopped in Hamburg, Emden, and a number of Frisian towns on the way to their ultimate destination, The Hague, where they intended to lobby the Prince of Orange and the Dutch States General. They found sympathy and good wishes wherever they went—even from the Lutherans in Hamburg—and plenty of offers for land. A gentleman in Emden offered land for one hundred families just outside the city, with promises of low taxes and three months of free food for all potential settlers. Across the border in the Netherlands they found vague offers of land near Leeuwarden and Groningen, and even vaguer promises of money from both the Prince of Orange and Pensionary Gaspar Fagel, the nominal head of the States General. Nonetheless, Mirmand had to admit that the entire journey had failed to raise any real money. With war raging between France and the partners of the League of Augsburg, solid promises of assistance were hard to come by. Land was worthless if the refugees did not have the resources to reach it.[85]

In the meantime, conditions in Switzerland deteriorated. Unlike Brandenburg or the Netherlands, the Protestant cantons had neither extra land nor abundant resources to share with the newcomers. Moreover, as time passed most of the refugees with skills or money had moved on, leaving their poorer or sicker neighbors to depend on dwindling public assistance. They were joined by two waves of additional migrants, first from the valleys of Piedmont in Savoy and then by another flood from France when Louis XIV released from prison and exiled a number of most recalcitrant Protestants in 1688.[86] A series of poor harvests in the late 1680s and early 1690s made matters worse. By this time Bern was spending one fifth of all its public revenues to care for poor Huguenots, most of whom lived in Vaudois towns and cities like Lausanne, Nyon, and Vevey, while just outside the borders of the confederation in Neuchâtel authorities took the step of hanging "sachets" at the entrances to churches in hope of getting enough spare change to keep their guests housed and fed.[87] Alongside fears of starvation lay another anxiety. Huguenot leaders worried that their flocks would grow desperate and return to France, where Louis XIV offered restitution of estates to those who abandoned their faith. This possibility terrified leaders of the Refuge. After losing so many souls to the mass abjurations in France, it seemed that even many of the remnant who had kept their faith were about to "plunge back into idolatry, in returning to France, as has been seen in many examples in Geneva in recent times."[88] These fears were not ill founded; in December 1688 the new French resident in Geneva reported that eleven refugees passed through town on their way back to Languedoc. Others were sure to follow, he believed, since "I learned that those [Huguenots] who are in Switzerland have been reduced to an extreme misery, and that many would not stay except that they lack money to return home."[89]

In the midst of this crisis, however, a miracle occurred. In November 1688 the Prince of Orange led an invasion fleet to England, and after a few months succeeded in expelling England's Catholic king James II and taking the British thrones for himself and his wife Mary, James's eldest daughter. This "Glorious Revolution" changed the European balance of power and cemented William of Orange's status as the head of the anti-French, Protestant interest in Europe. From the perspective of the Swiss Huguenots, the elevation of one who had espoused their cause—and who had surrounded himself with French Protestants both in The Hague and now in London—promised great possibilities. The heads of Lausanne's French committee wrote a fevered letter to two representatives in London, expressing great joy about the "wonders that have just happened in England," and hoping that "the royal beneficence of your august monarch" could finally help the poor refugees. Many did not even wait for offers of assistance. A Genevan minister reported that during the summer of 1689 "a great part of the refugees" left for England, sometimes four to five hundred each week, many of them young men who intended to enlist in William and Mary's army.[90]

Beyond the possibilities of military service, the British Isles became the new theater for Huguenot colonial ambitions. In April 1689 the new monarchs declared that "all French Protestants that shall seek Refuge in, and Transport themselves into this Our Kingdom" would receive not just "Our Royal Protection" but also unspecified help "in their several and respectable Trades and Ways of Livelihood, as that their living and being in this Realm may be comfortable and easie to them."[91] The next year members of the French committee were actively brainstorming ways to bring the beleaguered refugees from Switzerland to Britain, where they could find "uncultivated" land for the newcomers or encourage them in "new manufactures." The overall goal was charitable, to "give [the refugees] a retreat where they can pass their days in peace and quiet, without having to move from place to place without and fixed, secure home."[92] Nonetheless, applying the same theories from Germany to England would be difficult. English authorities frowned on the creation of autonomous Huguenot communities, preferring to disperse the refugees in smaller numbers to towns where they could help the local economy. They certainly did not desire the "disorderly assemblies of the French" that crowded London in 1689, "in the last stage of misery."[93]

There was another possibility, however, that eventually became the great hope of the refugees. By 1690 the front lines of the fight between William and Louis had moved to Ireland, where many of the refugees ended up fighting in "French regiments" alongside their Anglo-Dutch champion. The eventual cessation of hostilities left Ireland desolate and depopulated—not unlike the former war zones that the Huguenot colonists worked to improve in Brandenburg and other German states. Moreover, one of the key leaders of the Huguenot senate, Henri de Ruvigny, served as a leader of William's army in Ireland, and for his service received lands in Ireland and a new title as the earl of Galway. Ruvigny became the champion of a new scheme to use Switzerland's demographic problems to solve the very different problem in Ireland. Perhaps that war-torn kingdom could become the new center of Huguenot colonization.

Ruvigny laid out the possibilities of the program in a late 1691 letter to Henri de Mirmand. While he resisted the overblown language of a "land of milk and honey" that had characterized previous Irish colonization tracts, he lauded the possibilities of settlement there. There was plenty of cleared land that was vacant of people, and Protestant landlords were so desperate for settlers they saw the Huguenots as "the only means to reestablish their country, depopulated for a long time and even more so since the late war." Ruvigny admitted the voyage to Ireland was "long and hard," but insisted that those who formed "colonies" there could "enrich themselves in a short time with little effort."[94] What was more, English officials fully supported the plan, as it would withdraw more people from France and "contribute very much to a raising security of the peace of that kingdom."[95]

Huguenots were happy to capitalize on the situation in Ireland to further their own designs. Some intrepid refugees had settled in the kingdom before the war, and they quickly penned petitions promoting themselves as the ideal saviors of the troubled island. One undated proposal adopted the language so common in the earlier German petitions. The potential migrants began with a political economic argument, noting that "the multitude of peoples is the happiness of kingdoms," and that the most fertile lands would present "only horrors to our eyes" without "the industry of men" to cultivate the countryside, build great cities, and encourage "the sciences and arts" that distinguished Europeans from "the barbarous nations of the world." Moving to the case at hand, the petitioners noted that Ireland was a land with many natural advantages that remained nearly in a state of nature, largely because its native inhabitants, lazy and bigoted by Catholicism, refused to civilize the land. "The most certain way to remedy all these disorders," the Huguenots added, "and to make Ireland useful to you is to plant good colonies of new inhabitants with the opposite religion and morals to those of the Irish, and who can by their numbers and their diligence smother the spirit of revolt that is in them." The French were the best potential colonists: they were good, industrious Protestants who suffered for the faith, and helping them would serve "Christian charity" and the interests of the state. Finally, the petitioners added that many other European princes, including the elector of Brandenburg, had made similar offers—a subtle call for the kinds of promises of land and autonomy that were common in Germany.[96]

The emergence of Ireland as a possible retreat could not have happened at a more opportune time. During the winter of 1691 town authorities in Zurich broke the news to the French minister Paul Reboulet that the Huguenots could not stay. After a string of bad harvests had depleted the city's stores they could no longer afford to care for several thousand poor strangers. Reboulet feared that the other cities of the confederation would soon follow suit.[97] Several weeks later, Swiss leaders met with the English ambassador Thomas Coxe, who had been assiduously but unsuccessfully working to bring the Swiss into a firm alliance with William and Mary. They urged the ambassador "th[a]t the Refugiéz may be invited into Ireland, upon such termes as the King shall judge expedient," and that other Swiss be allowed to emigrate and join the "Colony" as well, all those who "cannot subsist any longer here, by rason of the extreme dearth of all things."[98] Coxe urged Zurich and Bern authorities to rethink their decision to expel the refugees—a strategy that was ultimately successful—but he worked for the Irish colonial designs as well. As Coxe saw it, removing the refugees from Switzerland was a diplomatic necessity, because the presence of thousands of French "fugitives" made it financially impossible for the Protestant Swiss to join the League of Augsburg.[99]

In the meantime, officers of the Huguenot senate sprung into action. Henri de Mirmand traveled to London, where he met with Henri de Ruvigny, and then to William III in The Hague where he secured a large amount of money to move the Swiss refugees to Ireland. Soon afterward Ruvigny, who had received a new title as the earl of Galway, went to Dublin to form a French committee to see to the refugees' needs once they reached Ireland. The general strategy remained the same for much of the decade: the earl of Galway suggested that William III grant a portion of confiscated land to a group of Huguenot lords and worthies, who would populate it with industrious Huguenots. Galway looked especially to Connaught, where he promised to set up linen and hemp manufacturing, while avoiding wool, since that would compete with domestic English production. Nonetheless, similar schemes appeared in virtually every corner of the kingdom, as local officials and Protestant nobles learned of the new possible source of settlers.[100]

In particular, Irish Protestant lords jumped at the opportunity to attract industrious Protestant settlers to lands that remained largely vacant after the war. One was Richard Coote, earl of Bellomont, an ally of William and Mary who received lands in Ireland for his troubles but had little means to make them profitable. In 1691 the earl embarked on a campaign to tempt Huguenots to settle on his holdings in the western province of Connaught and County Sligo, sending a description of his lands and terms to ministers in Switzerland. The lands were "proper for all sorts of agriculture," Bellomont wrote, "and very well situated for trade, being only two miles from the sea and five miles to Sligo which is a seaport." The earl offered to receive one hundred French families and provide them materials to build houses, with no taxes for the first year and very reasonable ones after that, with settlers able to take out long leases (lasting three generations) on their plots of land. Finally, he offered to bring in a French minister and build a church. While the terms made no mention of French political autonomy, they drew heavily from the "colonial" plans common in Germany the previous decade.[101]

Despite the hype, leaders of the Swiss Refuge insisted on completing their research before committing to sending their people to such an uncertain refuge. In one unsigned memoir, refugee leaders insisted on exact reports on "the situation of these places" where land was available, the numbers of families they could support, and the kinds of people who could thrive there. Beyond that, they called for more information on how exactly people could transport themselves from Switzerland to Ireland, especially during a time of war. All of this could best be managed, they noted, by sending a deputy who could report back on all these potential colonial settlements.[102] The person who answered the call was Charles de Sailly, a Burgundian gentleman who had already researched several schemes involving refugee colonies. In March 1693 Sailly headed to Ireland to judge the feasibility of moving large numbers of refugees to the kingdom.[103]

Sailly kept a careful journal as he traveled from Dublin through much of the southern part of the kingdom. Everywhere he went he saw a land scarred by warfare. Many of the places he visited were like the village of Goldenbridge, "which is a very good and beautiful place, on the river and the great road, but ruined and in need of rebuilding. In this country there are not cows, or sheep, or people, however rich or good the land." The war had ruined and depopulated much of the kingdom, leaving what Sailly saw as a blank slate for new settlers. Sailly also encountered dozens of Protestant nobles eager to find Huguenot settlers for their land. In each town he found local landowners willing to take ten, twenty, or a hundred families, and others who had traveled from miles away to offer terms to the French gentleman. One particularly optimistic lord said that "if things go well, he could receive and place more than a thousand families, and that there was no Protestant gentleman who would do so with as much pleasure." Sailly dutifully recorded all these offers and noted the advantages of the lands he traversed. He was especially taken with the seaside ports of Ireland's south coast, which he thought would be appropriate for merchants and artisans, and the "ruined and burned" cathedral town of Macroom, which he declared "the Montpellier of Ireland due to its healthy air." Sailly believed six hundred families could settle the area, where "One could make a good establishment and all sorts of manufactures."[104]

Despite Sailly's positive report, the settlement of Ireland had logistical problems that were difficult to overcome. Just as Swiss authorities relented on their plans to expel the Huguenots, English authorities kept delaying in providing money for transporting the migrants. Hundreds of refugees did settle in the kingdom, though most of them traveled from England or the Netherlands rather than Switzerland. A group of army veterans founded a town in Portarlington, to the southwest of the capital, while others settled in Dublin, Cork, Lisburn, and a few other locations. Nonetheless, the dreams of an Ireland populated by French refugees never came to pass—though they would reappear periodically during the eighteenth century. The Irish Refuge was important, however, in that it moved the Huguenots more explicitly into the world of imperial politics. Since Elizabethan times English leaders had attempted to "make Ireland British" by importing Protestant settlers, whether English Puritans or Scotch Presbyterians, to form what they usually called "plantations." The plan championed by Ruvigny and Mirmand represented a French variant of the same scheme. The Huguenots offered to become agents of the English empire in Ireland, as long as they could receive aid and some degree of autonomy. The same principles could be applied not just in Ireland but on any number of imperial frontiers. But settling on the edge of an empire, as Sailly noted, involved different challenges than moving to Berlin, Rotterdam, or the East End of London.[105]

———

The Ireland scheme was a strange culmination to Jurieu's ruminations about the coming Apocalypse. Nonetheless, one can see a continuous if winding path between the two phenomena. By promoting his people as special players in a political contest with apocalyptic implications, Jurieu helped to pave the way for Huguenot colonies around Europe, as Protestant leaders sought to provide aid to the suffering Protestants. Nonetheless, the great Rotterdam divine could not have been pleased with the way events played out. While he rarely commented directly on settlement schemes, his own gaze remained firmly directed toward France. The ascension of William and Mary in 1689 provided the first indications of great changes to come, and Jurieu became a tireless supporter of the new saviors of European Protestantism. He served as the master of a French spy ring that used Protestant informants to gather intelligence from French ports, and also championed the movement of ministers back into France to tend to the suffering Protestants still trapped there.[106] With the minister François Gaultier de Saint-Blancard, he lobbied the English to invade France, arguing that the Protestants in Dauphiné and Languedoc would join the invading armies much as the English had deserted their Catholic monarch in the Glorious Revolution. Jurieu understood the colonies as temporary expedients, places to lodge the people of God until things changed in France. He became nervous when he saw too many of his people leaving Rotterdam for England in 1689, to the point that he wrote a letter to Henri de Mirmand reporting "the deplorable state of the latest refugees in England" and urging them to stay where they were. For Jurieu, England was too far from France; it was better to keep the faithful close for the changes that he believed would shortly come to his homeland.[107]

While Jurieu remained true to his vision, other refugees gave up on the hope of apocalyptic change or an impending return to France. Instead, they began to see God's providence making other plans for them. Perhaps God did not intend them to engineer a French Reformation, but to be agents of the faith in other, more far-flung places. This was certainly one of the lessons from the life story of Jacques Fontaine. Back in Saintonge in 1685 the young Fontaine had counseled resistance against Louis XIV's dragoons. After escaping to the English West Country he allied with the Presbyterians and welcomed the arrival of William and Mary's armies. In short, his politics placed him firmly on Jurieu's side of the Refuge. And yet, by the late 1690s Fontaine had no thoughts of returning to France. He had given up on that sinful land. Instead he was settled on the very southwestern edge of Ireland, where he served, in his words, as the only agent of the "Protestant interest" in an impending struggle against Irish Catholic "Teagues" and French pirates. A man always attuned to the workings of God's providence, Fontaine saw this as his purpose: to witness for the faith in dark corners, where Protestant civilization barely reached. Several of his sons went even farther, across the ocean to the distant colony of Virginia. If France was lost, then the Reformation would need to move to new lands.[108]

2

Finding Eden

The Zurich minister Paul Reboulet looked out over the Refuge with a mixture of hope and fear. On one hand, as he reported to a friend in Geneva in 1687, many of the standard paths to safety were becoming more precarious. Refugees could no longer go to Bayreuth, Reboulet wrote, as "there are not the means to receive them there," while authorities in Ulm "no longer permit the Refugees to lodge there in passing." Amid all the bad news, there was a glimmer of hope. Reboulet had learned of a new Refuge, located not in Europe at all but thousands of miles to the south at the Cape of Good Hope, where the Dutch East India Company offered land and assistance to any Huguenots willing to dedicate themselves to life in that remote outpost. "The country produces everything," the minister noted, "and especially Wine." While the prospect of traveling so far to find peace and security could not have appealed to all refugees, Reboulet interpreted this latest news, in good Calvinist fashion, as a new expression of God's providence. "For a long time," he wrote, "I have believed that God's design was to disperse us to carry the Gospel to all the World."[1]

Reboulet's message indicated something interesting and important: the Huguenot colonial program had gone global. Over the previous several years refugees had streamed into Germany, the Low Countries, England, and Switzerland. They had founded colonies under the protection of various benevolent princes, and some had ventured out even farther, even to the eastern steppes of Russia or the marchlands of Ireland. Europe, however, was a troubled continent. Much of it remained crowded and impoverished, like Switzerland, or wartorn, like Ireland. Things worked out best in Brandenburg and other German states where leaders allowed the refugees to found their own semi-independent "colonies," but even there the proximity of non-French neighbors made life precarious. In the town of Erlangen, for instance, one of the most storied of the French colonies in Germany, the arrival of German-speaking refugees from the Palatinate in 1689 commenced a process that eventually made Huguenots an ethnic minority in what was supposed to be their town.[2] As Henri Duquesne, the leading advocate of Huguenot overseas expansion, wrote in 1689, it was better

The Global Refuge. Owen Stanwood, Oxford University Press (2020). © Oxford University Press.
DOI: 10.1093/oso/9780190264741.001.0001

"to live among men of the same Language, of the same Nation and of the same Religion, [among] which the humors consequently would be less incompatible, than among those who were born in different countries, which is almost always a source of divisions, of quarrels, and of many other inconveniences."[3] True peace could not come in someone else's land, but only by creating new lands.

In a sense, the push overseas came naturally out of the discourses perfected by Pierre Jurieu and other advocates for the refugees. The celebrated Rotterdam divine showed great interest in events happening on the farthest edges of the world, especially stories of successful Protestant missionaries. In one issue of his *Lettres Pastorales*, for instance, Jurieu printed a letter from the Boston minister Increase Mather, who offered a survey of the successful efforts to proselytize Native Americans. "Because by this we learn how God starts at last to accomplish his work." Jurieu noted, "that he started to send laborers in this great harvest, and that he animated the zeal of his Servants."[4] This "great harvest" of souls, of course, was one of the signs of the coming Apocalypse, and Jurieu was keen to add the imminent conversion of the Indians as yet another indication that Christ was about to return. In the English edition of his best-selling exposition on the book of Revelation Jurieu held forth that God had favored global commerce at this time in history and provided the technology to make it happen as a way of "fulfilling that great Promise that concerns the full *Conversion of the Gentiles*."[5] Since he already expounded at some length on the Huguenots' special role in the coalition that would bring down Antichrist and speed along Christ's return, it was not surprising that some refugees would make the same leap as Reboulet and assume that the refugees' dispersion was God's way to tell them to carry the faith abroad.

Beyond this millenarian backdrop, however, there was another set of beliefs that pushed Huguenots to consider striking off to new worlds. The seventeenth century was a great age of utopian thought among French writers, with Huguenots taking the lead in creating new, fictional societies that solved some of the looming problems in politics, economics, and religion in Louis XIV's France. Many of these utopias, like Denis Veiras's "nation of the Severambians," were perfect societies located, like Thomas More's original "Utopia," in faraway lands across the oceans. Veiras's narrator discovered the Severambians when his Dutch East India Company ship misfired and his company ended up in Australia. While these new-world utopias did not share all the same characteristics, they established the Indies as wondrous places where human beings could come close to achieving perfection. Apocalyptic thinkers also theorized earthly perfection, of course, and some Protestant utopians used biblical words like "Eden" and "Canaan" to describe their promised lands. Nonetheless, utopian literature did not have to be religious in nature. Indeed, utopias could only be possible if one believed that humans could shape their own destinies, at least to some extent, and many of the utopias decoupled morality from Christianity entirely. Veiras's Severambians, for instance, were virtuous pagans.[6]

There was a big difference between theorizing a perfect society and actually building one. For this purpose, the Revocation and diaspora provided opportunities that would not have otherwise existed. As it happened, Huguenots had particular ties to the kinds of exotic lands where utopian dreams might come to pass. Since the early sixteenth-century mariners from Normandy and La Rochelle had been leaders in French commerce in the Americas—and these men tended to be disproportionately Protestant. During the 1550s and 1560s Huguenots led prospective French colonies in Brazil and Florida, and then wrote about these failed experiments in narratives that defined French (and European) expectations of the Americas for decades to come.[7] In more recent decades, under the policies championed by Jean-Baptiste Colbert, Huguenots had taken the lead not just in the West Indies but in the East as well, where Jean-Baptiste Tavernier and Jean Chardin traveled and published about their experiences, and in Africa, where Jean Barbot worked for the Compagnie de Sénégal.[8] Huguenot commercial links gave them the necessary tools to strike out overseas, and their utopian mindset allowed them to imagine what they might find there.

If a turn overseas was a natural step for Huguenot refugees, it was not without dangers. For one thing, it broke decisively with the most cherished goal of Pierre Jurieu and other Huguenot leaders of a quick return and re-establishment in France. Once again, Henri Duquesne made explicit what many others surely believed, that even if they managed to convince the king to accept them back, they would always be "tolerated, but not dominant," waiting for the next tyrannical monarch to send them back to Babylon.[9] Abandoning the dream of return, however, came with dangers of its own. As the Huguenots quickly learned, moving overseas cast them headlong into a world of imperial intrigue and competition. While the Huguenot colonial program envisioned independence or at least autonomy along the lines of the storied German settlements, the refugees had no hope of gaining advantages without patrons, and to secure patrons the Huguenots would have to make themselves useful. Finding Eden in a world of empires would not be an easy task.

———

In the early 1680s no Huguenot possessed as much expertise about America as Charles de Rochefort. The elderly minister of Rotterdam's Walloon Church, Rochefort had published his *Histoire naturelle et morale des îles Antilles de l'Amérique* over twenty years earlier, and that massive guide to the West Indies had since appeared in two revised editions as well as Dutch, English, and German translations. The book presented a thorough if somewhat fanciful description of the Caribbean Islands, from the French establishments on Saint-Christophe, Martinique, and Guadeloupe, to the neighboring English and Dutch islands. The analysis even included the mainland, describing the probably apocryphal "colonie de la Palme," run by a French nobleman somewhere on the Gulf of Mexico, and the "country of the Apalachites," a mysterious Indian empire located in the mountains some hundred miles north in the Appalachian Mountains. The final 1681 edition included a new appendix extending the analysis into England's North American colonies, from Carolina to New England, which Rochefort depicted as lands of opportunity for potential migrants. Whether one wanted to travel to an island retreat like Tobago or a temperate mainland colony like Pennsylvania, there was no more complete guide in the French language.[10]

Rochefort's work drew from personal experience. In 1636 the young Rochelais minister traveled to the French West Indies as the chaplain to the Huguenot military engineer François Le Vasseur. While the details of Rochefort's residency in the Caribbean remain murky, he seems to have remained in the region for much of the next decade, residing on the islands of Saint-Christophe (St. Kitts to the English) and Tortuga and traveling around much of the region. He witnessed the first phase of French colonization in the Antilles, and much of the book concerned the great opportunities that awaited those who settled in the region. He was especially taken with Saint-Christophe, which he extolled as the jewel of the nascent French empire, a place "abundant in all things necessary for life." In the end, Rochefort did not stay in the West Indies—by around 1648 he had taken up his post in Rotterdam—but he still served as the foremost booster and expert on the Americas.[11]

Rochefort's enigmatic book provides a useful overview of how Huguenots viewed the West Indies across the seventeenth century. While the moniker "West Indies" covered a large swath of lands, from the arctic reaches of Canada to the tropics of Brazil, the most interesting parts for Rochefort were undoubtedly located in and around the Caribbean Sea, on the islands that were then becoming very important to the European economy for the production of sugar and other cash crops. Rochefort's Caribbean was a place of economic opportunity as well as wonder and danger. His book contained a vivid description of the landscapes, flora and fauna, and people of these strange islands. One (probably contrived) testimonial at the beginning of the book's 1665 edition summarized Rochefort's argument: these countries were "so beautiful and so gorgeous" that they resembled nothing as much as "the fortunate isles that are praised in the fables." Readers would have no choice after reading Rochefort on the Indies than to "voluntarily resolve to go and see them, to compare the excellent descriptions they have at hand with the real thing," and experience the "true delights" of the Americas.[12] In his glowing descriptions Rochefort followed other authors. Another witness, Capuchin missionary Hyacinthe de Caen, described the

Antilles as an "earthly paradise," a magical place where summer lasted all year, the fields and trees were perpetually green, and even the animals were "always . . . in love, and procreated continually without stopping, just like the earth did in the production of its plants."[13]

While Rochefort studiously avoided any direct reference to European religious politics, Huguenots constituted the primary audience for his work. They were an interested audience, moreover, because the French Antilles had always teemed with French Protestants. After the failure of the sixteenth-century colonies led by Huguenots in Brazil and Florida, French officials had made moderate efforts to exclude Protestants from their nascent empire. The point of the Edict of Nantes, after all, had been to restrict the practice of Protestantism to places it already existed, not to let it expand to new lands. Nonetheless, enforcing these provisions proved very difficult. Protestants still abounded in both the French Navy and the merchant marine, and local officials were too hungry for settlers to turn away potential migrants, especially those with financial resources. This proved especially true in the Antilles, where Protestants gathered in large numbers in both Saint-Christophe and the nearby island colony of Guadeloupe. In 1671, for instance, Protestants constituted 10 percent of Guadeloupan landowners and owned nearly 25 percent of the island's land. More Protestants worked as mariners, shopkeepers, or *engagés* (fixed-term laborers in the style of English indentured servants).[14]

In fact, many Protestants hoped that the Caribbean could become something more than just a place to make a living. As conditions slowly worsened for Protestants in France itself, Huguenots took advantage of the comparatively lax attitudes in the Indies to build better lives there. In the 1640s the primary champion of the Protestant cause was François Le Vasseur, Rochefort's employer. The Huguenot engineer acted as a ringleader for Saint-Christophe's Protestants, even securing a temporary decree of freedom of worship from the Catholic governor, Philippe de Poincy. Poincy faced political troubles for favoring these "heretics," so in 1640 he encouraged Le Vasseur to go on an expedition against the island of Tortuga, off the northern coast of Hispaniola, where a number of English privateers had established a small colony. Le Vasseur expelled the English and established what the Jesuit Jean-Baptiste du Tertre described as a "new Geneva" on the small island. He persecuted Catholics with great fervor, the priest claimed, tearing down a chapel that Catholic colonists built and expelling two priests, while his personal minister Rochefort led Protestant services. Not surprisingly, Rochefort himself never referenced Tortuga in his books, since by 1650 the island had become something of an embarrassment. In 1652 the experimental Huguenot republic ended with Le Vasseur's assassination at the hands of two men he had adopted as his heirs. Thus concluded the last Huguenot colony under the auspices of the French crown.[15]

Even after the fall of Tortuga, the French West Indies remained a fairly friendly place for French Protestants. While officials half-heartedly attempted to enforce Catholic orthodoxy on the islands, they allowed Protestantism to continue in the breach. Guadeloupe was one place where Protestants did quite well; Jean-Baptiste du Tertre complained of a quarter of Guadeloupe "where there is neither priest, nor churches," and thus no Catholics, who feared dying without sacraments. "The Huguenots on the other hand not being held back by the fear of this danger, established themselves there all the more since they would have more liberty to practice their religion."[16] Saint-Christophe proved even more attractive to Protestants. Since the island was split between French and English quarters, and the two nations lived in close proximity to each other, Huguenots could easily pass over to English churches for services, marriages, and baptisms (just as Irish and English Catholics made the opposite trek to the French quarter). It was probably no coincidence that Saint-Christophe appeared in Rochefort's book as the jewel of the French Antilles, the "most noble and most ample colony that our nation has planted outside the limits of France."[17]

While the first edition of Rochefort's work focused mostly on the French islands, the focus shifted as he prepared a second edition in 1665. The minister dedicated the new edition to the Dutch governor of Tobago and significantly expanded the section on that island, lauding "the goodness of the air that one breathes there, the incomparable fertility of the soil," not to mention "the ravishing beauty of the trees and the clear flowing rivers and springs that abound." Rochefort made the island's advantages clear: on Tobago Protestants could attend French-language services in a local Walloon church, but they would not need to fear that they were betraying the king, since Louis XIV had acknowledged the Dutch proprietor Adrien Lampsins as "Baron of Tobago."[18] In 1660 the French minister on the island, François Chaillou, sent a letter home that would have confirmed much of what Rochefort wrote. Chaillou reported that Tobago was "very fruitful in all that was sowed or planted, but especially in sugar," and he urged leaders of the Walloon churches to encourage any "poor people who can work" to move there. As far as the church went, Chaillou reported that he had appointed French elders and deacons, and even begun some halting efforts to convert African slaves and Carib Indians.[19]

In a separate, expanded treatment of Tobago published the following year, Rochefort went into even more detail about the island's advantages. He paid particular attention to a part of the island called "les Petites Anses," which could be referred to as the "French quarter" because so many French planters lived there. Rochefort spent pages describing the French settlers' beautiful plantations, fine houses, and families so large "to witness that honest women are just as fertile in America as in Europe." He also noted the orderly church governance, and a just government that met all the inhabitants' needs. It was a utopia, but a particularly Calvinist one, in which everyone worked hard and could not expect gold, pearls, or "an infinity of superfluous riches," but all that was necessary for an honest living. Rochefort ended the tract with a veiled exhortation to the persecuted of Europe, noting that sometimes God wanted people to be "transplanted from one place to another" in order to "profoundly unroot them from this miserable earth" and plant their gazes on "their true country, heavenly Canaan." Rochefort viewed Tobago, and the New World in general, as a suitable retreat where Protestants could serve God in peace.[20]

The other major additions to Rochefort's second edition reinforced his sense of America as a possible refuge for distressed Protestants, albeit in a more abstract way. The first edition had contained a brief digression on what Rochefort called the "country of the Apalachites," an Indian empire with historical links to the Caribs located in the mountainous interior of North America some days journey north from Florida. The minister's description of this perhaps fanciful empire drew heavily from previous utopian speculations. The Apalachites lived in peace and plenty in a land filled with mountains, lakes, and precious metals. More than that, they had a history of accepting European refugees to live among them—first a group of Huguenots who fled Florida in the wake of the Spanish massacre of the short-lived French colony in 1565; the second English and Irish refugees fleeing the 1622 Powhatan Revolt in Virginia. These refugees settled in the heart of the Apalachite realm, in the stunning "royal city" of Melilot. The Europeans had inspired the king of the Apalachites to embrace Christianity, and they enjoyed good treatment under his benevolent rule.[21]

The 1665 edition included an expanded "digression" on the Apalachites. In addition, the book included two testimonials, one from an "Edouard Graeves," supposedly one of the European refugees who lived in that country, and another from a Frenchman named Le Val Croissant, the governor of a French settlement called the "colonie de la Palme" located near the Apalachites. While Rochefort left any specific interpretations up to the reader, the Country of the Apalachites presented a sharp contrast with Louis XIV's France. For one thing, this was a land with ample resources and little social conflict, largely isolated from the rest of the world by mountains, and guarded by vigilant sentries who kept enemies from entering their refuge. In addition, the country presented a model of benevolent monarchy, where the king not only accepted the Huguenots but even converted to their faith, just as the Huguenots' own king moved toward persecution. Rochefort did not encourage anyone to set out for the country of the Apalachites—they had closed the doors to new arrivals, he claimed, and the lack of precious metals would keep money-hungry Europeans from settling there anyway—but the existence of this mysterious kingdom could only have reinforced America's appeal as a wondrous place of possibilities for travelers and migrants during a time of persecution.[22]

Figure 2.1 Charles de Rochefort included this depiction of the Country of the Apalachites, a classic New World utopia, in the second edition of his book *Histoire naturelle et morale des îles Antilles de l'Amérique* (Rotterdam, 1665). Courtesy of the John Carter Brown Library, Brown University.

During the 1680s Huguenots in the Antilles continued to hope that America could provide something of a refuge. In fact, Jesuit missionaries in the islands worried that the comparatively permissive environment in the islands would attract persecuted people from France. An anonymous priest reported that there were "many Huguenots" on the islands who dominated commerce in the 1680s, coming as they did from Dieppe and La Rochelle, two towns "strongly infected by heresy." Even worse, French heretics found plenty of opportunities to live their faith in the West Indies. On Saint-Christophe the Huguenot lieutenant's wife led a convoy of French Protestants to the English side for Protestant services, and did not even try to hide what she was doing, which tended to diminish the strength of the true Catholic Church, especially as Protestant planters spread the faith to their slaves as well. The priest especially feared that if such laxity continued, the islands would soon become a magnet for "many of those in France who are no longer tolerated there or even those who converted only under duress . . . especially the Huguenots who have fled to Holland or other foreign countries but on arrival did not find them to be good." In short, he feared that Saint-Christophe and Guadeloupe could turn into French versions of Massachusetts or Maryland, where religious groups who faced strictures at home could find toleration or even become dominant.[23]

Perhaps in response to such reports, the king's ministers sought to ensure that their deputies in the islands used the same methods against Protestants there as were practiced in France itself. In March 1685 the king issued what later became known as the Code Noir, a set of laws regulating slavery that also served to clarify the place of religious minorities in the empire. The first article of the law expelled the islands' Jewish minority, and the second and third made clear that while Protestants would not be forced to convert, they could under no circumstances openly practice their religion. The Code also sought to protect the souls of the large enslaved population by prohibiting Protestants from proselytizing them, and establishing their rights to Catholic sacraments.[24] Of course, seven months later the Revocation of the Edict of Nantes pushed matters farther. No one quite knew what the Revocation would do in the islands, since they were outside the bounds of the original Edict, but Louis made clear that he intended officials in the Antilles to use whatever methods available to force the island's Protestants to convert, including legal penalties and even dragonnades, and to prevent the king's subjects from leaving the islands.[25]

Nonetheless, extending France's campaign of repression proved difficult. For one thing, the only military force in the islands were the *troupes de la marine*, many of whom were Protestants themselves, and who had plenty of other duties defending the islands from foreign invasions and slave insurrections.[26] More than that, local authorities did not want to enforce the Sun King's orders, because they feared—correctly, it turned out—that Protestants would simply decamp for nearby English and Dutch colonies if the law turned against them. This problem was particularly acute on Saint-Christophe, where only an undefended land border separated the Huguenots from religious liberty. In July 1686, undoubtedly appraised of the situation at home, Saint-Christophe's Huguenots began to desert to the English side of the island, fearing that persecution would soon extend to the Antilles. The local governor attempted to stop them, claiming that "we have received no orders concerning them, and they can continue their commerce as usual."[27] While he adopted a cautious tone in his missive to the king, the official's letter made clear that he hoped he would not have to enforce the Edict of Fontainebleau in his jurisdiction. The islands always had trouble attracting white settlers, and the Huguenots held a fair share of the colony's wealth and slaves. Losing people would be disastrous for the Antilles, especially with the neighboring English governor, Nathaniel Johnson, offering good terms to French Protestants who agreed to settle in the English Leeward Islands.[28]

Instead of agreeing to turn a blind eye to Protestants in the colonies, Louis XIV and his ministers took a more controversial path. They continued to direct their underlings to force the conversions of the islands' Protestants, even as hundreds of them dispersed to neighboring English and Dutch possessions. At the same time, they made America the testing ground for a new project in forced conversion. For decades, European rulers had experimented with forced servitude in the Caribbean as a penalty for political or religious prisoners. The English islands abounded with former Irish and Scottish rebels, for example, who worked terms as laborers and, often lacking other options, stayed in the islands after their terms ended.[29] In 1686 the most recalcitrant Huguenots either wasted in prisons like the infamous Tour de Constance in Aigues-Mortes or worked as "slaves" on the king's Mediterranean galleys along with other criminals, debtors, and captive Muslims from North Africa. That year, however, the new administrator of the galley fleets had an idea. Michel Bégon had previously served in the Antilles, and he knew how difficult it was for the islands to attract white emigrants. Rather than be galley slaves, who tended not to live long anyway, perhaps the worst Protestants could go to the West Indies, where they would help to enrich the empire with their labor while they hopefully learned to give up their heretical practices.[30]

In 1687 the king's ministers put Bégon's plan into operation. Close to five hundred Protestants traveled to the Antilles on five ships over the course of the year, along with a number of invalids too weak to work on the galleys and a smattering of other prisoners.[31] Many of these exiles came from rural provinces of southern France, most notably the Cévennes region and Vivarais, places with no maritime tradition. The purpose of the transportation, the king's minister made clear, was not necessarily to punish the prisoners but to use them to build the imperial economy. In addition, by removing the Huguenots from prisons or galleys into a comparatively gentle American exile, the Sun King's ministers hoped they would keep these heretics from turning into martyrs for the Protestant cause. The French needed settlers in a number of places, most especially the colony of Saint-Domingue, where many of the prisoners ended up. Others went to Martinique, the seat of the colonial governor. Wherever they went, "his Majesty recommends that Governors distribute land to them so they can make a living and become habitants." The king hoped they would soon turn into productive planters, not slaves, but he urged authorities above all not to allow them to return to France under any circumstances. For this reason, none of the prisoners traveled to Saint-Christophe, where flight across the border was too easy, or to the nascent colony of French Guiana on the South American coast, located too close to Dutch Suriname.[32]

Whatever the benevolent intentions of Bégon and others, the transportation of Protestant prisoners did not play well with the Protestant public. Forced exile soon took a place alongside the dragonnades in lamentations for the Huguenot martyrs. Many of the stories originated in Cadiz, the Spanish city where the prisoners' ships waited before crossing the Atlantic—a port that abounded with Dutch and English merchant ships. In April 1687, for instance, a "certain French gentleman" working as a merchant on a Dutch ship visited the *Nôtre-Dame-de-Bonne-Esperance* while both ships waited for the wind to change off the Spanish coast. The Frenchman was shocked to find on board many of his coreligionists, who he described as Christian slaves to be sold to the highest bidder—a "most horrible and cruel" scheme that he falsely claimed "has never been heard of, except in this miserable age." The merchant gained an audience with several of the women and girls on the ship, one of whom heroically asserted that she went to America because she would never "worship the beast" or bow down before images.[33] This encounter was not an isolated incident. When the prisoner Samuel de Pechels passed through Cadiz some months later he also noted visits from sympathetic English and Dutch merchants, and letters and reports from these observers spread stories of the poor Huguenots heading to Caribbean exile. By early 1687 an English newsletter writer commented on the four hundred Protestants "sentenced to be sent slaves in America."[34] If Louis and his ministers intended to keep the prisoners from becoming martyrs, they failed miserably in their aim.

Writings from the exiles themselves only underscored their status as Protestant martyrs. One prisoner, Etienne Serres of Montpellier, published a lengthy account of his escapades in 1688, while another, Samuel de Pechels, wrote a manuscript of his experiences that did not see publication for nearly two centuries.[35] In addition, a number of letters and accounts from Huguenots in the Antilles made their way into the hands of Pierre Jurieu, who published them as part of his series of "Pastoral Letters" chronicling Huguenot suffering and resistance.[36] In all of these accounts, the Huguenots' American exile proved only one step in a long journey, beginning in every case with the dragonnades, continuing through imprisonment and various tests of faith, and ending for Serres and Pechels with deliverance (and for several of Jurieu's letter writers with martyrdom).

The image of America depicted in these letters and narratives differed starkly from Charles de Rochefort's glowing account. Rather than Eden, America functioned as the kind of howling wilderness that Moses's people had to cross on the way to the promised land. The trials started on the Atlantic crossing, where the prisoners crowded into a small space below deck where those on Pechels's ship faced "stifling heat" and "a frightful number of vermin who devoured us." Even worse, they endured terrible treatment from the officers and crew, who boasted that those who did not convert would be hanged once they reached the Indies, or "delivered to the savages," who many European believed to be cannibals.[37] The *Nôtre-Dame* faced similar conditions, according to Etienne Serres: nineteen of the Huguenots died en route, and "even Turks and devils" showed sympathy for the prisoners' plight. Matters got even worse when the ship reached the Caribbean. Due to poor navigation, the ship wrecked on an island near Martinique, killing many of the prisoners and leaving others, like Serres, clinging to pieces of the shattered ship and riding them ashore.[38] Another prisoner, Pierre Issanchon, related the story of his encounter with local Caribs, who "appeared to us to be very touched by our sufferings" and shared their cassava and fish with the distressed Protestants. Compared to the savagery of Louis XIV, the once feared Caribs were tender and merciful.[39]

Soon Serres and the others were back in the hands of their persecutors, and the Huguenots showed little love for either the people or the environment in the Antilles. Pechels went first to Saint-Domingue, which he labeled "very disagreeable due to the heat and the insects."[40] Etienne Serres complained of the "spirit of cruelty" shown by the governor in Martinique, the comte de Blenac, but the sun proved to be the greatest persecutor. "The sun had so burned my body," Serres claimed, "that I retained nothing of my natural color; its rays had so roasted my skin, that it seemed I had passed through a raging fire."[41] According to Issanchon, one man named Jacques Bernard actually died from extreme exposure to the sun, while several others faced the same kinds of pressure to convert that were common in France. Two gentlemen found themselves imprisoned in a dungeon and then converted in response to "a promise to be let free in Martinique"—an offer that, needless to say, the crafty Jesuits did not keep, sending the men to Saint-Domingue instead. Even for heroes who had braved prison and the galleys in France itself, the rigors of Caribbean captivity could prove dangerous not just for their bodies but for their souls as well.[42]

In the end both Serres and Pechels found silver linings in their captivities. For one thing, it was clear that the Protestants had a great deal of autonomy. Both men ended up in Saint-Domingue, and found that the conditions of life in a frontier colony were far different than those in France or even Martinique. The local governor treated the Huguenots with respect, probably happy to get white settlers of any kind. And reading between the lines of the two prisoners' stories of their tribulations, it seems clear that they had almost complete freedom of movement. In short, whatever the protests of Protestant propagandists, the men's lives bore no resemblance at all to the legions of African slaves who made the Caribbean economy. Both men realized that they could use their relative autonomy to win freedom and learned that the best place to do so was Île à Vaches, a small island off the colony's southern coast frequented by English ships on their way to or from Jamaica. Pechels got lucky when the governor sent him to work there, and he soon found passage to Jamaica and then London with an English merchant.[43] Serres had to cross a hundred miles of jungle to reach the island, but he had enough resources to hire two *boucaniers*—the famous buccaneers who first settled Saint-Domingue—to guide him to freedom, with a small cache of weapons to ward off attacks by maroons or wild boars. He eventually contracted with a Dutch merchant and, after stops in Curaçao and Saint Thomas, reached refuge in Amsterdam, "where, by the grace of God, my true liberator, I saw myself delivered from the hands of my persecutors."[44] By the end of 1688 most of the survivors of the project had found similar paths to freedom. The Caribbean was distant from France, but its borders were too porous to hold prisoners—at least if those prisoners were white. Soon Louis XIV called an end to the design; by April 1688, according to rumors heard in Geneva, the king had released all of the West Indian exiles and allowed them to leave the kingdom.[45]

In most respects the imprisonment of Huguenots in the Antilles seemed like a reversed image of the New Canaan imagined by Charles de Rochefort. Serres, Pechels, and their fellow prisoners were forced migrants, so they experienced America as a trial rather than a refuge. Still, the schemes did have some interesting parallels. Rochefort and Louis XIV had similar purposes: to solve the kingdom's domestic and imperial problems in one fell swoop, by using unwanted people in France to populate vulnerable frontiers. What was more, even the narratives of the prisoners themselves, who viewed America as a prison rather than a potential homeland, still sometimes adopted the language of the Rotterdam minister. In one remarkable digression, Etienne Serres concluded that "if France did not possess authority in this region, our chains would not be as heavy as they were in France." The Carib Indians, he claimed in an almost exact paraphrase of Rochefort, were gentle souls who had even rescued and fed several of the victims of his shipwreck. "If France did not reign in America, America could become our France" and the Indians "our compatriots." If even Etienne Serres could retain a vision of America as a promised land, then clearly the images from authors such as Rochefort had penetrated the Huguenot consciousness.[46]

————

If the Antilles rested in the hands of the persecutors, there were other prospective retreats for migrants who wished to set off for Eden. The final 1681 edition of Rochefort's book detailed the most promising possibilities. Over the course of the seventeenth century the English had built "many beautiful colonies" on the eastern coast of North America. While the French and Spanish empires largely prospered on indigenous or enslaved African labor, the English had managed to attract European migrants to their colonies and formed communities that resembled towns and villages back home far more than the sugar plantations further south. Rochefort wrote a thorough survey of these diverse colonial societies, which he titled "An Account of the Present State of the Celebrated Colonies of Virginia, Maryland, Carolina, New York, Pennsylvania, and New England." In this appendix Rochefort removed any doubt as to the purpose of his book: his intended audience included those who wished to "transport and establish themselves" in North America, and he spoke to those who did not own land in Europe, or whose land was so unproductive that it would not furnish a living. North America provided a welcome retreat for the poor of Europe, Rochefort underscored. "Those who work the land," the minister wrote, "will be rewarded with bread."[47]

North America represented a different kind of utopia than either the French Antilles or the country of the Apalachites. Unlike those strange places, British North America was a familiar paradise. It suited European constitutions, Rochefort wrote, because the seasons, climate, and produce of the land did not differ greatly from Europe. French migrants would not have to give up the bread or wine that served as the staffs of their diet, since even grapes "grow there naturally without any human labor" and would certainly produce excellent wine.[48] In short, "all this vast continent of *North America* enjoys an extremely agreeable and temperate climate and is stocked with all the things *most necessary* for life." It resembled nothing so much as an ideal version of a European province, a place where people like Huguenot refugees could live in peace and plenty without fear.[49] Moreover, the existence of benevolent governors and religious toleration ensured that refugees would be free to live as they wished. In Virginia and South Carolina, for instance, foreign migrants received "the same liberty and franchise as the native English" and could enjoy "the same religious forms and ecclesias-tical discipline that they have been accustomed to profess in the countries they have come from."[50]

Rochefort identified a number of advantages for those migrants who traveled to North America. Some were economic in nature. In Virginia and Carolina, for instance, the minister highlighted the possibilities of silk culture in the colonies. Mulberry trees grew naturally there, providing nourishment to the "innocent little worms" who produced the cocoons that could be made into raw silk. In Carolina, Rochefort added, the king had already received eighty "foreign Protestant families" to establish silk manufacturing as well as "the culture of grains, wines, and olive oils."[51] French people would be able to make an easy living, and they could also acquire land. In the new colony of Pennsylvania, Rochefort reported, the proprietor promised one hundred acres to anyone who transported servants to the colony—and each of these servants would receive fifty acres of their own on the completion of their terms.[52] He concluded that English North America was a good country for those who could work—not a place of easy riches, perhaps, but of an easy competency. The image on the title page of the appendix exemplified this interpretation: a lone woman stands in a field, holding a bible in one hand and a tool in the other, with the Latin motto "Labore et vigilancia" below her.[53]

Beyond economic opportunity, Rochefort lauded North America's spiritual climate. Like most Huguenots, the minister had little understanding of the complicated religious politics that tore the British world apart in the seventeenth century.[54] Nonetheless, he understood that some diversity existed from one colony to another in terms of religion, but that all of them were broadly Protestant and willing to allow strangers to worship as they wished (which was usually if not always accurate). He paid particular attention to New England's distinct church establishment, which he described as a form of "true and ancient Christianity" that differed from the larger Church of England only in "several points concerning discipline and the governance of their assemblies," but that otherwise "agrees with all the other Protestants of Europe in all the essential and fundamental points of pure doctrine." Rochefort's language for describing New England would undoubtedly have appealed to the more devoted of France's Calvinists. Dancing and gambling were forbidden, Rochefort noted, and the Sabbath kept holy, while ministers had translated the Bible and converted many local Indians. If anyone had the desire, like Zurich's Paul Reboulet, to spread the faith to the heathens of the world, New England was a good place to do it.[55]

It was not surprising that Rochefort mentioned Indian missions as a central benefit of North America. Conversion of Native Americans was already a hobbyhorse of many Huguenots, including Rochefort himself. Back in 1668 a Parisian Protestant merchant named Henri Mouche decided to pledge some of his fortune to the cause of evangelizing America's indigenous people. He first gravitated toward funding missions in "Virginia" (by which he seemed to mean all of English America), but then decided to put his gift in the hands of the Walloon Church of Leiden, under the logic that the Netherlands was a center of global commerce, and Leiden as a university town would supply young ministers willing to make Mouche's vision a reality.[56] Rochefort was one of the consultants who tried to figure out how to use the merchant's gifts, and he did so in part by writing to London to find out "the true state of religion on the North American continent." He must have been satisfied with what he found out, because by 1678 he suggested that some of the gift go to missionaries in New England, following up on an earlier proposal that some "predicants" from Leiden go to the colony to learn the best methods of conversion. Seen in context, the New England section of his "Récit" suggested that prospective missionaries, who intended to bring the gospel to the pagans, were one possible audience for his work.[57]

As it happened, Rochefort's description of English America was just the first volley in a propaganda war that lasted through much of the 1680s. Unlike French or Dutch colonial authorities, English colonial interests had a long history of issuing propagandistic tracts to attract potential colonists or investors, and during England's Restoration period the number of publications increased and the audiences became more diverse. The most astute propagandists were the proprietors of Carolina and Pennsylvania, the two newest colonies in the empire. Both had come about as the result of royal grants—in the case of Carolina to a group of English and Scottish nobles known as the "Carolina proprietors," and for Pennsylvania to the prominent Quaker gentleman William Penn. Aside from publishing numerous tracts for English, Scottish, and Welsh readers, leaders of both colonies looked beyond the three kingdoms. Penn had trained at the Huguenot Académie de Saumur and had extensive contacts in Germany and the Netherlands, and the Carolina proprietors also had connections to Dutch exiles. As a result, French-language pamphlets advertising the colonies appeared in the Netherlands, Switzerland, and London, marking the first times that English colonial planners explicitly targeted Huguenot refugees. If Rochefort's book came at an early point, after the Poitevin dragonnades but before the mass exodus began, most tracts appeared after 1684 and specifically aimed at the masses of vulnerable people languishing in English, Dutch, or Swiss cities. Some of them simply translated English-language publications, while others collected material purposely tailored for French audiences.[58]

The Carolina tracts tended to emphasize some of the same benefits that Rochefort described. The air was healthy there, propagandists claimed, to the point that local natives lived longer than in Europe. All things grew there in abundance, the government was "very reasonable and moderate," and English and foreigners alike enjoyed "an entire Liberty of Conscience." The weather was moderate to the point that even summer seemed like "a continual spring."[59] The colony had very little sickness, one writer falsely claimed, and what did exist came about only from the English planters' immoderate use of punch, their preferred drink.[60] To sum up, wrote one propagandist, "One must agree that there is hardly a Country more proper than this one, for establishing a good Colony, as the Climate is good and healthy, proper to the labor of Negroes, the earth fertile and abundant in Rivers, the government gentle and without charge, safety complete, comfort assured, and the Indians good and tractable."[61]

By 1686 French readers would already have an understanding of what a colony was, based on the numerous French colonies in Germany. In fact, the pamphlets deftly combined the Edenic imagery of utopian literature with the practical features of the German colonies. After lauding the climate the pamphlets almost always focused on the benefits that the proprietors offered to would-be settlers. The Carolina proprietors offered good terms for land and relief from taxation, as well as the opportunity to become naturalized subjects and thus gain all the "privileges" available to other English settlers.[62] They also desired large groups of newcomers; one author suggested that refugees form "confederations" with people of different social positions and economic competencies, who could lay out French villages in Carolina, like the colonies that existed in Europe but placed in a much more salubrious location.[63]

The Pennsylvania tracts focused more explicitly on religious liberty and political autonomy. The most important book, titled *Recueil de Diverses Pieces, concernant la Pensylvanie,* appeared in The Hague in 1684, and included French translations of a number of tracts that appeared in English and German, with a few additions specifically for French readers. The description of the province underscored its good location—on the same latitude as Montpellier and Naples—as well as its "clear and agreeable" air and good soil that could produce everything from silk to linen. The country was well suited for "ingenious Spirits" of "low condition" in the old world, skilled people held back by the rigid social and political structures in Europe. In two to three years, the tract claimed, these newcomers could easily make a living as farmers, protected by William Penn's beneficent frame of government, which the proprietor described in a lengthy letter appended to the tract. From a refugee perspective, perhaps the most salient section appeared at the end of the first section, when the author noted that God himself called colonists to Pennsylvania, who were destined to follow "the example of the blessed Patriarchs, the glory of God, and the instruction of those who are in the shadows." The new arrivals would settle in "ease, abundance, and plentitude, in order to attract the blessings of salvation to these ends of the earth."[64] For a people already primed to view themselves as chosen people on a holy mission, this was a tempting message.

Over the course of the 1680s similar accounts of New World Edens circulated around the Refuge. Printed tracts, usually produced by the proprietors themselves or their allies, tended to grossly exaggerate the advantages in the colonies they described. Nonetheless, there were other ways to advertise these prospective settlements. One preferred method was by circulating letters, usually through networks of Huguenot ministers, describing conditions of life across the world. The best example is a letter from New England in 1687, which provided a description of the province that diverged from the overblown rhetoric of the pamphlet literature. The anonymous author, who arrived in the vanguard of several hundred Huguenot settlers to the province, warned prospective emigrants not to expect any sort of special favors in New England, but added that "Living is exceedingly cheap, and that with a little one can make a good Settlement." He included lengthy descriptions of the three refugee communities in the province, each of which had different advantages. The wilderness town in the "Nipmuck Country," for instance, was a bucolic rural retreat with "little rivers and ponds . . . fruitful in Fish, and Woods full of Game." The settlement at Narragansett on the Rhode Island border was closer to water and had "more Commerce with the Sea Islands," while Boston itself had close trading links to the Caribbean and Spain. He concluded that migrants to New England could live in "the greatest Liberty," but could not refrain from a dig at his English hosts. "If our poor Refugee Brethren who understand tilling Land, should come hither," he wrote, "they could not fail of living very comfortably and getting rich, for the English are very inefficient, and understand only their Indian Corn and Cattle."[65]

A similar manuscript tract from the mid-1680s took the form of a set of "questions and answers" about the colony of Carolina. The fictional dialogue imparted practical information—who to visit to buy land in the colony, for instance—as well as detailed reports about the economic opportunities in the province. The author also stressed the availability of liberty of conscience, as well as the general healthiness of the climate. While the answers may not have all been truthful, the questions help to elucidate what prospective migrants wished to know about Carolina. One query, for instance, asked specifically about women and their ability to raise families in the colony—an important topic if the colony was to survive into a second generation. "The beauty, bounty, and sweetness of the climate," responded the writer, "allows women to bear themselves admirably well and they are very fertile." The manuscript may have been intended for print, but its existence shows the numerous ways that both proprietors and refugee leaders circulated information about the various opportunities to find land and form communities in corners of the Protestant world.[66] By 1687, a prospective migrant would be awash in information about various American retreats. They only needed to decide where to go and how to get there.

———

In the midst of all this colonial speculation Henri Duquesne conceived the idea for his Isle of Eden, the most ambitious of all the Huguenot colonies in the 1680s. In some ways, Duquesne's speculations fit nicely with the wave of colonial plans that swept the Refuge during the late 1680s. Duquesne began his published description of Eden with reference to the incessant talk of "colonies and new establishments" in Germany, North America, and southern Africa, and Duquesne's own writings displayed many of the features of a promotional tract. He wrote at great length of the natural advantages of his retreat, the plan of government there, and the economic opportunities, and he provided exact instructions on how prospective settlers could get in on the scheme. Yet at the same time, Duquesne explicitly rejected the logic behind all previous colonies. Unlike every other establishment, the Isle of Eden was not someone else's land. It was instead an uninhabited island, a place with neither indigenous inhabitants nor colonizers, a tabula rasa where Huguenots could build a republic of their own. Duquesne was quite insistent that, however grateful he was to the Protestant patrons who had given the Huguenots refuge, they would be better off in their own state, allied with but not subject to other Protestant powers.[67]

Henri Duquesne was well placed to realize such a monumental scheme. His father, Admiral Abraham Duquesne, had been the greatest French naval officer of the seventeenth century, sometimes considered the founder of the modern French Navy. Abraham was an old-school Huguenot; he saw no difficulty in reconciling his Protestant faith and his love for the Sun King, and in return for his service the king allowed Abraham to die a Protestant in his Paris house in 1688. Louis also granted Henri a one-way ticket out of the kingdom, as he did for a number of prominent Huguenot nobles, an offer the younger Duquesne accepted in June 1686. His father purchased Henri the barony of Aubonne, in the Swiss pays de Vaud just east of Geneva, and so Henri and his wife Françoise Bosc, the daughter of another leading ancien régime Huguenot, took up residence in a stately castle on the shores of Lac Léman, where Henri became the titular ruler over several hundred Vaudois villagers.[68]

The young baron dreamed of new worlds from the time he reached his Swiss exile. While he did not share Abraham's talent for naval combat, Henri had served as both a naval officer and later as an ambassador. The Sun King's marine included numerous world travelers as well as Huguenots, and Henri undoubtedly learned a lot about far-flung parts of the world from his fellow officers and sailors. Even the Aubonne castle conspired to turn Henri's thoughts toward the east. Its previous owner, Jean-Baptiste Tavernier, was a Huguenot explorer famous for his lively writings on Persia, the Middle East, and the East Indies. On acquiring Aubonne Tavernier built a new addition: a tower in a Middle Eastern style, supposedly so that he could always remember where his wealth and position came from. Perhaps because of such spending, Tavernier was unable to hold on to his barony, selling it to settle his debts in 1685. But the tower remained, a visible reminder of previous Huguenot encounters with the wider world, and one that Henri Duquesne must have looked on as he conceived his own scheme for a Huguenot republic in the East.[69]

The roots of Henri Duquesne's Eden experiment are difficult to decipher. According to one biographer he theorized an overseas retreat for his coreligionists as early as 1683, perhaps at the urging of his wife, but the first solid evidence of the scheme appeared in the late 1680s. Duquesne wrote four separate small pamphlets about his colony, which he circulated through established networks of refugee ministers in Switzerland. In 1689 a printer in Amsterdam issued a combined edition titled *Recueil de quelques mémoires servant d'instruction pour l'établissement de l'île d'Eden* ("Collection of several memoirs serving as instructions for the establishment of the Isle of Eden") The book combined elements of a promotional tract with many of the conventions of utopian literature, all wrapped up in an obvious Calvinist package.[70]

Duquesne's vision drew directly from the conceptions of Pierre Jurieu and others of the Huguenots' special status. The baron believed his people to be God's chosen, destined to do great things in the world. Unlike the Rotterdam minister, however, Duquesne did not think the Huguenots' destiny lay in France. Duquesne clearly aimed at Jurieu when he declared early in his tract that a return to France was unlikely and undesirable, since the political calculus there remained unchanged from the 1680s. Looking around Europe, Duquesne saw little to indicate an impending deliverance of Protestantism on the continent, despite the positive news of England's Glorious Revolution. To the contrary, Catholics were everywhere gaining dominance, leading him to believe "there is more cause to fear a general persecution in all of Europe, rather than an imminent deliverance of the Church."[71] Rather than wait around for apocalyptic changes in Europe it was better for the people of God to make their own paradise, far away from that troubled continent.

If he rejected return to France, Henri Duquesne was equally skeptical of finding permanent refuge in other people's states. He was cognizant of the many "inconveniences" that came from living among people of "different humors," a sentiment he probably developed in Aubonne, where he quarreled with townspeople who refused to give allegiance to their new baron. Duquesne was quick to laud the efforts of all his fellow Protestants who had offered charity to his brethren, but he did not believe that refugees could live indefinitely as "fugitives, wandering from country to country to find some asylum among their brethren and some subsistence from their work." It was better for these "poor sheep" to be "gathered into a flock" so that they could worship God and "eat their bread with joy, without being a charge to their brothers, but rather be helpful to the afflicted and welcoming to the unfortunate."[72]

Instead of depending on charity Duquesne suggested that Huguenots form a new France overseas. Like most utopian thinkers, he paid particular attention to the political structure of his "republic of Eden." Duquesne's political theory displayed the same confused amalgam of monarchism and republicanism that defined Huguenot thought during the late 1600s. Many Huguenots—especially those like Duquesne with close links to the Sun King's government—had been proud absolutists, and while some of them gradually moved toward limited monarchy as an ideal form of politics, they remained creatures of the old regime.[73] Duquesne proudly labeled his new polity a republic, but wanted nothing that resembled a democracy. Instead, his state was something of a Protestant aristocratic utopia. The leader of the polity would be an elected leader, a "chief and conductor of our republic," who would lead with the council of twelve notables, "the wisest and most prudent among us." By balancing a unitary executive with an appointed senate, Duquesne aimed to avoid the pitfalls inherent in both monarchies and republics, nearly stumbling on a theory of separation of powers. He recognized that all governments were "ordained by God," but noted that "excesses" could occur if power concentrated "in the hands of a single man."[74] The new republic even had a peculiar mechanism for popular participation in government. On the second day of every year the chief and senate invited ordinary people to write down suggestions and complaints and anonymously submit them to their governors. In this way each person, of whatever station, could comment on public affairs.[75]

While he laid out the rudiments of a state, Duquesne insisted that he did not intend to threaten anyone else's peace. Apparently rumors surfaced in 1689 that the baron meant to use his Eden project to build a kind of Huguenot army that would join with the Vaudois Protestants to invade the duchy of Savoy and perhaps France itself. Duquesne vociferously denied these charges, claiming he "has no design to invade the States of any King, Prince, or Republic." Instead, the Eden settlers intended to give "to Caesar what belongs to Caesar," intending only "to give God what belongs to him, in enjoying the gifts that he gives us with his grace, and we would be very ashamed to start such an establishment with an injustice, where we claim that justice and piety will rule in all things." Duquesne carefully contrasted his project with virtually all other European imperial endeavors in the Americas and Asia, which sought to bring riches and glory to the home country, even if accomplishing those goals required the use of violence against indigenous peoples or European rivals. Colonizers were rarely content with "mediocrity," but his Huguenots were not ordinary colonizers; they sought only "a life of moderation and tranquility of conscience," while others found themselves victims to "their unbounded ambition." Drawing on but going beyond Charles de Rochefort's earlier colonial vision, Duquesne declared that the Eden colonists wanted lives of peace far from the cares of the world. They hoped that all Protestant powers would support them in this goal, since it would remove the need for charitable donations, while "among others who see us as objects of disdain and scorn" —clearly Louis XIV and his allies— "they must be well satisfied to have us removed from their sight."[76]

Duquesne's anti-imperialism continued in his discussion of the Isle of Eden's economic character. Nearly every promotional tract focused heavily on economic opportunities. The Carolina publications, for instance, stressed the possibilities of cash crops like wine, silk, and olive oil, while offering tempting suggestions of undiscovered mines of precious metals in the American interior. Duquesne did not offer any such "pompous description of some country abundant in pearls and in precious metals, or of some lake where the sand is only gold, like some have made us believe there was in Peru." His was a different kind of paradise. Like Rochefort's country of the Apalachites, Eden provided everything one needed to live in comfort, but not in opulence. Moreover, potential colonists needed to know how to work. There were no "cultivated fields, or planted vines," only a healthy, forgiving land waiting for good workers to turn the wilderness into paradise. Duquesne did mention tobacco and sugar as possible crops on the island, but in general his was a very Calvinist utopia. The Eden colonists would work hard, worship God, and lead simple, godly lives. They would be "a society composed of honest men, established in a fertile and agreeable place, with health, liberty, the tranquility of conscience, justice, charity, and finally the hope of safety [*salut*], which are the true goods which are worth whatever efforts one makes to acquire them."[77]

In his first three pamphlets Duquesne carefully hid the exact location of his Isle of Eden. He feared that, since he intended to settle one of "the most agreeable and best" parts of the world, others might read his descriptions and beat him to it. In the final tract, he finally revealed Eden to be Île Mascareigne, or Île Bourbon, an island several hundred miles east of Madagascar in the South Indian Ocean now known as La Réunion.[78] Duquesne undoubtedly knew about the island from his father and fellow naval officers, as that part of the Indian Ocean had been a French preoccupation for much of the seventeenth century. At several points the French had founded colonies in Madagascar, and in 1658 Étienne Flacourt published an account of his time there that included a short but glowing description of the island that Flacourt himself had christened Bourbon, after Louis XIV. Flacourt described Bourbon as an "earthly paradise," the best country on earth to sustain a colony of Europeans. The air was pure, the water clear, and the land abounded with animals that were good to eat, but it was blissfully free of the snakes, crocodiles, and insects that plagued so many tropical locales. Flacourt related the story of three Frenchmen who had spent three years on the island and found the air so healthy that not only did they not get sick (an unusual experience in the tropics), but even found their previous ailments cured. The men resolved to remain there, even though they had no "shirt, clothes, hat, or shoes." They found they had no need of clothing, they never got sick, and they easily subsisted on the wild pigs and giant tortoises that abounded on the island.[79]

Despite Flacourt's glowing description, the French had little success making a permanent establishment on the island in the subsequent decades. A few stragglers did settle there but it remained a distant periphery, an aspirational outpost for French planners who wanted to raise the kingdom's profile in the East Indies, a part of the world where the Dutch and English had a much larger presence. Aside from being "the best country there is in all the Indies," according to one French witness, the island sat in a prime strategic location, halfway between the Cape of Good Hope and the Indian subcontinent.[80] The Dutch already had a small outpost on the nearby island of Mauritius, but the French thought they could set up a provisioning station on Bourbon that could eventually rival the Cape Colony. Others speculated on all the produce that could come from the salubrious island: indigo, sugar, tobacco, even wine that could then be traded with the great empires of the East. These hopeful speculations reached a climax in the early 1680s, at a time when Henri Duquesne himself worked within the government. Successive reports cast Bourbon as the key to the East Indies, and lamented that all of the settlers who had gone there lived "in the mountains

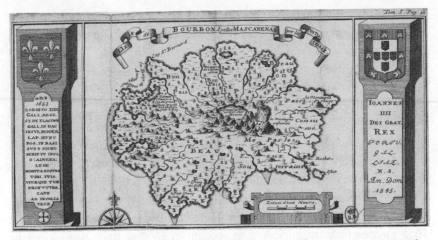

Figure 2.2 François Leguat included a map of Île Bourbon, otherwise known as the Isle of Eden, in his 1708 narrative of his travels, *Voyages et avantures de François Leguat, & de ses compagnons, en deux isles désertes des Indes orientales* (Amsterdam, 1708). Courtesy of the Bibliothèque Nationale de France.

completely nude like the Negroes." The island needed order, various officials noted: a military government, perhaps, and priests to ensure that the inhabitants did not drift into "libertinage."[81]

It was perhaps no surprise that Duquesne refashioned Île Bourbon as the Isle of Eden, shedding the name of the persecuting royal family in favor of humankind's original paradise. Although his Calvinist sensibilities and aristocratic bearing would certainly not condone "libertinage," his vision for the island was very different from that of the French crown. Duquesne teased the obvious theological meanings out of Flacourt's secular description of the island. Here was a place where the people of God could reclaim their birthright. The island had "all the commodities and charms of life that one could reasonably hope for," but its most important gift was good health, without which nothing else was possible.[82] In short, it was a place where the people of God could reclaim the innocent days before the fall of humankind, where they could "create a colony and go all together to live in a good country where they can live as good Christians and enjoy the blessings of life."[83] He summed up his offer to potential colonists by holding out the hope of *salut*, a word that could mean either physical safety or spiritual salvation. Certainly the double meaning would have been obvious to refugees who had escaped the lion's den of France only to find themselves struggling to stay out of poverty in Protestant Europe.[84]

The Isle of Eden represented both a culmination and a divergence from the other Huguenot overseas schemes of the 1680s. Like Charles de Rochefort, Duquesne advanced a glowing description of an exotic new world, a place where his persecuted brethren could find relief far from the troubles of Europe. But unlike Rochefort or any of the Carolina and Pennsylvania proprietary boosters, he painted his colony in explicitly religious terms. The founders of Eden recognized God as "our conducter, and our protector," and pledged themselves to his service. In an echo of Paul Reboulet's refrain regarding the Cape of Good Hope, Duquesne claimed that the Huguenots of Eden would be "instruments in [God's] hands for spreading the Gospel among the nations, and making his name renowned among the most remote peoples of the earth."[85]

The utopian thirst for new worlds both drew from and challenged the colonial program championed by European Huguenot leaders. On first glance, the objectives were almost identical: the preservation of a French Protestant church in exile. Duquesne's colony of Eden, after all, was the most explicitly Calvinist of all the Huguenot colonies, a place designed to be a bastion of God's grace in a sinful world. The colonies in Carolina and Pennsylvania, while less obviously religious in nature, also existed in places with liberal religious regimes, where refugees could practice their faith as they chose. On the other hand, these colonies were very far from France, the homeland that many Huguenots still hoped to return to someday. Moreover, for Pierre Jurieu and his followers, France was still the likely theater for the next great phase of Protestant history, when Babylon fell and began the series of events that would end with the collapse of the Catholic Church and Christ's return.

As it happened, Duquesne's scheme inspired some opposition from other Huguenots. In March 1689 the French resident in Geneva, Charles-François d'Iberville, reported on Duquesne's efforts to sell his Swiss barony and form a "principality" in the South Indian Ocean. The resident strongly disapproved of the plan, which he claimed came from a combination of "secret ambition" and "his natural anxiety." Moreover, he claimed that others agreed with him, even those within the Refuge. The design was "so visionary," he wrote to the king's chief minister, that it was "strongly opposed by all men of good sense."[86] While diplomatic correspondence is always difficult to interpret—diplomats tended to tell their bosses what they wanted to hear—d'Iberville seems to have understood the mood of the Refuge on Duquesne's project. Especially among prominent men and women, the members of the Huguenot senate who attempted to lead, the design did seem foolish and counterproductive.

The only direct evidence of this disapproval is embedded in Duquesne's own correspondence. In February 1689, before d'Iberville informed the king of Duquesne's scheme, the baron wrote a letter to Henri de Mirmand. The surviving letter was the last in a series that the two men exchanged over the course of a few months, probably starting when Duquesne sent Mirmand one of his pamphlets describing his new project. Clearly Mirmand did not approve, and in the final letter Duquesne attempted to answer his objections. In particular Mirmand took issue with Duquesne's chief contention: that the Isle of Eden would provide a place of safety for the thousands of refugees who ventured there. To Mirmand, apparently, the Isle of Eden looked more like a trap, a place where the refugees would become sitting ducks open to attack from the Sun King's fleets. Duquesne admitted that his scheme was subject to certain "inconveniences," but pledged that he would be able to prevent them. The island was "so far from France" that it was "beyond all reason and appearance that they could come and trouble us."[87] The argument centered more than anything on the issue of distance, on whether it was safe or unsafe to venture so far from Europe. While no other Huguenot leader left a record of their thoughts on Duquesne's scheme, one can imagine many other objections. In a decade when return to France remained the leading goal of many refugees, many must have considered the plan as visionary.

Moreover, this general opposition to overseas settlements went beyond Duquesne's admittedly eccentric design. American colonial plans also moved refugees too far away, threatening the treasured goal of an eventual return to France. The clearest indication of this sentiment appeared in one of the most interesting colonization tracts, written by a man known as Durand of Dauphiné. When Durand finally found himself on a ship toward London and refuge, he began reading tracts about the New World and caught the Carolina fever to which so many fell victim during the 1680s. When he got to London, however, some people discouraged him from continuing his journey. In particular, Durand visited Isaac de Bordieu, the elderly former minister of Montpellier who had taken a post at the French Church of the Savoy in Westminster. Bordieu advised against a trip to Carolina, saying that he could find Durand work in London for "two or three years," after which time "we should return to France." Durand ignored this advice and embarked for America, but he never fully extinguished the feeling that he should be back in Europe. Despite receiving offers of land in Virginia the gentleman decided to go back to London. He did so because "on leaving for America I had bought the accomplishment of the prophecies by Monsieur de Jurieu." Durand was quite taken with the minister's predictions, so much so that he resolved to return, as he "wished to be a witness of the restoration of the Religion in my country, as I had been of its affliction & its ruin."[88] As long as leaders of the Huguenot senate held on to return as a cherished goal, they would do what they could to keep refugees from ranging too far.

Despite Jurieu's popular appeal, many ordinary Huguenots followed Durand to overseas colonies during the 1680s. Moreover, many of them must have shared his enthusiasm for the promotional tracts that bragged of new Edens in faraway places. The most compelling evidence comes from the testimonial of another memoirist, François Leguat, who answered Henri Duquesne's call and became the leader of the first installment of colonists to the Isle of Eden. In early 1689 the Burgundian gentleman was in Amsterdam, after receiving leave to exit the kingdom from Louis XIV. Despite its offers of freedom, the Netherlands did not provide the resources to make a comfortable life, so he "gave my self up entirely to Providence, and determin'd humbly and patiently to make use of the Means that offer'd for me, perhaps to preserve my Life." Leguat's chief goal was to "endeavour to live in a Place where I might be free from the common and frequent Dangers to which I was expos'd."[89] His narrative presented a next step in the history of the chosen people: God would guide them to a new retreat, far from the cares of the world, where sufferers like Leguat, who had given up everything, could find the magical gift of *salut*.

Leguat found this mystical new world when he read Duquesne's description of the Isle of Eden. The account of the island "made me conceive so good an Opinion of it that I was tempted to give it a Visit, resolving to end my Days there in Peace, and out of the Care and Confusion of the World, if I found 'twas but in some measure so Pleasant and Commodious as 'twas describ'd to be." He did as the tract instructed and presented himself to the "gentlemen" gathering settlers for the colony, and Leguat found he was not alone; two sizeable ships sat in Amsterdam waiting to take settlers to the colony, and Duquesne had many recruits. Interestingly, many of those destined for Eden were not young men or soldiers, but those who had little other means of support. Leguat himself, though a gentleman, was in his fifties, a single man who had abandoned his estate when he left France. He reported that many of his fellow passengers were "women, and other persons who cou'd not defend themselves" —the very kinds of people who would be attracted to a quiet, peaceful retreat.[90] In the end, the two ships did not leave the harbor; reports of a French expedition to the Indian Ocean made Duquesne worry for the safety of his colonists. But the very fact that so many people answered his call demonstrated the powerful lure of new worlds to ordinary Huguenots.

Even more refugees followed Durand to America—a fact made clear in scraps of paper produced by "French committees" from Switzerland to London. These committees gave small bits of relief to thousands of refugees over the 1680s, many of whom specifically requested money to journey to America. In Schaffhausen in 1686, for example, a gentleman from Picardy named Guillaume Lemoir asked for a small amount of assistance on his way to Dutch Suriname.[91] Far larger numbers received aid from the Royal Bounty and the Threadneedle Street Church to travel to British America—and while refugees listed many colonies as potential destinations, Carolina predominated. Between the summers of 1686 and 1687 officials of the Royal Bounty offered aid to 137 refugees "in order to go to Carolina," a group of travelers that included almost every type of person and family arrangement. Some were single men, artisans or laborers, who probably had trouble finding work in London, but many men traveled with their wives and children. A surprising number of single women joined the crowd as well. One of them, Jeanne Soumain, intended to "find her husband" who had apparently already gone to Carolina, but others, like Judith Gascherie, traveled independent of male relations. Gascherie took along her niece, not unusual among female travelers who found safety and comfort in numbers.[92]

These Carolina dreams spread around the Refuge, from England to the Netherlands. In 1686, for instance, a French spy in the Netherlands reported on a massive plot to smuggle Huguenots out of the province of Saintonge and move them—and, perhaps more critically, their wealth and goods—to the colony of Carolina. The mastermind was a former La Rochelle merchant in Rotterdam, Jean Faneuil, who the French ambassador described as a "very zealous Huguenot who often acts against Your Majesty's interests." In June 1686 a ship waited in Haarlem, ready to go to Rochefort and then London en route to the new overseas Refuge. One can imagine that this design may have inspired the number of manuscript descriptions and inquiries that appeared around that time.[93] For instance, the manuscript "Questions et Reponces faites au sujet de la Caroline" (a copy of which ended up in La Rochelle's library) specifically asked "if all that is said in the printed relations is true," answering that "there is not a single exaggeration in all that is said there," and that those in the colony "notice a thousand advantages that have not been spoken of."[94] Another manuscript set of queries noted that there were "many families who suffer for religion in Poitou and Aunis," in La Rochelle's hinterlands, and that they wondered "if the relation of Carolina that has been circulated in France is sincere" and if newcomers would receive naturalization upon landing in the colony.[95] All of this evidence attested to the wide distribution and power of the Carolina tracts. At the same time, refugees remained discerning customers and wanted to make sure the accounts were not exaggerated.

The power of propaganda can also be gleaned from one set of travelers who headed toward Virginia in 1687. The Royal Bounty granted funds for twenty-one refugees—ten from a single family, the Renauds—to travel to Virginia, an unusual destination at the time since most American travelers preferred Carolina or, in some cases, New England and Pennsylvania. Some of this money went directly to Nicholas Hayward, an English gentleman who owned land in the colony and arranged for the Renaud family's naturalization, which in turn allowed the family to purchase land.[96] These migrants almost certainly responded to the descriptions of Virginia in Durand of Dauphiné's book. Due to bad weather Durand had never reached his intended destination of Carolina, but instead spent some time in Virginia, where he was quite taken with the salubrious lands of the piedmont, which he considered appropriate for a colony of his country folk. Moreover, he found himself barraged by offers of land and aid for a French colony, and Hayward was one of the people who approached him, as he "had been commissioned to offer lands at a reasonable price to any Frenchman wishing to come, & even to advance money to help build houses for those who had no funds, as well as corn for their sustenance during the first year." Hayward even added a description of his terms and of the land at the end of Durand's tract, assuring readers that "the said land is extremely healthful, good & very fertile, producing all kinds of grain, such as wheat, barley, oats & others as in Europe, grapes & all sorts of good fruit, & the waters are excellent."[97] Apparently the Renauds read these lines and determined to go there, becoming nearly the only settlers in a place named Brent Town after one of the English owners. In so doing, they helped Hayward in his larger goal to make money. As one of his business partners, William Fitzhugh, noted to Hayward, the design was "to help the distressed" but also "to make profit of your Purchase."[98]

One major lesson of the decade was that propaganda worked. The turmoil of the 1680s turned Huguenots' lives upside down, and many of them looked to the Indies for opportunities to set them right again—not a surprising development, given that Huguenots had played leading roles in exploration and travel going back over a century. But the dreams of Eden revealed by the tracts represented only one aspect of a complicated story. However appealing the promotional tracts made the Indies appear, many people did not want to move halfway around the world to find peace and quiet. Thus the move toward America and Asia came at least in part out of desperation. As European cities filled up with refugees, as offers for new colonies in Germany were not forthcoming, refugees had to get more adventurous if they hoped to find any land and aid at all. More to the point, they had to make themselves useful. As a result, the Edenic dreams in the promotional tracts had to exist alongside the ambitions of organizations like the Carolina proprietors or the Dutch East India Company, who offered refuge to the Huguenots not primarily out of charity but out of self-interest.

The Huguenots' desperation appeared in the margins of a number of documents. In 1686, for example, two young ministers named de Joües and du Berrion sought ordination and employment in the Church of England. Their design failed when the Bishop of Bangor in North Wales refused to ordain the men, probably because he feared "to draw a burden upon himself." Basically, there were no jobs. The men turned to the neighboring Bishop of St. Asaph with a new plan. Since they were brought up to be ministers they intended "as soon as they are in full Orders & have competent use of the English tong . . . to go for some of the Plantations, where their Ministery may be of use as well to the

French as to the English that live there." The Bishop of St. Asaph declared this to be a "laudable" design, since they could serve God in America without being a further charge on the bishop's own resources.[99]

If men of God went to the Americas, those with military or commercial experience viewed the East Indies as a similar refuge for the desperate and unemployed. The French in Holland intercepted one Huguenot letter that told such a story. The writer's nephew, a young soldier named Nicholas La Rose, resolved to travel in the "quality of a soldier" to the "Grandes Indes" or East Indies. He decided on this extreme step for a simple reason: there was no longer work for him in the Netherlands or Germany. The East India Company, on the other hand, was always hiring, so hundreds of young Huguenot men like La Rose found themselves headed East by necessity rather than choice.[100]

The English East India Company launched a similar scheme to attract Huguenots during the late 1680s. Probably because of the prominence of Jean Chardin, a refugee and East Indies expert who joined the company's employ, it sponsored a number of plans to move Huguenots to Asia. In 1688 company leaders suggested sending French soldiers to Bombay and Madras to strengthen the Company's regiments there, as well as ministers to tend to the soldiers' spiritual needs, whose transportation charges would be paid out of the Royal Bounty. They even went so far as giving commissions to the commander and ensign of a French regiment in Madras, Francis de la Serre and John du Brois. The design seemed to go nowhere, however. Two of the designated ministers deserted before ever leaving for India, making off with the money that was supposed to pay for their voyage, and no record exists of the refugees actually reaching Madras. In the end, Chardin populated Madras not with Huguenots but with Armenians, members of another Christian diaspora with deep connections to the Persian and Ottoman empires.[101]

Desperate men and women looked toward the Indies because increasingly that was where they could find the most advantages. And that occurred because English and Dutch leaders believed that the refugees could do the most good on the edges of their empires. For England in particular, the 1680s was an era of imperial reckoning, when officials had to decide how best to manage an expanding but poorly organized empire. One key issue was the issue of population. Many analysts lauded the possibilities of colonies, especially in tropical locales that could produce crops impossible in England, but feared the deleterious effects the colonies could have in draining England of its people. A common line of argument held that England was underpopulated and "undenyably must now be far lesse populous than ever," wrote William Petyt in 1680, "having so lately peopled our vast *American Plantations* and *Ireland*."[102] This belief put advocates of plantations like East India Company President Josiah Child on the defensive. He believed the benefits of colonies outweighed their detriments, especially since many who traveled overseas were poor people or persecuted minorities who could serve little useful purpose in the home kingdoms. Nonetheless, Child advanced another argument that could neutralize those of opponents like Petyt. He advocated the welcoming of persecuted "strangers" from throughout Europe to England, where they could lend their skills to the accomplishment of any number of state goals, from improving the manufacturing sector in England itself to finding new laborers for imperial peripheries.[103] Another writer put the matter bluntly: "The Numbers of Refugees here, and in other Countreys near us, are Objects in this Case, both for our Charity to them, and Advantage to our selves."[104]

Dutch ambitions were never quite as lofty as those of the English. The Dutch overseas empire ran on trade rather than settlement. Most of its colonies were mere trading stations, and they endeavored to send only the number of people necessary to sustain mercantile links. Those Huguenots who joined the East India or West India Companies, therefore, tended to do so as individuals for fixed terms. Nonetheless, the refugees could perform a number of key functions, which came to center on two regions. In Suriname settlers could help jumpstart a Caribbean plantation economy in a frontier colony located uncomfortably close to French, English, and Spanish rivals.[105] In the East, meanwhile, refugees provided a means to solve an even more longstanding problem. The Dutch East India fleet had difficulty providing their ships with inexpensive grain and wine, since their voyages took them so far from home. If they settled an agricultural way station on the way to the Indies, they could save the Company a great deal of money. A set of reflections on the Company's predicament expressed the exact same sentiments regarding charity and interest that appeared in English political economic tracts. The Company was moved above all "by compassion and charity toward all suffering people," but they also considered that helping out the suffering refugees "could be of some use to [the Company]." These were good subjects with relevant skills and few options, the perfect people to travel halfway across the world to realize the Company's schemes.[106]

It was this desire for settlers to provision their fleets that inspired the design that Paul Reboulet learned of in 1687. The Dutch outpost at the Cape of Good Hope stood in a strategic locale between the Atlantic and Indian Oceans, almost at the halfway point for Dutch ships traveling to the eastern trading capital of Batavia. Since settling an outpost at the Cape in the 1650s leaders had tried to concoct schemes to make the colony useful, but most had failed, for the simple reason that no one wanted to relocate to the remote African outpost. The Huguenot persecution thus provided a great opportunity. The East India Company issued a printed notice, perhaps the most uninspiring promotional tract of the decade, laying out the terms they would offer to prospective French Protestant migrants. The tract avoided the overblown rhetoric of the Carolina tracts; indeed, it failed to describe the colony at all. It did underscore that the company would pay travelers' passages and help them make a living "by whatever art or profession there might be." The only conditions were that migrants take an oath to serve the Company and stay in the colony at least five years.[107] When Reboulet heard about this opportunity he naturally integrated it into his narrative of the refugees as chosen people, going off to find their destiny in the farthest parts of the world. Yet there was no doubt, to anyone reading the East India Company's invitation, that the Huguenots who traveled to Africa would do so as part of someone else's scheme. The simple truth was that the Company wanted wine and grain for their ships, and the Huguenots had the skills to provide it. Thus appeared a tension that would characterize all Huguenot overseas settlements, a tension between the refugees' dreams of Eden and their patrons' dreams of profit.

Dreams of Silk and Wine

Durand of Dauphiné was obsessed with the New World. After a circuitous escape from Provence he found passage to London in 1686, and while on board
the ship he determined to follow in the footsteps of many of his compatriots and
head to Carolina. He already knew how he would make a living in that faraway
colony. Durand befriended a woman on the way to London whose husband had
abjured his faith and abandoned her. He took the woman under his protection,
and together the two refugees decided to enter the silk business. "She was from
the country & liked the city no more than I," Durand wrote, and "she understood
thoroughly the management of a farm, & told me that on her own estate she had
very successfully raised a quantity of silkworms." The Carolina tracts they had
read on the ship confirmed that Carolina possessed "plenty of mulberry trees"—
the sole source of food for the worms that spun the cocoons that became silk—
so the pair had no doubt that they could make build comfortable lives running a
silk plantation in North America.[1]

Durand's dreams of silk never came true. His female companion died en route
to America, and winds shifted his boat off course to Virginia, some hundreds
of miles to the north. As he traveled around that colony, however, he began to
believe that his earlier ambitions had been misplaced. Virginia was a far better
colony than Carolina, and the route to wealth and comfort was not through silk
but through wine. Especially as he toured around Virginia's piedmont, Durand
noticed wild grapevines everywhere and theorized that with the expertise of
those who knew the crop—such as several hundred or thousand Huguenot
migrants—these now neglected vines could produce "very good income."
He waxed poetic as he traveled around Rappahannock County with his host,
leading planter Ralph Wormeley. "I was extolling upon the beauty of the place
we had just seen, the same lovely hills whence flow fountains & brooks, & broad
meadows below, always covered with wild grapevines," Durand wrote. "I was
saying that fine vines could grow upon these slopes & that doubtless the wine
would be excellent. Monsieur Wormeley replied that if I could find some means

The Global Refuge. Owen Stanwood, Oxford University Press (2020). © Oxford University Press.
DOI: 10.1093/oso/9780190264741.001.0001

to bring Frenchmen there, he would sell the whole of those ten thousand acres of ground he owned on both sides of the river for one écu an acre."[2]

Durand was not the only Huguenot who designed to make a living making silk or wine in an overseas colony. Nor was Wormeley the only patron who sought to attract French people with special skills to a particular plot of land in the New World. Indeed, during the late 1600s and afterward the language of silk and wine became ubiquitous in nearly any conversation that involved the refugees. From Virginia and Carolina to the Cape of Good Hope, imperial projectors came to believe that French refugees could provide special skills that would make their colonies economically successful. Silk and wine, after all, were Mediterranean commodities, both especially common in France, but impossible to produce in England or the Netherlands. Northern Europeans tended to assume that most French people possessed the requisite knowledge to work in these pursuits, and for their part, the refugees did nothing to dissuade their patrons from this belief. They bragged of their facility in silk, wine, olive oil, salt, and other particularly French industries, and some of them, like Durand's unnamed female companion, probably did have some relevant experience. Far more of them, like Durand himself, were bourgeois people who perhaps had trafficked in wine and silk and certainly had consumed these things, but had no real idea how to make them. Nonetheless, they were perfectly willing to play up their ability to do so, especially once they realized, like Durand, that the language of silk and wine tended to open the purses of otherwise stingy patrons.

The story of these silk and wine colonies illustrates how the Huguenot migration became tied to the political economy of states and empires. The first refugee appeals for land and aid stressed the Huguenots' status as the persecuted people of God, symbols of the international Protestant brotherhood. These missives had some effect, especially from rulers like Elector Friedrich Wilhelm I or William of Orange who had political reasons to embrace the French Protestant cause. Nonetheless, appeals to common Protestantism only went so far. The coffers of European charities drained quickly during the 1680s, leaving many refugees in increasingly desperate positions. They soon found that they could gain assistance if they promoted themselves as chosen people in an economic sense. There had always been strategic considerations behind Huguenot colonies—the Great Elector, for instance, had sought to settle refugees on depopulated lands, and refugee leaders often wooed patrons by appealing to their desire for new settlers. By the late 1680s, however, Huguenots were generally going beyond these boilerplate arguments about population to promote their particular skills and aptitudes. France was the greatest producer in Europe, a "rich, populous, and plentifull" land abounding in natural and human resources. Much of its riches came from a few things, and foreign observers tended to look especially at "corn, wine, and many sorts of fruits," along with a variety of manufactured goods, including "silks, linen-clothes, laces, and many other rich commodities." The refugees learned that by playing up their purported skills—their economic Frenchness, so to speak—they could gain even more advantages for themselves.[3]

Thus the Huguenot migration ran headlong into the set of ideas labeled as mercantilism. Pioneered by a cadre of European political economists during the seventeenth century, mercantilists tended to view economic life as a competition between states for a finite amount of the world's wealth. In order to win the competition, a prince needed to be a kind of accountant-in-chief, ensuring that the kingdom's exports exceeded its imports. This positive balance of trade would mean that the victorious nation brought in excess gold and silver—real wealth, in the eyes of most mercantilists. This language originated in France, but gained increasing currency in seventeenth-century England, where writers decried the "voluptuousness" of a country that was addicted to consuming foreign, and particularly French goods, to the detriment of its balance of trade.[4] Fine silk garments and French wines were especially bad: whenever English people drank foreign wine, William Petyt claimed, "we *swallow* and *piss* out inestimable treasures."[5] The only solutions to these problems involved reducing consumption or increasing domestic production in these particular commodities, but neither proved practicable. Upper-class English men and women had no desire to curb consumption, but they continued to view silk and wine production as mysterious arts that northern Europeans could never master. If they could import those who did have the requisite knowledge— say, Protestant refugees from parts of France with traditions of viticulture and sericulture—then English people could go on consuming and have their balance of trade too.[6]

There was one more problem, however. Despite years of experimentation, it was clear that neither England nor the Netherlands provided fertile ground for grapes or mulberry trees. Thus, if refugees were going to win advantages for themselves by making silk or wine, they would have to do so in foreign plantations located in friendlier climes. The logic of political economy pushed the Huguenots into the arms of state planners, and then in the direction of overseas colonies, since these were the only places where they could realize their patrons' economic ambitions. Such visions of profit often appeared alongside the dreams of Eden that also pushed Huguenots overseas. Charles de Rochefort, for instance, boasted of American vines that "grow there naturally without any human labor," while Paul Reboulet noted that the Dutch colony at the Cape of Good Hope "produces everything, and especially wine."[7] To realize their dreams of Eden, these writers realized, Huguenots might need to make some useful things along the way. While there was no particular reason that Eden and profit could not coincide, the political economic logic of empire did not always dovetail with the refugees' desires for *salut*. These tensions between Eden and empire only became more acute as Huguenots scattered around the world, enlisted in various projects in America and Africa.

———

Understanding the economic forces behind Huguenot emigration requires a detour back to the early days of colonization. Europeans began dreaming of silk and wine almost as soon as they encountered new worlds. Exploring what would later become South Carolina in 1563, for instance, the Huguenot René Goulaine de Laudonnière noted that "the trees were all entwined with cords of vines, bearing grapes in such quantities that their number would be sufficient to render the place habitable."[8] Some decades later English witnesses reported bushes "so overgrowne with Vines, we could scarce passe them."[9] If French eyes interpreted grapevines as a sign of habitability, English ones viewed them as possible profits. As Thomas Harriott reported from the soon-to-be lost colony of Roanoke, just to the north of Laudonnière's plantation, "When [the grapes] are planted and husbanded as they ought, a principall commoditie of wines by them may be raised."[10] After the sixteenth century turned such descriptions only became more glowing. Virginia's early explorer and governor John Smith marveled at vines that "climbe the toppes of the highest trees in some places" while another booster of the colony added "we have eaten there as full and lusheous a Grape as in the villages between Paris and Amiens."[11] If "skillfull vinearoons" came to the colony, noted Virginia's Council in 1610, they could "make a perfect grape and fruitfull vintage in short time."[12]

Evidence of the promise of silk was less obvious than the vines but no less exciting. As nearly everyone knew, raw silk came from the cocoons of silkworms, delicate animals that subsisted on the leaves of mulberry trees. Explorers thus kept a close watch for these trees as they ranged across the new continent, and they were not disappointed. Laudonnière believed that he saw both white and red mulberry trees in Florida, "and on the tops of these many silkworms."[13] John Smith reported on "some great Mulberry trees" in Virginia, occasionally "found growing naturally in prettie groves."[14] No one proved happier to hear these reports than England's king, James I. Impressed by the efforts of his rival across the Channel, Henri IV, who jumpstarted France's silk industry, James hoped to do the same in England. In 1607 he instructed officials in English counties to require landholders to plant mulberry trees, and to show that he was no hypocrite, the king took the lead himself, hiring a man to oversee the planting of the trees in Westminster outside his royal palace.[15] Given his enthusiasm for silk, the king must have encouraged the Council in their first efforts to make the commodity, which occurred as early as 1610. John Smith reported on an "assay to make silk" during his time in the colony, which seemed to be going well before the expert employed for the task became ill and died. The silkworms ended up providing what must have been very small snacks to the colonists—a sad and fitting end during a winter when Virginians ate everything from rats to each other in a desperate attempt to avoid starvation.[16]

These efforts had little chance of success without the help of foreign experts. English people simply did not understand the secrets of silk and wine, a fact that the king admitted when he employed a Frenchman named John Bonoeil to oversee silkmaking efforts on both sides of the ocean. Bonoeil wrote two tracts instructing Virginians in the ancient art of silkmaking—first describing how to build "houses" for the delicate worms and then providing exact instructions on how to cultivate mulberry trees. The king ordered copies of the book sent to every head of household in the colony, while also trying to enforce the old provision that each landowner plant at least six mulberry trees and some vineyards.[17] Those who actually read Bonoiel's tract might have been forgiven for believing the task to be hopeless. The silk trade was far from easy. For one thing, Bonoeil advised planters that the worms' dwellings "must be made spacious, lightsome, pleasant, neate, and wholesome, farre from ill sents, damps, fogs, and humidities: warme in cold, and cold in hot weather." The worms should not live on the top or bottom floors, but in between, to avoid extremes of hot and cold. As far as mulberry trees went, planters had to grow at least two to three thousand trees to provide enough sustenance for the worms and had to plant them in neat rows with enough exposure to the sun.[18] Once the worms produced cocoons, spinning the silk required another set of exacting practices. While it appeared more straightforward, wine making proved complicated as well. One could not simply pluck grapes off the vine and turn them into wine. As John Pory lamented to an English correspondent, "There belong so many severall skills to the plantinge and dressinge of a vineyard and to the making and preserving of wines, whereof our nation is ignorant."[19]

To remedy this situation the Virginia Company arranged for "eight French Vignerons" to help turn the colony into a silk and wine mecca. Little information remains about the French colonists. They came from Languedoc, apparently, and by 1620 or so they had taken residence in Virginia. Their main task was to take control of the colony's nascent vineyards and also provide counsel about the "orderly planting of *Mulbery*-Trees."[20] Company officials apparently assumed that the presence of these experts would finally bring the scheme to perfection. In 1621 they counseled the new governor, Francis Wyatt, to "plant mulbury trees, and make silk, and take care of the French men and others sent about that work."[21] The Company underscored that neither they nor the king would tolerate any deviation from these silk and wine designs. The land was appropriate for these commodities, they heard from so many reports, and the combination of the French migrants, sent "at our great charge," and the wide distribution of

Figure 3.1 In his guides to silk production John Bonoiel included visual aids, such as this illustration of how to build platforms for the silkworms, lined with their preferred food, mulberry leaves. Bonoiel, *His Majesties gracious letter to the earl of South-Hampton, treasurer, and to the councell and Company of Virginia heere: commanding the present setting up of silke works, and planting of vines in Virginia* (London, 1622). Courtesy of the John Carter Brown Library, Brown University.

Bonoiel's book meant that no English planter could feign ignorance. Virginians needed to "imploy all your indevours to the setting forward those two Staple Commodities of Silke, and Wine; which brought to their perfection, will infinitely redound to the honour, benefit, and comfort of the Colony, and of this whole Kingdome."[22]

Despite the admonitions from king and company, silk and wine culture did not take off in early Virginia. Local apologists listed all sorts of excuses: the

Indian attack of 1622; the sourness of the grapes; the existence of "a prickle" in the leaves of local mulberry trees that injured too many silkworms.[23] Most of all, people blamed the French. In 1628 the House of Burgesses claimed that the French migrants had either lied about their viticultural skills or intentionally botched the job after reaching the colony, and three years later the assembly passed an act specifically prohibiting the French from planting tobacco. The act alleged that the Frenchmen had "spoyled and ruinated that vyniard, which was, with great cost, planted by the charge of the late company," an act that had "dishartened all the inhabitants here."[24] Another French Protestant nobleman, the baron of Sancé, attempted to restart the design in 1629. He petitioned the Privy Council on his intention to move to Virginia with a retinue of French Protestants skilled in vines, olives, silk, and salt, and asked for an official invitation as well as letters of denization for himself and his son to make his emigration easier.[25] This design never got off the ground, and Sancé's ambitions soon moved to an adjacent territory called "Carolana," in present-day North Carolina, though the baron never ended up moving there either.[26]

The real problem, as some commentators realized, was that Virginia had already found its cash crop. By the 1620s most planters had turned to tobacco, taking advantage of the rising English penchant for that addictive substance. Looking out on the colony just after taking it over from the beleaguered Virginia Company, the king lamented Virginians' single-minded affection for that noxious weed. "This Plantation is wholly builte uppon Smoake," the king scolded, "Tobaccoe being the only meanes it hath produced, and that so easie to be turned into aire." As he noted, some English landowners were trying to grow tobacco at home, and even at this early date tobacco prices proved unstable. To build a colony on any one crop seemed foolish, according to leaders in England, and tobacco was especially risky. The king recommended that the governor use his authority to "moderate" the production of tobacco while encouraging diversification, including mining iron and "The planting of Vines."[27]

Events over the subsequent decades only validated the king's worries. Tobacco brought a great deal of revenue to the crown and individual planters, but proved especially liable to cycles of boom and bust. During the 1650s two tracts appeared that sought to use the old standbys, silk and wine, as tools to diversify Virginia's economy and serve the national interest. The most ambitious work, written by a planter named Edward Williams, laid out in new detail the dream of an English Mediterranean on the shores of the Atlantic Ocean. He began by noting a geographic fact: Virginia lay on the same latitude not just of Spain and Italy, but also China, Persia, Japan, and Cyprus—many of the places that produced the most treasured goods in the world. Virginia possessed the "same bounty of Summer, the same milde remission of Winter, with a more virgin and unexhausted soyle." So naturally, with very little effort planters would be able to produce all of the goods that came from the Mediterranean and the East, starting with wine and silk.[28]

Williams set out an elaborate plan to turn Virginia into one of the most fruitful corners of the world. It would begin by clearing the vast American woods, creating ordered fields of rich Virginian soil, where "the Vine and Olive which Naturally simpathize together, will thrive beyond belief." This pursuit would not prohibit ordinary agricultural activities, Williams claimed, because grapes had their own harvest cycle. The felled trees could easily provide wood for the barrels that Virginian vintners could use to send their wine back to European markets. Williams also recommended two expedients to ensure that the new crops prospered as he believed they should. First, he suggested bringing in European vines; Williams understood, as others had before him, that the American grape varieties did not have the same properties as those in the Old World. Second, he advocated the immigration of more experts, "some Greeke and other Vignerons . . . to instruct us in the labour." With the right grapes and the right people, Williams did not doubt that Virginia could produce enough wine to rival France and Spain and make England the "happiest Nation in Europe." In perhaps his boldest suggestion, Williams even proposed that Virginia's position between Europe and Asia would put it a good position to introduce wine to China.[29]

A second tract echoed Williams's plans in specific regard to silk. Published under the auspices of the great projector Samuel Hartlib, *The Reformed Virginian Silkworm* repackaged many of John Bonoeil's suggestions for the 1650s. Hartlib repeated many of the tips on how to care for silkworms, but avoided the exacting instructions in that earlier work, stressing that anyone could raise silkworms— after all, poor peasants in Italy managed to provide shelter for their worms. While he echoed Williams in his advocacy for economic diversification, urging Virginians to build an economy on a "reall-royall-solid-rich-staple Commodity" rather than "smoak and vapour," he saw a turn to silk as more than just an eco- nomic expedient. Indeed, he even saw it as the beginning of a religious trans- formation in America. Silk culture was so easy and profitable, Hartlib averred, that even Indians could master it. Hartlib advised the English to "incourage them . . . that for every pound-weight of Silk-bottoms they bring unto you, you give them (as well it deserves) 5 *shil.* worth in any Commodities they desire." Soon the natives would dedicate themselves to silk of their own volition, "And thus by the blessing of Almighty God, there may be good hope of their civilizing and conversion; so that they may be likewise great gainers both in body and soule by this thing."[30]

Boosters of silk and wine in America had utopian ambitions. They aimed to transform the Virginian and then the imperial economy, to turn America from a howling wilderness into an orderly, pleasant, and profitable garden. The tur- moil of England's Civil War, which extended to the colonies as well, put a hold on many of these plans, but after the Restoration of Charles II the silk and wine speculation continued, driven by a new push for empire and a rise in political economic speculation. English commentators were divided on the usefulness of overseas colonies, but nearly all agreed that if the kingdom did maintain these distant outposts, they should at least produce raw materials that England would otherwise import from rival nations, thus improving the kingdom's trade balance. These authors raged against the English taste for luxury, noting that "national gaudery" had increased to the point that even ordinary people clamored for French silks and wines, turning those hated rivals into the "Lord Mayors of the Continent." Colonies provided a possible solution to the problem, if English consumers could not be content with woolens and good English ales. Whig theorist Carew Reynall advocated "the planting of Mulberry trees, Vines, and Olives, as they begin in *Carolina*, by which means they would produce Silks, Wines, and Oyls, which would turn to a greater account; and besides our Commodities that we cannot raise, and so would breed a better commerce."[31] By turning the colonies into silk and wine producing bastions, the English could use the empire to finally solve the problem of foreign consumption.

The design found an early champion in Virginia's governor Sir William Berkeley. The governor shared the common misgivings about basing the colony on one fragile crop and from his own plantation of Green Spring continued some of the longstanding experiments to diversify Virginia's economy. He noted in 1662 that planters "fix their hopes only on this vicious weed of Tobacco, which at length has brought them to that extremity that they can neither handsomely Subsist with it, nor without it." His answer, in keeping with frequent advice from the crown, was wine and especially silk. He made his own wine at Green Spring, bragging to the earl of Clarendon that "I drank as good of my own planting as ever came out of Italy," but he doubted that Virginia could rival France or Spain in wine production due to the vagaries of moving wine across the ocean.[32] Instead, he focused on silk as Virginia's next great cash crop. Over the course of the 1660s Berkeley worked with the planter Edward Digges to produce samples of raw silk that would demonstrate to the king the feasibility of the pursuit. In 1663 and again in 1668 Digges and Berkeley sent samples to Charles II, who pledged to make the Virginia silk into a garment "for our own Person" to wear in court, in the hope that "our Subjects shall not need to fetch it from Persia, but may trade, and be Cloathed with those native and rich Proceeds of our own Dominions."[33] Digges also reported on his efforts to the Royal Society, speaking out against some of the previous rumors regarding Virginia silk. He argued, for example, that tobacco smoke and thunderstorms did not kill the worms, as previously believed, nor did the presence of menstruating women harm them.[34]

Despite their glowing reports, Berkeley and Digges understood the great barriers to silk culture in Virginia. The main problem, Berkeley demonstrated, was lack of expertise. Authors like Hartlib and experimenters like Digges tried hard to say that anyone could make silk, and they were technically correct. To produce the commodity in large enough quantities to make money, however, was nearly impossible without outside assistance. Berkeley made that argument repeatedly to the crown, requesting help in locating "skilful men to instruct us." At one point he asked the king for financial assistance so Berkeley himself could travel to France to find experts willing to follow him to Virginia and instruct planters in silk culture.[35] When this design led to nothing, he suggested that the crown work through foreign consulates—possibly Naples and Sicily—to identify skilled foreigners and pay for their transportation to the colony. Berkeley represented the lack of experts as the last obstacle to producing this "hopeful and Honorable commoditty" in Virginia. "Had we some skilful men from Sicily or Naples or Marseillies that could enstruct us a neerer and better way than we know," Berkeley concluded, "I speake it confidently in ten or fifteen yeares we might make and send for England five hundred coarse cloaths."[36] Once again, Berkeley received no satisfactory answer. While the king and his ministers continued to insist that their subjects make silk and wine, they proved reluctant to provide any sort of practical or financial encouragement.

As Berkeley tried and failed to diversify Virginia's economy, new possibilities appeared in Carolina. The new colony to Virginia's south represented one of the boldest new designs in the Restoration empire, an attempt by a group of noblemen known as the Carolina proprietors to realize many of the deferred dreams of Virginia and other plantations.[37] From the beginning, the proprietors, including William Berkeley himself, emphasized diversity. They hoped to avoid the monoculture of Virginia and the Caribbean islands, which were increasingly turning to sugar. In particular, they aimed to use Carolina as a theater to finally realize England's ambition to produce silk and wine in America. Explorers in the region reported the same natural features that had abounded in reports of Virginia. One of the first English explorers in the area noted "the Country abounds with Grapes, large Figs, and Peaches" as well as "severall Mulberry-trees."[38] Two years later another witness observed seeing silkworms on some trees near the Cape Fear River.[39] In 1672 Joseph Dalton reported to one of the proprietors on the best possibilities for cash crops in Carolina and focused on "wine, oil, and silk, which may be propagated to great perfection and profit, which the land seems to promise by fostering so many old vines and mulberries for want of better."[40]

The Carolina Proprietors made the development of these commodities their most treasured goal. They granted a seven-year moratorium on duties for any wine, silk, oil, or raisins produced in the new colony.[41] Tracts about the colony, whether in English or French, inevitably stressed Carolina's Mediterranean qualities. "I take *Carolina* to be much of the same nature with those delicious Countries about *Aleppo, Antioch,* and *Smyrna,*" noted Samuel Wilson, "but [it] hath the advantage of being under an equal English Government."[42] Another author predicted a "great Concourse" was coming to Carolina, drawn among other things by "the likelyhood of Wines, Oyls, and Silks."[43] Perhaps the most compelling evidence of the centrality of silk and wine in early Carolina came from philosopher John Locke, who served during the 1670s as the secretary to Anthony Ashley Cooper, earl of Shaftesbury, the most important of the Carolina proprietors. During the mid-1670s Locke traveled throughout France, ostensibly to regain his health but with the clear secondary purpose of collecting information on silk, olive oil, and wine production to share with his employer. Locke provided exacting descriptions of the process from his own observations. He noted, for instance, the importance of placing vineyards on hills with proper drainage, and the precise (and sometimes disgusting) methods used by peasants in the juicing and fermentation processes, when grapes gradually became wine. Regarding silk, Locke narrated the four "sicknesses" that silkworms endured as they moved through their life cycle, with particular attention to the spinning process, "a thing that cannot be taught without seeing."[44] Locke sent back eight different vines from Montpellier, adding specific instructions on their cultivation, but taken as a whole his treatise seemed to support the belief of Berkeley and others that without proper teachers, the English would not get very far in producing these mysterious commodities.[45]

This mania for Mediterranean commodities soon dovetailed with another key plank of the Carolina proprietors: their commitment to religious toleration. Whether Whig or Tory, most political economists decried persecution, which they believed pushed away good, productive subjects. In particular, they pointed to the Netherlands, whose economic mastery came about at least in part from serving as "the common refuge of all miserable men," who came for freedom of conscience and "fill'd their Cities both with People and Trade."[46] Many authors encouraged Charles II to emulate the Dutch in attracting productive, persecuted strangers, and this advice inspired the king's courting of the Huguenots during the 1680s. Nonetheless, the Stuarts and their allies could not fully abide freedom of conscience, which provided an opening to the Carolina Proprietors. If England would never become another Holland, perhaps they could build their own, subtropical Holland in the Carolina Lowcountry, one that could gather the oppressed of Europe and put them to work for the English imperial cause. As a result, the Fundamental Constitutions of Carolina stressed religious diversity, inviting anyone to settle in their colony regardless of creed and neglecting to exclusively establish the Church of England.[47]

In truth, the earl of Shaftesbury probably had something in mind beyond religious neutrality. While a conformist himself, the earl was the leader of the Whig cause during the 1670s, a champion of Protestant dissenters, and an advocate for the exclusion of James, duke of York, from the line of succession on account of his Catholicism. While Shaftesbury certainly had economic goals, he had religious ones as well, and he intended Carolina not just as a colony in an English empire, but also as a bastion of the Protestant cause. In this he probably followed the line of many Whig political theorists, who advocated attracting Protestant dissenters to England not just because they were people with relevant skills, but because Reformed Protestants made better migrants. For example, Carew Reynall adopted a common Protestant argument when he labeled the Reformed as the best traders and workers, since "it is observed that where the Protestants are countenanced, there all manner of Trade and improvement follow more than in other places, as well as advancement in Reason and Philosophy." This transformation occurred because Protestants were "a rational and industrious people, not having their Souls or manne[r]s inflam'd to superstitious Principles, which makes them hold to all ingenious prosecutions: but having their minds free, and ready to embrace any improvement, learning or Trade."[48] Slingsby Bethel agreed, claiming "it is the undoubted political Interest of all Trading Countries, to countenance and advance by all honourable and honest ways the Reformed Religion, as those of that perswasion are of active and industrious Principles."[49] Shaftesbury clearly concurred with these two thinkers, as he dedicated himself to attracting all sorts of Calvinists to Carolina—Huguenots as well as aggrieved Scottish Covenanters, who were embroiled in their own battle with Charles II and the Scottish Episcopal Church.[50]

All of these factors combined to push Huguenot refugees into the arms of America, and particularly into the arms of the Carolina proprietors. The design to produce silk and wine in the New World, to correct England's balance of trade with colonial products, stretched back nearly a century, but had led to nothing. While environmental factors probably had the most influence on this lack of success, projectors on the ground refused to admit defeat, instead insisting that with proper experts these dreams of silk and wine would come to pass. The persecution of the Huguenots suddenly provided a huge number of potential migrants from Mediterranean Europe, desperate people searching for advantages in an unsure world. In addition, the religious connections of leading Whigs like Shaftesbury made them especially eager to attract oppressed Calvinists, who they believed to be sufferers for the faith and natural political allies against the forces of popery and absolutism. Finally, many Huguenots proved all too willing to play the part that the proprietors wrote for them. They began to portray themselves as silk and wine masters, the very kinds of people who could transform the empire into the new Mediterranean paradise so desired by English projectors.

———

Huguenot refugees quickly learned to adapt themselves to the economic rhetoric that abounded in the English court. From their first petitions to foreign princes in the 1680s, the refugees understood that they needed to make themselves useful, to convince powerful people to grant them aid—whether by stressing their status as the people of God or their practical expertise in various industries. In England, this meant mastering the language of silk and wine, and they did so with great acumen. Of course, Huguenots had spoken of their skills with various commodities well before the great wave of persecution started—the 1629 petition of the baron of Sancé was a case in point—but after 1679 the number of Huguenot petitions for land and aid on imperial peripheries increased exponentially and nearly all of them mentioned silk, wine, or olive oil.

The first and in some ways model of these petitions came from René Petit and Jacob Guérard in 1679. According to the petition itself, Petit was the English king's representative in Rouen, and Guérard a "Norman gentleman." Both had longstanding connections to England, and the fact that they were in London before the dragonnades started indicated that the two men were far from typical Huguenots. Nonetheless, their appeal became a model for future migrants who sought opportunities in the far reaches of the British empire. Petit and Guérard began their appeal with religious metaphors. England was an "evangelical Israel," they underscored, a promised land where the persecuted people of God could find peace. But things were not perfect there. The men lamented that in England itself they would always remain strangers, perhaps liable to new waves of persecution in the future. The best solution seemed to be to find an overseas retreat, and they pledged that if they received land in America the Huguenots would become "one Nation and one people with those who already under the dominion of Your Majesty," all working together to "augment His power and glory by augmenting [the number of] his Subjects." Moving beyond this general political economic argument, Guérard and Petit added that as French people the refugees could build the imperial economy in particular ways that the king and his ministers would find especially valuable. The French were "accustomed to the culture of vines, of grains, of cloth and in many places the making of Silk," skills that they could easily transport to Carolina. In a shorter English version of their petition they specifically underscored how their design would help the nation's balance of trade, since they would supply the kingdom with "Silkes, oyles, Wines and such other things which they are forced to purchase of forraign Nations."[51]

Of course, the two men asked for a great deal in return. In a policy derived from earlier efforts in Virginia, the Carolina proprietors already guaranteed land to anyone who could transport themselves or male servants to the colony, but transatlantic passage was expensive, especially for people who had left their homes and most of their fortunes behind. Guérard and Petit thus asked for the king to provide royal frigates to transport eighty French families to Carolina, along with rights of naturalization. They also requested some money to cover expenses, which would be taken out of the higher customs duties that would inevitably flow into the king's coffers "by bringing into England the Commodities of the groweth of that same Plantation." With these policies, Carolina could soon "serve as a retreat for an infinity of people oppressed in their conscience from French colonies in the Antilles as well as Hispaniola and Canada where they suffer under the Cross until it pleases God to find them a refuge."[52]

The response to the Normans' petition in the English court was almost uniformly positive. For their part, the Carolina proprietors understood that the proposal fit nicely with their own ambitions to turn the colony into a center for producing Mediterranean commodities. They maintained to the Committee on Trade and Plantations, which was a subcommittee of the king's Privy Council responsible for colonial affairs, that "both our Interests & his Maj[esti]es Dominions there & Customs here may receive great advantage by these Gentlemens goeing both by their skill and Example in planting vineyards, Olive Trees and making of Silk." The proprietors also hoped that the coming of these first migrants would encourage future exoduses of "forreigne Protestants," whose skills and labor would lead to greater revenues for the king and proprietors alike.[53] The proprietors undoubtedly saw additional advantages in the Huguenots' petition. The appeal came during the panicked year following revelations of a "Popish Plot" against the king and realm, a cause that the earl of Shaftesbury made his own as leader of the parliamentary opposition to James, duke of York. Given the paranoid fears of a Catholic takeover in England, it is not surprising that the earl would welcome fellow sufferers against Catholic tyranny from across the Channel, or that he would attempt to settle as many good Protestants in Carolina as possible.[54]

More surprising than the proprietors' endorsement was the reception of the petition in the various dark corners of Whitehall. English official bureaucracy was a labyrinthine maze, difficult to navigate for those without proper connections. Against the odds, Petit and Guérard's appeal moved fairly smoothly through its various ordeals. Like all petitions involving the colonies, it first went to the Lords of Trade and Plantations, who then sent it along to the Lords of the Treasury to gauge its fiscal viability. Treasury then sent the missive along to the Commissioners of the Customs, since the Huguenots had asked for an advance out of future customs revenues, and the Lords wanted to make sure such a plan was likely to succeed.[55] Finally, after each office had added its opinions, the petition returned to the Lords of Trade and Plantations, who issued a detailed recommendation to the king. They enthusiastically endorsed the French gentlemen's plan, which would be "of very great advantage & importance to the Trade of this Nation & increase of Yor Revenue." They especially applauded the fact that these particular migrants would "carry on and improve the Manufactures of Foreign Countries." The Lords did set some conditions: they recommended only giving aid to those who had come "from beyond the Seas" especially to join the new colony and specified that "many of them [be] skilful & practised in the manufacture of Wines Silks & Oyls." In the final step, the king approved the petition, ordering that two royal ships take the Huguenots to Carolina, and that the Treasury issue an advance on future customs to help the refugees establish themselves in the colony.[56]

The success of Petit and Guérard's petition set a tone for future Huguenot missives. The supplicants learned that they could open the coffers of the English crown by asking for land on the edges of empire and specifically by playing up their facility in producing silk and wine. Of course, this required some sleight of hand on the part of the petitioners. Both Petit and Guérard came from Normandy, which was perhaps the French region least appropriate for silk, wine, and olive oil. Normans made some wine, but they preferred cider, and the rainy climate was about as appropriate for silkworms as England itself. In addition, it was clear to anyone watching closely that the Huguenots quickly broke the conditions of their contract. The first ship of colonists left London on the frigate *Richmond* in December 1679, and the ship contained many people who did not come to England specifically to embark for Carolina. Many of them had lived in England for years and probably had not migrated specifically to avoid religious persecution. Jacob Guérard, for instance, appeared in the records of the French Church in Southampton as early as 1671.[57] In short, the petition seems to have represented something of an official fiction: the Huguenots pretended to be skilled *vignerons* and silk makers fleeing French persecution, while English officials conveniently ignored the fact that most of the petitioners were trying to play the system for greater advantages. The game worked because each side got something they wanted: the Huguenots got land and passage across the sea, the proprietors got to develop their colony, and the crown appeared to help the Protestant cause and fix the balance of trade in one fell swoop.

The success of the petition ensured that the language of silk and wine would become a regular feature of Huguenot appeals in England. In 1682, after the Poitevin dragonnades had started, a refugee named Gabriel Rappe presented a similar petition to the Committee on Trade and Plantations, "praying liberty to build Salt Panns, plant Vineyards, & Sow Hempe & Flax in such places wth in his Ma[jes]tyes Dominions in America, not yet used for those or other usefull purposes." In return, Rappe requested free passage for himself and any other "poore french Protestants" who joined his community. By listing so many possible economic pursuits Rappe seemed to be attempting to keep his options open, and he was equally flexible in terms of location, asking for a retreat between 36 and 52 degrees north latitude, a span that stretched from North Carolina to Newfoundland.[58] In this case the Lords of Trade proved reluctant to grant any land to Rappe, but did forward his petition to the duke of York, recommending that the Huguenot receive a license to make salt in New York.[59] No response from the duke survived, but Rappe did eventually find his way to America, settling in Pennsylvania by 1683.[60]

A more interesting, if mysterious relation of the mindset behind these proposals appeared in an anonymous "Memoire" submitted to Henry Compton, the Bishop of London sometime during the 1680s. The author wrote in French and probably belonged to London's Huguenot community. Whoever he was, his proposals represented the most well developed example of a Huguenot global economic vision organized around the growth and production of various commodities. The author began by recommending the formation of a committee in London to deal with the problem of the growing number of refugees and to decide where they should go—a sentiment that reflected the Bishop of London's ongoing interest in distributing refugees to various parts of England. Like many officials, the author looked especially to East Anglia, specifically to the seaside town of Little Yarmouth. He suggested settling "tradesmen, merchants, and mariners" in the town itself and finding "vacant lands" outside of town for farmers with skills in "the making of hemp and cloth."[61]

After describing his proposed East Anglian colony, the author's vision moved overseas. He admitted that not all refugees were suited for the types of trades and agricultural pursuits possible in England itself. It was necessary also to establish "a Colony in Carolina" that would be linked to the one in East Anglia. The Carolina migrants would be people "not proper for England," including especially "Vignerons and raisers of silkworms." The author believed that many of these migrants could come from the valleys of Piedmont in Savoy, a region wracked by religious and political strife during the late 1680s, and a place filled with peasants who understood the making of silk and wine. He also included "men of letters" as potential Carolina migrants, since they could devote their time to converting Native Americans to Christianity. With this exception, though, the point of these two colonies was entirely economic, and in fact represented the mercantilist ideal in miniature. The East Anglian manufacturers would be able to sell some of their goods to these captive consumers in Carolina, who in turn could send their raw materials back to East Anglia and the rest of England. By scattering people across the empire based on skills and inclinations, this engineer of the Refuge hoped to create a linked international system. This global network of Huguenot colonies would serve to give everyone a good job, and it would also help to enrich the British empire and fix its balance of trade.[62]

Over the course of the 1680s these dreams of silk and wine moved beyond just Carolina. A particularly interesting manifestation of the vision implanted in Pennsylvania, the place where the petitioner Gabriel Rappe ended up. The proprietor William Penn attempted to lure Huguenot refugees to his colony, engaging in something of a pamphlet war with the Carolina proprietors. As early as 1681 he expected to attract "many [migrants] from fra[ance]," and he worked especially with the well connected apothecary Moses Charas, who was one of the original purchasers in the new colony.[63] Alongside the usual offers of land and religious liberty, Penn made particular promises about Pennsylvania's productive capacities. The leading French pamphlet about the colony included a number of dubious claims about Pennsylvania's viticultural promise. It was on the same latitude as Montpellier, the tract asserted, and abounded in vines and mulberry trees. Among the list of people appropriate for the colony, the authors began with "laborers, wine-makers, and industrious and laborious artisans," especially "men who know how to raise silkworms and prepare silk."[64]

In fact, the proprietor himself made viticulture a particular project. Since grapes grew in such large quantities in Pennsylvania, Penn believed, they could certainly be made to produce good wine if he could attract people with the right expertise. He set out to prove his hypothesis on his own land in Philadelphia. He employed a French refugee as his own personal vigneron, to use his knowledge of grapes to unlock Pennsylvania's potential as a wine country. He hoped, moreover, that by bringing in more Huguenots he could further both wine and silk in the colony. He called specifically for those who understood "the making of wines and cloth" to move to Pennsylvania, since he believed that "the French carry out [those things] better than others."[65] Like the Virginia Company and the Carolina proprietors, Penn had come to believe that the Huguenots were special people—not just for their role in sacred history, but also for their particular skills and aptitudes. This belief opened up a world of possibilities for individual refugees, who could find land and employment across the globe, as long as they could convince their patrons that they could produce things that the empire needed.

While the rhetoric of silk and wine proved especially important in English and North American circles, it could pull Huguenots to even more exotic locales. In general, the Dutch empire resisted the mercantilist logic that defined its English and French counterparts. As an English observer noted, the Dutch gained economic mastery not by producing things of their own, but by becoming the "common carriers of the world," moving things that other people produced from one place to another. In fact, silk and wine were two particular strengths of the Dutch carrying trade. The powerful Dutch East India Company brought large quantities of raw silk back from Persia and other parts of the Far East—some of which was then manufactured by Dutch artisans—while an even larger European trade brought gallons of French wine and brandy into the Low Countries and from there to other markets in Europe. As long as these trades were strong, the Dutch had little reason to want to make silk or wine of their own.[66]

During the 1670s and 1680s, however, a number of factors conspired to change that situation. To be sure, the Dutch never considered the large-scale production of Mediterranean commodities in the far reaches of their empire; they were content to preside over an empire of trading posts rather than agricultural settlements. But the coming of war with France had damaged the wine trade, and the geographical extensiveness of the East India Company's domains produced unique challenges. By the late 1600s the Company sent dozens of ships a year on long-distance trading missions that stretched the limits of geography and technology. The journey from Amsterdam to the Company's eastern capital of Batavia (modern-day Jakarta) took over six months, and provisioning ships with adequate food and drink proved complicated and expensive—cutting into the Company's profit margins. To solve this problem, the Company set up provisioning stations at strategic locations where ships could stop to refuel. The most famous of these way stations lay at the foot of Table Mountain, near the southern tip of the African continent, where the Atlantic and Indian Oceans came together. In 1652 the Dutch established a small fort, and within several decades a village eventually known as Cape Town grew up alongside it. The town and its environs turned into the most ambitious exercise in settler colonialism in the Dutch East Indies and became the site of an experiment in wine culture that eventually exceeded contemporary efforts in North America.[67]

The development of the Cape Colony did not happen quickly. European sailors had been stopping at the Cape for decades before the Company's governing council—a committee known as the *Heren XVII* or "seventeen gentlemen" —ordered their servant Jan van Riebeeck to establish a "fort and garden" on the site. Issuing their instructions in 1649, the gentlemen lauded the region, noting the convenience and possible profits that could come from having a "refreshment station" on the way to the Indies. In addition, the establishment would also "magnify the name of the Most Holy God and the spreading of His Holy Gospel," since the natives of the area were pagans with no knowledge of Christianity.[68] For his part, van Riebeeck agreed with his superiors. By the time he set out to the Cape he had extensive experience as a merchant and company servant in both the East and West Indies, and he believed the Cape to be one of the best lands anywhere. He predicted that "all sorts of trees and other fruit would thrive well in the valleys," especially since "the Cape climate is very similar to that of Japan, and the northern portions of China, which places have abundance of all kinds of fruit and cattle."[69] In early 1652 the commander and his small retinue arrived at the new outpost and built a fort and garden. While things progressed slowly, van Riebeeck remained confident. He found "everywhere fine garden ground," the commander noted in his journal, predicting that "thousands of Chinese or other agriculturalists would not be able to cultivate a tenth part of the country, which is so rich that neither Formosa nor New Netherland can be compared with it."[70]

Despite the Commander's high hopes, the settlement remained small for the next two decades. This was partly by design: many within the East India Company had no desire to conduct extensive agriculture at the Cape, preferring small garden plots sufficient to provision passing ships. In addition, resistance from the local seminomadic pastoralists, the Khoekhoe and San people (often lumped together as the Khoesan), effectively limited the Dutch to a small territory under Table Mountain. More than that, there was a problem finding qualified farmers who could make the colony profitable or even self-sufficient. As early as the 1655 the Company established a population of "free burghers" at the Cape—people who received a release from Company duties and land so they could engage in agriculture. Nonetheless, few people seemed to relish settling in the colony, especially since by law they could only sell to the Company at fixed prices. In 1685 the total population of free burghers and their families was merely 378 people, and Company officials complained that far from provisioning the fleet, the outpost could not even provision itself, relying on rice imports from Batavia each year to sustain its small population.[71]

The strategy changed under a new commander, Simon van der Stel. A true son of the Dutch East Indies, van der Stel had been born on the island of Mauritius to a company official and his Malay wife. In 1679 he took up his post as commander, and he devoted himself to two particular goals. One was the geographical expansion of the colony. Buoyed by the recent defeat of some of the Khoesan resisters, van der Stel led or authorized a number of expeditions to the interior. He found a particularly fertile valley some forty miles inland from Cape Town, which he christened Stellenbosch and sent a number of free burghers to take up holdings there.[72] As an adjunct to his expansionist program, van der Stel also championed agriculture, both in wheat and vines. In the latter pursuit the commander actually followed in the footsteps of his predecessor Jan van Riebeeck, who had planted European vines in the Company's garden as well as on his own farm and succeeded in making South Africa's first wine in 1659. Van Riebeeck had never managed to convince many of the Dutch burghers to devote themselves to the vine, so van der Stel began the campaign anew, harvesting grapes on his farm at Constantia as an example to the burghers.[73] By 1685 these efforts had borne some fruit. A French priest who stopped at the Cape on the way to Siam raved about the local wine, which was white and "very agreeable," resembling that of "the Genetin," a grape variety popular in the Loire Valley. He noted that over twenty-five ships each year stopped at the outpost, filling up their holds with "sheep, wine, fruit, and vegetables," most of which came from the East India Company's "beautiful garden."[74]

Even as the Frenchman raved about the Cape's productive capacities, Company leaders in the fatherland attempted to make them stronger. In 1685 the Seventeen Gentlemen resolved to send more colonists to the Cape in order to "encourage farming" and cut down on the expenses of the garrison.[75] Apparently sharing other witnesses' sanguine outlook, the Seventeen believed that Cape farmers could eventually supply many of the provisions of the passing fleets, which would lessen the Company's dependence on East Indian rice. In addition to grain, the Company clearly sought to strengthen the Cape's wine and brandy production. In this goal, the Seventeen closely followed the Carolina Proprietors, and they quickly arrived at the same solution. By October 1685 the Netherlands was already filling up with Huguenot refugees—many of them skilled in the very agricultural pursuits that could turn the Cape into a profitable outpost. With very few Dutch settlers willing to make the trek to Africa, the Company turned to these new, more downtrodden people to solve their population problem.

The Company issued their first call for refugee migrants to the Cape only days before the Revocation of the Edict of Nantes. In fact, they looked for a number of migrants—ordinary farmers from the Netherlands, female orphans, and also "French Refugees of the reformed religion, especially those understanding the cultivation of the vine, the making of vinegar and the distilling of brandy."[76] Reading between the lines, it appears that Company leaders viewed the French Reformed as one plank in a wider strategy to people the Cape with productive newcomers. The Dutch migrants—who received free land in return for the promise to stay fifteen years—would hopefully solve the colony's grain problem. The young orphan girls would fix the colony's skewed sex ratio and allow the population to grow. The French, meanwhile, would supply the wine and brandy—especially since successive champions of the vine had noted that the Dutch, like the English, had no facility with viticulture and had proved resistant to putting much effort into winemaking.[77] Simon van der Stel strongly approved of these efforts to bring people who "are acquainted with the vine stock and the planting of olive-trees, in order to teach the older settlers what they as yet do not know about the cultivation of these plants," who could "marvellously establish and strengthen this Colony, and generally rouse the highest emulation of the Netherlanders." In short, the French could serve in the same role as the "experts" in Virginia.[78]

As it happened, none of these early efforts amounted to much. Young girls proved just as reluctant to travel to the Cape as Dutch farmers, which led the Company to redouble its efforts to attract the third group, French refugees. Two years after its initial appeal, in October 1687, the Company tried again—this time targeting not only "French refugees" but also "emigrating Piedmontese," from the duchy of Savoy, the dalluyden (people of the valleys) or Vaudois who had proved

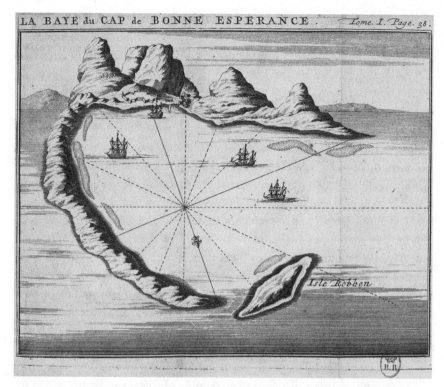

Figure 3.2 An illustration of Cape Town and Table Mountain during the 1690s. From *Voyages et avantures de François Leguat, & de ses compagnons, en deux isles désertes des Indes orientales* (Amsterdam, 1708). Courtesy of the Bibliothèque Nationale de France.

so tempting to English colonial projectors as well. This new appeal largely repeated the same terms from two years earlier, but gave the French and Savoyards somewhat better terms than their Dutch counterparts, only requiring them to stay five years at the Cape. The Company also attempted to advertise their scheme within the refugee community. They translated their call for emigrants into French and distributed it both to local Walloon Churches and through ministerial networks as far away as Switzerland—probably due to their fixation on refugees from Piedmont. To be sure, Dutch promotional activities never approached those of the Carolina proprietors or William Penn; they preferred to work through back channels rather than go straight to the public. Nonetheless, evidence suggests that the Company had a similar mindset to the English as they sought to construct their colony, and news of the opportunity got around not just to Paul Reboulet but to diplomats as well. In 1688, for instance, the king of Poland's ambassador in The Hague sent word that the States General had worked to send "a considerable number of Families" from Savoy to the Cape of Good Hope. French authorities, he noted, "appear not at all pleased with this design."[79]

The mindset behind this colonization scheme came through in a detailed set of "Reflections" that was unique in laying out the theory behind a Huguenot overseas colony. The document's provenance is difficult to determine; it consisted of lengthy ruminations on the East India Company's plan to send Huguenots to the Cape, but seems to have originated outside the Company itself. The fact that it ended up in the collected papers of the Walloon churches (and in French) suggests some collaboration between officials in those churches and company leaders, though the detached tone of the document itself means it was likely not written by an actual refugee. Whatever its authorship, the document functioned as both an endorsement of the Huguenot colonial endeavor and a blunt recommendation on how to make the design succeed. As such, it reveals much about how Dutch officials viewed the refugees as tools in a global economic strategy.[80]

Like the contemporaneous plan for linked refugee colonies in Carolina and East Anglia, the reflections began by ruminating on what sorts of Huguenots belonged in the Cape Colony. The first, and most important, were agriculturalists: "laborers, winemakers, gardeners, and generally all those who know how to cultivate the earth and make it productive." Since the colony centered around "the cultivation of the earth," these people should make up a majority, perhaps 90 percent, of the new settlers, and they needed to be "well suited for work, robust, of good manners." At the same time, the planners wanted an organic community. They called for a small number of artisans and craftsmen to accompany the farmers to the Cape, and they were particularly keen on attracting a few men of means—people who could serve as natural leaders over the farmers and artisans, who tended to be people of "mediocre capacities" and needed to be "guided and driven" by those with the "ability to put others to work." In sum, the colony should focus on agriculture but aim to recreate something of an ideal Huguenot village in the Cape Colony, with representatives from a variety of social classes and walks of life. This was necessary, the author implied, not so much to preserve the French church in exile as to preserve the public peace, which would be threatened by bringing in too many people from the middling and laboring classes.[81]

The author continued by reflecting on the possible difficulties that the Dutch could face in building a successful refugee colony. The first problem had to do with the nature of the Huguenots themselves. While planners hoped to attract refugees of all types, they understood that most would be "poor people who are having trouble finding their subsistence elsewhere" and who could therefore easily become charity cases for the Company rather than producers of revenue. This risk made it all the more critical to choose carefully who could go to the Cape—presumably by having Company officials examine prospective migrants. The Huguenot community, moreover, presented particular challenges for colonial leaders who wanted to ensure they did not attract "worried or turbulent" subjects. The refugees had all surmounted great obstacles in leaving France and possessed "courage and hardiness, and a great love of liberty." While these traits could be positive, too much liberty could undermine public order. One possible way to solve the problem was to favor refugees from particular provinces, since "some of them have more docile inhabitants than others." As in the similar Carolina proposal, the author especially recommended "those of the Valleys of Piedmont . . . who are naturally good and hard-working subjects."[82]

The author also noted that the liberty-loving Huguenots could be particularly unhappy in a place like the Cape Colony. Unlike "the other foreign Colonies," the Cape was not "free in its trade." A Company outpost, it existed solely to bring profits to its leaders back in the Netherlands. Like other free burghers, the Huguenots could only sell their wine, grain, and other produce back to the Company, who would in turn sell it to passing ships. The new settlers could not maintain their own trade either in the Indies or Europe, nor could they trade with the Cape's native people. In addition, settlers could only buy goods from the Company's stores, with prices fixed by fiat. While these policies existed to ensure that individuals did not profit at the Company's expense, they could also dissuade people with means—the leaders who would hold the community together—from going to the Cape when they had better options in Europe or North America. The author recommended relaxing these strictures by allowing settlers to trade in a limited way with passing ships, which would allow them to sell more of their produce at better prices and obtain goods that were unavailable in the Company stores.[83] The main problem was clear to see: it was difficult to balance corporate interests with the individual desires of refugees.

Over the next year the Company worked to find settlers for the scheme. Near the end of 1687 the Seventeen Gentlemen updated Governor van der Stel, saying that they had found "vine cultivators as well as those who understand the manufacture of brandy and vinegar, so that we hope that the lack of these articles so frequently deplored by you will now be supplied." They also resolved to send a minister along with the vignerons, so they could establish a stable community life. "They are industrious people, satisfied with little, and your Honours are to give them the same treatment as is laid down by us for freemen of our own nation at the Cape."[84] In a separate letter the company's Amsterdam chamber repeated the common assertion that the settlement plan would cut down costs and help the refugees themselves, since the new migrants included "men who understand vine-growing, who will be of value to the Company and themselves in the future." Seemingly responding to some of the earlier queries about the feasibility of the project, these officials hoped that "since these people are able to help themselves in a small way, that at the Cape they will be able to adapt themselves to the work, as finding themselves settled under a lenient Government, and feeling free from past persecution. This time alone can effect."[85]

In addition, Company officials enthusiastically courted refugees from Piedmont. By early 1688 several thousand Protestants had fled Savoy into Switzerland and adjacent parts of Germany, and many of them clustered in the city of Nuremberg, looking for appropriate retreats around Europe. While the community's leaders hoped to find land for most of the refugees in Brandenburg, a representative, a merchant named Jean Pastre, came to The Hague to see if the Dutch could find a place for five to six hundred of the Savoyards. The appeal quickly found its way to the East India Company, who believed that they had located their Cape settlers. Pastre presented an official appeal on behalf of the refugees, and attempted to negotiate their passage from Nuremberg to the Netherlands as well as passage to the Cape. While the details are murky, the design seemed to fail once the Savoyards learned where they were headed. Perhaps even more than the Huguenots, the Piedmontese hoped to return to their valleys, which would actually happen in 1689. When they received a good offer for land in Germany, they preferred that to an uncertain trip to the farthest reaches of the Indies. They were, after all, "averse to the sea."[86]

The loss of the Piedmontese meant that Company leaders would not be able to fill the valleys of southern Africa with refugees. If the Savoyards had traveled to the Cape, they would have more than doubled the size of the free burgher population and dominated the population there. As it happened, the Company was still able to find other Huguenots willing to travel to the colony. Perhaps the most important catch was the minister Pierre Simond. A native of Dauphiné who had served in the town of Embrun before the Revocation, Simond had fled to Rotterdam by 1686 and soon received a posting in the Walloon Church of Zierikzee in Zeeland. A man of around thirty-five, Simond belonged to the middle ranks of Huguenot pastors in the Netherlands. He was far from a luminary, but was well connected enough to publish one of his sermons in Leiden in 1687. He also may have traveled to Saint-Domingue as a young man, which could have whetted his appetite for overseas travel. Whatever his reasons for accepting employment with the Dutch East India Company, his involvement was critical for the design's success. By employing a minister, the Company indicated a willingness to form a Huguenot community in Africa—a goal that dovetailed with the suggestions in the "Reflections," but also appeared similar to the terms offered to Huguenot communities in Germany. Simond pledged to find settlers for the colony, including those skilled in wine production, which he did by appealing to friends in Zeeland as well as old contacts from Dauphiné and elsewhere. After the minister signed on the Company was able to attract nearly two hundred refugees, many of whom had personal connections to Simond. The colonists departed in several ships in 1688, and the Dutch dreams of wine and grain seemed poised to come true.[87]

As Simond and his neighbors prepared to go to the Cape, a similar plan appeared across the Channel in England. The great emulators and competitors of their Dutch counterparts, the English East India Company, stumbled on the same idea to build a provisioning station with the help of refugee agriculturalists. The EIC's "refreshment station" was the island of St. Helena, a small, fairly barren outpost in the Atlantic conveniently located on the sea route to Asia. The Company set up a post there during the 1640s, nearly the same time as the Dutch establishment of the Cape Colony, and hoped that they could produce enough to provision their ships heading to India. Much like the Cape, St. Helena operated in a strange limbo between east and west. It was a Company outpost, without any of the political liberties that defined English North American colonies, but at the same time Company governors there looked across the Atlantic for examples on how to run their colony—not least in their agricultural ambitions and early embrace of enslaved African labor. In 1683 Company directors expressed hope that the island could soon become a version of Barbados, since "the soil and climate of the Island is fit for production of commodities of a richer nature than cattle or potatoes, yams, plantains, &c."[88]

Soon the Company's ambitions switched from sugar to wine. They may have been inspired by the example of Madeira, the Portuguese Atlantic island that would soon become the key supplier of wines to North America. They knew about the Dutch experiments in the Cape Colony as well; in early 1687 company leaders noted the "good wine" produced at "the Dutch Plantation in Table-Bay at the Cape" and suggested to the factor at Surat that the English try to set up a similar wine plantation of their own, perhaps farther east on the South African coast.[89] By 1689, the EIC realized that their existing station at St. Helena could fill this role. "After diverse attempts to make some profitable productions upon that Island which may in some measure recompense the prodigious charge we have laid our upon it," the London office noted, they settled on "the planting of Vines, and the making wine and Brandy, which all men of what quality so ever, that ever were upon the Island that we have conversed with, do unanimously agree to be a feazable attempt." They noted, however, that the design would only work if they could find "Persons bred up in that Science, that know how to cultivate and dress Vines perfectly well, & how to make wine and Brandy." Not surprisingly, the Company settled on French Huguenots as the proper agents to turn St. Helena into a wine island.[90]

The St. Helena wine scheme centered around one refugee, Stephen Poirier. According to Company officials Poirier was "an honest man" who had "lived formerly in great plenty upon his own land in France where he made two or three hundred hogsheads of Wine and Brandy P[er] ann[un]," but after the Revocation he fled his home on account of religion and lost everything. While it is impossible to know if Poirier told the truth, he may have been related to several people of the same surname who fled Burgundy for Switzerland and Germany around the same time, which means he very well could have been experienced in viticulture. In addition, he found nine other "Vineroons," all French Protestants, willing to move themselves and their families to St. Helena.[91]

The Company's letters to both Poirier and the colony's governor revealed the same combination of high hopes and doubts that characterized the Cape Huguenot scheme. The Company instructions to Poirier—appointed as "Supervisor of all the Companyes Plantations Vineyards and Cattle" on the island—stressed the importance of setting up "a large Vineyard" in the part of Poirier's own land that he "shall apprehend most fitt for such a purpose." While it was their skills as "Vineroons" that made the French most valuable, the Company also hoped that they would "live sober & vertuous lives, that by their good Example They may be a means to draw those debaucht Planters unto a more vertuous Conversation." The Huguenots, then, were model settlers in that they were sufferers for the faith who also had special skills. Landing in a colony of drunken, quarrelsome misfits, they could only make things better. At the same time, the Company warned the island's governor to keep close watch on the French. They would make "excellent servants," the Company advised, "But are apt to grow insolent & negligent if they not be held to do their work as they are in France, & if you give them ear, they will never leave craving and asking." Like their Dutch counterparts, English East India Company leaders worried that the Huguenots possessed an excessive love of liberty and advised them to use a firm hand with the newcomers to keep them productive and compliant.[92]

The Dutch and English East India Company schemes were very different from those in North America. In both St. Helena and the Cape the refugees were Company servants rather than independent settlers, and in some ways the goals of the companies for the new arrivals were far more modest than the grandiose visions of economic mastery that brought Huguenots to America. At the same time, these eastern and western migration streams came from one single root: the desire of northern European leaders to master Mediterranean crops in their overseas colonies. Starting with the departure of the *Richmond* from London to South Carolina in late 1680, to the *Verschoten, Oosterland,* and several other ships leaving for the Cape in 1688, to the *Benjamin,* which stopped in St. Helena en route to India in 1689, hundreds of Huguenots scattered across the world to attempt to make these dreams of silk and wine come to pass.

———

It is tempting, with the benefit of hindsight, to view these silk and wine schemes as marginal experiments doomed to failure. After all, a vast majority of them did fail, due to climate and geography. Despite similar latitudes, Carolina did not resemble Languedoc. Nonetheless, the experiments did not all fail, and they continued to inspire imitators for decades. In fact, hundreds of refugees did relocate to colonies during the 1680s, and many of them dedicated themselves to silk and wine production. The trip to America or Africa was the beginning, not the end, of a story that stretched well into the next century, as French people, their offspring, and their non-French neighbors all continued to try and make farms and plantations in the Indies produce the kinds of goods that central planners had dreamed about for decades. These visions lived on despite massive evidence to the contrary and dozens of false starts. Despite so many disappointments, wine and silk remained at the heart of the Huguenots' New World endeavors.

In some ways, Carolina was the most hopeful, and the most disappointing, of these experiments. The first Huguenot settlers, who came as part of the original Petit-Guérard colony, arrived in 1680 at the new port of Charleston, where they found a colony unlike the one represented in promotional tracts. It was, for one thing, a frontier settlement with no sure economic purpose and difficult living conditions. Even five years later, a new arrival named Judith Giton described nearly the worst possible introduction to frontier life. Giton arrived in Charleston after a harrowing nine-month journey during which she lost her mother. After six months in the colony she had not tasted bread and "worked the land like a slave." Her brother, who had "nothing but Carolina on his mind" before the trip, succumbed to a fever, being unused to the backbreaking labor.[93] Another early witness, who may have been the nobleman Henri Auguste Chastaigner, confirmed Giton's impressions but put a more positive gloss on it. Carolina did not resemble the "flattering portraits" of the promotional tracts; one had to live there "without refinements," and even a privileged person like Chastaigner had to accept life in a small cabin without comforts like bread and wine. Nonetheless, this was a good country for those who expected little and only wanted "to live in peace." Chastaigner's portrait of the colony would have been easily recognizable to those who read the works of Charles de Rochefort or Henri Duquesne: it was a peculiar Calvinist utopia, not a place for idlers but ideal for those who wanted to work hard and receive the divine gift of *salut*.[94]

Alongside these paeans to the simple life lay dreams of profit, and Carolina's first Huguenots did not forget their pledges to turn the colony into a new Languedoc across the ocean. While many of the *Richmond* migrants were Normans who seemed to have had no real intention to make wine or silk, at least a few did apply themselves to those pursuits. François de Rousserie, for instance, a native of Montpellier, received 800 acres from the Proprietors in 1683 for "haveing wth great Industry aplyed himself to the propagation of Wine & other Usefull things in Carolina."[95] Another member of the Petit-Guérard contingent, Louis Thibou, left behind more evidence of his winemaking endeavors. Thibou was a native of Orleans in the Loire Valley who lived in Paris for many years before decamping to London in 1677, before the persecution began in earnest. He seems to have been a merchant, but he described himself as a *vigneron* in one document, suggesting at the very least that wine was his primary trading item— not surprising since his homeland, the Loire Valley region, supplied much of Paris's wine during the 1600s.[96] Whatever his background, Thibou did try and make wine in South Carolina, with mixed results. In his one surviving letter Thibou lauded the "fine climate" in Carolina, which he compared to Languedoc or Italy. It was particularly well suited to grapes, which "do wonderfully well," especially those made from cuttings brought in from Madeira, France, or the Canary Islands. "They produce excellent grapes which are sweet, wine-flavored [*vineux*], and full of juice," he wrote, and "There can never be a lack of them since they are nourished by warmth and soft rain." Overall, be believed that Carolina wine could surpass that of Europe. Nonetheless, it was clear that Thibou had planted no vines of his own—he lamented that "If only I had good vine-stock from Champagne, Suresne, and Argenteuil I would very quickly do well in this country for wine is very dear. . . . We only need labor and good plants to do a lot in a short time." With God's help, he hoped, his vines would prosper and allow him to live "like a gentleman." Nearly a decade later Thibou was still trying, according to his neighbor Jean Boyd. He had not yet produced wine, but hoped to make a vintage soon, since there were "all sorts" of grapes. "We no longer doubt we will be able to make very good wine here," Boyd concluded with confidence.[97]

Jean's own brother, Jacques Boyd, made similar attempts at viticulture. A family of mixed Scottish-Huguenot heritage, the Boyds were leading merchants in Bordeaux before the Revocation. At least two of the brothers made their way to Carolina, and in 1686 Jacques Boyd wrote a letter to a correspondent in England that offered a detailed portrait of life in the young colony, along with his personal hopes to profit in the wine trade. Boyd admitted that there were only four planted vines in the province, and that they were small in size, but insisted that they were "all successful." More than that, he hoped to soon make the vines central to his business; he intended soon to ship back "the first wine from native grapes made on English soil and even in all of America."[98] This was not the end of Boyd's wine speculations. Nearly a decade later in 1694 the Carolina Assembly awarded him 3,000 acres partly as a reward for his "great Charges in endeavouring the estab- lishment of a Vintage and severall considerable productions" in the province. He needed the land for an unspecified "matter of great importance" —though like François de Rousserie's earlier efforts, it is not clear if they amounted to an- ything. Interestingly, the family made more profits from the wine trade, not just before the Revocation but well into the eighteenth century, when they managed much of the commerce between Bordeaux and Dublin.[99]

Reports from other Carolina vineyards during the 1690s underscored the problem. As the exploration accounts and promotional tracts noted, Carolina abounded with wild grapes, but these were very different plants than the ones that flourished in European vineyards. The berries were small and "filled with seeds," noted Jean Gignilliat, a Swiss settler who experimented in viticulture in the 1690s. The answer, he and many other French people believed, was to find the right Old World vines and plant them in the New World soil. Louis Thibou had earlier experimented with cuttings from various places, and Gignilliat followed in his footsteps. Although he reported that vines from Bordeaux did best, none of them lived up to his expectations. He continued to have faith that with the right cuttings he could finally make good wine, suggesting to a correspondent that he needed Spanish or Portuguese vines, after which "we will infallibly make very good wine."[100] What he did not realize was that climatic and soil conditions were not optimal for these imported species. Some years later the new Charleston French minister Paul L'Escot reflected on the experiments to bring in various cuttings, all with little success. He expressed hope in the very thing that Gignilliat and others had found hopeless, that the native grapes could finally produce wine. He noted that some experiments had yielded small quantities of good wine, but not nearly enough for export.[101] One of these experiments did earn the approval of the English botanist William Salmon, who reported on an experience he had in the house of one "Garrat a French man" who had made a hogshead of wine "from Vines which grew Wild in the Woods." Salmon declared it "the pleasantest Wine I ever drank in my whole Life."[102]

If Carolina's wine industry developed slowly, silk proved even more problematic. Refugees on the *Richmond* carried silk "seeds" (the unhatched eggs of silkworms) to America with them, but as so often happened, the eggs died before reaching America.[103] This initial disappointment underscored a difficult reality of sericulture: even with proper experts, silk required a huge infrastructure, from thousands of mulberry trees to the silkworm lodgings that John Bonoeil had described decades earlier. As one refugee noted in 1688, all of this required a "great investment," and when new settlers had to clear land for houses and crops it was unlikely they would immediately turn their attention to silkworms. Nonetheless, there were those who tried. Several passengers on the *Richmond* had experience in silk, and other weavers arrived in the colony during the next decade. In Santee one Joachim Gaillard had devoted himself to the prospect, expecting to "make a very good trade here" once silk took off, and another of his neighbors had already planted more than twelve thousand mulberry trees.[104]

During the next decade the experiments continued. Some of the champions of sericulture were not Huguenots at all—the former governor of the Leeward Islands, Sir Nathaniel Johnson, settled in the colony on a plantation he named Silk Hope, where he planted groves of mulberry trees (as well as vineyards), even sending a sample of some of his silk back to the Proprietors in 1699.[105] By the first decade of the eighteenth century, Johnson (by that time South Carolina's governor) had inspired imitators, to the point that "Silk is come unto great Improvement," according to the former governor John Archdale, "some Families making 40 or 50 *l.* a Year and their Plantation Work not neglected; little Negro Children being serviceable in Feeding the Silk-worms."[106] Much of this activity centered on area known as the Orange Quarter, an area near Johnson's Silk Hope that served as one of the centers of Huguenot settlement in the colony. Some of the best evidence of the scale of the industry appeared in the ledger book of Nicholas de Longuemare, a Dieppois goldsmith who became an active merchant in silk, trafficking raw silk, eggs, and other materials to French weavers in the Orange Quarter.[107] None of these efforts were enough to turn silk into Carolina's cash crop—that honor would go to rice—but they kept hope alive.

While Carolina's Mediterranean dreams survived in spite of great obstacles, endeavors on the road to the East experienced similar twists and turns. The efforts to make wine on St. Helena, for instance, failed almost immediately. In 1689 John Ovington's ship *Benjamin* transported Stephen Poirier and his nine *vignerons* to the island. The captain predicted that their "Project for Planting Vines" would be a great boon to both the East India Company and the refugees, since they would provide "refreshment" to passing ships and "forget their Poverty, and remember their Miseries no more."[108] As it happened, the vineyard scheme never led to any significant profits. Inhabitants preferred to traffic in arrack, a liquor distilled from potatoes and other roots that did little to improve the island's reputation for drunkenness and debauchery. By 1695 four of Poirier's nine French employees received leave to return to London, and while he continued to work on the vineyard, he intended to use slaves rather than skilled vignerons for the labor, and he produced very little wine anyway. In 1698 Company leaders scolded Poirier, by this time the island's governor, for the vineyard's lack of success but resolved to send "some Vine plants," hoping "they will prove much better than what you have there Already." By the early 1700s officials were able to send back a small quantity of St. Helena wine, but it never lived up to the Company's grand expectations.[109]

The Dutch endeavors to make wine at the Cape proved far more promising. Later on the same voyage that took Poirier to St. Helena, John Ovington visited the Cape and found "fruitful wine," which the Dutch used "to supply their Ships, and to furnish the *Indies* with some quantity" —though Ovington found it "much harder and less palatable" than European wine and more "offensive to the Brain." He ascribed much of this industry's success to the presence of hundreds of those "sent hither by the *French* Persecution," who settled in the valleys beyond Cape Town where they "rear their Cattle, sow their Corn, plant Vines, and sedulously improve all things of worth to the best advantage." In Ovington's eyes at least, the Dutch design to use Huguenots to advance the Cape Colony had been an unqualified success.[110]

Of course, the Cape Huguenot experience had not gone as smoothly as the English captain believed. By the time he wrote nearly two hundred refugees had settled in the colony, most of whom had traveled in a number of ships in 1687 and 1688, armed with instructions from the Dutch East India Company that Commander Simon van der Stel provide the new settlers with "land, seed corn, and whatever else they require."[111] In keeping with the original plan, van der Stel sent most of the new arrivals to farms in Stellenbosch and the Drakenstein Valley. While the landscape was very different, refugees at the Cape experienced similar tribulations as their counterparts in Carolina. The clearest portrait of these struggles came from a lengthy letter by the minister Pierre Simond. Reporting to the Seventeen Gentlemen in June 1689, the minister thanked the Company for providing the "sweet and precious liberty" the refugees so desired, but he spared no detail in relating the difficulties of life on the Cape. On arrival, many of the Huguenots found the land they had been granted less than ideal for agriculture, and while the Commander obliged them by giving them new parcels, they still found it slow work to build farms in the wilderness. If Carolina colonists spent their time felling trees, those in the Drakenstein Valley could not find enough timber to build houses, and the lack of flour mills and sufficient transportation to Cape Town ate up time and money. The refugees received charity from the commander and eventually from the consistory at Batavia, but the newcomers had to put most of their energies into ensuring their survival.[112]

Nonetheless, the production of Cape wine and brandy increased significantly during the 1690s, and Huguenots played a role in the industry's expansion. While the Cape Huguenots came from almost every conceivable French province and many occupational backgrounds, the Company seems to have made good on its resolve to enlist at least a few experienced vignerons for the colony. In 1688 the Company's Delft chamber offered an endorsement of the Villiers brothers—Pierre, Abraham, and Jacob—who had particular skill in managing vineyards. The brothers seem to have originated in the village of Viviers-sur-Artaut on the northern fringe of Burgundy, and scattered evidence suggests they did have a family history of viticulture.[113] They were not the only ones. Isaac Taillefert, for instance, had grown vines in Chateau-Thierry, in the western part of Champagne, before heading to Middelburg and then the Cape on the *Oosterland* in 1688. By the 1690s he had recreated much of his old life on his farm just below Paarl Mountain. When François Leguat visited the Cape on his way home from his East Indian adventure in 1698, he lauded Taillefert as the Cape's best vintner. "This generous man receives and regales all those that are so happy as to come and see him," Leguat wrote, and his wine was "not unlike our small Wines of *Champagne*."[114]

Beyond these anecdotes, there was clearly a transformation occurring in the Cape's wine industry that went well beyond that in Carolina. Wine was becoming a significant staple of the economy. Leguat noted that many of the houses in Cape Town were "surrounded with Vines, Gardens, and Groves," and a decade later the German visitor Peter Kolb went even farther, claiming that "There is hardly a Cottage in all the Colonies without a Vineyard." Most farmers had enough wine to maintain vast personal stores for themselves, while also selling much of it to the East India Company (who in turn sold it to passing ships) or in some cases to local tavern owners. Many visitors did not show much affection for Cape wine: the Burgundian Leguat complained it was "none of the best," while a Dutch traveler noted that much of it had an "astonishingly bad, earthy taste" that he blamed on the varieties of grapes. Nonetheless, farmers made a great deal of money off of wine, which during the eighteenth century constituted the surest path to material comfort for free burghers, who utilized imported slaves and local Khoesan labor to manage vast vineyards.[115]

If Cape wine was successful, however, it is not clear to what degree the refugees themselves either brought about or benefited from that success. Certainly many French farmers maintained vineyards, and a few of them became quite successful in the wine business, but their Dutch and German neighbors also proved adept at wine making, and it was the old farm of Simon van der Stel, Constantia, that became known for making the best Cape wine, not any establishment of the Huguenots. While the refugees seemed to "peaceably enjoy their happiness," as François Leguat noted, they tended to live in somewhat more spartan conditions than their Dutch neighbors. Peter Kolb noted that one of the fears of two decades earlier had come to pass; many French refugees had become indebted to the Company. This circumstance meant that while some had "better Success than ordinary," they tended to live in small, simple houses, even as the leading Dutch burghers in Cape Town and Stellenbosch possessed "stately Seats and Pleasure-Houses." Like the first settlers in Carolina, the Huguenots of South Africa did not get rich, from wine, silk, or anything else, but lived in simplicity and, for the most part, peace.[116]

———

Durand of Dauphiné never returned to Virginia. During his last months in the colony he collected offers of land and aid from English planters from the Potomac to the James Rivers, practically from one end of the colony to the other. When he returned to England in 1687 Durand dutifully published the narrative of his experiences, which was as much a promotional tract as a tale of his escape and travels. He concluded by laying out the advantages of settlement in Rappahannock and Stafford counties, places where "grapevines . . . can be planted" and migrants could receive free land and the right to their own, French-language church services. Despite these good offers, Durand felt pulled back to

Europe, excited by Pierre Jurieu's apocalyptic speculations. In the summer of 1687, just after he returned to London, a "gentleman of Dauphiné" of the same surname appeared in the Royal Bounty records. He received £2 of charity to pay "the charges of his sickness." If this was in fact the same Durand, then his dreams ended in dramatic fashion. Struck down with illness, perhaps something he caught on board the ship back to London, Durand found himself depending on the king's charity to survive. He never again appeared in the records, and few people heeded his call to Virginia, at least for another decade. Louis XIV did not fall, Christ did not return, and Durand probably died a pauper in a city that he derided as cold and unfriendly.[117]

If Durand's scheme came to nothing, within a decade others had emulated his design to grow vines in the piedmont. In 1700 and 1701 a large retinue of refugees—more than the number to Carolina or the Cape—settled in a place called Manakintown on the upper reaches of the James River. Soon they had turned to vines. According to one report from less than a decade after the town's founding, the refugees produced "excellent wine . . . which will be very much to their own advantage and to the colony."[118] The planter and historian Robert Beverley described it as "a sort of Clarret" made from grapes that were "gather'd off of the wild Vines in the Woods." The result was "tolerably good," but inspired Beverley himself to go farther in the experiment, tending a few vineyards and making his own wine—and thus proving that Huguenots could in fact inspire their neighbors in the pursuit.[119] Thus, Durand's vision came to pass, and Virginia wine became a reality. At the same time, it was not just visions of Mediterranean crops that brought Manakintown into existence. The settlers in that town took a circuitous path to the colony, one that demonstrated the power not just of political economy but of geopolitics and military rivalry as well. By embracing the world of empires, Huguenots like the ones at Manakintown moved farther from the goals of autonomy and *salut* that attracted them to new worlds in the first place.

Refugee Geopolitics

Jacques de la Case spent the last twenty-five years of his life on the frontiers of empires. A Protestant merchant's son from the town of Nérac in Gascony, la Case left home in 1683 to enlist in the army of Friedrich Wilhelm, the "Great Elector" of Brandenburg. By 1689 he had left the elector's service and made his way to Amsterdam, where he joined a different scheme, the design by Henri Duquesne to settle a colony of refugees on the "Isle of Eden" in the Indian Ocean. La Case was one of the small band of men who served as the first settlers in what they hoped would be a Huguenot utopia in the tropics. They spent several years on the deserted island of Rodrigues, but eventually built a small ship and made it to the Dutch colony of Mauritius. There la Case's life took a darker turn. He and his fellow refugees got into a dispute with the governor, who imprisoned them for several years on a barren island before sending the men to Batavia for trial. Once acquitted, la Case finally returned to Amsterdam in 1698. From there he made his way to London and signed on to yet another imperial design, crossing the Atlantic to the new refugee colony of Manakintown, located on the upper reaches of the James River on one of the farthest edges of the English empire. It was there that the peripatetic Frenchman finally found some rest, living in the town until his death in 1708.[1]

La Case's extraordinary journey reveals some important truths about the nature of the Huguenot Refuge in the 1680s and 1690s. First of all, for many young men in particular, migration was tied to geopolitics, and more specifically to military rivalries in Europe and the wider world. La Case began his career as a soldier, and in this pursuit he joined thousands of his coreligionists who served in a number of theaters, from Ireland to Russia, during the late 1600s.[2] After he stopped being a proper soldier, la Case's movements still reflected other people's strategic motives. His trip to the Indian Ocean, for instance, was bankrolled by the Dutch East India Company, who hoped that the colony of Huguenots on the Isle of Eden would serve to defend their interests against France's push for influence in the region. Even his trip to Manakintown, where he served as a settler rather than a soldier, had a strategic component to it, as officials at the Board of

The Global Refuge. Owen Stanwood, Oxford University Press (2020). © Oxford University Press.
DOI: 10.1093/oso/9780190264741.001.0001

Trade and Virginia's governor hoped to use the Huguenots to strengthen one of the colony's most vulnerable frontiers and fend off attacks by French or Native American enemies. In sum, la Case's global journey reflected far more than his own preferences; he traveled almost exclusively to the places where Dutch and English leaders wanted to strengthen their borders.

As it happened, similar strategic considerations moved hundreds if not thousands of Huguenots to the edges of empires. If political economic visions of silk and wine propelled one wave of migrations, the geopolitical interest of defending and expanding borders inspired another, with small cadres of refugees heading off to any number of vulnerable frontiers. This process accelerated after 1689, when England and the Netherlands went to war with France in the War of the League of Augsburg. Given their antipathy toward Louis XIV, many Huguenots willingly served as soldiers against the Sun King. Beyond that, English and Dutch leaders increasingly believed that French Protestants were the best people to combat French Catholic designs for mastery in both the West and East Indies, and Huguenots were happy to portray themselves as experts in battling French domination. After all, many of them had served in the French military before the Revocation of the Edict of Nantes, and nearly all of them had lived in France and its empire. In the post-Revocation world they were poised to serve as experts in French objectives or even as spies and border crossers. This was just one more way that the refugees appeared as chosen people: their Frenchness made them valuable and allowed them to infiltrate enemy lines. Not surprisingly, Pierre Jurieu himself operated a spy ring that brought back valuable intelligence from French ports.[3]

At the same time, the Huguenots' Frenchness could be a liability during times of war. If the refugees could serve as spies behind enemy lines, it was also conceivable that French agents could infiltrate England and the Netherlands by pretending to be Huguenots, or that actual refugees might retain some of their affections for their home country in spite of everything. It was these suspicions, at least in part, that landed Jacques de la Case and the other Eden colonists in a Dutch prison for several years, when Mauritius's governor suspected them of harboring French sympathies. There were many other examples of French Protestants facing similar charges, sometimes in Europe but even more often on the edges of empire, where settlers felt especially vulnerable. Essentially, the Huguenots' neighbors did not know whether nationality or religion mattered more in cementing identity. Were the refugees trustworthy because they were Protestants, or suspect because they were French? Non-Huguenots debated this question among themselves, while the refugees themselves tried to blend in and make themselves useful to avoid ill treatment. Of course, the situation was complicated by the fact that a few Huguenots *were* spies and double agents.[4]

In sum, geopolitics partially made the Huguenot world and also threatened to unmake it at the same time. It pushed refugees to the margins of European empires, but also divided them from their non-French neighbors, and provided temptations for those who missed living among other French people and had tired of life in exile. Over the course of the 1690s especially, this drama recurred in many different parts of the Huguenot world—from the Caribbean to New England, and from the Mascarene Islands to the Cape of Good Hope. By the end of the decade, this precarious existence between empires had changed the Huguenot mission. Dreams of utopian Calvinist societies and autonomous French bastions faded, replaced by the desire to fit in—whether that meant returning to France or ceasing to be French altogether.

———

In 1682 a French frigate anchored in the harbor of Port Royal, on the English island of Jamaica. The ship was named *La Trompeuse*, and a Huguenot mariner from the Île d'Oleron named Pierre Pain piloted the vessel. It was not unusual during times of peace for foreign ships to visit English Caribbean ports, but Pain's visit was not typical. He had come to defect. Hearing of the "severe Persecution" against his fellow Protestants at home, Pain deserted his post in Cayenne, a French settlement in Guiana on the northern coast of South America. After arriving in Port Royal Pain presented himself to the island's lieutenant governor, the ex-pirate Henry Morgan, and offered to pledge his allegiance—and his ship—to the English cause. After some thought, Morgan decided to grant Pain's request, urging Jamaica's council to naturalize the Frenchman as an English subject. "I designed to follow in this the dictates of humanity as well as those of law and reason," Morgan reported to the Lords of Trade in London in justifying his decision.[5]

Even during peacetime, Pierre Pain understood his own strategic value. Early modern navies nearly always had trouble filling their ships, and the French represented something of a special case. The kingdom suffered from a perennial lack of skilled mariners, and a disproportionate number were like Pain—Protestants from the coastal communities of western France. The captain's act of rebellion thus had very serious implications for France's sea power, implying as it did that the persecution of Protestants could endanger national security.[6] At the same time, the peculiar circumstances of the Caribbean undoubtedly played a role in Pain's decision to desert his post, and Morgan's willingness to naturalize the stranger. The region operated as a strange extension of European geopolitics; settlers from various European nations lived in close proximity to one another, fighting each other during wartime and often preparing for war when they were at peace. Moreover, all of the islands had developed into societies based on plantation slavery, with large black majorities and a perennial fear of rebellions. Local officials in nearly every part of the region competed for white subjects, who could serve in militias either in the case of war or a slave revolt. As a military man with his own ship, Pain was the most valuable kind of subject, and he knew it.[7]

In the end, Pain's saga also demonstrated the danger in trusting strangers. While there is no reason to believe that the captain was not concerned about the plight of his people in France, he seems to have had more worldly reasons for moving to Jamaica. Only a few months after his naturalization Pain took *La Trompeuse* on a logwood trading expedition to the coast of Honduras. On the way to the coast some of the ship's crew "set up for pyrats" and went on a spree of looting and pillaging across the western Caribbean. Of course, this was a storied Caribbean, and especially Jamaican tradition—Morgan himself had made his fortune in a similar way, and authorities in Port Royal often turned a blind eye when pirates, and their goods, turned up in the port. This time, however, Pain was unlucky. A new governor, Thomas Lynch, had set up in Jamaica, with orders to curb piracy, which he and his masters in London viewed as a detriment to Jamaica's legitimate trade. Lynch apparently did not believe that Pain himself was an innocent party, and he cancelled the captain's naturalization. It did not matter anyway, as by that time Pain had fallen into the hands of the French in Saint-Domingue. Authorities charged him with baratry—essentially making off with the king's property—and sent him back to Normandy, where he hanged for his crime in 1684.[8]

Despite its curiosities, Pain's story was a prophecy of things to come in the Caribbean and other imperial borderlands. As persecution heated up during the 1680s, more Huguenots, whether mariners or planters, decided to cross borders and take refuge in English or Dutch colonies. Some of these people were genuine refugees, responding to persecution like their relatives in France—but with a much shorter path to freedom. Border crossers like Pain often received star treatment in the West Indies, since their demographic and military value was so much higher than in Europe. These opportunities undoubtedly tempted many people with less tender consciences to call on their religious status to win earthly rewards. This situation only became more acute after war came to the Caribbean in 1689, with France vying against England, the Netherlands, and Spain for mastery in the region. Huguenots found themselves especially valuable, but like all boundary crossers, they were also objects of suspicion. Each refugee appeared as a possible Pierre Pain—an opportunist looking for individual advantage—or, worse, as a French agent in disguise.[9]

The first theater of intrigue in the region appeared in the English Leeward Islands. Made up of St. Kitts, Nevis, Antigua, Montserrat, and a few small neighboring islands, the Leewards included the oldest English settlements in the Caribbean. They had not, however, become as populated or profitable as Barbados, partly because they lay in a contested imperial borderland. The French had their own colony alongside the English on Saint-Christophe, and Guadeloupe lay just to the south of Antigua and Montserrat. When war broke out, as in 1666 during the second Anglo-Dutch War, the English planters on St. Kitts found themselves dangerously exposed. In that war the French overran the English part of the island, eventually returning English plantations but keeping most of the slaves and goods they plundered. Governors and planters alike spent much of the 1670s and 1680s in fear that the same thing would happen again. When a French fleet appeared in the region in 1678, for instance, Governor William Stapleton sent numerous letters to the Lords of Trade demanding either more naval protection or permission to negotiate a separate peace with the French, which would allow the islands to remain neutral in case of a European war. The Lords demurred on the last request; the best they could manage was to send some Scottish convicted criminals to increase the number of men eligible for the militia.[10]

This constant tension and paranoia colored the way that English people in the Leeward Islands interpreted the Revocation of the Edict of Nantes. The nature of daily life in the islands meant that English and French planters and settlers—along with African slaves, Irish servants, Carib Indians, and visitors from any number of nationalities—saw and interacted with each other frequently. The French islands' many Huguenots were especially visible, since some of them were leading merchants and others came to English Protestant churches either for occasional services or for marriages and baptisms. When the wave of persecution intensified, Stapleton's successor, Sir Nathaniel Johnson, immediately began plotting to attract the French Protestants to decamp for the English islands. The same man who later championed silk and wine culture in Carolina, Johnson was a keen imperial thinker, and he realized the benefits of these new (white, Protestant) subjects. The project began as a charitable one. The implications of the Revocation did not immediately travel to the French Antilles, but by 1688 the island's French Protestants were worried enough about their future that they made "daily complaints . . . on their bended knees [to] implore His Maj[es]ties mercy here which he is pleased to grant their Brethren in England." At first Johnson worried about granting refuge to the French, in case any of them used the pretense of religion to escape debts or criminal sentences. He began to change his mind when one of his underlings, the governor of Nevis, sent an escaped Huguenot back to French authorities, who summarily executed him as a criminal. After that, Johnson decided to grant provisional protection to any refugees who came to see him, while awaiting further instructions from James II.[11]

Johnson's embrace of Huguenots had two other dimensions. The refugees' appeals came at the same time that the governor published James II's Declaration of Indulgence, a bold proclamation of religious toleration in the British realms. A dutiful royal servant, Johnson set out to enforce the declaration, even aiding the islands' many Irish Catholics as they sought to establish churches. Johnson believed that the Huguenots' appeals for religious freedom fit the spirit of the Declaration, but he may have also seen the political danger of turning away suffering Protestants as he was coddling Catholics.[12] Beyond that, Johnson frequently noted the demographic benefits of the Huguenot troubles. He asked for the power of denization —a somewhat less robust version of naturalization that the Governor of Jamaica possessed and had used in Pierre Pain's earlier case— because "it would be of great advantage for the Strengthening and setling of these Islands which are not one third part so well peopled as they were some years ago." The following summer he repeated his request and presented it as essential in the multinational competition for subjects in the region, as governors in neighboring Dutch and Danish islands welcomed strangers and "do very much strengthen and benefit themselves."[13] Johnson's thinking had changed: rather than having no place to go, the Huguenots had many places to go, and he needed to act fast or they would take their bodies, labor, and capital to rival islands.

Johnson's particular design, like his governorship, disappeared in the confusion of the Glorious Revolution. James II's ministers had more pressing concerns than the Leewards' demographic problems, and Johnson himself had to resign his position when he refused to pledge his allegiance to William and Mary in 1689. Many refugees did cross the border to the English side of St. Kitts, but most of them kept moving, especially to New York, where they made up the core of a rapidly growing new community called New Rochelle.[14] In the meantime Johnson's fears came to pass, as it was Dutch rather than English colonies that attracted the lion's share of migrants. Some went to the important entrepôt of Curacāo, but the most tempting retreat was Suriname. Here as well, demographic and strategic consideration propelled the movement of refugees toward a place that was anything but a peaceful retreat.

Like the Leeward Islands, Suriname had been a multinational melting pot for decades, with a marked history of French and Huguenot settlement. French, Dutch, and English agents had all tried their hands at founding settlements on what became known as the Wild Coast, attracted by Walter Raleigh's visions of El Dorado as well as more practical desires to build sugar plantations in a region located between Brazil and the Caribbean Islands. The colonies never prospered in the seventeenth century, due to a combination of a terrible disease environment and frequent wars between the contending European powers and local native polities. Suriname, for instance, came into existence as an English colony during the 1650s and became Dutch in 1663, but remained a diverse place with

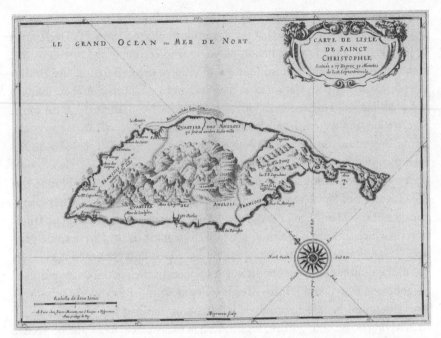

Figure 4.1 This 1667 map of Saint-Christophe clearly marked the borders between the French sections (on the east and west sides of the island), with the English section in the middle. *Carte de lisle de Sainct Christophle* (Paris, 1667). Courtesy of the John Carter Brown Library, Brown University.

English, Jewish, and Dutch planters working sugar plantations with African slaves on low, swampy ground.[15] Even before the 1680s a few Huguenots also joined the mix. In 1671 the minister François Chaillou, who had presided over a mixed French and Dutch congregation in Tobago, moved to Suriname, where he continued to preach in both languages. In 1673 Chaillou remarked that he had only forty auditors in his congregation, but hoped to gain more in the future, who would "one day eat our bread in peace, each person under his vine and fig tree."[16]

These small numbers increased after 1682 when a new regime came to Suriname. In contrast to the broad reach of the Dutch East India Company and its weaker Atlantic counterpart the West India Company, Suriname's administration fell to an odd coalition made up of the West India Company, the city of Amsterdam, and one Dutch aristocratic family, the Aarsen van Sommelsdijck clan. United in an organization known as the Society of Suriname, these three interest groups sought to realize Suriname's economic potential and safeguard Dutch interests in that volatile region, and they chose for their leader Cornelis Aarsen van Sommelsdijck, a powerful noble and representative of the colony's new leading family. This choice ensured that Huguenots would serve a leading role in the colony's reimagination. Sommelsdijck's wife was a French Protestant and one of the leading patrons of refugees in the Netherlands, and he surrounded himself with Huguenot allies, many of whom shared his goal to strengthen religion in a colony often considered a den of immorality. The governor was, as an eighteenth-century historian of the colony put it, "very austere," with "an ardent zeal to make religion respectable and even redoubtable in the eyes of the colonists."[17] In 1683 and 1684 two new French Calvinist ministers made their way to the colony. The first, Pierre Albus, went with the blessing of the Walloon Churches, probably to replace Chaillou. Albus promised to send regular reports on his efforts to "carry the light and the love of virtue into the souls and the hearts of these miserable people, who live in brutality and idolatry," but he died on his way to the colony.[18] The other, a Genevan named Gédéon Flournois, fared little better, succumbing to sickness within a year of his establishment in Suriname.[19]

These ministers were not the only Huguenots to go to Suriname. Sommelsdijck clearly looked to refugees as a key source of ordinary settlers, probably working through his wife's connections. He brought a few French craftsmen with him on his arrival in 1683, and two years later, during the time of the Revocation, a larger number of French settlers came to the colony. Unlike their contemporaries who went to North America or the Cape Colony, the circumstances and motivations of the Suriname Huguenots remain somewhat mysterious. No promotional tract attempted to woo prospective migrants, nor did the Society of Suriname issue a specific call for refugees. Unlike other prospective colonies in tropical locations, the founders do not seem to have had ambitions to make silk, wine, or olive oil; they simply needed settlers, good Calvinists if possible. Nonetheless, word of the settlement must have spread as far as Switzerland, since in 1685 one refugee appeared before the French committee in Schaffhausen reported that he was heading to the colony. If he ever made it, he would have joined around five hundred Huguenots who lived there by the turn of the seventeenth century.[20]

The lives of the Huguenots once they reached the colony are even more difficult to recover. A plethora of French plantation names—from the classically Calvinist "La Providence" to "Picardie," "Bellevue," and the highly ironic "Liberté" —testified to the presence and relative affluence of the Huguenot settlers in the colony, as did the French surnames of several eighteenth-century governors. An early eighteenth-century history listed the French as one of four groups of white inhabitants in Suriname, along with Dutch, Germans, and Jews, and noted that they worshipped with the Dutch in a single Reformed church in the capital of Paramaribo, where services alternated between the two languages.[21] After the deaths of Albus and Flournois, the next minister seems to have been Jean Briffault, a former pastor in Guyenne who served in Suriname for much of the 1690s, promising on his arrival in 1687 to work to attract more settlers to the colony. He even claimed to have sent numerous letters to contacts around the Refuge lauding conditions in the colony.[22] In 1697 Pierre Saurin replaced Briffault and dedicated himself to another strategic purpose, the conversion of the natives. Using money from the same fund that had bankrolled earlier ministers in Tobago, Saurin even took time to learn the local Galibi language, though he left no direct testimonial of his missionary effort, and probably spent more time with French settlers than with the Indians. He had plenty to do; a register of marriages in the capital of Paramaribo indicated that 15 percent of the town's white population was French during the 1690s.[23]

If the Suriname settlement had a purpose, it was as a defensive bastion against the French. The stretch of land to the west of the Amazon delta had been a zone of conflict for years, and the French possessed their own small outpost at Cayenne, just 250 miles to the west of Paramaribo. Even before France and the Netherlands went to war in 1689, French soldiers began deserting their posts in Cayenne and taking refuge in Suriname. In May 1685 the French governor in Guiana wrote to Sommelsdijck to report that two soldiers had fled to the Dutch colony, and he asked that Sommelsdijck return the two men and make sure not to admit any new arrivals from Cayenne unless they had passes from the governor.[24] Sommelsdijck never responded, and a year later the French commander sent a representative to collect the men. The Dutch governor, in the company of a Huguenot minister, explicitly refused the French captain's request, stating that returning the men was "against the laws of mankind." To make matters worse, one of the captain's Huguenot crewmen decided to join the deserters, "because he was there in the liberty of his Religion."[25]

The logic of Sommelsdijck's decision to harbor deserters became clear three years later when war came once again to the Caribbean. The governor had died in 1689—killed by rebellious Dutch subjects—but his successors had to deal with the renewed threat of French attacks. That same year the War of the League of Augsburg began, pitting the Netherlands, England, Austria, and Spain against France—a conflict known in America as King William's War after the coalition's chief mastermind. The French sent an expedition from Cayenne to take Suriname, finding both a new Dutch governor and Sommelsdijck's son, the marquis de Chatillon, who had come to collect his dead father's things. The Dutch managed to beat back the French assault, showing the wisdom of Sommelsdijck's policy of peopling the colony with refugees who had both the knowledge and the motivation to fight against their former masters.[26]

The English adopted a similar strategy in the Leeward Islands. While Nathaniel Johnson had left the islands, many Huguenots did remain in the region, and they found themselves at the center of the deadly conflict between France and England in the Caribbean. As on the Wild Coast, the French struck first by invading the English sector of St. Kitts in July 1689, finally vindicating the fears of past governors like William Stapleton. Then the French menaced nearby islands—including Montserrat, a place with a large Irish Catholic majority that the English feared would defect to the enemy.[27] Faced with its own internal threat from the Irish, English leaders sought to cultivate the Huguenots, who could carry intelligence from beyond enemy lines. Some of the refugees, after all, were valuable men: people like M. Bourgeois, who had served as a translator in meetings between the English and French governors before the war and then deserted to the English for the sake of religion. Bourgeois seems to have acted as a kind of double agent, delivering letters to Martinique and returning with critical intelligence.[28] The following year the new commander of the English expedition to regain St. Kitts, planter Christopher Codrington, consulted Huguenots before planning an invasion of the French island of Marie-Galante.[29] In short, the refugees had valuable expertise, since they had lived beyond enemy lines and some of them clearly continued to move back and forth across borders.

Much as they bragged of their facility in making silk and wine, refugees promoted their military value to their Dutch and English masters. In particular, they tried to leverage their service to the English crown to gain economic and political advantages, most especially naturalization or denization as English subjects. Because of the restrictions of the Navigation Acts, foreigners could not freely trade in the English Atlantic, and Huguenots asserted that their service to the English cause had proven their value as potential subjects. In 1698, Stephen Duport implored the Lords of Trade to lobby governors in the West Indies to give the Huguenots "the necessary priviledges to live Comfortable among the English," since they had "served in all expeditions in thoze parts during the late warr, to the satisfaction of their commanders."[30] In fact, Duport's missive was part of a campaign that went beyond the Caribbean, as Huguenots attempted to use their service to gain advantages. One published broadside lamented that even though the refugees who went to America worked the land, paid taxes, and fought for William and Mary in "the Attacks of *Quebeck, Martinico, Guadalupa, Jamaica,* and *St. Domingo,*" they still did not enjoy the status of English subjects. Indeed, a bill before the House of Commons threatened to prohibit the French from acting as "merchants or factors."[31]

As the petitioners showed, the Huguenots' tribulations went beyond just the Caribbean. In North America as well, French refugees pledged their service to fighting for the English against their former master, and there too they tried to use their service to gain advantages. At the same time that their status as French people made the Huguenots strategically valuable, it also made them objects of suspicion. Many English people had trouble trusting anyone with ties to their hated rival. What, after all, prevented a French agent from infiltrating the English colonies by disguising himself as a Protestant? Thus, war made life doubly difficult for refugees, and nowhere more so than on the edges of the empire.

———

During the 1680s hundreds of refugees settled in the English colonies of Massachusetts and New York. Unlike the migration streams to Carolina or the Cape Colony, those who went to the Northeast tended to come in smaller numbers, and not as the result of any concerted campaign to attract them—though the Huguenots found particular champions in both colonies. New York's French Protestant history predated the 1664 English conquest of the colony; many of the original settlers of New Netherland had been Walloons, and a number of other French-speaking Protestants had crossed the ocean to join them over the years. During the 1680s, it was newcomers from the French Caribbean, especially Saint-Christophe, who dominated the community, probably because New York was a strategic port city that allowed them to continue their commerce in the West Indies.[32] Massachusetts, on the other hand, was a colony of English Reformed Protestants, who closely followed the tribulations of their fellow Calvinists around the world. Puritan leaders followed the French persecution with particular interest and felt that "it may be for the credit of Religion" to help the refugees.[33] At the same time, there was another critical context for the Huguenot migration to the Northeast: this, like the Caribbean, was a borderland between the English and French empires.

The borders between New France and the English colonies of New York and New England had always been porous. English and Dutch merchants conducted extensive, if often illegal, trade in Quebec and Acadia, and many French traders crossed the woods from Montreal to the outposts of Albany, Schenectady, and even New York City. All of this occurred in a complicated imperial landscape where political boundaries were more imagined than real. In most of New York, for instance, Dutch colonists outnumbered their English counterparts by a large margin, and some Dutch institutions—for instance, the Reformed Classis of Amsterdam responsible for sending ministers—still had jurisdiction in the colony. Beyond the imperial and colonial establishments, meanwhile, native polities remained critical to the region's stability. In particular, two powerful Indian confederacies, the Iroquois and the Abenaki, lay between the English and French colonies and often played the two empires off of one another.[34]

Huguenots had long had a place in this melting pot of cultures. To be sure, authorities in France banned Protestants from settling in Canada or Acadia, but these provisions proved difficult to enforce, especially when many Protestant (or former Protestant) merchants from La Rochelle dominated the Canada trade. In fact, hundreds of Huguenots lived in Canada either on a seasonal basis, which was permissible before 1685, or on a permanent one by feigning conversion to Catholicism and staying under the radar.[35] French officials in Quebec occasionally noticed these circumstances, especially the indefatigable bishop François-Xavier de Montmorency Laval, who warned officials of the presence of Protestants throughout the period between the 1660s and the 1680s. In 1682, for instance, he urged the king to "prevent the Huguenots from establishing themselves in this country" or in neighboring Acadia, due to "the proximity of the English and Dutch."[36] Laval perceived the Huguenots as threats to colonial security as well as Canada's spiritual state. These heretics could not be allowed to settle in such a strategic borderland.

Events during the 1680s gave some credence to the archbishop's worries. The French and English contended for power in the Iroquois country between New France and New York that both nations claimed as their own. New York's Governor Thomas Dongan dedicated himself to strengthening the Iroquois alliance and cementing the English claim on their lands, and one way to weaken New France was to tempt some of its disgruntled subjects to cross the border and take up residence in New York.[37] The French governor in Quebec, Jacques Brisay de Denonville, noted in 1686 that a variety of "libertines" deserted New France for New York—and while most of these border crossers seemed to have been economic migrants, attracted by the freer markets across the border, religion provided another rationale for emigration. In 1685 echoes of the Revocation of the Edict of Nantes reached Quebec; ministers in Versailles instructed Denonville to make sure that all Protestants in New France abjured their faith, especially the Protestant soldiers stationed in the colony. The governor dutifully reported that "no inhabitant of the Pretended Reformed Religion" remained in Canada, but it was clear that some of New France's Protestants chose flight over conversion, joining the "libertines" who had fled to New York.[38] In 1687, for example, a merchant named Gédéon Petit moved from Quebec to Albany. A native of La Rochelle, Petit had converted to Catholicism in 1673 in order to stay in New France, and according to Denonville he made his money by trading with the English and running a "house of ill repute" near Montreal. The governor did not identify Petit's religion when he complained of the merchant's defection, and perhaps he did not migrate for religious reasons at all. In some ways, however, that was not the point. Whatever his level of piety, Petit knew that by declaring himself a religious refugee he would get good treatment in Albany. Like Pierre Pain in the West Indies, his experience on the other side of the border was a decided asset.[39]

Even as they lamented the loss of "scoundrels" like Petit, French officials in Quebec noticed a more alarming trend: the arrival of hundreds more French refugees in both New York and Boston. Denonville learned in 1686 that fifty to sixty Protestant families from Saint-Christophe had arrived in New York, and a number of other families in New England's capital. The governor worried that these newcomers would provide "fresh material for banditti," disgruntled people who would undermine the French cause in the Northeast.[40] Over the next few years these newcomers presented a number of petitions for land and aid in New York and New England that seemed to promote their strategic value. One refugee named Pierre Baudouin, for instance, asked for and received land on a vulnerable frontier in the territory of Maine, while a group led by Jean Boutillier sought trading privileges in part by claiming they could "bring in others who could then greatly augment and prove valuable to these countries."[41]

Some refugees were willing to use their strategic value as a cudgel to beat anyone who refused to give them aid. That is what happened in the case of Pierre Reverdy, who in 1686 presented a petition to the Lords of Trade and Plantations asking for "sole making of Salt" in New York. The committee passed the petition on to New York's governor Sir Edmund Andros, who apparently opposed it, at which point Reverdy unleashed an ad hominem attack on the governor. Reverdy noted in a petition to the Archbishop of Canterbury that many Protestant soldiers lived in New France during the 1680s. "Several did Indeavour to Come to New York," but instead of helping them do so—an act that would have been a charitable good as well as a strategic boon to the colony—Andros colluded with the French governor to prevent the Huguenots from coming to the colony. Even worse, Andros made a ruse of employing some of the deserters as his gardeners but when the men presented themselves "he sent them to the westward Islands," presumably as prisoners or slaves. Reverdy's petition reflected a new strategy. He still implied that those who opposed Huguenot designs were bad Protestants— this was, as it happened, a common charge against Andros, whose loyalty to the Catholic James II made him appear suspect. More than that, Reverdy claimed that Andros had proven himself a poor commander by rejecting his and other refugees' entreaties. The French were about to become "masters of all those Countreys," but wise governors who knew their proper interests could strengthen the English cause. Reverdy came very close to claiming the Huguenots were the key to conquering the continent.[42]

Reverdy's petition never received much consideration, but another Huguenot, Gabriel Bernon, used the same implicit arguments in an attempt to build an establishment for refugees in the Northeast. Another La Rochelle merchant, Bernon was active in the Canada trade before 1685, working in partnership with his brothers. After the Revocation Bernon asked to be allowed to remain in New France, and Denonville apparently valued the "merit of this family" enough that he sent his petition to Versailles for consideration, but he did not receive a satisfactory answer.[43] Luckily, Bernon had another plan. Even before this time, he was probably the chief actor behind an appeal by La Rochelle Protestants to find "what advantage we can have" in New England, a place for which they had "great estime."[44] Soon after he had to leave New France, Bernon settled in Boston, a strategic location for someone who wanted to continue his American trading activities. While he could easily have devoted himself to his own trade and blended in quite easily in the port town, he instead attempted to become something of a patriarch for the Huguenots of New England. And like Pierre Reverdy, he used his people's strategic value to get them advantages.

Bernon's ambitions soon centered on a plot of land in a town called Oxford, some hundred miles west of Boston. Located in the country of the Nipmuck Indians, Oxford was a vulnerable frontier of Massachusetts, ravaged by native warriors during King Philip's War the previous decade. In partnership with another of his countrymen, Bernon received 750 acres of land from the Massachusetts General Court to build a refugee town in the woods.[45] He intended to use the settlement to satisfy one of the key imperial ambitions in America—the making of naval stores, including masts, tar, pitch, and turpentine. Alongside silk and wine, naval stores production was one of the most treasured dreams of political economists, since England depended on imports from Russia and the Baltic to build its navy. During the 1690s, in fact, a very similar vision to Bernon's appeared in the pages of a tract by Francis Brewster. "*New England* is Superior to any of the *Northern* Crowns for Timber and Masts, Pines and Firr, to make Pitch and Tarr," Brewster claimed, and the creation of such an industry "would make *New England*, of the most useless and unprofitable Plantation of this Nation, the best and most advantageous to this Nation."[46] Brewster specifically recommended "Foreign Protestants" as the leaders of this economic experiment, and Bernon meant to make good on this vision. He sponsored the migration of a number of settlers, like Pierre Cornilly of Saintonge, who signed an indenture to work at Oxford for three years in 1688, or Jacques Hipaud of Poitou, who pledged two years of service and brought his wife and daughter along with him.[47] By 1687 a French visitor noted that the colony already had fifty-two people and a minister. Settlers received land for free, and "it is very true that Living is exceedingly cheap, and that with a little one can make a good Settlement."[48]

In addition to helping build the Royal Navy, Oxford had another key strategic purpose. Most English officials realized that the French conquered America with priests as well as soldiers. Jesuits had set up missions throughout the interior, and the English believed that by converting Indians the French effectively turned them against England. A company of ministers from New England sought to counter these efforts by sending English missionaries to the backcountry, but they could find few willing to dedicate themselves to mission work. French Protestant ministers seemed to provide a perfect solution to the problem. Many interior Indians already knew some French, due to their interactions with both

Jesuits and French fur traders, so Huguenot ministers could easily communicate with them. In 1688 the Company for the Propagation of the Gospel in New England employed Oxford's minister Daniel Bondet in this task, hoping that Bondet could "instruct some ingenious converted Indians in the french tongue and principles of Religion," who could then be sent "to further the worke among those Indians that converse with the french." Soon Bernon joined the board of the Company and continued to promote his people as suitable missionaries.[49]

The most interesting artifact of these efforts was a peculiar printed book that appeared in Boston in 1691. Sometime during the previous year a cache of Jesuit documents surfaced in Albany, including a detailed catechism and some correspondence between members of the order. Through a circuitous path the materials found their way into the hands of Boston minister Cotton Mather, who in turn shared them with the town's French minister Ezechiel Carré. The Huguenot wrote extensive manuscript notes on this "small sample of poisonous principles" that constituted an expert's exposition of how the perfidious Catholics tricked people into believing their false doctrines—undoubtedly a favorite subject of a minister who had probably seen many of flock fall to the same temptations back in France. A version of his notes soon appeared in print, constituting the first French-language publication in North America. While the tract focused on Jesuit conversion practices, it obliquely endorsed a Protestant mission program, setting it in an apocalyptic context that would have pleased Pierre Jurieu. In addition, Carré subtly suggested that he and his countrymen had sufficient expertise that would allow them to counteract Jesuit trickery and win converts among the natives.[50]

Carré, Bernon, and others made a constant case for the usefulness of the Huguenots, but they faced increasing challenges as war came to the region. From 1689 on New York and New England endured a number of attacks from French and Indian raiding parties, and a retaliatory invasion of Quebec ended in bitter failure in 1690. Under these desperate conditions, French people found themselves objects of suspicion. As early as 1688 residents of Narragansett, a refugee town located on the Massachusetts-Rhode Island border, faced bad treatment from English neighbors who stole their hay, "laying open their inclosures and destroying their meadows," while three years later residents of Salem levelled witchcraft charges against French-speakers like Philip English, a native of Jersey whose ties to New France made him unpopular.[51]

More worrisome were the efforts of the Massachusetts Assembly. In 1691 the General Court worried that there were among the refugees those "who pretend to bee protestants . . . that are papist & Enemies to theire Maj[es]ties." An act the following year ordered that "none of the French nation" could live in the colony without the governor's leave or conduct trade without permission of local selectmen.[52] To be sure, some English argued in the refugees' favor. In a preface to another of Ezechial Carré's tracts Cotton Mather lauded the author as "a *Christian* and a *Protestant*," while Carré himself noted that "persons may easily perceive" that the refugees "cannot reasonably pass for Papists . . . and it is uncharitable and uncompassionate to accuse them as such."[53] Nonetheless, it was clear that many English people did just that, making life difficult for the French.

In some ways the French made life difficult for themselves. While much of the prejudice against French refugees was groundless, some of the Huguenots did use their position in an attempt to play both sides. One example was a mariner named John Reaux, who attempted to play the same game as Pierre Pain but in an even more dangerous age. Reaux had moved to New York and received naturalization there at some point during the reign of James II and, using his newfound rights as an English subject, became master of a sloop. Soon after, the captain intentionally sunk his own ship and made off with over six hundred pounds of stolen goods before ending up in a Boston prison. While in custody Reaux befriended some of the French prisoners of war, and together they successfully escaped to Canada and then La Rochelle, where the former English subject received a new commission from Louis XIV. At that point Reaux looked like a simple turncoat, but the story soon became more complicated. Apparently Reaux's family still lived in La Rochelle, and during his time there he brought them on board his ship and transported them back to New York. The governor balked when the Frenchman showed up in town and sought to try Reaux as an enemy of the state. The case failed due to lack of evidence, and the Frenchman ended up doing quite well in his dangerous game, winning the ability to live in peace with his family as an English subject.[54]

The case of Abraham Boudrot showed many of the same characteristics. A native of Acadia, Boudrot was one of the many merchants who traded freely across the border between Port Royal and Boston. Of course much of this trade was illegal, and during wartime it appeared to be treasonous as well, as Boudrot supplied goods to England's enemies. Throughout the 1690s officials collected evidence against the French merchant; in 1691, for example, one of his English crew presented detailed information on one shady trip to Acadia in which Boudrot had sold goods to the French and even stopped at a Catholic chapel for services. Three years later the collector of customs in Boston, Jahleel Brenton, seized Boudrot's cargo and apprehended him, all of which inspired a violent response from Governor William Phips, a champion of the refugees who claimed Boudrot and his partners "were as good or better Englishmen then the Collector."[55]

As it happened, it was Brenton rather than Phips who read Boudrot correctly. Soon after the incident a fellow Acadian warned officials in Boston "not to put any trust in Abraham Baudrot, who gives advise of what passes wth you and makes you believe he doth the like wth us."[56] Across the border, Acadia's French governor Joseph de Villebon bragged of Boudrot's aid in his letters to Versailles, noting the merchant's value in bringing back detailed information about the English post at Pemaquid, a key target of the French. Apparently the merchant had specifically volunteered to supply the governor with "reliable news of what was going on."[57] With dangerous characters like Boudrot in the borderlands, it was no wonder that even an old friend of the Huguenots like Richard Coote, earl of Bellomont, began to have second thoughts. Bellomont knew Bernon and had attempted to settle refugees on his lands in Ireland. As governor of New York and Massachusetts he started to change his mind, noting that the French were "very factious and their number considerable," and wondering if it was safe to allow them to settle on the continent's "cheife frontier towards Canada."[58]

By the end of the decade, most of the Huguenots' grand ambitions in the Northeast lay in shambles. The Narragansett community had folded under pressure, and Ezechiel Carré left Boston for the Channel Islands, chased out by his own congregants.[59] In Oxford, meanwhile, French-allied Indians attacked in 1696, where they "burnt and Distroyed several of the people, and the rest have been forced to fly, and leave their habitations, and Improvements."[60] Bernon returned to London where he sought more aid to rebuild the colony and realize his ambitions of producing naval stores, so that the land "may be secured & Protected Against the french and Indians."[61] The colony did reform, but few seemed to want to be there. The minister Daniel Bondet took his money from the Company for the Propagation of the Gospel and decamped to New Rochelle, while his replacement, Jacques Laborie, despaired that the Indians preferred Catholicism to Protestantism because they found it "more beautiful," and the Jesuits gave them "silver crosses to put around their necks."[62] By the dawn of the eighteenth century Bernon had tired of both grand ambitions and most of his fellow refugees. His naval stores plan foiled for the last time, Bernon moved to Providence, where he became a leading merchant and joined the Anglican church. He spent much of the rest of his life petitioning to get back some of the money he lost in the Oxford debacle.[63]

———

Part of the tragedy of the Huguenots' tribulations during the 1690s reflected the difficulties of finding peace in an age of war. The refugees dreamed of retreating far from the political and religious storms that divided Europe. In order to move anywhere, however, they needed patronage, and as war consumed the continent after 1689 the refugees found that only by claiming some sort of strategic purpose could they find support for their schemes. Nowhere did this paradox appear as clearly as in the sad ending of Henri Duquesne's search for Eden in the Indian Ocean. According to the detailed tracts justifying the colony, the Isle of

Eden was to be a quiet retreat, a place for the people of God to live in health and safety away from problems of Europe. Of course some in Louis XIV's court suspected the baron of Aubonne had less pure motives, and that he intended to use his coterie of refugees as an invasion force, whether in Europe or somewhere else in the world. Not so, countered Duquesne. He hoped that his would be a colony without an empire, a place that would be a threat to no one, where downtrodden migrants could build lives in a corner of the world that no one else cared about.[64]

Duquesne may have truly believed his rhetoric, but it proved impossible for him to remain aloof from the competition of states and empires. The problem, as for so many Huguenot schemes, was money. Duquesne could not move hundreds of refugees halfway around the world without large infusions of cash, and he could not get the support he needed without support from individuals or institutions with abundant resources and the means to transport large numbers of people. In Duquesne's case, his only choice was to approach the Dutch States General and the East India Company, the most prominent European interest in the East Indies. In 1689 Duquesne traveled to The Hague with his brother Abraham and a key ally from the Swiss Refuge, Charles de Sailly, in search of Dutch help to build his colony on the Isle of Eden.

Duquesne's audience in The Hague happened at a peculiar time. War with France was imminent, and the Dutch East India Company worried that Louis XIV intended to attack Dutch outposts in the East Indies. In 1688, before the coming of war, a French expedition to Siam lodged at the Cape of Good Hope for a time, raising worries that the rival fleet was collecting intelligence to use in case of war. Soon after that, the Dutch intercepted a large cache of French documents that only exacerbated these fears. One letter told of a supposedly French Protestant gardener in the Company's service at the Cape who pledged to return to the service of Louis XIV—showing the danger that supposed refugees might be unreliable subjects.[65] More alarming were the letters from colonists at Île Bourbon, the small French outpost in the Mascarene Islands. Bourbon had not so far lived up to French expectations, but it was clear from the documents that at least some in France wanted to build the island into a center of power in the Indian Ocean. Such an establishment would not only threaten the nearby Dutch island of Mauritius, but would also give France a means to attack Dutch ships as they crossed the Indian Ocean. Company officials could not let that happen.[66]

Luckily for Dutch leaders, Duquesne's proposal gave them a relatively inexpensive way to solve their Mascarene problem. He proposed to settle his colony of Huguenots on Île Bourbon, the very place that so worried Dutch officials. This in itself gave Duquesne's proposal a very good chance of moving quickly through the Dutch bureaucracy, but there was one problem. Duquesne had sold the project to prospective settlers as a Huguenot utopia on a deserted island, but the Company knew that the island was not uninhabited. Receiving news of the French ambitions in the Mascarenes did alter Duquesne's approach—he resolved, for example, not to send the numerous women and children who had gathered in Amsterdam en route to Eden—but he did not abandon the project. Instead, he changed it to suit the needs of his patrons. Duquesne's contract with the States General belied all of the peaceful intentions he boasted of in his published work and earlier correspondence. Instead, he represented the Eden colonists as an invasion force. The baron and his brothers pledged to "arm several ships at their expense" and take them to Île Bourbon, "which the French have occupied for several years." The refugee fleet would then use "the right of reprisals against those who have so unjustly taken their goods," essentially claiming from the French settlers of the Mascarenes what Louis XIV and the dragonnades had taken in France. The States General and Dutch East India Company accepted the offer, as long as the colonists would take an oath to serve the Company, and agreed to provide ships for the colonists. The venture would begin with the departure of the *Hirondelle*, a small ship that would take an advance party of ten Huguenot men to scout out the island and make an initial establishment.[67] In a letter to the commander at the Cape, Company officials clearly stated their goal of using Duquesne's colonists to establish a refreshment station on the Mascarene Islands and prevent French attempts "to cripple us as much as possible at the Cape and India."[68]

The *Hirondelle*'s voyage did not progress smoothly. Duquesne granted command of the ship to Antoine Valleau, a mariner from the Île de Ré who had initially abjured his faith but recanted when his French ship fell into Dutch hands. This was enough to make Valleau an object of suspicion to François Leguat and the other Huguenots on board the ship, but to make matters worse, Duquesne seems to have only shared the true mission of the voyage with the cagey captain. Leguat still believed he was heading to a peaceful Eden beyond the seas, making Valleau's actions on the voyage seem more and more alarming. The passengers feuded with the captain for months—the worst offender was Jacques de la Case, who refused to share meals with Valleau and almost ended up in irons for his repeated insubordination. After an awkward sojourn at the Cape Colony, the voyage reached its conclusion in the Mascarene Islands. Valleau approached the fabled Isle of Eden, which Leguat later described as a paradise to the senses, "perfum'd with a delicious odor" and "enamell'd with a charming Verdure." For reasons inexplicable to Leguat, Valleau refused to land his ship in that paradise and instead took the men to a different island, Rodrigues, where he left them with a cache of supplies in April 1691.[69]

Valleau's actions after dropping off his troublesome passengers attested to the strategic goals of his mission. The captain immediately returned to Île Bourbon, where he collected intelligence on the French presence on the island to take back to Duquesne and Dutch officials. As he ranged around the island Valleau encountered a free African man named Arré or Athenas Garel who lived among the French, and promptly kidnapped him in order to provide a first-hand report to Duquesne. On the way home Valleau returned to Cape Town, where he seems to have worked on another angle of the invasion plot. If Duquesne still meant to bring refugees from the Netherlands, he also designed to use the refugees already resident in the Cape Colony as part of his invasion force. Valleau tried to find possible recruits among the Cape Huguenots for an impending expedition against Île Bourbon. All of these designs failed when Valleau fell into French hands on the way back to Europe. The captain quickly recanted his recantation and provided a detailed narrative of his recent movements to the French. Nonetheless, he did hide some details of the mission. For instance, he neglected to tell the French about the ten Huguenots he left on Rodrigues Island, and he claimed that "he knew only two men among the French who had the intention of offering their services to the said Sr Duquesne." Valleau's prisoner Arré gave testimony that contradicted some of Valleau's statements. The African noted that Valleau "had told him Sr. Duquesne had the design to seize the said Île Bourbon, and that he had taken him to present him to the said Sr. Duquesne in order to inform him about the state of the island." He also claimed that there were four hundred French refugees in the Cape Colony who "say that they await the said Sr. Duquesne in order to offer themselves to him to go and conquer Île Bourbon."[70]

The capture of the *Hirondelle* spelled the end of the Dutch-Huguenot design against the Mascarene Islands. Without proper intelligence Duquesne could not go forward with his plan, and with the war raging in Europe, Dutch officials had little time or money for refugee schemes that seemed to have little chance of success. Historians have tended to blame Duquesne for the failure, but at least one oblique piece of evidence cast aspersions elsewhere, on the States General. A manuscript note on the first page of the only surviving copy of Duquesne's Eden tract claimed that "everything was nearly ready to go" when the States General abruptly "revoked their donation and thus brought about the end of the project." It is impossible to know if the anonymous writer was correct, but it does give evidence of a particular memory of the project, one that testified to the danger of Huguenots placing their trust in foreign governmental bodies that did not always have their true interests at heart.[71]

Duquesne soon left The Hague to return to his castle in Aubonne, but his colonists remained in the East Indies. On the deserted island of Rodrigues, the eight survivors of the *Hirondelle* expedition made a life that, at least as Leguat reflected on it over a decade later, seemed to realize his dreams of finding peace in a remote corner of the world. Rodrigues was a small island, without the strategic utility of Bourbon, but "this little new World seem'd full of Delights

Figure 4.2 This depiction of life on Rodrigues Island portrays a paradise for refugees. The central pillar reads "Nos Patria Pulsos" (we were driven from our homeland), a reference to a line in the *Aeneid*. From *Voyages et avantures de François Leguat, & de ses compagnons, en deux isles désertes des Indes orientales* (Amsterdam, 1708). Courtesy of the Bibliothèque Nationale de France.

and Charms." Leguat thanked Providence for allowing him to end up in such an "Earthly Paradise," where "if we wou'd, we might be rich, free and happy; if contemning vain Riches, we wou'd employ the peaceable Life that was offer'd us, to glorifie God and save our Souls." The men built a small settlement that Leguat described in jest as "our *Republick*," though the most pressing decisions concerned what to eat for dinner. The only problem with this paradise was the lack of women, and for Leguat's young male companions, this was an unacceptable circumstance. "Had there been Women amongst us," Leguat wrote, "100 years hence, instead of seven Hutts, one might have reckon'd seven Parishes." But after two years passed with no word from the outside world, the men despaired of receiving reinforcements and decided (against Leguat's advice) to build a ship and try to sail to nearby Dutch Mauritius. With the benefit of hindsight, Leguat cast the decision as a major blunder. "What can be imagin'd more happy," he asked his companions, "after having groan'd and suffer'd under the Yoak of Tyranny, than to live in Independence and Ease, without danger of Worldly Temptations[?]" At the end of the day, earthly temptations won out, and the men eventually reached Mauritius after a harrowing voyage that claimed the life of one of their number.[72]

When the travelers arrived at Mauritius they traded paradise for the violence and paranoia of an imperial outpost during wartime. While the small way station of settlers, slaves, and prisoners did not much resemble New England, the same anxieties appeared there, and instead of a sympathetic governor like William Phips, the Huguenots found Roelef Diodati. Despite his own family roots in Geneva, Diodati was extremely suspicious of the seven refugees who turned up on his island. One of the men, Jean de la Haye, had transported a large piece of ambergris—a secretion from sperm whales, highly valued as an ingredient in perfumes—but had unwittingly sold it to a Dutch goldsmith, not knowing its true worth. La Haye then complained to the governor, but at least according to Leguat, Diodati plotted with the Dutch colonist to keep the ambergris for himself. At the same time, it was clear that the governor had other suspicions about the strange French newcomers. He burned their makeshift boat to prevent their escape and imprisoned the men in servant's huts with only leftover food to eat. At this point Jacques de la Case and another of the men, Jean Testard, plotted to steal one of the company's small boats and escape to Île Bourbon, the fabled Isle of Eden that they knew very well to be in French hands. In short, they decided to flee their new oppressor and take their chances with the old.[73]

This escape attempt confirmed every ill feeling the governor had about the refugees. Clearly they were French agents, working for the enemy—even those men, like Leguat, who claimed to have no knowledge of the plot. Diodati placed the men on a "Desert[ed] and frightful Rock" off the coast of the island, where they had to live in "a vile Hutt." The prisoners languished there for three years, losing another of their number to illness. The men only received relief when Paul Benelle's family back in the Netherlands learned of his plight and insisted that the men be transported to Batavia and tried for their offenses. Finally acquitted in 1696, the three survivors set sail for Europe, by way of the Cape Colony, the following year. On their way home the men learned of the Peace of Ryswick, ending the War of the League of Augsburg. Their global peregrinations had coincided almost exactly with the length of the war, but according to Leguat, "we could not help thinking that this Peace would not last long."[74]

The Eden colonists were not the only ones who aroused the suspicion of Dutch officials in the East. At the Cape, Governor Simon van der Stel soured on the Huguenots quickly, and a big part of his sentiment seems to have come out of his persistent fear of French attack. He repeatedly reminded the refugees of their oaths to the East India Company and tried to scatter the French around the colony rather than placing them together in one town. While much of this paranoia was misplaced, there were those, like in New England, whose actions suggested that van der Stel might have had something to fear. During the mid-1690s several Huguenots began conducting illegal trade with the Khoesan—not an act of treason exactly, but certainly a violation of their oaths. One of these men was Jean de Seine. While he never appeared in Leguat's book, de Seine was another passenger on the *Hirondelle*, probably a native of the valleys of Piedmont, who stayed at the Cape rather than going to Rodrigues. In a crowd of refugees in 1695, de Seine expressed an unfortunate opinion. If the French invaded the Cape, he would not resist, but join them. This utterance landed de Seine in legal trouble; soon the council banished him to Mauritius for ten years, which was fast becoming a prison for the Cape's undesirable people. There Jean de Seine also met the ire of Roelef Diodati. After de Seine tried to escape in a storm, the commander ordered him shot to death.[75]

By the time Simon van der Stel handed power to his son Willem Adriaan in 1697, his impressions of the French had soured considerably. In a set of instructions, the departing governor recommended that his son favor migrants from "such Germanic nations as are not engaged in sea traffic, lest you expose your Government to the danger of a revolution. Should the Colony be populated by other nationalities, each individual would hold fast to his own, and all our defensive arrangements and precautions become futile accordingly." Of all the nationalities, he noted, the French were "the least to be trusted." They were poor agriculturalists, and not the most loyal of subjects. Clearly years of war had taken its toll on French-Dutch relations in the East. No longer the ideal immigrants, the Huguenots had become liabilities.[76]

———

Jacques de la Case returned to Europe during a time of uneasy peace. And yet he was not destined to remain long on the continent of his birth. With no surviving correspondence, we can only speculate on what drove la Case to enlist in yet another Huguenot overseas colony, especially after the last one had ended in disaster. He may have fallen under the influence of Charles de Sailly, a man who had worked to promote Duquesne's earlier colony, as well as efforts to move refugees from Switzerland to Ireland during the middle part of the 1690s. By the end of the decade Sailly had teamed up with an eccentric English physician, scientist, and former colonial governor named Daniel Coxe. The Englishman had inherited a large claim to a colony called Carolana, which theoretically covered most of the continent's Southeast, from Florida far into the interior. Coxe framed his project as both an act of charity and a strategic boon, since he aimed to use refugees as settlers in a scheme that would occupy the Gulf Coast and the North American interior and thus prevent the French from claiming the continent. Coxe and Sailly's plan combined many of the mixed motivations from all of the decade's Huguenot colonies in one exciting package. Carolana would finally succeed where other ventures had failed.[77]

The outcome of the Peace of Ryswick represented a significant defeat for the Huguenot cause. Refugee leaders lobbied negotiators to insist on the reestablishment of the Edict of Nantes as a condition of peace, to remember "the deplorable state of the Reformed Protestants of France, chased from their country, deprived of their property, transported by force to barbarous lands," but they had not done so, and with the war over the prospects of a return to France seemed dimmer than ever.[78] At the same time, after more than a decade some of the Huguenots' patrons had tired of their guests. The situation was especially acute in Switzerland, where a series of poor harvests during the 1690s and diplomatic pressure from France combined to make the Huguenots' place in the cantons precarious. As early as 1692 the English ambassador reported that Swiss peasants and the poor were "extremely inragd agt the fr[ench] Refugiéz, chiefly by reason of the . . . present dearth" of grain.[79] By the end of the decade authorities in the cantons decided they could no longer support Huguenots without the resources to pay their own way. They needed to move along—to Brandenburg, or Ireland, or wherever else they could find succor. Assistance, however, was hard to find anywhere. Many found themselves in the same position as one Monsieur Sondreville, who told authorities in Zurich that he had "wandered through all of Europe in search of bread" but "could no longer find help in any place."[80]

A number of English schemes during this period sought to take advantage of the uncertain climate. One centered on a familiar territory, the island of Tobago. Since Rochefort had lauded the colony some decades earlier, Tobago had gone through a dizzying number of changes, some driven by dynastic exchanges in Europe and others by invasions during the late war. By the late 1690s it was in the hands of a Lithuanian noble named the duke of Courland, but an Englishman named John Poyntz claimed rights to the island based on a grant from one of the duke's predecessors. In 1699 he proposed a colony that would combine strategic considerations with charity. He would settle Tobago with "the poor of this Kingdom" as well as "the French Refugies," and then use some of the revenues from the island to fund a number of charitable projects, from a hospital for London's "blind poor" to the "Conversion of the Indians to the Christian

Faith." Poyntz's scheme picked up on the appetite for moral reform that proved so popular during the decade, while also acting "for the security of his Majesties Neighbouring Plantations in time of warr." The design seems not to have gone anywhere. Perhaps Poyntz's claim was not clear enough, and Tobago was not yet a proper English colony anyway.[81] The same principles appeared, however, in Daniel Coxe's proposal, which had a greater possibility of success.

Coxe's idea drew from decades of American experience. The idea for the colony seems to have originated around a decade earlier, when Coxe, at that time absentee governor of New Jersey, entered into a partnership with a number of French merchant explorers, including the Huguenot Jacques Le Tort, who had settled in the Pennsylvania backcountry, and Pierre Bisaillon, a former member of La Salle's western expeditions who had also briefly partnered with another Huguenot, Gédéon Petit. The men proposed to form a partnership called the New Mediterranean Company that would claim the North American interior for England, centering on the Great Lakes region but trading "as far as New Mexico." Le Tort himself may have gone off on a scouting expedition on the Company's behalf, perhaps even as far as the Mississippi. While Coxe and his partners had trouble finding official encouragement for their scheme, the critical place of Huguenots like Le Tort showed the strategic value of French Protestants, who sometimes had knowledge and experience in the vast interior of North America.[82]

By the late 1690s Coxe retained the same general goals but changed his approach. Rather than settling directly on the Great Lakes, he would begin his colony on the Gulf of Mexico and move north and west from there—a reflection of the fact that Coxe no longer had an interest in New Jersey, but had inherited an old patent for most of the North American Southeast. He still retained his strategic goal of taking land that would otherwise be claimed by the French, and he also maintained that Huguenots would be the best partners and settlers for such a project. The vast American interior, Coxe maintained, was among the most fruitful lands in the world. For one thing, it abounded with "Vines of divers sorts" that would yield good wine, and the climate was appropriate for silk as well. From an initial settlement on the Espiritu Santo River (now the Apalachicola), Coxe aimed to occupy the whole interior, from the Ohio River Valley to the semimythical "great western lake" of his earlier dreams, which he believed to be a short distance from the Pacific Ocean, thus opening up the Asian trade. He thought that from the lake one could easily reach "the great gulph of Nova Albion" and the "better half of the Island of Calefornia," places claimed for England by Sir Francis Drake in the sixteenth century, and close to "the Seas of Tartary and Japan."[83]

Coxe and his partners worked assiduously to gather funds and support for what one writer labeled the "New Empire." In their efforts to gain funding and support, the designers of "Carolana Florida," as the colony often appeared, used almost every method in the colonial booster's toolbox. Coxe began by lauding the productive capacity of the land in question, not only in producing those old standbys of silk, wine, and olive oil, but also naval stores, fruits of all kinds, furs, and precious metals from mines.[84] Coxe also appealed to the charitable intentions of officials in both the Church of England and dissenting congregations, promoting his colony, like Poyntz's Tobago, as a peaceful retreat for the poor, debtors, and orphans as well as refugees. He also envisioned his colony as a center for evangelizing Native Americans, and indeed he worked closely with several men also active in the New England Company. Nonetheless, it was the refugees who would form the nucleus of the colony. Coxe specifically noted that in the late 1690s "Protestants Refugees" had become "a charge and a burthen to those Princes and States, under whose protection and government they live." Once they were established in Florida, these refugees would become productive and useful subjects, providing "a due value for the Nation." Planners of the colony initially hoped to send 250 Huguenot families to the new colony, augmented if needed by English and Germans.[85]

Whether from desperation or real enthusiasm, plenty of Huguenots volunteered to be settlers in Coxe's new colony. Unlike the Carolina proprietors or William Penn, Coxe directed his promotional tracts to English investors rather than prospective French settlers. Instead, he seems to have attracted settlers by cultivating a number of Huguenot gentlemen, who then advertised the colony through established refugee networks. His two main partners were a minor nobleman named Olivier de la Muce and the enigmatic Charles de Sailly. The latter man in particular had become one of the Refuge's most ubiquitous characters, serving as a conduit of information from Switzerland to Ireland and beyond. He had acted as one of Henri Duquesne's lobbyists in The Hague, and after touring Ireland in 1692, he became closely associated with perhaps the most powerful man in the British Refuge, Henri de Ruvigny, the earl of Galway. While Galway never lent official support for the scheme, he was probably a silent partner, as Coxe directly appealed to those refugees, especially in Switzerland, that Galway had earlier tried to move to Ireland.[86]

Even by the standards of that sorrowful decade, the refugees' path to Carolana Florida was unusually difficult. In 1698 a committee formed to manage the transportation of Swiss refugees to the colony. It contained many noteworthy names from the Swiss and Irish Refuges—M. Reboulet, probably none other than the Zurich minister, was one of the chief agents, and other signatories included Elie Bouhéreau, by this time the earl of Galway's secretary, and the Irish minister Jacques Fontaine. The group advertised through French-language newspapers in the Netherlands, urging charitable people around Protestant Europe to contribute to their cause. In the meantime Charles de Sailly found seventy-two refugees in Bern willing to go to Carolana. The Huguenots made the difficult trek through the Rhine Valley to Rotterdam, where Sailly was supposed to meet them and accompany them to the colony, only to find that their benefactor had already left the port. Alarmed by yet another betrayal, representatives of the families petitioned the States General, complaining that they had been "deceived by the high hopes they had been given," and that they now languished "in such a deplorable state, that they would all have perished of misery and hunger without the help of some charitable people who had assisted them." The States collected some money to send the unfortunate people to lands in Germany and Ireland. Their vision of Florida, as a nineteenth-century historian put it, was little more than a mirage.[87]

The design went forward even without these particular settlers. In fact, another center of recruitment existed in New York, where some members of the refugee community feuded with the English governor, Richard Coote, earl of Bellomont, and expressed a desire to avoid their problems by retreating to the place they called "Mechasipi." It is unclear if any of them actually made the trek, but by 1699 Coxe had found enough people to send a scouting expedition to find a location for the settlement on the Gulf Coast. A small warship stopped in Charleston and then continued up the coast, carrying a number of French refugees, including the Marquis de la Muce and two sons of Charles de Sailly, along with an English captain and crew. Coxe's self-serving retrospective account said that the ship sailed up the Mississippi and took possession of the land for England, and "found neither French Settlements or any sign that any French had been settled in any part or place upon the said coasts in all the said Tracts."[88]

French sources reveal much more about the voyage. In fact, officials around the French empire had been following Coxe's schemes from the outset and managed to gather a large amount of fairly accurate information. While stationed in La Rochelle in 1698 the Canadian captain Pierre Le Moyne d'Iberville learned from contacts in London of an English design "to go and make an establishment on the Mississippi," an expedition that would include "four companies of French protestants" and their ministers, who would teach the gospel to the Indians.[89] D'Iberville used this news to advocate a new royal expedition to cement France's claim to the Gulf, and he soon gained an ally in New France's Governor Louis Hector de Callières. The governor learned from a spy in Albany that because of "the predicament the English faced in providing subsistence to the French of the [Reformed] Religion," William III had sent three ships to "take possession of the Mississippi." Callières later noted that a refugee establishment "would be just as dangerous for the good of this Colony as if it was made up of Foreigners," and that France had to work to contain the threat.[90]

Ministers in Versailles were loath to devote many resources to colonial adventures, but they did deputize d'Iberville to lead several expeditions to the

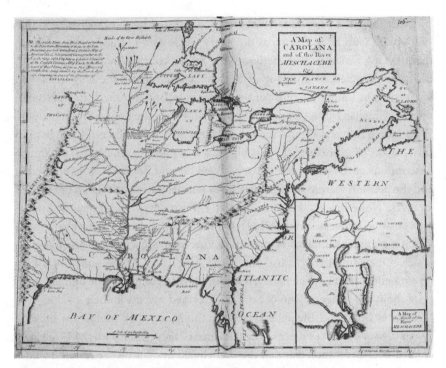

Figure 4.3 Daniel Coxe Jr. simply grafted this 1722 map of "Carolana" on a contemporary French map of Louisiana. It gives a good idea of the vast territory that his father hoped to settle in the 1690s. "A Map of Carolana and of the River Meschacebe." Courtesy of the John Carter Brown Library, Brown University.

Gulf. He made the first establishments in what would soon become the colony of Louisiana, settling a small post at Biloxi and exploring the lower Mississippi Valley. By the time of his second voyage d'Iberville knew many of the details of Coxe's expedition to the Gulf, including the names of the three ships' captains. The English commander, he learned, was none other than William Bond, a "scatterbrain" who d'Iberville had previously captured in Hudson's Bay. As it happened, d'Iberville's brother Jean-Baptiste Le Moyne de Bienville encountered Bond's ship as the Frenchman led a small fleet of birchbark canoes up the Mississippi from Biloxi on September 15, 1699. Bienville was in no position to press any claim, but the two captains exchanged threats, each pressing their king's right to the region, and Bond promised to return the next year to make an establishment.[91]

The initial reports of the encounter made no mention of Huguenots being on board the ship, but d'Iberville's journal added details on the refugees that demonstrated the complicated geopolitics involved in the settlement of what would become Louisiana. The captain claimed that a French Protestant traveled with Bond and privately approached Bienville. The unnamed refugee told

Bienville that "the Frenchman was greatly distrusted by the English," and that "he wished with all his heart, as did every single one of the French refugees, that the king would permit them to settle in this country, under his rule, with liberty of conscience." The Huguenot then asserted that if the king welcomed Huguenots in Louisiana, most of the refugees in British America would settle there, as "English rule . . . could not be sympathetic to the French temperament." While some refugees clearly shared the sentiment that d'Iberville assigned to this person, the encounter probably never happened. The most proximate descriptions of the encounter between Bienville and Bond never mentioned it, and the petition mentioned in d'Iberville's journal never surfaced in the French archives. Nonetheless, the passage neatly illustrates the Huguenots' precarious position between empires. In fact, d'Iberville was probably trying to make a subtle argument in favor of extending liberty of conscience in the colonies, which some administrators had advocated since 1685. At the same time, if his report ended up in English hands, it would serve to confirm some of their worst fears about the refugees, who occasionally seemed suspect in their loyalties.[92]

Even as Bond and Bienville argued on the Mississippi, officials in London began to sour on Coxe's design. The presence of French ships on the Gulf Coast confirmed the common fear that the French had designs on the American interior, which could threaten all of the English plantations from New England to Carolina. Nonetheless, officials at the newly formed Board of Trade felt it unwise to push English claims in the region. In a report the Board advised the king that "the settling of a Colony in that part of the world, as proposed, does not appear to be a strengthning of Your Majesty's other plantations." They worried that the settlement might also anger the Spanish at Pensacola, and besides, "the multiplying of distant Plantations tends to the incouragement of illegal Trade; and affords a greater opportunity for the reception of Pirates." If the Board thought Carolana a bad idea, the involvement of Huguenots in the scheme seemed to make it even more precarious. The Board had learned "that a considerable part of the persons designing to engage in this Undertaking are French Refugees," and they believed that "without a constant military force" they "will be lyable to be molested or attack'd by them of a different Religion, who bear no good will to them." If earlier proposals had understood the Huguenots as a strategic boon for the empire, the Board of Trade now saw the refugees as liabilities, since they would attract unwanted attention from French authorities and make military confrontations more likely.[93]

With his Florida plans in disarray, Daniel Coxe settled on another solution. Along with the patent for Carolana he had also received title to a smaller tract of land in Lower Norfolk County, Virginia, on the border with North Carolina. This new plan was far less ambitious than a design to claim the interior of a continent and remake the global economy, but it still found a retreat for the refugees and provided Coxe settlers for some of his holdings. In 1699 and 1700 champions of the colony, including Olivier de la Muce himself, tapped into the charitable networks of the Church of England to find aid for individual refugees, "French and Vaudois," who hoped to go to Virginia.[94] The chief agent in this endeavor was Sir William Ashurst, a Whig member of the Corporation of London who had longstanding family connections to both overseas colonization and the dissenting interest. Ashurst was able to open up the coffers of the Corporation's collections for refugees. During the spring and summer of 1700 the Archbishop of Canterbury coordinated with Ashurst and the Corporation to distribute several thousand pounds from the old Royal Bounty to refugees heading to Virginia, at the rate of £6 per person, as well as a special fund for maintaining a church and minister, which went to a man named Benjamin de Joux.[95] During the summer the first colonists, a contingent of 170 men, women, and children, left London in the *Peter and Anthony*, reaching Jamestown in September, where they met a small advance party, including La Muce and Sailly, who were already in the colony.[96]

When the refugees reached Virginia they found another surprise. The governor, a Tory military man named Francis Nicholson, had decided that the land set out for the colonists in Lower Norfolk County was not suitable. As early as 1698 Nicholson's ally William Byrd II, then in London, had lambasted the plan, arguing that their proposed retreat was "low Swampy ground, unfit for planting and improvement, and the air of it very moist and unhealthy, so that to send Frenchmen thither that came from a dry and Serene Clymate were to send 'em to their Graves." Byrd suggested instead that the refugees settle not "in that Fag-end of N. Carolina" but on the upper part of the James River, a more salubrious climate that also happened to be an exposed frontier region whose leading settler was none other than Byrd's father, William Byrd I.[97] When the colony's leaders arrived Nicholson greeted them and instructed them not to go to the "unhealthfull place" they had expected, but to Manakintown, an abandoned native village on the upper James River. In a letter justifying himself, Nicholson cited "Strengthening of the Frontiers" as the main reason to send the newcomers to Manakintown.[98] Nicholson himself had made military preparations against the French one of his main projects, and Byrd had long tried to attract more settlers to his neighborhood. Beyond that, Byrd was not unfamiliar with the refugees' story. While not a particularly religious man, he had requested a copy of Pierre Jurieu's *Accomplishment of the Scripture Prophecies* some years earlier. It was that book, of course, that had convinced Durand of Dauphiné to leave Virginia for Europe in 1687. Perhaps at the same time, it inspired the Virginian planter Byrd to try and find some Huguenots to become his neighbors.[99]

Jacques de la Case joined the crowd of some hundreds heading toward the new colony. He booked passage on the *Nassau* in late 1700, traveling alone with

191 people, mostly French but also including Swiss, Germans, and Dutch. By March 1701 la Case had made the difficult trek into Virginia's backcountry to the new town. The new settlement was no Eden, but a struggling frontier outpost. The refugees cleared out as much land as they could, while Byrd tried, mostly without success, to raise charitable collections for the Huguenots around the colony. "They are very poor, and I am not able to supply th'm w'th Corne," Byrd noted, "yet they seem very cheerful and are (as farr as we could learne) very healthy, all they seem to desire is th't they might have Bread enough."[100]

Jacques de la Case's long journey epitomized the process that brought so many Huguenots to the edges of the European world in the late 1600s. The young man had sought employment, but beyond that, security in an uncertain era, and like many refugees, he responded to utopian visions of new worlds, whether east or west. The search for utopia, however, cast him headlong into the world of empires. His movements reflected not his own desires, but those

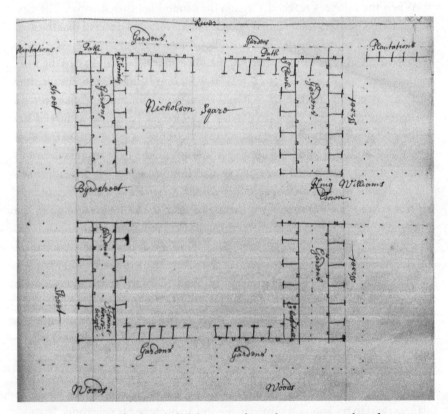

Figure 4.4 Virginia officials included this map of Manakintown in a packet of papers for the Board of Trade (CO 5/1312). The place names indicated the role of local and imperial patrons in the town's development. Courtesy of the National Archives.

of his patrons, who decided where la Case should settle based on their own strategic considerations. Even the map of his eventual home reflected that imperial reality. The town's central square was called Nicholson, after the governor
who barely tolerated the refugees, while the main street was named after William
Byrd. Even William III, the British king and Huguenot champion, had a lower
profile in the town than their local, Virginian patrons.[101] This was an effective
symbol of how imperial administrators everywhere viewed the refugees, from
the Cape of Good Hope to New England. They were pawns in a great geopolitical game more than allies or even objects of charity. Individual refugees like la
Case had to figure out how to prosper in this imperial world, once their dreams
of Eden had died.

Disappearing to Survive

During the eighteenth century Huguenot communities in the Indies seemed to disappear. The coherent French Protestant settlements of the seventeenth century shrank in size, as refugees moved elsewhere and many of their children married outside the community. French churches had trouble finding pastors, and many of their flocks chose to join other congregations, from Anglican churches in New York and South Carolina to Dutch Reformed ones in the Cape and Suriname. On the linguistic front, most second generation Huguenots stopped using French in official life, and some of them forgot the language altogether.[1] Perhaps typical in this respect was the history of the Laurence or Laurens family. The first migrant, André, fled La Rochelle for England, soon moving on to Ireland and New York before settling in South Carolina in 1715. André left his small estate to four sons and a daughter, who chose different paths. "Some of them retained the French pride of family," recalled André's grandson Henry Laurens, "and were content to die poor." Not so Henry's father John, who "learned a Trade, and by great Industry acquired an Estate with a good Character & Reestablished the Name of his Family." For John Laurens, success meant leaving his heritage behind. His children spoke little French, and to his son's chagrin, John threw out most of his old papers. "He looked upon them as incapable of producing any real benefit," Henry noted, "& had no inclination to gratify his Vanity by a retrospect of any little Grandeur which might have existed, before he was born, among his Fore fathers."[2]

Similar stories appeared from one end of the Refuge to another and have often suggested weak bonds at the heart of the Huguenot community. After all, the engineers of the Refuge intended that Huguenot communities abroad would keep the French Protestant church alive, in anticipation of either a return to France or the creation of a new France overseas. By turning their backs on their heritage and abandoning their communities, Huguenots like John Laurens seemed to betray the very ideas that had brought them across the ocean in the first place. Such an interpretation is tempting, but ultimately fails to account for the diversity of refugee experience in the eighteenth century. In fact, families

The Global Refuge. Owen Stanwood, Oxford University Press (2020). © Oxford University Press.
DOI: 10.1093/oso/9780190264741.001.0001

like the Laurenses did not simply assimilate; they went through complicated transformations. Some did retain their Frenchness, even if they often did so in their private rather than public lives, and even if being French meant sacrificing some degree of political or economic power. In addition, those who seemed to blend in, like John Laurens, did not completely divorce themselves from larger Huguenot networks. Even his son Henry, who did not possess the confidence to write in French, had close ties with refugees in both America and Europe, and used his transnational heritage to attempt to build his business. Many other Huguenot merchants did the same, using their ethnic and religious connections to build trading regimes that transcended empires and continents.[3]

In fact, one may perceive assimilation, whether partial or complete, as just another strategy used by refugees to navigate competing political allegiances. This tactic appeared nearly as soon as Huguenots left France. In 1686 minister Jean Tirel wrote a number of letters from his prison cell that circulated in manuscript among the refugees. One of the letters reflected on the different countries where the Huguenots could find refuge, noting their various strengths and weaknesses. Tirel advised refugees to blend in and to learn from the positive attributes of their various retreats—Dutch frugality, for instance, or the "deep wisdom" of English theologians and philosophers. "God has dispersed you," Tirel wrote. "Do not tell me that you do not want to be dispersed. God has separated you, like a good Father separates children who he finds waste their time together." The refugees had to accept their state by serving, loving, and respecting their protectors. Tirel did not want the Huguenots to abandon being French, but he did suggest that the experience of living in exile could create a better, more godly people, who combined the best traits of their natal culture with that of their adopted one. "The homeland [*patrie*] is a venerable thing in the society of men, but when it comes to God, homeland is nothing more than a name, an idea that falls to the consideration that Scripture teaches all the earth belongs to the Lord of Lords."[4]

Tirel died in prison, but the process that he identified—of assimilation in order to build a more perfect Christian society—continued to play out in a variety of national contexts. To be sure, not everyone agreed with Tirel's program. National prejudices were hard to break, and Huguenots tended to divide, like most other Europeans, between those who embraced cosmopolitanism and those who instead stressed the superiority of their own language, culture, and religion. Nonetheless, the act of dispersion usually necessitated blending in, and the difficult history of the 1690s encouraged most refugees, especially those on the edges of empires, to be discreet about their Frenchness. While the Huguenots faced far less discrimination than many other early modern minority groups, fingers tended to point the refugees' way when anything unpleasant happened. When several buildings in Boston caught fire in March 1701, for instance, English neighbors immediately blamed "the frensh people here among us," who they believed to be "Imployed by the Jesuites to burn us & ruin us." With such sentiments widespread, Huguenots had more reasons to take Tirel's advice and imitate their neighbors as much as possible.[5]

This drama played out differently in the various corners of the Refuge. In New York, for instance, Huguenots found themselves in the middle of a complicated civil conflict, one that divided refugees as it did the polyglot colony's other ethnic groups. In Virginia and the Cape Colony, the Huguenots were at odds with hostile local authorities who resented their independence. In South Carolina they sought political rights and representation, largely through the pursuit of naturalization as British subjects and membership in the Church of England. Refugees in each of these colonies steeped themselves in the local political cultures that they encountered, and their stories were far from identical from place to place. But the end result tended to follow Tirel's suggestion. Huguenots learned how to work in a variety of local contexts, and their communities slowly blended in with those of their non-French neighbors. But it was clear that this was far from accidental, but a deliberate decision that foretold the transformation of the Huguenot Refuge.

———

Eighteenth-century refugees had to tread carefully when they made public statements. One of London's most public Huguenots, Abel Boyer, learned this lesson in 1703 when he began to speak out on behalf of his brethren in the Cévennes. That mountainous region of Languedoc had become the center of a fierce war between Huguenot peasants, known as Camisards, and Louis XIV's armies. While most French Protestants had abandoned open resistance, the Camisards accelerated the fight, inspired by a millenarian religious vision that the end times were near and the Antichristian empire, embodied by Louis XIV, would soon fall. The Camisard cause attracted a number of adherents, including the elder statesman Pierre Jurieu. From his home in London, Abel Boyer was one of the prominent refugees who urged foreign Protestants to assist the Camisards. He argued, in language that resembled that of Jurieu in an earlier era, that all good English Protestants needed to support the rebels in the Cévennes, "for the advancement of the Protestant religion, the Prosperity of this happy and powerful Nation, and the Good of the Common Cause." The Camisards were direct heirs to the Huguenot cause, another kind of chosen people picked by God to continue the fight. Any people who opposed helping them, Boyer claimed, were "but a short remove from frenchifyed papists."[6]

Unfortunately, Boyer soon found out that such arguments were more problematic than they had been a decade or two earlier. For one prominent Tory politician, the Duke of Nottingham, Boyer had gone too far, and the duke summoned the Huguenot writer to appear and explain himself. Nottingham himself was not a supporter of the Camisard rebels. Their dependence on religious prophecies worried many English Protestants, who feared that such "enthusiasm" could quickly lead to the overturning of all established order. He issued Boyer a warning: that "We french gave our selves great libertys, though we were but strangers tolerated by the Government, That the Queens subjects were not permitted to Reflect upon any body, and as for a stranger it was presumption in him, to Characterize even the greatest Villains in England." Nottingham seemed to stumble a bit in figuring out why exactly Boyer was dangerous. He might be a millenarian radical, a denier of Queen Anne's authority, or perhaps he was a spy for the Sun King, but in any case he was not to be trusted. Boyer's appeals to common Protestantism, and his references to past charity by English kings and parliament, did not go very far in calming Nottingham's fears.[7]

Those who lived on the edges of empires faced similar troubles. One illustration is the life of a man who seemed to be one of the more successful imperial Huguenots, Stephen Poirier. Back in 1689 Poirier traveled to St. Helena, the English East India Company's remote Atlantic refueling station, to be the director of vineyards on the island. That wine scheme failed more quickly and completely than most similar designs, and most of Poirier's fellow Huguenots returned to Europe by the end of the 1690s. For whatever reason Poirier himself stayed in St. Helena, and he must have done something right, as in 1698 East India Company authorities appointed him governor of St. Helena and captain of the local militia. He probably rose to that position for the simple reason that he was a gentleman in a place with a very small population of competent men, but it made him the first refugee to gain a position overseeing non-French underlings. He had a tough task on his hands. St. Helena was a famously ungovernable place, even by the standards of the seventeenth-century empire. Company officials noted two problems that they hoped Poirier would remedy. First off, St. Helena was frightfully immoral, its people prone to "drunken profane swearing and riotous excesses." Indeed, soldiers had even murdered one of the previous governors. Company leaders hoped that Poirier would get matters under control with a full-blown campaign of moral and religious reformation, especially by enforcing laws to keep the Sabbath. Second, its economy was a mess, with the vineyard scheme, like everything else, leading to no profit. Officials in London resolved to send Poirier even more "Vine Plants," hoping that these new ones would succeed where the others had not.[8]

Governor Poirier's term did not go smoothly. In 1698 he gave a speech to the island's court that showed he took one of his charges, that of promoting religion and morality, very seriously indeed. He lambasted some on the island who mocked the practice of religion and claimed "it is [being] a bussy body to medle with such trifelous affairs" as the people's godliness and proper behavior. Poirier countered by reminding his listeners of Sodom and Gomorrah, noting that God could smite the settlement at any time.[9] The soldiers and other inhabitants of the island did not appreciate Poirier's campaign, especially when he declared that the making of arrack, the only liquor produced on the island, was contributing to the low moral standards. Moreover, they often pointed to Poirier's Frenchness as a reason not to trust him. One Captain Bright spread rumors about the governor, claiming he would "have been hanged in France in effigies and that it was not for Religion sake but for Treason or rebellion." In short, as a Huguenot he was a natural rebel—a slur that to Poirier showed Bright's sympathies with the French who were always trying to downplay persecution and slander the Huguenots.[10]

In addition to Captain Bright, Poirier feuded with Anglican ministers on the island. The most telling dispute pitted Poirier against the newly arrived chaplain John Kerr in 1703. According to Poirier, Kerr aimed to bring him down, saying that "he came here on purpose to ruin the French rougue and refugee—meaning the Governor." He hated Poirier for his religious beliefs and his politics. Kerr criticized the governor because "he stood up in Church in time of Divine Service like a French Hogonot proud fool," when he should have kneeled. He also claimed that Poirier had been a "traitor to his own king" in France, and questioned whether he could be trusted to remain loyal to England. While Kerr raised trouble, others accused Poirier of making certain political statements. One said he claimed the Stuart monarchs "were an unfortunate family and never did any good for England," and that he would have preferred the elector of Hanover to take the throne instead of Queen Anne. Another contended he had refused to condemn Oliver Cromwell, that old hero of the Puritan cause. With the exception of the slander of the queen, none of these statements were that shocking; they were typical opinions shared by English Whigs who distrusted the Stuarts and supported the Hanoverian succession. Nonetheless, to his opponents such declarations smacked of the religious radicalism and political disloyalty that was on display in the Cévennes—two traits they believed to be common among Huguenots.[11]

In addition, others accused Poirier of the opposite crime—favoring Louis XIV and the French. The coming of the War of the Spanish Succession in 1702 put the island at risk. In 1706 the French attacked and captured a ship in St. Helena's harbor after sailing in under Dutch colors, and the East India Company's board back in London reacted by fulminating against Poirier, claiming that "our Governor has been unaccountably careless about the Fortifications" and that he had previously welcomed the French on St. Helena and allowed them to survey the waters around the island. Poirier vigorously denied the charges, but they only demonstrated more clearly the dangers of being a Huguenot in the early eighteenth century. Whether he was a spy for Louis XIV or a rebel against him, there was clearly something wrong with the Frenchman. The chaplain Kerr spoke for many when he screamed at Poirier before the council "you Hogonist go[,] go to your own Hogonist countrey to command your Hogonist Ministers." In fact, Poirier did soon leave, but not for his own country. In 1707 he got sick and died, and in his will Poirier left a poignant statement about his time as a refugee. Poirier thanked God for allowing him to escape persecution in France— which he described as "the slavery of Babylon" —and "for having provided me an Azile protection and entertainment under good and auspicious masters the Right Hon[ora]ble East India Company." He had been "loaded perpetually of trouble and vexations by traitors and unjust Enemies," but had sought nothing more than to serve his masters well.[12]

The parallel, but very different circumstances of Boyer and Poirier demonstrated the problems with being Huguenot, whether in a cosmopolitan city like London or in a distant imperial outpost. But the refugees faced problems beyond the ire of their non-French neighbors. The stress of living in someone else's land led to serious tensions within Huguenot communities, largely over the issue of how they should relate to their foreign hosts. For both Boyer and Poirier, being Huguenot was important, and while both men considered themselves loyal English subjects, they advocated for the French Calvinist cause, whether by advocating for the Camisards or pushing a typically Calvinist campaign for godliness and morality. Other Huguenots took Jean Tirel's advice to blend in much more seriously. The most dramatic confrontation occurred a year after Boyer's conversation with Nottingham, when a number of newcomers from southern France began preaching in London. These "French prophets" advocated for a militant, millenarian version of Christianity that actually resounded more with ordinary people in England and Germany than with the more genteel, conservative types who dominated among the refugees.[13]

The coming of the prophets divided London's French community, and the divisions had as much to do with politics as religion. To be sure, many Huguenots disagreed with the millenarian "enthusiasm." At the request of Bishop of London Henry Compton, for instance, the conformist French Church of the Savoy sent a minister to examine the prophets, who was not pleased, finding them dangerously unorthodox.[14] Beyond the religious objections, however, the refugees felt that they needed to denounce the prophets to satisfy critics like the Duke of Nottingham, who already believed that all Huguenots were susceptible to such extreme and dangerous forms of religiosity and used the actions of a few people to represent the entire Huguenot community. More and more refugees sought to blend in, choosing the safe moderation of the Church of England over the maintenance of separate independent congregations like the Threadneedle Street Church. Nonetheless, not everyone agreed, and the main question for debate—to maintain a distinctive community or blend in—divided London's refugees. At the Church of the Savoy, which began to overtake Threadneedle as

the center of the English Huguenot world, ministers and elders took the position that the French should, as one petition stated, "spread into the body of the
State" rather than maintain their independence. Whether for principle or out of
necessity, the old dreams of autonomy were becoming hard to preserve in a new
eighteenth-century world.[15]

These disputes hit Huguenot communities on the edges of empires particularly
hard. Stephen Poirier was one man without a community, so any prejudice impacted him and him alone. The London refugees were great in numbers and
attracted plenty of ill will, but they could blend in to the crowded city, and their
economic value as artisans, especially in the Spitalfields silk business, blunted
the bad treatment. In the colonial world, however, Huguenots had labored to
set up semiautonomous "colonies" whose populations, if small compared to
their coreligionists in Europe, were large enough to make a decided impact on
the colonies they inhabited. They did this, moreover, during an age of imperial
consolidation, when all of the European empires, but particularly the English,
sought to streamline and simplify the administration of colonies. This program
argued against creating "states within a state" on the edges of empire.[16] Finally,
while Huguenots had promoted themselves as critical to the imperial economy,
the spotty record of productivity in their colonies meant that fewer and fewer
people sought to defend them. As a result colonial Huguenot communities faced
even more acute challenges than those in London—they encountered resistance from authorities as well as their neighbors, and they divided into factions.
Local circumstances determined a lot about how these communities' histories
progressed.

Strangely, the most classic example of the conflict occurred not in the British
empire but in the Dutch colony at the Cape of Good Hope. As an outpost of
the Dutch East India Company the Cape did not seem to be subject to the same
centralizing pressures as colonies in the English empire.[17] Nonetheless, the
Company demanded obedience, especially if its leaders thought that the liberties
of individuals might cut into the Company's profits, and the autocratic style of
Governor Simon van der Stel led to conflicts with the refugees. The Huguenots
were not political radicals, but they clearly expected to form a coherent community and receive many of the same advantages they had come to expect in
places like Brandenburg. When several shiploads of refugees arrived in the
colony in 1689, however, the governor scattered them around the Drakenstein
and Stellenbosch valleys. Van der Stel pledged to "receive them with love and
kindly feeling, and unsparingly lend them a helping hand," but his method was
to settle the French alongside Dutch neighbors, "to amalgamate them with our

countrymen, that the one may impart to the other his own particular knowledge and experience, and in that manner agriculture may be promoted."[18] The French received their own church in Drakenstein, but no separate consistory, and the Reverend Pierre Simond split his time between the French church and the Dutch one in Stellenbosch. The distance between them—and the poor quality of land that some of them received—was a major theme of Simond's plaintive letter to the East India Company's Seventeen Gentlemen in June 1689, just after the refugees' arrival.[19]

The minister and his flock sought to remedy this situation in two ways. Most especially, he called for the redistribution of land so that all of the refugees had tracts that were fit for agriculture and in close proximity so that they could easily attend one church and school under Simond's direction. In the meantime, another group of prominent refugees sought to go one step farther, establishing an independent church consistory. According to the governor's later resolution on the subject, Simond opposed this last step—a somewhat surprising assertion given his clear preference for a separate refugee settlement—but he agreed to represent the men before the governor anyway. While Simond's appeal for autonomy and aid made its way back to Amsterdam, he and several of his neighbors presented a request for a church council to van der Stel and the council. These demands looked very similar to requests in other parts of the Refuge, especially those in Brandenburg and other German states, where French communities always received the right to adjudicate their own churches and communities.[20]

The governor not only rejected the request, but raged at the refugees for their impertinence. In a dramatic resolution, he noted that the Huguenots had asked for "a separate Church Council" and took that as evidence that they "were very much minded to elect their own magistrate, chief, and prince of the land, & thus withdraw themselves from the allegiance which they owed the Company." More than that, van der Stel claimed that the petitioners, like most of the refugee community, were useless as well as disloyal. They came to the Cape "under the cloak of being zealous members & supporters of the Protestant faith, to live a lazy & indolent life." The Company had seen to all of the needs of the French—indeed, they had been treated "better than our own nation" —but instead of behaving as loyal subjects they set out to establish their own, independent authority, which was a clear violation of the oaths of allegiance they had taken to the Company. Van der Stel responded to the petitioners simply by handing them a copy of the oath they had signed and warning them "in future to beware of troubling the Commander and Council with such impertinent requests."[21] In a later complaint against the refugees, van der Stel showed that he could use the refugees' favorite biblical analogies against them. "They resemble the children of Israel," he noted, "who, fed by God's hand in the wilderness, still longed for the *onion* pots of Egypt."[22]

The conflict between the refugees and van der Stel encapsulated all of the possible disputes that those in the Netherlands had predicted. After all, earlier commentators had warned that the Huguenots had too great a "love of liberty" to make tractable subjects, especially in a restrictive atmosphere like the Cape Colony where the Company's profit was the first and perhaps only motivation among the leadership.[23] For the autocratic governor, any pretensions of independence detracted from the Company's authority. He sought complete obedience and made clear that the purpose of the Huguenot project in the colony was to further Dutch objectives, not to build any sort of refugee utopia. Such a perspective was most unwelcome to Simond, who reportedly asserted that van der Stel's "tyranny" was just as bad as that of Louis XIV.[24] Interestingly, administrators in Amsterdam took a much softer line. Once word of Simond's requests reached them, they instructed van der Stel to allow the creation of a separate French church council, though they empowered the governor with appointing some of its members, all of whom should be conversant in both French and Dutch. They agreed with the larger goal of assimilation, arguing that by teaching French children Dutch they could "unite our nation." But perhaps because of the continued clout of the Huguenot lobby in Europe, they allowed the refugees to preserve at least some of their dreams of autonomy.[25]

Despite this small victory, the Cape Huguenots did not live happily ever after. The next round of drama involved not a dispute with the governor but internal strife. As the tiff with van der Stel demonstrated, Pierre Simond had worked to make himself the chief power broker of the Huguenot community. As minister, he was responsible for the refugees' spiritual health, while as an officer of the East India Company he acted as an official conduit between settlers and authorities at the Cape and beyond. Nonetheless, it was hard to keep the peace during the 1690s, as the community split into factions. The root cause was a bitter but confusing feud between Simond and Jacques de Savoye, a highly ranked refugee who had been one of the minister's collaborators in the earlier attempt to gain an independent church council. The lack of a paper trail makes the details difficult to recover, but it seemed to start when Savoye believed that Simond was acting as an imperious ruler over other refugees, in particular by pressuring French settlers to bake their bread in Simond's oven. For this and other reasons, Savoye began circulating "scandalous calumnies" in letters about the minister to friends in Europe. Clearly Simond heard about them, because when Savoye's daughter brought her newborn son to his church for baptism, Simond refused to allow Savoye to be a godparent, which divided the community. Some people thought that the minister was being too controlling—administering sacraments, after all, was the most important task a minister could perform, and setting conditions on them put people's souls at risk. Many others—fifty-six in one petition—favored the minister and lambasted Savoye for criticizing the leader of his own community.[26]

The correspondence left by the two men demonstrates much about the issues that divided refugees during the 1690s. Coming out of the crisis surrounding the Revocation, the key issue was faithfulness to the cause. So many French Protestants had abandoned the faith, either temporarily or permanently, that the greatest slur was to suggest someone was not a genuine Protestant. That was exactly the charge Savoye made in his letters against Simond, claiming that the minister set himself up "as a pope" and calling him a "tarfuffe, hypocite, Jesuit, [and] Jew."[27] But Savoye may have made these charges because he was open to similar accusations himself. Unlike most of his fellow refugees, Savoye had not come from France at all but from Ghent in the Spanish Netherlands, where he had lived as a successful merchant in that Catholic city for much of his life. Simond did not directly charge Savoye with being insufficiently Protestant, but the allegations must have been circulating, as Savoye felt compelled to write back to Europe for testimonials about his religious zeal. One letter, from François Simon, a minister "under the cross" in Flanders, attested that Savoye was a committed Protestant, "well instructed in the mysteries of salvation, and also capable of defending and maintaining the truth against the errors of the communion of Rome." Simon and three other witnesses claimed that it was the efforts of angry Catholics, led by the Jesuits, that chased Savoye out of Ghent and forced him to take refuge in the Netherlands and then the Cape, making his story sound similar to those of his Huguenot neighbors from France itself.[28] Dutch officials in Cape Town looked on the feud as a mere annoyance. "We only wish that the Rev. Pierre Simond and Jacques de Savoye would bear themselves towards each other more peaceably and amicably," the governor wrote back to the Seventeen Gentlemen, but "being stubborn," they refused to settle their quarrel. Van der Stel did suggest he may have seen Savoye as the more reasonable party. He complained that Simond interfered too much in the "private affairs and those of the public in general" and reminded him that "they must be satisfied to remain as they were, a branch congregation of the [Dutch] church of Stellenbosch."[29]

These sorts of internal divisions only made life more difficult for the refugees as they attempted to preserve their autonomy against an imperious governor. Indeed, the next years witnessed a gradual decline in the French community's integrity, starting with the church itself. In 1700 Simond was ready to leave Africa, and by 1702 he had returned to the Netherlands, where he struggled to find employment while he published a new translation of the Psalms he had worked on in the Cape Colony, which he titled *Les Veillées Africaines* ("African Vigils").[30] Back in Africa, authorities used Simond's absence to further promote the absorption of the Huguenots into the larger Dutch burgher population. In 1701, as they looked ahead to Simond's departure, officials in the East India Company's Amsterdam chamber did recommend finding a minister who understood both Dutch and French, but "not as we take it to preach in the latter language, but only to be of service to the aged colonists who do not know our language, so that he may visit, admonish and comfort them, in order that in the course of time the French language may die out, and be, as it were banished."[31] It was the most explicit statement one could imagine in favor of cultural assimilation, which did proceed apace during the eighteenth century. In 1713 the Classis of Amsterdam said they would try to find a pastor who could preach in both languages, but recommended that the French "do their best to learn the Dutch language."[32] As the population aged, that is exactly what happened; French turned into a language for the elderly. By the time the Frenchman Nicholas de la Caille visited in the 1750s, he noted that only the children of the original refugees, themselves quite old by this time, retained any facility with the language. Within twenty years, he predicted, "there will be no person in Drakenstein who will know how to speak it."[33]

While this assimilation most definitely occurred, albeit slowly, it did not mean that the French community ceased to have any influence. In fact, the opposite may have occurred—by becoming closer with their Dutch neighbors, the refugees were able to increase their political clout. The key event occurred in 1706 and involved Willem Adriaan van der Stel, who had succeeded his father as governor. The son inherited many of his father's autocratic tendencies and was increasingly at odds with the colony's freemen, both Dutch and French, after he built a large plantation for himself that monopolized much of the Cape's lucrative provisioning trade. A free burgher named Adam Tas led a movement against the governor, lodging an official complaint that eventually made its way back to the Netherlands, despite van der Stel's best efforts to suppress it through the arrest of Tas and some of his allies. Many of Tas's most prominent supporters were Huguenots, including François du Toit, a heemraad (local councilor) and militia captain. In 1706 Tas wrote a letter to du Toit, in French, that lauded the refugee's "virtue and constancy" in the face of van der Stel's attempts to silence him. The episode demonstrated the degree to which Dutch and French burghers had become allies in the same cause—and the result was the removal of a governor who had repeatedly labeled the French as bad subjects. Perhaps the van der Stels had been correct when they complained of the Huguenots' excessive love of liberty. That liberty, however, came not through separation but alliance with Dutch neighbors.[34]

A similar drama occurred around the same time across the Atlantic in New York. Here too the refugees had to deal with the central question that appeared in all their communities: should they maintain autonomy or seek to blend in? That task was made more difficult by the fact that the refugees did not know exactly what they should be blending into—after all, the colony was famously diverse, with Dutch, German, and British inhabitants of several denominations rubbing shoulders with a substantial population of enslaved

Africans and native Americans. The Huguenot population in the colony even differed from those in other parts of the Atlantic world. Many with French surnames descended from Walloons who had moved to the Netherlands decades earlier, while other French speakers from the German Palatinate had founded their own distinct community in New Paltz that had little to do with the parallel migration of refugees from France and the French Caribbean.[35]

The first test of Huguenot loyalties came in 1689, and standing in for Simon van der Stel was the new lieutenant governor, Jacob Leisler. While he came from Germany, Leisler in fact had family connections to French Protestantism. His father, Jacob Victorian Leisler, had been the minister to the French Protestant church in Frankfurt, which became such an important conduit on the refugee circuit in the 1680s. The younger Jacob traveled to New Amsterdam as a soldier with the Dutch West India Company, and after the English conquest he made a tidy fortune as a merchant, due largely to his connections with family back in Europe. The Glorious Revolution radicalized Leisler and brought him into provincial politics. He accused local leaders, who refused to acknowledge his hero William III as the new English king, of being dupes of Louis XIV who aimed to deliver the colony to France. Leisler and his allies led a rebellion that seized power in the colony and installed a radical Protestant caretaker governorship, led by himself, to preserve New York until William and Mary could send a legitimate governor. This rebellion divided the colony largely along religious lines, especially as Leisler accused more and more people of being "papists" in league with the French and filled the prisons with his enemies.[36]

One would think that New York's Huguenots would be natural Leislerians. Not only was the new lieutenant governor a fierce opponent of the Sun King and a seeming adherent to the kind of Protestant politics favored by Pierre Jurieu, but he was also a particular friend to the refugees. It was the increasing persecution of Huguenots in France, as much as anything, that pushed Leisler toward his radical anti-French politics, and he showed his colors by sponsoring the settlement of refugees in his province. As a powerful merchant with transatlantic connections, Leisler was in a position to make it happen. He donated much of the land that became New Rochelle, a new settlement that formed in 1688, just before his rise to political power.[37] Given his politics and genealogy, it was not surprising that many refugees took up arms alongside Leisler and his fellow "rebels." Peter Reverdy, who had earlier tried to win a grant to make salt and slandered New York's Governor Edmund Andros, was an early adherent to the cause, urging Bishop of London Henry Compton to acquire a "Kings letter" to legitimate Leisler's governorship. He presented Leisler's cause as identical to that of the refugees. "The French for certain have a designe upon New York," Reverdy wrote, and "there [are] 200 French families about New York which will be putt to the torture if the french takes itt."[38] The fear of French attack brought many Huguenots under Leisler's banner, and it was not an unreasonable anxiety. Indeed, the following year some of the Sun King's ministers advocated just such an invasion of New York, with the clause that all the colony's French refugees would be sent back to France in chains.[39]

Reverdy's appeal on Leisler's behalf did not work. While William and Mary's ministers forgave similar rebellions in Massachusetts and Maryland, they sent a new governor to New York who decided to make an example of Leisler. Tried and convicted of treason, Leisler died on the gallows beside his son-in-law and partner in 1691. Not all the refugees wept for the fallen rebel. The anti-Leislerian side also included many French names; indeed, Leisler's chief opponent, Nicholas Bayard, descended from Walloon Protestants. If many refugees wanted to take the fight to the French in Canada, others wanted to avoid conflict altogether and live quietly under the rule of their imperial masters. Huguenots had been loyal subjects even under Louis XIV, and while some had abandoned neutrality for Pierre Jurieu's brand of confrontational, apocalyptic politics, others maintained their old quietism. Among the latter group was New York's French minister Pierre Daillé. A former teacher at the Huguenot academy of Saumur, Daillé had fled France in 1683 and ended up in New York. True to his Huguenot roots, Daillé counseled Leisler to rule with moderation at a time when he was imprisoning many of his political opponents. In reaction, Leisler allegedly cursed at the French minister in the middle of a church service, screaming "Diable vous porte," or "the devil take you."[40]

Most of the French congregation seems to have followed their minister's lead and attempted to stay out of the conflict, and as soon as the new governor arrived they continued to offer petitions asking for special treatment. In short, most refugees were not eager to take sides in a complicated political dispute. They were interested in patronage and willing to support whoever granted it to them. This seemed to be a sound strategy in such an uncertain political climate. After Leisler's execution as a rebel in 1691, his erstwhile political allies became outcasts, driven from power and in some cases thrown in prison. By May of 1691 a group of refugees had already begun petitioning the new governor, Henry Sloughter, who had just arrived two months earlier and was already presiding over Leisler's trial and punishment. In a style typical to their appeals on both sides of the Atlantic, the Huguenots reminded the governor that they were "refugiate in these parts of the world, to avoid the Popish yoak, and to enjoy the freedom of their Conscience, and the liberty to profess the Protestante Religion under the Royal Protection of their majesties William and Mary." They asked simply to be made "burghers," so "they may enjoye the freedom, privilege, and prerogative of the same." The refugees did not wish to make a scene; they wanted to become like other English subjects.[41]

Nonetheless, in the topsy-turvy world of New York politics this opportunism did not always serve the refugees well. In 1698 the anti-Leislerians lost power when the Irish Whig Richard Coote, earl of Bellomont arrived as governor of both New York and Massachusetts. Bellomont saw himself as a friend of the refugees— he had tried to settle refugees on his Irish lands, and through his acquaintance with the earl of Galway he made contact with a number of Huguenots in the colonies, including Gabriel Bernon and Oxford's minister Jacques Laborie. While he cultivated refugees in New England, he feuded with those in New York, especially ministers and elders in New York City and New Rochelle, who joined other divines in protesting when Bellomont unilaterally dismissed one of the colony's Dutch ministers, blurring the lines between political and ecclesiastical power. In one letter to the Board of Trade the governor lamented that the French had "ran in with the Jacobite party" and accused them of passing intelligence to New France. During the subsequent row the governor refused to pay the New Rochelle minister Daniel Bondet's salary and questioned the loyalty of New York's refugee leaders, inspiring several of them to consider moving to Daniel Coxe's Carolana.[42]

While it appeared to be a straightforward rift between French and English, a letter from Gabriel Bernon to the consistory of the New York's French church complicates that picture. Bernon took Bellomont's side, and in doing so he presented a classic Huguenot argument about the necessity of submitting to authority, whatever that might be. "Like you I abandoned my possessions and our country for the sake of religion, just like many of our refugee brethren in various parts of the world," wrote Bernon. "Each of us needs to submit to the government that we encounter," he continued, adding that "it is for us a great happiness, and a great honor, to be able to proclaim ourselves good subjects of our Sovereign, King William, as God commands us to be." Of course, Bernon was far from a disinterested party; he himself was petitioning Bellomont to become a partner in his ongoing scheme to produce naval stores in New England. Nonetheless, he represented one Huguenot political approach—the impulse to obey whoever was in power and gain advantages by working behind the scenes. He advocated a version of Jean Tirel's argument, claiming that the duty of refugees, wherever they were, was to give their allegiance to their protectors. The elders of the French church, meanwhile, sought to preserve the interests of their community, even if that meant bucking the colony's leaders every now and then. For them some degree of autonomy was essential, even if it meant they had to abandon their current refuge and set out to a new one.[43]

None of the New York French ever followed through on their threat to move to "the Mississippi." After all, that colony never became a reality, and its organizers, for complicated reasons, ended up not on the Gulf of Mexico but in Manakintown in Virginia. As that town developed in the first years of the eighteenth century, it exhibited many of the same issues as New York and the Cape of Good Hope during the previous decade. In Virginia, too, Huguenots struggled in their relations with official authority, especially on the question of autonomy, and the community itself divided into opposing factions. The main difference, however, was that some of the Manakintown Huguenots did what the New York refugees would not in the face of Bellomont's persecution: they left. Migration became another strategy refugees used to deal with strife, whether it came from persecutory governors or community divisions.[44]

Like nearly everyone who settled on an imperial frontier, the Manakintown colonists had to deal with their own difficult governor. Francis Nicholson had been the chief royal official in New York at the time of Leisler's Rebellion, when he had to sneak out of the port to avoid arrest. After regaining his reputation Nicholson returned to North America, first to Maryland and then to Virginia, where he took the post of lieutenant governor. A high Tory, Nicholson fiercely defended the royal prerogative and the Church of England, and had little sympathy for radical Protestants like Jacob Leisler or New England's Puritan leaders. At the same time, he was one of the most vociferous opponents of French pretensions in North America. He believed, rightly it turned out, that Louis XIV and his ministers had a design to dominate the interior of the continent and isolate the English on the Atlantic coast. This combination of anti-French vitriol and distrust of Reformed Protestantism had the potential to complicate relations between Nicholson and the Huguenots who arrived in his colony in 1700. They had common interests in defeating the Sun King, and the Manakintown migrants embraced the Church of England, but as Abel Boyer's difficulties indicated, refugees tended to be associated with Whig politics and dissent in England, and their desire for autonomy could be particularly unwelcome in an exposed frontier region like the Virginia piedmont.[45]

While the situation was never as dramatic as in the Cape Colony, the Manakintown colonists did clash with Nicholson on the question of autonomy. Unlike their African coreligionists, the Virginian refugees resided in their own town, distant from most English settlers, and they had their own "distinct parish" that had to conform to the Church of England, but offered them a great deal of practical autonomy.[46] Still, Nicholson made clear that he expected the refugees to be good imperial subjects and not autonomous actors. Like their counterparts around the Refuge, the leaders of Manakintown wrote frequent petitions to the government. The community's leaders Charles de Sailly and the marquis de La Muce complained that the captain who transported them to America had made off with their money, while other petitions asked for the government to send a surveyor and grant newcomers the same "liberties" as the first colonists.

Nicholson and his council granted some of the petitions, but their language annoyed him. The Council noted that "the said french Refugees in their Peticons to his Exc[ellenc]y do frequently Call themselves the french Colony." The language of their petitions implied independence, and in the Council's estimation this pretension of autonomy led to dissensions within the community, as various French factions vied for power. "His Excell[en]cy was pleased to ordr that the said Refugees shall not hereafter use the title of a Colony," the Council journal noted, "and that for the future all peticons they shall present to his Exc[ellenc]y be in the English tongue."[47]

The Council's riposte offered two distinct challenges to refugee independence. First off, it specifically proscribed the word "colony" to describe Huguenot communities in North America. That word had particular significance in the history of the refugee diaspora, as leaders in Brandenburg and elsewhere had specifically defined their independent towns as colonies, implying a level of autonomy and isolation from the larger, dominant culture.[48] While the word did not always travel to places across the seas ("plantation" was another frequent label for overseas settlements), it did frequently appear in North America. In 1691, for instance, New Rochelle's minister had signed a letter as "Pastor of the French Colony" in the province.[49] By directing the Manakintown colonists not to refer to themselves as such, Nicholson and the Council explicitly rejected the autonomous designs of the old German colonial schemes. Second, the order specifically targeted the French language. This was not quite enforced assimilation on the model of the Cape of Good Hope—Manakintown retained a French-language church and school—but it implied that Virginia's leaders expected a measure of acculturation, at least when Huguenots interacted with the state. One possible piece of evidence for this linguistic imperialism appeared in a catalog of books in Manakintown's library in 1710. The list included most of the Anglican classics, from the Book of Common Prayer to theological works by luminaries like Gilbert Burnet and Thomas Bray—but not a single French-language book.[50]

While the refugees never responded to the Council's criticisms, the stresses of living in someone else's land had similar effects on Manakintown as it had in the Cape and New York. The community divided, and even if the sources of their divisions remain somewhat elusive, they seemed to concern the question of assimilation and autonomy. The key player, as in the Cape Colony, was the minister, in this case Benjamin de Joux. As early as February 1701 Olivier de la Muce complained that de Joux circulated a "Factious and scandalous Petition."[51] The minister apparently disagreed with the way Sailly and La Muce administered the town and moved with some of his adherents just outside the village, where the two leaders complained they have "given unto us great many subjects of Complaints in troubling and vexing us."[52] De Joux's allies, on the other hand, spoke of Sailly in particular as "odious and insupportable," and unwilling to give aid to refugees unless they backed his chosen candidates for justice of the peace positions. They also complained that Sailly misused or extorted funds that had been raised for their relief in England. In general, the refugees complained that they were "languishing under misery and want," since their lands were unsuitable for tobacco and they could not "drive a trade in wings, flax, Silk and hemp, and other effects of their industry, which they aime at," without considerable time and investment.[53]

Virginia's leaders attempted to get the refugees to overcome these "private differrences" by commissioning two of them to be magistrates. Matters seem to have calmed down, but some of that may have been due to Charles de Sailly's death in 1701 and the subsequent sickness of Benjamin de Joux. By 1702 a new minister, Claude Philippe de Richebourg, had arrived to help him carry on his duties, and within a few years de Joux died as well.[54] Unfortunately, Richebourg proved just as fractious as his predecessor. After he had taken over as minister of King William Parish in 1707, he engaged in a bitter dispute with Abraham Sallé, one that nearly led to the breakup of the community. Sallé won appointment as a magistrate sometime in the middle part of the decade, and his dispute with Richebourg centered on the power of the vestry, the twelve-person council that administered the parish. By 1707 a faction of the vestry led by Sallé had begun to protest the minister's "unusual and irregular conduct" at meetings, and matters came to a head in March of that year when the clerk of the vestry, an ally of Sallé, confiscated the church's book of christenings. The minister exploded, demanding the return of the book and threatening to excommunicate any members of the vestry who opposed him. He was not alone. A group of Richebourg's parishioners, led by the vestry member Jacques de la Case, supported the minister against Sallé, and the scene nearly turned into a brawl. According to Sallé, Richebourg's partisans "took the liberty to utter many injurious things against me," with some saying "we should assassinate that damn'd fellow with the black beard, and that bougre de Chien [damned dog] ought to be hang'd up out of the way."[55]

In the wake of this dispute Richebourg petitioned the Council to dissolve the Vestry and arrange for the appointment of a new one. Much of the dispute may have simply been the clash of strong personalities. La Case, after all, had engaged in similar arguments with Huguenots and non-Huguenots on and between several continents. Nonetheless, there were important principles at stake as well. Sallé's letter claimed that he and Richebourg disputed the structure of church governance, with the minister contending that members of the vestry had been "chosen for one year according to the way of electing Elders in france." Richebourg's claim rested largely on language. The vestrymen had been called "anciens" in the French style, so the minister assumed they had the duties and responsibilities of a proper French-style consistory. Sallé countered that they only used the French word "ancien" because there was no proper translation for "vestryman," and that they were just like any other English parish, meaning that members served at the pleasure, in Virginia, of the council. The dispute, therefore, struck at the heart of Reformed ecclesiology and concerned whether the Manakintown church should operate based on French or Anglican rules. The irony is that both sides felt obligated to go to the English council to resolve the dispute.[56]

In the wake of this dispute two things happened in Manakintown. On the one hand, the town became steadily less French. The surviving parish records demonstrate the change, beginning in the 1710s when a few English names appeared in the lists of tithable inhabitants in the parish, to 1738, when nearly half of heads of household (39 out of 79) had English surnames.[57] This demographic change accompanied a gradual transformation of the landscape, as a rude frontier settlement became a more recognizably Virginian place. A Swiss visitor in 1702 found a remote but promising settlement, where things grew "in such abundance that many Englishmen come a distance of 30 miles to get fruit, which they mostly exchange for cattle."[58] By the 1720s, however, the community had turned toward slavery and tobacco farming. In the three short years between 1720 and 1723, for instance, the population of slaves increased from five to twenty-three, making them over 20 percent of the tithable population (which included all adult men along with nonwhite women). This percentage was still far lower than the tidewater counties to the east, but proved that King William was becoming just another Virginia parish. At the same time, the church became more typically English. In 1718 the minister began preaching in English once every six weeks to satisfy the growing English population, but by 1730 every fourth sermon was in English.[59] By the end of that decade Manakintown no longer had a regular minister, and the visitor tasked with delivering sermons was an Englishman named Anthony Gavin. Of his seventeen yearly sermons in the community, four were to be in French. A few decades later, the French community was mostly remembered in the surnames of a dwindling number of inhabitants—a situation not dissimilar to what the Frenchman Nicolas de la Caille had found at the Cape of Good Hope.[60]

There was, however, another side to the story. Those who objected to the community's leadership often voted with their feet. Within a few years of Manakintown's founding, a number of its leading people were ready to move on. In 1703, for instance, two representatives traveled to Charleston to ask what aid they could find to transport forty families from Virginia to Carolina. Some in the South Carolina Assembly recommended paying to bring the Huguenots to the colony, noting that "these people when here will add a Considerable french [population] to our Collony, wch in this time of war we have a great need of and will noe less add to its manufacture, production & trade."[61] In the end the assembly decided not to send a sloop, and only a few Virginia Huguenots ended up in South Carolina, but the episode indicated that American refugees, like their brethren in Europe, were still quite willing to shop around to find the best situation, which would presumably include greater autonomy.

A few years later, after Richebourg's incident with Sallé, more of them decided to leave. The minister himself led the emigrants, who intended to settle this time in North Carolina on the Trent and Neuse Rivers. Probably not coincidentally, these lands were not far from those in Lower Norfolk County that Daniel Coxe had promised the refugees before Francis Nicholson and William Byrd conspired to send them to the piedmont instead. In addition, North Carolina was one of the most ungoverned corners of the empire, so it is not surprising that refugees who treasured independence would travel there, or that they would subsequently leave very few traces in the records.[62] The best evidence of their existence came from John Lawson, who passed through their town on a tour of Carolina in 1708. As North Carolina's leading booster, Lawson was thrilled that so many of Manakintown's settlers had chosen to remove there. "They are much taken with the Pleasantness of that Country, and, indeed, are a very industrious People," Lawson wrote. "At present, they make very good Linnen-Cloath and Thread, and are very well vers'd in cultivating Hemp and Flax, of both which they raise very considerable Quantities; and design to try an Essay of the Grape, for making Wine." Clearly, the North Carolina Huguenots realized that by bragging of their facility with wine they could find good treatment. Richebourg assured Lawson that "their Intent was to propagate Vines," thus bringing the rhetoric of Huguenot viticulture to yet another American province. The newcomers never did grow many (or any) grapes, but the small numbers who moved to North Carolina seemed to have found peace and quiet nonetheless.[63]

Richebourg did not stay long with his flock in North Carolina. Instead, he was one of the few who ended up in its sister colony to the south, where he took up a job as a minister to the existing French Protestant Congregation at St. James Santee. He probably went for the money, as that church, which around that time joined with the Church of England, provided Richebourg a better living, but he ended up in yet another colony that was dealing with the question of Huguenot autonomy, both in a political and religious sense. South Carolina was a younger colony than Virginia or New York, with perhaps the largest refugee community outside of Europe. A fairly comprehensive census of the Huguenot community in 1696–1697 identified 196 adult refugees, 40 percent of whom were women and most relatively young. Over the period from 1680 to 1718, almost four hundred French Protestants came to the colony. Only in the Cape did Huguenots make up a similar percentage of the population, but unlike that Dutch outpost, Carolina had a traditional English colonial political structure, with an elected assembly holding a great deal of influence. If the refugees could classify them-selves as political insiders, they had the potential to become a critical interest group in the colony. Figuring out how to do so, however, would be no small task.[64]

The fullest indication of the problems came from a remarkable series of let-ters written by Jacques Boyd. Like Richebourg, Boyd lived in the part of the colony sometimes called "French Santee," the most recognizably French part of the province, where he had lived as a merchant and experimented with viticul-ture over the previous decade.[65] As a leader of the refugee community, Boyd was in a good position to reflect on the circumstances that had brought the Huguenots to South Carolina. In a 1695 letter he gave newly arrived Governor John Archdale a history lesson. The French had come not on their own volition, Boyd noted, but as special guests of Charles II and the Lords Proprietors, and the "Incouradgements the Lords offered to the French were that they should be here, in all the same priviledges as Naturals English, either for Charges or possessions of Lands." The French had then purchased lands in good faith, as-suming they held the same rights in them as all other English subjects, and they naturally took places on juries and as magistrates—all of the trappings of "English liberty."[66]

The refugees were surprised, therefore, when some in the province claimed they possessed none of these rights after all. Indeed, the Huguenots witnessed an all-out assault on their political and religious liberties across the whole decade. First, English neighbors attacked their right to vote and hold office. One English letter lamented that the population of Craven County was "only French," and that as a consequence all six of the county's representatives were Huguenots "which hath been very Dissatisfactory to the English here." The councilors hinted as an expedient that Craven County should not be allowed to send any representatives at all.[67] The following year two refugees attempted to vote in a 1696 election only to be refused by the sheriff, who claimed that they could not vote without "let-ters of naturalization or denization," whatever had been the practice in the past.[68] Soon the attacks went beyond the political. Some English people threatened the French by claiming they could confiscate their estates when they died, and those who had not been naturalized could not legally enter the colonial trade or even hold land. Since the French were "aliens," the argument went, they did not enjoy the same inheritance rights enshrined in English law. During another episode, some English neighbors challenged Huguenot ministers' authority to solemnize marriages.[69]

Boyd saw more than simple politics at play in the dispute. He believed that the targeting of Huguenots was partly done out of prejudice, probably driven by the stress of a decade of war. Their opponents argued for the refugees' exclusion from political life not simply because they were "Strangers," Boyd wrote, but because "We were Devells" and "Traitors." The language he used suggested both religious and political divisions—Huguenots in South Carolina, like Stephen Poirier in St. Helena, were unfaithful subjects and re- ligious radicals. He countered, of course, with the usual declaration of the Huguenots' demographic and economic value. Non-English migrants had built South Carolina, not just the French but also "the Scotch Suissers Dutch &c.," and without political rights they could not be expected to contribute to the colony's development, and South Carolina would be ruined. In a separate letter he claimed that after the coming of peace hundreds more Huguenots would probably want to set out for the colony, but not if they faced such prej- udice and persecution.[70]

Matters were worse because, as in New York, the Huguenots had settled in the midst of a factionalized colony. Even by English standards, early Carolina was a place riven by divisions, from the Tory, Anglican "Goose Creek Men" to a strong dissenting interest dominated by Puritans and Presbyterians. Beyond this struggle loomed the Lord Proprietors, heirs to the earl of Shaftesbury's vision, distant masters in England resented by everyone, whose real power dwindled every year. In their early years in the colony, the Huguenots gravitated toward the Proprietors' interest—it was their Lordships, after all, who had arranged the refugees' transportation and given them such good terms. Boyd himself wrote to Lord Ashley, Shaftesbury's son and heir, in addition to his missive to Archdale, calling on him to advocate for the Huguenots' cause.[71] The Proprietors did fre- quently take the refugees' side, still believing that they could be the colony's ec- onomic saviors. When some of the French complained of ill treatment at the hands of the assembly in 1693, the proprietors responded that they desired the French to be "upon an Equall foot wth Englishmen," with the same polit- ical rights, and cast themselves as the only people who could will "protect you against the Envy and Injurys of the people" in Carolina.[72] The Proprietors did not offer this assistance for free, however. They urged their Huguenot subjects to work toward the ratification of the Fundamental Constitutions, the governing plan for the colony that had been frequently rejected or ignored on the ground. This, however, probably did the Huguenots more harm than good, as English neighbors came to associate the refugees with the hated Proprietors. Indeed, opposing the Huguenots' "liberties" was a direct blow at the Fundamental Constitutions, since that document had explicitly granted the refugees their rights to naturalization.

It was that issue, naturalization, that most animated the Huguenots' political struggle. That legal process, by which a "stranger" became a legal English subject, was a necessary step for anyone wishing to obtain economic and political power in the English empire, especially in an age when the Navigation Acts attempted to retain the empire's wealth for English subjects alone. The earliest Carolina tracts usually noted the ease and importance of naturalization, and some Huguenots found ways to acquire it in England or the colonies, but the legal procedures around the act remained vague. As the Huguenots' Carolina opponents noted, naturalization did require an act of Parliament, but the king had the power to make people "free denizens," which granted most of the rights of naturalization without its letter. Both of these practices inspired debate in England itself between those who believed more subjects would lead to more revenue and others who feared the deleterious influence of hordes of foreigners. These conversations proved even more complicated in the colonies, where governors and local legislatures occasionally naturalized foreigners, including Huguenots, from the 1680s onward. Both naturalization and denization brought key economic and political benefits, and most refugees sought it, but not without qualms. Before 1697, according to an English witness, many Carolina Huguenots resisted naturalization because they believed that "the warr betweene the Crownes of England and France canot End but with the Restoracon of all the French P[ro]testants to their Native Kingdom and Estates."[73]

After the disappointment of Ryswick, however, the Huguenots changed their political approach. Given the clear risks of remaining neutral, they embraced colonial politics as a way to retain their estates. In doing so, they chose surprising allies. While the Proprietors had been useful in the past, it was becoming clear that they were more of a liability than a benefit for the embattled refugees. The French needed new friends. One possibility was to cultivate imperial officials like Edward Randolph, who visited the colony during the late 1690s. Pierre Girard did just that, complaining that unnaturalized Huguenots were "denied the benefit of being Owners & Masters of Vessells." Girard justified the refugees' inclusion in the political nation in economic terms, and Randolph was convinced, as he added his own note that "I find them very Industrious & good husbands," and that if the refugees could be all "made Denizons" South Carolina "would be the most Usefull to the Crown, of all the Plantations upon the Continent of America." To underscore the political economic argument for naturalization, Randolph enclosed a reckoning by Girard himself, who included two sets of numbers. First he included a census of the Huguenot community, listing the numbers of refugees in each of the colony's four church communities, adding up to a total of 438 useful subjects. Second, Girard added an unrelated note that "I may undertake my self To Procure Every year at the End of The bridge of Charlestowne fiveteen hundred barrels of Good Tarr at 88 p barrel, fifty Thousand weight of Pine Gumme at 106 p ct And A Parcell of Cyprus mast for The Second & Third Rate of the English man of warr." In a clever twist, he attached his own proposal to become active in the naval stores trade to an argument for naturalization. Huguenots had not forgotten how to argue for their value with their imperial masters.[74]

Nonetheless, it became apparent that the Huguenots would need to do more than charm imperial officials if they wanted to win their battle for recognition. It was local power brokers, in particular the anti-proprietary Goose Creek faction, who increasingly held the balance of power in turn-of-the-century South Carolina. In 1698 one of their number, James Moore, attained the governorship, replacing Archdale. His largest goal was the establishment of the Church of England in the province, and he courted the Huguenots to do so, astutely realizing that the combined forces of French and Anglicans would outnumber Carolina's sizable English and Scottish dissenting community. The refugees were happy to support establishment in return for political legitimacy, which earned them the ire of the dissenters. In one volley in the tract war between the two sides, a dissenter complained that Moore and his successor Nathaniel Johnson allowed "Strangers, and Aliens" to vote, and particularly "*almost every* Frenchman *who had never taken the Oaths to the Government*."[75] The Huguenots hated the dissenters in return. In 1707 a number of them made public statements attesting their belief that "the Gentlemen presbetarians would bring Tyrany upon us as pharoh did upon the Children of Israel," primarily by taking away the French community's right to vote and inherit property. The dissenters denied having any such plan, but the whole episode revealed something remarkable. Huguenot refugees had often used the language of Egyptian cruelty against their Catholic persecutors, but here they were turning it against English Presbyterians, whose ideas about theology and church governance resembled the refugees' Calvinism more than the beliefs of the established church. Politics made strange bedfellows and stranger enemies.[76]

The alliance between Anglicans and Huguenots succeeded in changing Carolina's political and religious landscape. In 1704 Nathaniel Johnson pushed through the Church Act, which finally established the Church of England in South Carolina. After strident opposition the Proprietors vacated the act, but a revised version passed two years later, setting up the structure of parishes and an advisory council that would exist for the better part of a century.[77] The colony's French population supported the acts, and for at least some of them, this support was more than just a political move. Like their brethren in other parts of the empire, Carolina Huguenots gravitated toward the established church during the early 1700s. The 1706 act turned two of the colony's three French Protestant churches into Anglican parishes, leaving only the church in Charleston outside the Church of England. The Huguenot enthusiasm for Anglicanism has long stood as a puzzling problem for historians of the early American refugees. As Calvinists, they should have preferred the dissenting side of English religious life, and many in Calvinist-majority places like New England and New York did just that, at least at first. As time passed, however, they increasingly abandoned their particular Calvinist churches for membership in the wider established church community. Virginia's Huguenot church was always part of the Anglican communion, and during the first decade of the 1700s New Rochelle's church turned, like those two parishes in South Carolina, to episcopacy. Even in places like Boston, many individual Huguenots abandoned their own church for the local branch of the Church of England.[78]

The Huguenot turn toward Anglicanism appears as the ultimate act of assimilation. Independent churches had been the primary requirement of the first refugee colonies, since their purpose after all was to preserve the French Protestant church for its ultimate return to the homeland. That would seem to be impossible in the context of the Anglican church, with a liturgy based on the Book of Common Prayer and a church hierarchy very different from the system of synods and consistories that had governed the old Protestant churches in France. Such a reading of Anglicanism as assimilation is overly simplistic. First of all, Huguenots were divided on how much autonomy to give up. And second, even within the Anglican fold, the refugees were able to negotiate a great deal of autonomy. In essence, their outward acceptance of "common prayer worship" allowed them to continue in the breach to follow their old liturgy. This was made possible by the fact that most of the French Protestant churches within the Anglican communion, from the Savoy Church in London to those in New Rochelle, Manakintown, and South Carolina, continued to operate fully in French, beyond the comprehension of any English observers.[79]

The story of Claude Philippe de Richebourg, the pastor who fled from Virginia to South Carolina, helps to demonstrate the process. It is difficult to decipher much about Richebourg's particular religious orientation before coming to America. One document described him as a "former Roman," implying that he had been a recent convert from Catholicism, but in the strange world of late seventeenth-century France, when Protestants (and some Catholics) crossed confessional lines frequently, it is hard to know exactly what that meant. His short tenure in Manakintown, where he seemed to advocate for a more traditionally French method of church governance, suggests that he was more of a traditionalist than some of his fellow refugees, but once in South Carolina he seemed to abandon all that. His new parish, St. James Santee in a heavily French part of the colony, was one of the two French-language parishes created by the Church Act of 1706. He took up his post there in 1712 and also took responsibility for occasionally ministering to the French minority in a neighboring parish, assisting the English minister Thomas Maule.[80]

On his arrival Richebourg appeared to be genuinely attached to the Anglican cause. An English divine, the commissary Gideon Johnston, reported that the people of the parish "had frequently declar'd, and were fully resolv'd to join intirely in Communion with the Church of England for the future," and the new minister shared in that goal. But clearly there were problems afoot at St.

James Santee. In late 1712 another refugee minister, Francis Le Jau, reported that the church had divided, like Manakintown before, into two factions, with "divisions and Quarrels and Swords drawn at the Church door." Le Jau presented Richebourg as a victim rather than the cause of the disturbances, but Johnston came around to a different opinion. He focused his critique on Thomas Maule's parish, where he alleged that the French parishioners had gone back on their pledge to conform. Maule had allowed Richebourg to preach in French, but soon discovered that the minister abandoned the "Cannons & Rubrick" of the church to embrace "the Geneva way." Richebourg allegedly criticized the decision of the French to join with the English in the parish, suggesting they should have remained separate to preserve a purer Calvinist church. Beyond that, Johnston believed that Richebourg's St. James Santee congregation was nearly united against the Church of England, along with a sizable proportion of the other French parish of St. Denis. As he put it pessimistically, "I have intirely lost their friendship without the least hope of ever recovering it again." Their hearts, he claimed, "are not with us, but at Geneva or Elsewhere."[81]

Significantly, Johnston had a much more positive opinion of the most prominent real Genevan in South Carolina, the Charleston minister Paul L'Escot. The child of French refugees, L'Escot trained as a minister with the noted divine Jean-Alphonse Turretini. While he had evidently been a good student—his lengthy correspondence with his former teacher is one of the most voluminous remaining records of Huguenot life in America and England—he had trouble finding gainful employment, which is why he ended up in Charleston's church in 1700, where he replaced the original pastor Élie Prioleau. Johnston claimed that despite being the minister of a nonconformist church, L'Escot supported the Anglican side in the dispute. He did so, moreover, in a way that recalled Tirel's directive to blend in. "He said every Church & Party of Christians had their own waies," Johnston said of L'Escot, "which they strictly & religiously adhered to; And why they, who were Members of the best of Churches, shoud not do so too, he coud not tell, nor coud he call their lukewarmness or tergiversation in this matter by too hard a name." Johnston also claimed L'Escot said "he woud not live a day without Episcopal Ordination, coud he bring his People to it, & heartyly wish'd, that all his countrymen were so wise, as to lay aside their ground-less prejudices, & once for ever to join in full & perfect comunion with the Church of England." In sum, he believed the Anglican Church to be the better church, especially if one chose to live in an English place, but stayed outside of it only to gratify the wishes of his Calvinist flock.[82]

L'Escot's surviving correspondence with Turretini confirms many of Johnston's impressions of the minister. He often described his close ties with various leading Anglicans, both in Carolina and England, and even forged

connections with the Bishop of London, who possessed ecclesiastical authority over the colonial churches. At one point he attempted to use his Swiss
connections to find a conforming minister for St. James Santee in 1709, at the beginning of the search that ultimately brought Richebourg to the parish.[83] His letters from Carolina gave lengthy descriptions of the province—probably to serve
as information for potential migrants in Geneva—but little commentary on
Carolina's religious divisions aside from mentioning the existence of conformist,
Presbyterian, and French churches.[84] After he left Carolina for England in 1719,
however, he gave some hints about how he had tried to manage divisions in the
colony. He complained to Turretini about a former acquaintance in Carolina,
an unnamed Parisian, who "declared himself my enemy." The man shared "certain extravagant religious visions" with L'Escot, but the minister had not reacted
favorably. The man was a fanatic, the pastor claimed, who had "made the circle
of Religions" and tended toward visions and prophecies, but in fact he clearly
resembled the French prophets who had preached in London not long before-
hand. L'Escot worried that the man had substantial power to harm his reputation, especially through the influence of a wealthy and well-connected sister.[85]

 This marginal complaint suggests a world of religious radicalism that lurked
beneath the surface of Carolina's Huguenot community. If most refugee
leaders, like L'Escot and Richebourg, claimed to reject radicalism and separation in all its forms, and desired, like Jean Tirel, to blend in with their English
neighbors, there were evidently some Huguenots who disagreed. A smattering
of radicals had found refuge across the ocean, and other refugees, while perhaps not embracing the extravagant visions of L'Escot's purported enemy,
still had little real affection for Anglicanism. As John Lawson reported on the
residents of Santee in 1708, just after they officially turned Anglican, "they are
all of the same Opinion of the Church of *Geneva*," and wished above all to live
"as one Tribe, or Kindred."[86] Ecclesiastical conformity, like naturalization, was
a strategy that some refugees used to find their way in an alien world. Some
undoubtedly did blend in, but others retained many of their old beliefs and
practices in the breach. Assimilation, in other words, was far from a quick or
simple process.

———

In 1713 the War of the Spanish Succession ended and peace returned to Europe
and its colonies. Few were more jubilant than the Huguenot refugees, who had
suffered so much during the previous decades of conflict. Only two years after
the end of hostilities another signal event occurred, as the old persecutor Louis
XIV met his demise. His great-grandson Louis XV, a boy of five, took the throne,
leading to a period of uncertainty as regents assumed control of the kingdom.

Writing to his brother in Normandy, New York merchant Thomas Bayeux reflected on these changes. He hoped that the Sun King's death would lead to a
relaxation of laws against Protestantism, and he "prayed to God" that he would
forgive and bless the *nouveaux convertis*, the poor Protestants who had become
Catholic to stay in France. While he hoped for improvement, he did not believe
that he himself would ever return to his homeland. He earnestly desired to "have
occasion to see you again and embrace you and your dear family," but he and his
family were "so well established and so attached here," and the voyage home was
too long. Indeed, his descriptions of his life made Bayeux somewhat resemble
John Laurens, another merchant he may have known personally. In other letters
to his mother he made clear that he was raising his children to be good English
subjects. They did study in a local French school, but he also made sure they
learned the empire's dominant language, and he intended to send his children to
England for schooling when they reached the proper age. Bayeux retained family
and business ties to Europe and France, but he plainly declared where his own
allegiances lay. He was a New Yorker and more importantly, a subject of King
George I.[87]

Bayeux's letters suggests a kind of end to the history of the Huguenot refuge.
The diaspora formed in order to preserve the French Protestant churches in
exile. Ministers like Pierre Simond or even Claude Philippe de Richebourg, as
they cozied up to their Dutch and British patrons, tried to preserve some level
of autonomy in their communities. For Bayeux and others, though, the rewards
of blending in were just too great. For their children, often raised in a bilingual
environment with no memories of the homeland, the process was even more
rapid. In the second generation, as numerous historians have attested, levels of
outmarriage were quite high among the Huguenots, and by mid-century many
of the French Protestant churches were gone, as they had few people left in
the pews. With a return to France now out of the question, Huguenots had no
reason to remain French any longer. They became British, or Dutch, or German,
and gradually their ancestry became a point of pride but little more than that.[88]
This was undoubtedly the case for some refugees. But it was not the universal
experience, and indeed, in some isolated cases refugees *did* manage to go home
again, even as they held on to their Protestantism and, paradoxically, their status
as subjects of another king's empire.

The people in question were the Huguenots of Saint-Christophe, or St. Kitts.
For nearly a century that small island was divided between French and English
sections, and the sizable Huguenot minority on the French side frequently
crossed the undefended border for church services—and many of them did the
same after the Revocation of the Edict of Nantes, settling around English America.
A significant number of islanders settled in New York, where they constituted

a key part of the refugee community; several were powerful merchants. After that exodus, St. Kitts became an important theater of war. During the 1690s and early-1700s the French and English conquered and reconquered the island several times in succession, until the Treaty of Utrecht finally brought calm in 1713. France then gave up its rights to Saint-Christophe, making the whole island British. In the wake of that treaty, officials in the Leeward Islands moved into the former French parts of the island, seeking to distribute land to deserving applicants—mostly English subjects who had lost their plantations in the late wars and felt they needed compensation.[89]

After the peace of Utrecht a number of Huguenots submitted petitions to the British Board of Trade. The documents tell an interesting collective story of families ripped apart by the Revocation and further inconvenienced during several decades of destructive conflict. Most of the petitions, significantly, came from women. One of them, Alletta de Coussage, was the wife of a Frenchman who had retired to the English side of the island and entered "in your Majesty's Service." She asked for the rights to her deceased father's plantation in the former French quarter of Cabesterre.[90] Two sisters named Mary and Margaret de Nampon asked for restitution of the family plot in the same area, noting that the family had to flee their land before the war "upon account of the Persecution."[91] Another woman, Martha Assailly, requested her father's former property "on Behalf of her Self Mother and Sisters." Her late father Peter had retired with the family to Boston after the Revocation, returned to St. Kitts in 1690 when the English briefly occupied the French part of the island, then departed "upon account of his Religion" again in 1697 when the Treaty of Ryswick returned parts of the island to France.[92] Some of these women had stayed on St. Kitts on the English side of the island during the war; others had scattered around the English Atlantic. But for all of them, the Treaty of Utrecht provided an opportunity to undo the dislocations of the last few decades and regain their old property.

The petitions rested the case for restitution on two pillars. One was the refugees' steadfast commitment to the Protestant faith. Each petition made sure to mention that it was religion that forced them out of their plantations. In addition, most of them mentioned their long service to the English cause in the subsequent two wars. Stephen Duport stressed that he was a "close prisoner of warr in France" at the time he lost his plantation, and that the French plied him with offers to change sides, but that he rejected them all "upon account of his Zeal & steddy fastness to the English government & the protestant Religion wherein he & his familly were ever brought up."[93] Another petitioner, Paul Minvielle de Bonnemere, made similar arguments in his attempt to obtain the land of his deceased relatives. The eldest, Daniel de Bonnemere, had abandoned his plantation after the Revocation, and his son, also named Daniel, had joined "Lord Rabys Regiment of Dragoons" and died in the English service. Minveille asked for the plantation in compensation for "what the fammily have suffered & Lost on ac-count of their steedy adherence to the protestant Religion and Constant Zeal for your Majesty's Government."[94] Another petitioner, Elizabeth Renault, "was Offered to be Restored to her whole Estate if she would change her Religion," but chose exile instead, since living in the English empire with her children "in a very Miserable Condition."[95]

The Board of Trade granted virtually all of the petitions without ques-tion. They only hesitated in the case of Madame Maigne, who had been a Catholic during the wars but had since married a Protestant and converted. All the others were "found to be fit Objects of His Majestys Compassion and may deserve his Grace & favour on account of their steady Adherence to the Protestant Religion."[96] Nonetheless, as in previous episodes in Huguenot his-tory, there was more to it than just charity. After two decades of warfare, St. Kitts was largely depopulated and unproductive, and making this key sugar is-land profitable was one of the Board of Trade's greatest priorities. Not surpris-ingly, the Huguenots presented themselves as the chosen people who could make the island productive as well as Protestant. There was an important dif-ference, however. In St. Kitts, these French Protestants were not striking off to new lands, with all the dislocation and labor that required. Instead, they were regaining their old estates—vast sugar plantations worked by slave labor that would now bring profits to the British rather than the French empire. These petitioners, unique among the tens of thousands of refugees who fled France and its empire, managed to maintain their faith and win back their homes at the same time.

Of course, most Huguenots were not so lucky. There would be no home-coming for Thomas Bayeux or the thousands of others who had escaped France. Nonetheless, the story of the St. Kitts Huguenots indicated the creative responses of the refugees to the fluid circumstances of the early 1700s. Assimilation was one practical measure that Huguenots took to fit in, but it was never complete, and sometimes it allowed the refugees to preserve important parts of their heritage beneath the surface. Moreover, even as Huguenot communities in the Americas, Africa, and Europe began to fade, individual refugees and their children became more and more prominent. By the middle of the eighteenth century, for instance, John Laurens's son Henry had become one of the most im-portant merchants in South Carolina. He did not speak French, but nonetheless acted as a benefactor to his father's countrymen and women who arrived in the colony during the 1760s, encouraging experiments in viticulture in the Carolina upcountry. More than that, by 1774 he decided that his father's attempts at as-similation had been mistaken. Henry made contact with family members back in

La Rochelle and even sent his son to Geneva, not London, for an education that would include the French language.[97] "French Protestans tho expatrioted ought not to be so negligent of their Origin," wrote one of Laurens's fellow Carolina Huguenots, as "it may sometimes be of service to them."[98] During the middle of the eighteenth century being a Huguenot could still be an asset. Assimilation was not as complete as it seemed.

Making the Empire Protestant

In the eighteenth-century world one encountered many characters with French names who were not quite French. One of those men was Pierre Simond the younger, a prominent British merchant. Simond was born in the Cape Colony, the eldest son of the minister to the Huguenot settlers in the Drakenstein Valley. The family moved back to the Netherlands in 1702, and Pierre spent much of his adolescence in various Dutch and Flemish towns where his father ministered to Dutch troops during the War of the Spanish Succession. Finally, after an apprenticeship to an Amsterdam merchant house, Pierre made his way to England, where he forged a business career, first in stock-jobbing but eventually in transoceanic trade. He was, like many of his Huguenot brethren, quite successful in that task. He built a firm, eventually known as Simond Hankey, that specialized in colonial commerce, especially the trade in sugar and slaves. By the end of his life in 1783, Peter Simond—as he became known—was one of the leading merchants of the British empire, as well as the owner of several plantations on the Caribbean island of Grenada. His French ancestry had proven no impediment, and indeed, few people remarked on Simond's Frenchness at all. He appeared to be a perfect, assimilated Briton—a model of how Huguenots blended in to their new host societies. Simond did not just survive; he thrived.[1]

He was not the only one. Dozens of Huguenots became leading merchants in the British and Dutch empires during the eighteenth century, turning families like the Faneuils, Bowdoins, and Jays into members of a nascent imperial aristocracy. Huguenots dominated outside of commerce as well. In the Church of England, for instance, many refugees or their children became ordinary ministers or even missionaries in Europe as well as places like South Carolina and New York. In politics and the military the children of refugees had even more success. Men with French surnames like Paul Mascarene and John Ligonier rose to the top of Britain's military establishment, often taking postings on the edges of the empire. The ranks of colonial governors and other high officials included a number of French people, who ruled places as diverse as St. Helena, Nova Scotia,

The Global Refuge. Owen Stanwood, Oxford University Press (2020). © Oxford University Press.
DOI: 10.1093/oso/9780190264741.001.0001

Suriname, and the Cape Colony. Given their relatively small numbers, the ubiq-
uity of Huguenot descendants in the military, commerce, and the church speaks
to a phenomenal ability to advance in foreign institutions.[2]

And yet, it has always proven difficult to fit these characters into a larger
story of the global Huguenot diaspora. Unlike their forefathers and mothers,
the refugees of the eighteenth century rarely wrote or spoke about their
experiences as Huguenots. Their talent came in blending in and pretending to
be the same as their English and Dutch neighbors. Many of them wrote more
often in English or Dutch than in French, ceased attending French church services, and gave up any hopes of returning to France to re-establish their church.
They appeared to be perfectly assimilated immigrants and thus dropped out
of the Huguenot story altogether. Genealogists have long noticed the many
Huguenots who rose to positions of prominence, but historians have rarely
followed suit.[3]

Nonetheless, there is plenty of evidence that the rise of many refugee
descendants to imperial leadership was far from a coincidence. The Huguenots'
impressive ability to blend in had something to do with it, but there was more.
French Protestants did not simply give up their Frenchness when they took
posts in the British or Dutch empires. Rather, they used their Frenchness
to their advantage. This process has been most appreciated in the case of
merchants, who utilized family and community networks to build trading
connections that joined empires together—even trading with France itself and
maintaining links to family members who stayed behind. These same sorts of
connections proved useful in politics, as leaders who could speak French and
work with French subject populations provided critical skills in an era of war
punctuated by uneasy peace. Even in the church, the cultural heritage of French
Protestantism—a faith that defined itself in relation to Catholic neighbors—
gave certain advantages to those ministering or missionizing on the edges of
empires.[4]

This story of Huguenot imperial mastery was primarily centered on the
British world. Since William of Orange crossed the Channel to England in
1688 many refugees had begun to see that kingdom as the center of Protestant
power, and English military prowess and the development of the economy
furthered this process. Two other events—the Act of Union of 1707 creating
the United Kingdom and the Hanoverian succession of 1714 that brought a
family of German Protestants to the throne and excluded all Catholic heirs—
only solidified the new United Kingdom's place as a leader of the Protestant
cause, as did the kingdom's strong performance against Louis XIV in the
War of the Spanish Succession. Of course, the Netherlands, Germany, and
Switzerland did not completely drop out of the story. Many merchants and
military men maintained their Dutch connections in particular, and most

refugees retained business partners and family members around the Protestant world and beyond. For the most ambitious or the most desperate, nonetheless, Great Britain and its growing empire provided the best opportunities for personal success.[5]

More than just personal ambition motivated these refugees and their descendants. As the empire naturalized these men—and virtually all of them were men, not women—they naturalized the empire as well, making it less of a singularly British institution and more of a force to further global Protestantism. This process was most clear in the Church of England. As an explicitly national faith, there was nothing about Anglicanism that lent itself naturally to global expansion, and even in Britain's own early empire the Church had a somewhat small footprint. This changed in the eighteenth century, as church leaders sought to turn it into a global institution. Huguenots proved particularly useful allies in this project since they possessed close connections to Protestants around Europe and experience in missionizing; they gave a veneer of credibility to the Anglican Church's attempt to cast itself as a primary catalyst for global Protestantism. This mission extended beyond the church to the military and political spheres as well, in which British leaders defined the empire as not just a national institution but a Protestant one. Many Huguenots who had gravitated to the empire in the wake of the Glorious Revolution shared the dream of turning it into a force for the advancement of godliness, especially by taking territories that had previously belonged to the French or other Catholic empires. Finally, merchants like Simond proved critical partners in this task, since their transnational commercial activities kept the empire profitable and often explicitly depended on Huguenot networks that transcended any one state or empire.[6]

The Huguenot mastery of British imperial institutions would seem to contradict the colonial vision that had dominated the Refuge since the first refugees had set up colonies in Germany during the 1680s. In some ways that was certainly true; refugees like Simond or officer Paul Mascarene had little interest in living in homogenous French communities and had given up on the old dream of preserving the French Protestant church in order to return to the homeland. Nonetheless, these seemingly assimilated Huguenots did not completely abandon their brethren in France. Beyond a general care for persecuted Protestants around the world, these well-connected men hoped that the British empire would support their persecuted coreligionists back in the homeland. In addition, they continued to advocate for Huguenot colonization of the New World, promoting their people as Protestant heroes with particular skills and aptitudes. After a lull in the early 1700s, Huguenot colonization plans reemerged in the 1720s and 1730s, eventually leading to a new age of refugee settlement schemes in the middle of the eighteenth century, one that was largely conceived and planned by these seemingly integrated refugees in the church, government, and commerce.

———

In 1708 Claude Grosteste de la Mothe believed that the Protestant world was on the cusp of a great breakthrough. For the last two centuries European Protestants had been mainly on the defensive, fighting a Catholic menace that had attempted to stop the progress of the gospel. Protestantism had survived all its trials, however, and in a new century la Mothe hoped godly people would move on to the next great task: "bringing the light to the very ends of the world." Catholics ridiculed Protestants for their lackluster record in creating overseas missions, but la Mothe would have none of it. After all, Protestants rejected the use of force in conversion, which precluded them from the huge "harvests of souls" bragged of by Catholic missionaries. In any case, the Protestants had been facing intense persecution of their own at the hands of Catholic enemies, especially Louis XIV. La Mothe called on the world's Protestants—particularly French-speaking ones—to devote themselves anew to extending God's kingdom to the farthest stretches of the globe. The shadows were gradually lifting, and soon the non-Christians of the world, including Jews, Muslims, and especially the pagans of the Indies, would come to Christ.[7]

The minister believed that Great Britain was providentially destined to lead this project. He paid particular homage to William III, the late king who had done so much to protect true religion in Europe by taking on Louis XIV's global ambitions and expelling the Catholic James II from the British throne. As important as these milestones had been, la Mothe cited another of William's accomplishments that may have been even more important. In 1701, only a short time before his untimely death, the king had chartered the Society for the Propagation of the Gospel in Foreign Parts (SPG), an Anglican missionary society that stood poised to lead the charge to turn the world Protestant, to "make conquests in the most distant countries." La Mothe called on all his French Protestant brethren to do what they could to help the SPG in its designs. Very few, he admitted, had the resources or skills to actually travel to the Indies to convert the pagans, but others could aid the effort with prayers and financial support, and by acknowledging that England—especially the Church of England—had attained the status as the institutional home of international Protestantism. "What glory to Great Britain," la Mothe wrote, "that God wants to use her to begin and execute his grand design to enlighten the universe!"[8]

In some ways, la Mothe's testimonial was not that surprising. The minister in Rouen before moving to London in 1685, la Mothe eventually gained a post as pastor in the French Church of the Savoy, the most prominent conformist

Huguenot church in the empire. A grateful refugee, la Mothe lauded the English acceptance of the French Protestants as one of the marks of their virtue. Ordinarily, he noted, "there is a kind of antipathy between neighboring countries," which stemmed from wars and "difference in manners." Nonetheless, the English had embraced the Huguenots as brothers and sisters in the faith, even supporting poor French Protestants out of their own coffers. This singular beneficence demonstrated England's special role in the Protestant world, as a "source of light for other Nations." If it was a typical expression of refugee gratitude, la Mothe's tribute to the SPG represented a transitional moment. Earlier ministers like Pierre Jurieu had also praised William III, but had not expressed such feelings for the institutional Church of England, nor usually for the principle of foreign conversion. La Mothe, on the other hand, seemed to tether the Huguenot cause to both the practice of conformity in England and the extension of Anglican Protestantism overseas.[9]

In fact, many Huguenots did take up la Mothe's call and join the SPG. During the eighteenth century a disproportionate number of refugees and their descendants became missionaries, ministers, or supporters of the society, and more than a few traveled to the Americas under its auspices. This movement was related to the general migration of Huguenots to the Church of England in both Britain and the colonies.[10] But it also represented a tactical, symbiotic alliance between the Society and some refugees. Leaders in the church recognized or at least believed that Huguenots would be especially good missionaries and advocates for their vision, especially in the New World. The refugees, meanwhile, were on the lookout for powerful institutions that could help them meet their own goals: whether it was managing their own congregations or bringing the faith to the "heathens" of America. The partnership between the SPG and the Huguenots represented strong continuity from earlier decades when the refugees had tried to promote themselves as key actors in the global Protestant community, and perhaps even agents in turning the rest of the world Protestant, as Paul Reboulet had expressed when he hoped refugees would "carry the Gospel to all the World."[11]

The SPG's particular mission made it especially eager to enlist the refugees in its work. In 1701 the churchman Thomas Bray founded the Society, a chartered organization that would manage the church's missionary efforts overseas, particularly in England's growing colonial empire. The Society had three main aims. Its first and most important was to combat the efforts by Catholics, especially the hated Jesuits, to convert the world's people. In this goal the SPG was little different from the earlier Company of New England, which had been organized by dissenters. Thomas Bray made particular note of the "*French* of *Canada*," who "draw over so many of these *Indians*, both to their Religion, and their Interests."[12] Beyond bringing the heathen peoples into the Church, the SPG also hoped to encourage conformity in colonial places where the established church had little sway, and dangerous dissenters like Quakers, Baptists, and Presbyterians deluded too many people with their errors. Finally, the SPG joined the larger campaign for a reformation of manners in both Britain and its colonial extensions, encouraging morality and discouraging vice, continuing the work of its sister organization, the Society for the Propagation of Christian Knowledge, and a plethora of other moral reform organizations around Britain.[13]

Huguenots could help the Society's mission in a number of ways. First, they had gained a reputation as effective missionaries. Some of this association may have simply come from their Frenchness—French Jesuits, after all, were the key rivals of the SPG and other Protestant missionaries in North America. But that was not the only reason. Since they had lived for decades as a Protestant minority in a Catholic country, Huguenot ministers were more adept than their English counterparts in arguing for the truths of Protestant Christianity, especially against the most common Catholic responses. In addition to their facility as controversialists, Huguenots had value for their status in the Protestant world. In the early eighteenth century the Church of England was still overcoming its past reputation as a persecutory institution that had targeted Calvinist dissenters in particular. By bringing Huguenots into the fold, the Church could establish itself as a bastion of international Protestantism. Then its leaders could convince dissenters to give up their separate congregations and rejoin the national church. This program involved a great deal of international outreach, especially to the Protestant pastors of Geneva and Switzerland, who seemed sympathetic to the Church of England's mission, especially in overseas efforts, and played such an important symbolic role in international Protestantism. La Mothe himself reprinted a testimonial from one of Geneva's leading ministers granting approbation to the SPG's efforts.[14]

Even before la Mothe's endorsement appeared in print, Huguenots were already active in the SPG. One of the first and most exceptional was the merchant turned catechist Élie Neau. Indeed, Neau was probably the most famous refugee in British America at the time, as his inspirational story of keeping the faith while a prisoner in Louis XIV's galleys had attracted a wide Protestant readership in both French and English. In 1703, for instance, the former Dutch Reformed minister in Albany Godfrey Dellius sent a copy of Neau's book to the secretary of the SPG from Amsterdam "to satisfye your curiosity."[15] The book in question was probably the lengthy French-language account of Neau's captivity that had appeared in Rotterdam three years earlier, a gripping devotional tract that combined letters from Neau throughout his captivity with testimony of his character from his childhood pastor Jean Morin, who had since taken up a post in Bergen-op-Zoom in the Netherlands.[16] The most complete account, the book chronicled Neau's capture and five years of imprisonment in the galleys and dungeons of France. A shorter version in Neau's own words had been published in London in 1699, and the Boston Puritan Cotton Mather issued his own tract using Neau's trials as an example of Protestant steadfastness in the face of popish persecution. By the time Dellius wrote, Neau needed no introduction at the SPG's headquarters. They had already been corresponding with him for some time about missionary techniques in North America, and in March 1703 the Society decided to hire Neau as a catechist in New York, where he would work toward the religious instruction of all who needed it, but especially young people, Indians, and African slaves.[17]

Neau's gradual migration into the Church of England revealed much about both Neau and the Anglican Church at the dawn of the eighteenth century. In 1704 he was still a member of the Consistory of New York City's French (Calvinist) Church and a favorite of everyone from New York's French minister to Puritans like Cotton Mather. He gave no indication of being on the verge of conversion, and indeed the published accounts of his imprisonment were replete with Calvinist themes of sin and redemption. Nonetheless, Neau himself claimed that even in the dungeons of Marseille he was beginning to move toward Anglicanism. His chief comfort during his imprisonment came from an English bible, with parts of the Book of Common Prayer appended to the end. "I had learnt in my Dungeons part of the English Liturgy by heart," reported Neau in a letter to the SPG's secretary, and that had made him resolve to join the Church of England "through a Principle of Conscience." He represented his final act of conversion, when he cut off all ties to the French churches that had sustained him for his whole life, as merely the formalization of something that had started long before, in the dark times of his captivity. The story could only have appealed to the heads of the Church, since it established Anglicanism as a tool of resistance against Catholicism, and perhaps even as the natural leader in the international Protestant movement.[18]

Nonetheless, there is something slightly too convenient about Neau's story. It is difficult to accept that self-interest did not play some role in Neau's sudden move toward the established church. After his return to New York, Neau dedicated himself to the design of a "reformation of manners and propagation of the knowledge of God" in the English world. As early as 1701 he was promoting this design to his fellow refugee Gabriel Bernon, sending along tracts for distribution in Rhode Island that may have come from the SPG's sister organization, the Society for the Propagation of Christian Knowledge. Neau's plan was not overtly sectarian; he seemed to be hoping for something of a return to first principles that could unite all Protestants—an outcome not unlike that advocated by Huguenots like Claude Grosteste de la Mothe or by latitudinarian Anglicans. He may have believed early on that there was no great problem with remaining active in the French Church while also courting the

Elias Neau *in the Dungeon,*
as described in Page 48.

Figure 6.1 Élie Neau's steadfastness for the Protestant faith during his French captivity made him a hero on both sides of the Atlantic. This illustration from a 1749 edition of his book portrays his time in a Marseille prison. From *A Short Account of the Life and Sufferings of Elias Neau* (London, 1749). Courtesy of the Beinecke Rare Book and Manuscript Library, Yale University.

support of an Anglican organization like the SPG. In any case, he ascribed to the common belief that he and his fellow refugees were well suited to help bring about this moral reformation. He thought that as someone who had also abandoned his country and sacrificed everything for God, Bernon would be especially willing to join the cause.[19]

Neau obviously believed that the SPG represented the best path forward for his project for the reformation of manners in the New World. For their part, the Society proved just as enthusiastic about Neau as he was about them. They resolved to hire him as a catechist even though he was not an ordained minister—probably because he had important connections in London, especially to Claude de la Mothe, and his fame in the Protestant world made him a good catch. Nonetheless, there were some conditions attached to his employment. Early on, some Anglican officials in New York opposed his appointment. Everyone agreed that he was a "good man" and a model Christian, but some, including the city's Anglican minister William Vesey, worried about appointing a merchant from another church, and a Calvinist one at that. His English was poor and he had "never yet communicated with us," meaning that he did not attend Trinity Church, the city's conforming congregation. Vesey worried that encouraging Neau would only embolden the myriad nonconformist preachers who worked in the colony and undermined the church's mission.[20] Nonetheless, the Society's leaders in London overrode Vesey's objections, and by the end of 1705 the minister promised to work with Neau, who had by this time broken all ties to the French church and joined the English one. This move assuaged his conscience, Neau reported, even if it earned him the ire of his former brethren in the Huguenot congregation.[21]

It was unclear how Neau came to feel so passionate about missionizing New York's non-Christians. It may have come from his belief in moral reform, since he viewed both Indians and Africans as morally suspect—though he blamed traders and slave owners for many of those moral lapses. At any rate, he placed conversion of both groups of non-Christians in a confessional context as part of the struggle between Protestants and Catholics. The contest for Indian souls was a central part of the SPG's propaganda—champions of the Society like White Kennett held up the example of the "Black Legend" of Spanish cruelty, explaining that the Spanish had brought about conversions by fire and sword, while the English would use only love and persuasion.[22] Apparently the SPG first corresponded with Neau by asking him about techniques for converting America's natives, especially the Iroquois, but he was uninterested in the task. A successful missionary would need to learn the language, and most Indians lived far from New York City. Connecting the SPG to earlier missionary efforts, Neau claimed to have known New England's "Apostle to the Indians" John Eliot, saying that while Eliot was a devoted Christian, Neau "never saw any [Indian] that was truly converted."[23]

Instead, he advocated for a less glamorous mission, to New York's enslaved Africans. Mostly due to the negligence of their masters, Neau reported, most of the city's Africans lived in ignorance of Christianity. Unlike Indians, they resided in the city and could easily be catechized, at least if their masters consented to sending them for instruction. Combating the standard fear that Christianized slaves would seek their freedom, Neau countered by using the example of Catholic colonies, especially the French islands where he had spent most of his teenage years. If the French slaves could come to the church but remain in slavery, so too could those in New York and other English colonies, and indeed Neau lobbied for a law that specified conversion would bring no change in a slave's status. This change largely brought reluctant slave owners on board, and over subsequent decades Neau worked to convert dozens of enslaved New Yorkers. The program did not always go smoothly. A foiled slave insurrection in 1712 led some whites to denounce Neau's school as a possible venue where slaves could plot rebellion, but the school survived, making Neau a key figure in the early history of black Christianity in North America. As late as 1718 he was reporting on the progress of his mission to the Bishop of London, while still complaining that masters "do not care in the least for the salvation [*salut*] of their domestics."[24]

While justly famous for his efforts to evangelize slaves, Neau performed other functions for the SPG as well. For one thing, he was on the vanguard of their effort to bring French Protestants into the Church of England. The church's efforts focused especially on Daniel Bondet and his New Rochelle congregation. Bondet had been a missionary to the Indians in Oxford before moving to New York, and like Neau had connections both to New England's Puritan leadership and prominent Huguenots like Claude Grosteste de la Mothe. In 1707, through la Mothe's intercession, he managed to gain the ear of the SPG. Bondet needed a new church building for his congregation, and the SPG was willing to help, but with the predictable condition that the New Rochelle Huguenots join the Church of England. With Élie Neau's strong support, Bondet embraced the established church, even though it caused an immediate and serious rift in his congregation. Bondet left no testimonial of his spiritual reasons for embracing the Anglican Church, but for him, as for many Huguenots, it was a way of maintaining community while also developing links to official power.[25]

South Carolina was perhaps an even more important mission field for the SPG. As in New York, Huguenots played a disproportionate role in the Society's efforts. Missionary Francis Le Jau, unlike Neau, was not famous and never in his correspondence did he remark on his refugee past. Indeed, he appeared as an almost perfectly assimilated Briton. A migrant to England and then Ireland as a young man, Le Jau studied at Trinity College Dublin and eventually attained a doctoral degree before finding employment at one of London's Huguenot churches. By 1700 he had earned the attention of Henry Compton, the longtime advocate for refugees who as Bishop of London enjoyed jurisdiction over the colonies. Compton recommended Le Jau for a posting in the Leeward Islands, where he became a minister and missionary and must have rubbed shoulders with some of the dozens of Huguenots who found homes there, especially in St. Kitts. After delivering a lengthy report on his experiences there to the SPG on his return in November 1705, Le Jau headed to a new posting. The Society "were of opinion" that he would be a good candidate for a ministerial position in Goose Creek, a rural parish just outside Charleston, South Carolina.[26]

Le Jau's primary responsibility was to minister to the region's English majority, but his Huguenot ancestry undoubtedly proved valuable for an Anglican missionary in that particular colony. After all, there were many French Protestants living there, and the established church was in the middle of a pitched ideological battle with English dissenters about whether to officially establish the Church of England in the colony. The French could hold the balance of power in the dispute, and Le Jau was one of the key actors who sought to bring the colony's Huguenots over to Anglicanism. Henry Compton himself noted that one of Le Jau's tasks was "to take care of the French Colony," and early in his tenure he paid several visits to preach to the Huguenots.[27] In April 1708, for instance, he visited the French congregation in the Orange Quarter, where he "settled their Vestry and school" and promised to provide the French with bibles and books of common prayer in their language. Thus the Anglican church added another parish, and soon another French church, that of St. Denis, joined the conformist fold as well.[28] This was especially welcome since, as Le Jau reported, the colony was awash in various heresies.

Nonetheless, ministering to the French was not Le Jau's main function. Along with his normal duties to the English, he dedicated himself to la Mothe and the SPG's favorite task of converting Carolina's non-Christians. He proved more sanguine than Neau about the eventual conversion of Native Americans. He erroneously identified a local language, Savannah, as a kind of American lingua franca, suggesting that if missionaries learned the tongue they could easily convert large swaths of the continent's peoples, as far north as Canada. He even shared a version of the Lord's Prayer in Savannah with his colleagues in London. Early on in his mission he viewed the Indians positively—he claimed they "do make us ashamed by their life, Conversation and Sense of Religion," and needed only Christ to make their lives complete. The main impediment to that work, he claimed, came not from the Indians themselves but from English traders who corrupted the Indians' morals and encouraged an intertribal slave trade that destroyed communities. Indian slavery was widespread in South Carolina, and while Le Jau, himself a slave owner, believed the slaves performed a "necessary service," he worried they were "the price of great many Sins."[29] Events were to prove him correct, when the Yamasees, who he considered apt targets for conversion, turned against the colonists and temporarily forced Le Jau from his parish. While in good Calvinist style he blamed the people's sins for the calamity, he singled out "the manner how the Indian Trade has been Carry'd," and indeed the slave trade in particular played a key role in the conflict.[30]

The African slaves who formed a majority in Goose Creek occupied more of Le Jau's attention. Though Le Jau never mentioned Élie Neau's contemporary efforts in New York, he sought to do much the same thing in his parish, inviting Africans to become catechumens and eventually even communicants in the church. Like Neau, he saw this task as part of a larger emphasis on moral reform. "All vice reigns here scandalously," he reported, and he defined his project as the promotion of Jesus Christ "in that part of the World where I am afraid Mammon has hitherto got too many Worshippers."[31] Though no opponent of slavery, he saw both masters' resistance to Christianizing slaves and their brutal treatment of them as moral failures. "Indeed," Le Jau wrote, "few Masters appear Zealous or even pleased with what the Missionaries try to do for the Good of their Slaves, they are more Cruel Some of them of late Dayes than before, They hamstring main & unlimb those poor Creatures for Small faults."[32] Despite this opposition, Le Jau slowly increased the number of black communicants in his parish, an achievement that he believed to be an important one in the work of moral reformation for all the colony's inhabitants. By early 1716 Le Jau bragged that his enslaved catechumens "have behaved themselves very well upon all occasions, so as to disarm and silence Envy itself." Those who could read the bible prayed with those who could not "and took no notice of some Profanne men who laught at their Devotions."[33]

One group of converts stood out among Le Jau's students. A number of slaves in the colony were baptized Catholics, and the missionary took particular notice of them, suggesting that he retained the desire to argue with Catholics that defined so much of the Huguenot project. In 1711 he reported on "two poor Negroe Slaves born & brought up among the Portuguese that are very desirous to Abjure the popish heresy's." Le Jau instructed the slaves for two full years before bringing them into communion with the church, reporting with pleasure that one of them served as "a pattern of faithfullness & Sobriety to all the slaves in the Parish."[34] Two years later he hoped to "receive the abjuration of a Negroe woman that had been bred in Guadelupe, but now Expresses a great desire to serve God according to his Word."[35] In welcoming these former Catholic slaves into the Anglican church, Le Jau was not just glorifying God by attracting more converts, but winning souls that had been lost to popery, a key goal of both Huguenot ministers and the SPG.

Le Jau and Élie Neau represented Claude Grosteste de la Mothe's vision in perfect terms. Though not English themselves, they embraced the Church of England and the SPG as institutions that would be best poised to bring about the tasks of moral reformation and conversion of the world's peoples that were common to many in the Huguenot diaspora. Their embrace of this foreign institution represented a tactical alliance, since the Society benefited from having such zealous and talented men within the fold. For other Huguenots who gravitated to the SPG and the Church of England, however, the relationship involved less principle and more interest. Such was certainly the case for several other South Carolina Huguenots supported by the Church of England in the early 1700s. For these clerics, the Church represented less a way to change the world than to secure a living.

As the Huguenot churches turned to conformity a number of French ministers came to the colony in search of stable employment. One of them, a Swiss minister named James Gignilliat, disgraced himself in fairly short order, leaving his parish to marry an elderly refugee widow, who he then deserted before returning to

Europe with much of her money.[36] Others were less brazen opportunists. Albert Pouderous, who took up a posting in the colony in the early 1700s, noted that he "abandoned every Thing for the cause of the Gospel" and eventually joined the Church of England, "finding her [to] Conform with the word of god and with the primative church." After several years preaching in London he moved to Saint James Santee, South Carolina, where he pieced together a living with the meager salary provided by the SPG and other public and private sources. He claimed that he ministered to eighty families, nearly all French, along with an "indiens man bound a christian that I instruct" and one black slave. The church ceremonies "we observe exactly by the canons and Constitutions of the church of england," though entirely in French. Indeed, Pouderous could barely write in English. The Church of England and the SPG provided a path to a competence, if not to opulence.[37]

Another episcopal minister in the colony, John La Pierre, was a slightly more ambiguous character. Little is known about La Pierre's early life; he may not have been a refugee at all, but a descendent of Huguenots who migrated to England in earlier times. Like Le Jau, he attained a degree in theology from Trinity College Dublin and came to the SPG's attention when they began the search for a conformist pastor for the French parish of St. Denis, located in the Orange Quarter.[38] His linguistic competencies and connections to highly placed people, including once again Claude Grosteste de la Mothe, secured his appointment. While he was undoubtedly qualified, he did seem to really need the work. Two of his parishioners reported on La Pierre's arrival in August 1708, noting that the minister had "a blind Wife and a very pretty little Girl." His flock voted him some aid in the meantime, including an enslaved woman to keep the house, while he waited for his £50 salary promised from "the Publick fund of the Country." The congregation loved La Pierre's inaugural sermon and reported that "Mr de la Pierre is as much admired & esteemed by the English as he is by the French, for besides his sweet and affable Temper he is counted one of the most able Preachers in French that ever appeared in this Colony."[39]

La Pierre's mission was very different from that of his friend and colleague Francis Le Jau. In a letter to la Mothe back in London, he rejected missionary work in the most explicit way. He knew that evangelizing Indians and slaves was a key aim of the Society but he believed both tasks to be impossible. The natives were an "a confused heap of vagabonds with no fixed places, whose occupation is hunting and fishing," and who frequently conspired against Europeans. African slaves, meanwhile, were "not proper for conversion, because once they gain understanding, it is then that they become insolent, and when they convert to the faith they still retain the practice of polygamy." In short, he gainsaid Le Jau in almost every particular, and directly contradicted la Mothe's own insistence that a charitable Christian must try to keep the heathens from going to hell. Instead, La Pierre preferred to wage the fight for Anglicanism against "enthusiasts" of all sorts. He noted that a tract of the French prophets—the fanatical, millenarian French Protestants who la Mothe and other "respectable" refugees did so much to combat—had circulated in the colony. "I occupy myself above all," La Pierre concluded, "in refuting him from the pulpit to prevent his venom from infecting the spirit of these poor people."[40]

The minister waged a long but at times half-hearted struggle to keep his congregation in the conformist camp. Like many Huguenots, the people of Saint Denis parish divided over how much to accept Anglicanism. Many, like their minister, viewed the Church of England as an important partner in the international Protestant movement, but others agreed with the nonconformist pastor in New Rochelle who said "he finds our [Anglican] Church & that of Rome, as like one another, as two Sisters can be."[41] La Pierre performed a delicate dance in an attempt to keep both his parishioners and his English overlords happy, stressing his Anglican credentials in letters to superiors while making church practice in St. Denis look more like the French Calvinism the people of the parish expected. More than anything, however, he wanted a higher salary. As early as his letter to la Mothe he was complaining that he could not live on what he was paid, and by the 1720s he had left the French congregation altogether, setting off for North Carolina where he ministered in a number of English parishes. While he was far less remembered, it may have been La Pierre rather than Le Jau who represented the most typical Huguenot divine. While generally attached to the Protestant episcopal cause, he was mostly just willing to work with any institution that could guarantee him a steady living.[42]

Nonetheless, the Huguenot impulse to missionize did not die, and appeared again later in the century in some unlikely places. In 1750 the missionary Jean-Baptiste Moreau received an SPG subsidy to go to Nova Scotia. A convert from Catholicism who had moved at some point to England, he eventually ended up in the town of Lunenberg, which was the center of the government's plans to use foreign Protestants, both Huguenot and German, to settle the province. Moreau's initial task was to serve the town's sixteen French families, but he went far beyond that charge, eventually preaching to the Germans as well and attempting to unite the town's diverse inhabitants under one Anglican umbrella. His mission included even Catholics and the local Mi'kmaq Indians. In 1760, for instance, Moreau presided as a Frenchman named Dominic Du Laurier publicly abjured "the errors of the Church of Rome . . . before a crouded Congregation of French, Germans, & English."[43]

With the Indians he made an even greater effort. The Mi'kmaq had welcomed Catholic missionaries for decades, and Moreau, like many British leaders, considered these missionaries key impediments to peace in the region, since they blackened the reputation of the British and encouraged the Indians to commit acts of violence. Moreau believed that by bringing the Mi'kmaq to Anglicanism he could make them faithful subjects, and he engaged in a bit of a spiritual warfare for these Indian souls with French Jesuits and Acadians, who were based in Newfoundland and Canada. In 1766 Moreau baptized twelve children while also combating the false propaganda of the Catholics, who circulated a fictitious letter from Jesus Christ that the Indians were supposed to wear next to their hearts. The letter "threatned [them] with eternal Damnation, if they fail in any point of the Romish Religion" and required them to "separate from those with a different opinion." For Moreau, the front line of confessional conflict was the battle for Mi'kmaq souls, which could end up determining if the Indians became friends or remained foes.[44]

A similar plan materialized around the same time thousands of miles across the ocean. Samuel Poirier, a spokesperson for a group of British merchants trading in Africa, wondered how to bring Senegal, a region dominated by the French, into the British fold. His answer was to contact the SPG and urge them to dispatch missionaries to the region. It would be impossible to "attach the Inhabitants of this place in any degree to our Interests," Poirier argued, until the British could "wean them in some measure from the French, & from the supersition of their Religion." The best person to fulfill the plan would be "a French Huguenot Clergyman, or one capable of preaching in that language," since the West Africans, like the Mi'kmaq, already had extensive experience with French traders and Catholic missionaries. The fact that Poirier made this particular suggestion was significant. He himself was the son of a refugee, the former governor of St. Helena and wine experimenter Stephen Poirier. Members of the second generation continued to believe in the special status of Huguenots, destined to travel the world and use their cultural competencies to bring more people into the Protestant communion.[45]

In the end, Claude Grosteste de la Mothe's dream of converting the world's people to Protestantism did not come to pass. Despite the efforts of Huguenots like Le Jau and Neau, the Anglican missions to slaves and Indians never rivaled those of the Catholics in their success. Even in the more modest task of bringing dissenters, including French Calvinists, into the church, the SPG's successes were incomplete. From New Rochelle to Saint Denis Parish and elsewhere, almost every French congregation resisted the coming of common prayer worship. Nonetheless, the stories of missionaries like Neau, and even of ordinary ministers like La Pierre, were important milestones in the development of the Refuge. These refugees saw the institutional Church of England less as the true church and more as a powerful institution that could distribute largesse or help the world's Protestants achieve their common goals. To be sure, embracing the church could be a powerful tool of assimilation, especially at a time when the enthusiasm of the French prophets made Huguenots suspect. Nonetheless, there was more to the actions of these ministers than a desire to assimilate. If the church made them more English, they also made the Church and the SPG more cosmopolitan, anchoring it to an international Protestant cause and the task of converting the world's peoples.

———

As Élie Neau sought to convert slaves in New York, another Frenchman named Michel de Monsegur put forward a very different kind of scheme. An officer in the French marine, Monsegur served in Newfoundland during the 1690s, when that remote colony, split between England and France, saw a number of skirmishes in the War of the League of Augsburg. At some point after that he defected to England, where he inhabited the circle of an eccentric "marquis" named Guiscard, a French Catholic who was allied with Pierre Jurieu and hoped to lead a French and English invasion force into the heart of France itself.[46] Monsegur's plan was perhaps not quite that bold, but it demonstrated the ways that French defectors, especially Huguenots, could be useful in times of war. Of course, many refugees served in the British, Dutch, and German military forces in their wars against Louis XIV. Huguenot men of all ranks, but especially gentlemen like Monsegur, had rallied to the banners of William of Orange and the Elector of Brandenburg. Like the churchmen who joined the Church of England, these military men mixed principle and interest when they pledged their fealty to foreign princes. They believed their new masters to be guardians of the international Protestant cause, but they also needed work, and the military was one of the key routes of advancement for men of a certain class with few financial resources.[47]

These Huguenot military men often ended up on the edges of empire. French regiments in Ireland played a key role in the Williamite wars there during the 1690s, and Huguenot officers joined both the Dutch and English East India Companies. In addition, many of the refugees had served in the French colonies, which is where Monsegur's ambitions lay. He recommended a bold design on the settlement of Plaisance (Placentia to the British), the main French settlement in Newfoundland. It was "the most beautiful colony in all of America, and the best place for commerce, and an admirable retreat for ships of war."[48] He believed that Great Britain could easily conquer the small but strategic colony, and the key was its governor, a French officer named Daniel de Subercase. Subercase came from a Béarnais Huguenot family, and remained a "good Protestant in his soul," according to Monsegur. The Subercase family had faced intense persecution after the Revocation, and Monsegur knew that the king's actions bothered Subercase because he had seen some letters that the governor had written to his father from Canada in the 1690s. In 1708

Monsegur still believed that Subercase's Protestantism made him a possible ally. With the governor's defection, the British could take Newfoundland without a fight.[49]

Monsegur laid out an intricate plan to bring Subercase over to the cause. First the British would send a ship to Plaisance under French colors. The captain and crew of the ship would be French—or at least proficient enough speakers to pass as French. The supposed French commander would give the governor two letters. The first, a fake, would lay out the ship's fictitious mission to undertake raids against English settlements to the south. The second would reveal the ship's true purpose: to come in the name of Queen Anne, "the protector of Christianity," to extend the same protection to Subercase "that she has already done for the many poor Christians in France." After the governor signed on, more ships, still under French colors and with French crews, would descend on the port, and once they revealed themselves to be British, Subercase would have no choice but to surrender. Moreover, the governor could retain his honor, since he could tell the French that he was honestly tricked by the British ruse, believing them to be his own men. Thus Newfoundland would become completely British, and Subercase would avenge his family's bad treatment.[50]

Of course, Monsegur believed himself to be the perfect man to lead such an expedition. He had served the queen with distinction in Ireland, he said, and spent years planning his Newfoundland design. He claimed to act for two intertwined purposes: first, "the legitimate grounds of Christianity and religion" had drawn him to Queen Anne's service. Once there, he also claimed to act for "the good of the Nation." As the queen's ministers repeatedly ignored his entreaties, Monsegur became more and more strident about the benefits of his design. It would not just bring a new colony into the British empire; it could be the decisive turning point in a war that had stretched on for years with little resolution. The cod fishery, Monsegur claimed, was so central to the economy of maritime France that its failure would lead to widespread distress. The economy would collapse, and ordinary people would rise in revolt, which would then pave the way for a British invasion of France which, if it focused on maritime regions with large populations of former Protestants, could easily succeed. Monsegur's plan thus related to those by his patron Guiscard and others to take the fight to France itself, while also revealing the central importance of overseas trade in winning the war. For their part, British authorities were rightly skeptical and gave no support to the plan. Daniel de Subercase, meanwhile, never wavered in his loyalty to Louis XIV.[51]

Even though it never happened, Monsegur's planned invasion of Newfoundland perfectly demonstrated the ways Huguenots could make themselves useful in foreign militaries. After all, no one knew the enemy better. It was Monsegur's special knowledge of Subercase's family circumstances and snooping at his letters that inspired the design in the first place, and only French people like him were capable of manning the faux-French ships that would lead the invasion force. In addition, Monsegur demonstrated the particular aptitude of French officers and soldiers on the colonial peripheries. It was there, after all, in the borderlands between British and French colonies, where the intercultural talents of the Huguenots proved especially valuable. In addition, Monsegur was far from the only refugee with experience in France's overseas empire. The French Navy had employed a number of Protestants, even in very prominent positions. As with the missionaries in the SPG, there is no reason to think that these people were not sincere in their attachment to the British state and the Protestant cause. At the same time, they saw these kinds of foreign military adventures as paths to personal profit. Monsegur admitted as much when he noted that aside from the benefits to queen and church, the Plaisance expedition "would be a great increase of glory for me."[52]

The British and Dutch military establishments abounded with characters like Monsegur. After the Revocation a plethora of young French gentlemen flooded into the Netherlands or German states. Lacking any kind of practical skills and too high born to be laborers, many of them pledged their services to the largest Protestant armies—the Elector of Brandenburg was one key candidate, but more of them went to the Prince of Orange. When the latter invaded England and became William III, many of them, including Monsegur, moved with their king across the Channel and joined the famous "French regiment" in Ireland during the 1690s. By the turn of the century French officers had earned high places in the English army, and others held similar positions in continental forces. While the most well connected found postings in European capitals, others ended up on the peripheries, from the Dutch East Indies to English America.[53]

The Huguenot exodus into foreign armies did not end with the Glorious Revolution and the Williamite Wars. Younger Protestant sons continued to cross the border to pledge their services well into the eighteenth century. One interesting Dutch example was Joseph de Grandprés, born around 1700 in Valenciennes in northern France, who somehow migrated to the Netherlands as a teenager, where he signed on as a soldier of the East India Company. He ended up in the Cape Colony, where he rose to the office of secretary of the Political Council. Known by this time as Josephus de Grandpreez, he conducted a lengthy correspondence during peacetime with the French governor of the Mascarene Islands during the 1750s and 1760s, before the outbreak of the Seven Years' War. The documentary record is silent on how this ordinary French soldier reached the upper rungs of Dutch officialdom, but clearly his Frenchness was an asset in his dealings with the Mascarene governor. He maintained an active trade with the French colonies in the Indian Ocean, sending them wine and grain—the two things the Cape produced in quantity—in exchange for wood, which was sorely lacking. On an imperial borderland, as Grandprés demonstrated, intercultural competency could go a long way.[54]

Even more interesting examples of these competencies appeared in the British empire. While a number of Huguenots rose through the ranks, the phenomenon is best seen through the fortunes of two men from the same town, Castres in Upper Languedoc, who both migrated to the Netherlands in the 1690s and ended up in England. The elder man, Jean-Louis Ligonier, was born in 1680, the heir to minor nobility in that majority-Protestant town. His father made a tactical decision to convert to save his estate in 1685, while many others in the family chose exile, including a number of young Jean's maternal uncles who entered the Prince of Orange's army. The younger man, Jean-Paul Mascarene, entered the world in 1685, right as the drama of the Revocation unfolded. Unlike Ligonier's father, Jean Mascarene the elder stayed true to his faith, and after an initial sentence of life in the galleys Louis XIV expelled him from the kingdom. He escaped to the Netherlands, where two of his brothers had, like the Ligonier brothers, signed on with William of Orange. Young Paul Mascarene's mother converted to Catholicism and therefore gained all of her departed husband's estate, leaving Paul to enjoy a comparatively privileged childhood, since his father had been a prominent lawyer.[55]

Thus Jean-Louis Ligonier and Jean-Paul Mascarene came of age as (official) Catholics in a town where most of the population consisted of recent converts to the king's faith, though neither really embraced Catholicism. Ligonier's family maintained private worship in the safety of their chateau, and while Mascarene's mother remained a nominal Catholic, his paternal grandmother made sure he did not stray from his godly roots, while also reminding young Paul of the heroism of his father's sacrifice. Even as a young child, Paul later recalled, he made imaginary rides to Utrecht on his "hobby horse" to see his absent father. Around 1696, each of these boys decided to leave the kingdom and join family members in the Refuge. Ligonier was sixteen when he left Castres to rendezvous with his uncle in Utrecht, joining another brother who made a similar journey. The timing was certainly not accidental: by 1696 it was becoming clear that the end of the War of the League of Augsburg would not bring a relaxation of conditions for France's Protestants and perhaps would bring the opposite. Paul Mascarene was only eleven, but his grandmother and uncle chose to spirit him out the country, first to Geneva to the hands of family friends and eventually, they hoped, to his father in Utrecht.[56]

Once the young men reached the Refuge, they needed family and community connections to ensure success in what remained a tough refugee labor market. Ligonier found these connections mainly through his maternal uncles, well-connected Huguenots who had gravitated to the military and served in Ireland during the last war. Soon after arriving in Utrecht his uncle there decided to send young Jean-Louis in that direction, thinking that "it will be easier to purchase some employment there [in Ireland], which will enable me to live better than in this country or elsewhere." By 1702, as looming war with France necessitated a larger army, Ligonier received his first commission as well as naturalization as an English subject.[57]

Mascarene's journey was more difficult. He found refuge in Geneva with close friends from Castres the Rapin family, who had connections to the top rungs of the Anglo-Dutch nobility. The Rapins then sent young Paul Mascarene on to Utrecht, where he tragically arrived two days after his father's death. Luckily for Paul, the Rapins maintained a residence in that city as well, and continued to care for him as he came of age. Like Ligonier's uncles, they had close connections to William III's army, and they used these links to get a posting for Mascarene, who by 1706 followed Ligonier to England in search of employment. The exact time-line is unknown, but by that year Mascarene received his first commission and naturalization, in the midst of what was quickly becoming a global war. He may have crossed the Channel somewhat earlier, however, since in a letter to his son he made reference to some time spent living in London's refugee community.[58]

Both Ligonier and Mascarene ended up in places where biconfessional, bi-cultural backgrounds proved useful. Ligonier traveled to the most important theaters of the war—the Low Countries and Spain—before ending up on the island of Minorca. British forces captured the island from the Spanish in 1708, eager to possess a strategic port not far from the French fleet's Mediterranean headquarters in nearby Toulon. The island was a bit of a backwater; its popu-lation had declined for some years, and it had few exports aside from a small amount of wine. Nonetheless, the British believed it could be a key to mastery in the Mediterranean, and by 1712 they determined to make it part of their growing empire, sending a military governor and maintaining a garrison in the port town of Mahón.[59] Jean (now John) Ligonier was one of the officers sent to keep order on the island after the Treaty of Utrecht gave possession to Britain while also preserving the civil and religious liberties of the Catholic, Catalan-speaking inhabitants. He was not the only Huguenot serving in that place so close, in dis-tance and appearance, to his southeastern French homeland. While Ligonier served as lieutenant governor of the main fort guarding Mahón, another man named Durand was engineer. Unfortunately, none of their observations on the island survive, but they must have had strong opinions about one of the island's central issues: the relationship between Protestant rulers and Catholic subjects.[60]

The same problem appeared several thousands of miles away in Paul Mascarene's posting. Luckily, Mascarene's voluminous observations clearly showed how his background as a French Protestant refugee colored his policy recommendations. Mascarene crossed the Atlantic in 1706 to New England,

and soon after that he participated in the conquest of Acadia, a sparsely settled French colony that became known as Nova Scotia. The circumstances of Nova Scotia's conquest were eerily similar to those of Minorca. The old French colony had been economically marginal, but its geographical position made it an important prize. In addition, it was inhabited entirely by French Catholic farmers and their Mi'kmaq Indian neighbors, and the Treaty of Utrecht also guaranteed them freedom of worship. As a result, the main challenge of British governance was to find a way to turn these French Catholics, many of whom were intensely suspicious of both Britain and Protestantism, into good subjects of George I.[61]

Perhaps not surprisingly for a Protestant refugee, Mascarene was not originally very positive about the Acadians. Serving as engineer in 1720, he submitted a lengthy report on the province to the Board of Trade, and he echoed many of the grim prognoses of his commanding officers. Most military officials there believed the French to be impossible to govern as long as their priests continued among them, since the clerics constantly plied the people, Acadian and native alike, with anti-British and anti-Protestant propaganda. Mascarene described the Acadians as being "in general of the Romish persuasion" and "entirely wedded" to what he called "the French Interest." They consistently refused, he noted, to take an oath of allegiance to the British king—an issue that became central to Nova Scotia politics for the next few decades. Mascarene outlined the pros and cons of allowing the Acadians to remain in the country. He agreed with others who cautioned that if the French Catholic farmers left Acadia's economy would collapse as the emigrants took their talents to neighboring French colonies in Canada or Cape Breton Island. Soldiers and officers made up the sole British inhabitants of the colony, and Mascarene knew that even Catholic subjects were better than none at all.[62]

Nonetheless, the problems with the Acadians impressed Mascarene more than their positive aspects. The biggest challenge was religious in nature. The Treaty of Utrecht guaranteed freedom of worship to Acadian Catholics, but Mascarene believed they would never be loyal with the priests whispering in their ears. The priests "have that ascendance over that ignorant people, as to render themselves masters of all their actions, and to guide and direct them as they please in temporal as in spiritual affairs." Moreover, they reported to superiors in the French colonies, which meant that their political interests would always be at odds with those of the British, even when the two nations were at peace. In the end, he recommended that Nova Scotia's leaders deliver an ultimatum to the French. If they took oaths of allegiance they could stay, but otherwise they needed to depart. An enlarged force of troops would administer the test and remove those who refused to comply, delivering their land to British colonists, who would be "far more advantageous to the settling this Province, and would besides the better improvement of it, for which their Industry is far superior to the French."[63]

Figure 6.2 John Smibert, "Portrait of Major General Paul Mascarene," 1729, Los Angeles County Museum of Art. Courtesy of Art Resource.

Mascarene's anti-Catholic attitudes echoed much of the correspondence of the time. Still, it is hard to deny that his status as a French refugee and a child of the Revocation colored his early understanding of the Acadian issue, especially in his fears of a dark alliance between priests and French authorities. His Huguenot bona fides came out more clearly in a scheme he tried to engineer several years later to fix the problems he laid out in his report. While he had recommended British migration, Nova Scotia did not prove attractive to many settlers from the home island, so he proposed another scheme involving a different kind of productive Protestant. Mascarene had deep connections in Boston, where his wife and family lived and he spent all his leave time away from Nova Scotia. While a member of the Anglican King's Chapel, Mascarene also was friendly with the minister of Boston's French church, Andrew Lemercier. In 1726 the two men began to collaborate on plans to move Huguenots into Nova Scotia. The new settlement, to be called New Caen after Lemercier's hometown in Normandy, would consist of one hundred French families brought both from New England and France. Mascarene and Lemercier advertised the scheme in Boston, but few Huguenot settlers wanted to take their chances on Nova Scotia.[64]

In the end, Mascarene's legacy would not be the creation of a Huguenot colony in Nova Scotia. Instead, beginning in the 1730s he began to change his perspective on the Acadians and advocated not for their removal but for their incorporation into the British state. This shift occurred gradually, but seemed to accelerate after Mascarene began to interact more frequently with ordinary Acadians. As a fluent French speaker, the officer became one of the key conduits between the colonial state and its francophone subjects. He built close relationships with the elected deputies in the French towns and even with a number of the missionary priests who served in the colony's Catholic churches. In 1740 these relationships became more critical when Mascarene unexpectedly rose to a position of leadership. Governor Lawrence Armstrong committed suicide, leaving Paul Mascarene as the senior member of the council and thus the de facto governor. Over several years in that role Mascarene adopted what was perhaps the most enlightened interpretation of the Acadian question of any British official in that colony's troubled history.[65]

Mascarene's stance toward the Acadians betrayed his refugee roots in a number of distinct ways. For one thing, he insisted on separating political loyalty from religious faith. This belief had been central to Huguenot politics in seventeenth-century France; Protestants insisted, against arguments to the contrary, that they could be good, loyal subjects to a king of a different confession. Now, Mascarene claimed the same in reverse: that Acadians could be good British subjects even if they remained Catholics. The key, however, was the recognition that ultimate sovereignty rested with the king. Mascarene continued to insist that subjects take loyalty oaths, but his main task was to curb the efforts of the missionary priests and "to hinder them from Establishing *imperium in imperio* which the Laws of Great Britain will not suffer." He had no problem with missionaries who performed only a "spiritual function," but he demanded that none of them claim authority from any master besides the king of Great Britain represented in the governor and council. During his time in power, therefore, Mascarene claimed the authority to approve the appointments of priests and to dismiss any who exceeded their proper role.[66]

Mascarene's relationship with Nova Scotia's priests moved well beyond being a simple overseer. In another reflection of his Huguenot roots, he engaged them in conversation, both about their duties to the state and, in one memorable correspondence, about theological questions. In 1734, well before rising to his ultimate leadership position, the officer began corresponding with a priest named Claude de la Vernade de St. Poncy. The conversation started when St. Poncy sent Mascarene a book by Jacques-Bénigne Bossuet, the Bishop of Meaux, denouncing the Reformation and the Protestant churches. Even though he was a "simple soldier," Mascarene took up the task of responding, since he noted that the English ministers who would be more qualified to answer the charges did not read or write in French. Over the course of hundreds of pages of theological argument, Mascarene proved himself to be far more than a simple soldier. He presented a lengthy exposition of the Thirty-Nine Articles of the Church of England, explaining its positions on everything from the Trinity to the Sacraments to the structure of the church, and followed that up with a spirited defense of the early Reformers, replete with the scriptural references and allusions to contemporary authors that were common in such works.[67]

While Mascarene wrote as an Anglican, and insisted he wanted "to live and die, God willing, in the communion of the Anglican Church," he also ventured into French religious politics. Answering the priest's claim that Protestantism bred immorality, he held up the example of French Protestants, thousands of whom "were obliged to abandon their goods and their homeland, and to go as refugees in foreign countries to avoid being persecuted for professing their faith." Those who failed to escape, he noted, faced the dragonnades, "galleys, the gallows, the wheel, or a thousand other kinds of torments, only for the crime of not being able to abjure the faith that they professed." He must have drawn on his own father's experience when he made these arguments, and indeed some of the points he raised with St. Poncy resembled those put forward by Jean Mascarene as he faced pressure to convert in 1685. Of course, now the tables were turned. The refugee had become a British officer, and the missionary priest served at the pleasure of a foreign government.[68]

The acting governor's plan to turn Acadians into Britons seemed to go well. He gave up on St. Poncy and took a hard line against priests in general, eventually expelling several of them, including his old interlocutor, for exceeding their authority. As Britain and France moved toward war in the 1740s he worried about the state of the colony, but in the end most of his Acadian neighbors stayed loyal. Even when the French occupied the town of Grand Pré, its French Catholic inhabitants issued a statement declaring that they lived "under a mild and tranquil government, and we have all good reason to be faithful to it."[69] After the occupation ended and Mascarene re-established authority, he admitted that Britain preserved the colony mainly because "our French Inhabitants refus[ed] to take up arms against us."[70]

By the dawn of the 1750s Paul Mascarene appeared to be a perfectly assimilated Briton. He married an English woman, his three children all married in the English community, and his son even studied at Harvard College. He worshipped in the Anglican King's Chapel and rubbed shoulders with leading officials like Massachusetts Governor William Shirley. At the same time, he never stopped being a Huguenot. That became clear when his son John traveled to London in 1752. Paul instructed John to make several stops in the capital in an effort to help him claim back salary from his time in service in Nova Scotia. Aside from English officials like Shirley and his successor in Nova Scotia, Edward Cornwallis, Paul recommended his son visit his old neighborhood in Dean Street, Soho, in search of a number of Huguenot men and women who he knew in his youth. Finally, he directed him to the most luminary refugee of them all, Sir John Ligonier. "You must take Coach and wait on Him, in the morning about ten or sooner," Paul Mascarene instructed. "You must give Your name and add, Colonel Mascarene's Son. You will soon find how Sir John is dispos'd. He can do a great deal if he pleases, I have reason to believe he will unless he has been prejudic'd by some malicious person." The two men had many mutual friends and relations back in Castres, and now Mascarene hoped to use those connections to advance his own interests.[71]

Since leaving Minorca decades earlier John Ligonier had indeed risen to the very top of the British military hierarchy. After serving for years in Ireland, he spent the 1740s making a name for himself as a military strategist—first in helping put down the Jacobite Rising in Scotland in 1745, then in continental campaigns during the War of the Austrian Succession. By the end of that war he moved to London and soon accumulated a stunning number of offices. He became a Member of Parliament and of the Privy Council—offices usually restricted to natural born Britons—and also joined the Royal Society as a fellow while retaining a plum military position as Lieutenant General of Ordnance. By 1752 when Mascarene sent his son to London, there was no more powerful Huguenot in the realm, and he was also the toast of the capital's high society, and a friend of the Whig hero Prince William, duke of Cumberland, the son of King George II.[72]

Ligonier appeared on the outside to have shed every vestige of his former Frenchness. But that was not the case. Around the same time he entered Parliament he also became the governor of the corporation of the French Hospital, one of the key institutions giving charitable aid to refugees and their descendants. His policy positions also occasionally reflected his Huguenot heritage, especially in the next global war with France, which began in 1754. Ligonier eventually rose to the top of the British military leadership, and while he never ventured to America, he took a keen interest in the conduct of the war there, and championed an approach that utilized foreign Protestants in particular as actors in the war—a tactic that resembled nothing so much as the earlier French Protestant regiments under William III.[73]

The best example of this phenomenon came in the formation of the Royal American Regiment. That organization was the brainchild of James Prevost, a Swiss officer of Huguenot ancestry who had served in a number of European militaries, most recently in the Netherlands, and proposed a regiment led by continental officers, especially Swiss and Germans, and including German-speaking soldiers from Pennsylvania. The plan met strong opposition from many within the British government, including the first minister William Pitt, but Ligonier supported it, and by 1757 Prevost and a number of other Swiss officers, including future leaders Henry Bouquet and Frederick Haldimand, had made it to America where they were especially active in frontier warfare. The regiment fit closely with the types of military strategies that had brought Huguenots into the empire in earlier wars, though now changing circumstances meant that central Europe rather than France supplied the bulk of new officers. Nonetheless, many of them, like Prevost himself, descended from families that had fled France at the end of previous centuries.[74]

Prevost's plan for the regiment indicated even more similarities with earlier Huguenot schemes. In addition to its military capabilities, Prevost imagined the Royal American Regiment as a vanguard of settlement. When peace came, he proposed that authorities send the regiment's soldiers and officers to some strategically important part of the colonies, where they would receive half pay for a time, become farmers, and "contribute to the security of the borders in the provinces of Carolina, Virginia, and Pennsylvania." These plans closely resembled the earlier establishment of Portarlington, a settlement of discharged Huguenot soldiers and officers in Ireland, and also recalled the many attempts to use refugees to populate frontier regions from New England to the Gulf of Mexico. The strategic value of foreign Protestants continued to motivate British policymakers.[75]

The intertwined stories of Ligonier and Mascarene indicated that the preponderance of Huguenots in the British Army was far from an accident. In an age of war with France, refugees both symbolized what the British were fighting for and provided important cultural competencies that would help them win the fight. At the same time, as Mascarene's negotiations with the Acadians showed, Huguenots could serve important roles in peacetime, especially in borderlands between the French and British empires. Nonetheless, it was merchants, more than military men, who made that system work, and who round out the story of how refugees influenced the empire.

In 1742 a Boston minister paid a glowing tribute to a recently deceased citizen of the town. Peter Faneuil was not just an ordinary Bostonian. His "*Largeness of Heart* equal'd, great as it was, his *Power to do Good*," intoned the minister, John Lovell, and indeed Faneuil had gained a reputation as the most charitable man in the city—not surprisingly, as he was also the richest. "His Alms *flow'd* like a *fruitful River*," Lovell continued, "that diffuses it's *Streams* thro' a *whole Country*." Its most lasting monument was the very building where Lovell gave his sermon: Faneuil Hall. Until the 1740s Boston had lacked a central market, despite being an increasingly important Atlantic port town closely intertwined with imperial networks. Faneuil donated the money needed to finally construct a market building, which Lovell defined as a monument to empire. "May Liberty always spread its *joyful Wings* over this Place," he hoped, "*Liberty* that opens *Men's Hearts* to *Beneficence*, and gives the *Relish* to those who enjoy the *Effects* of it. And may Loyalty to a King, under whom we enjoy this *Liberty*, ever remain *our Character*. A Character always *justly due to this Land*, and of which our *Enemies* have in vain *attempted to rob us*."[76]

Lovell never mentioned Faneuil's refugee heritage in his sermon. In fact, the most generous of Bostonians was not a native of the town at all. Peter Fanueil was the leading member of one of the British Atlantic's most prominent Huguenot families. The Faneuils hailed from the port city of La Rochelle. A cadre of Protestant families with international ties had dominated trade in that town back to the sixteenth century, making money not just from trade across the Channel with England but off colonial commerce as well. When the persecution hit in the 1680s these merchants were well-positioned to escape, since most of them owned ships and had connections and investments in Protestant ports like Rotterdam, Amsterdam, London, and Bristol. The difficulties of controlling their movements appeared clearly in the correspondence of Pierre Arnoul, the royal administrator given the thankless task of policing Protestants and new converts in the port and surrounding countryside after the Revocation of the Edict of Nantes. Arnoul could not shut down La Rochelle's commerce without damaging the local economy, but he suspected that many Protestant merchants pretended to convert to Catholicism only so they could have more time to make arrangements to leave. He made particular note of the Baudouin family (who as the Bowdoins would eventually become another branch of New England aristocrats). One of them had converted to Catholicism, but everyone knew he had brothers and other relations in the Netherlands, and Arnoul believed that a planned trading expedition to Newfoundland was just a ruse to allow Baudouin to safely leave France without giving up too much of his estate.[77]

Like the Baudouins, the Faneuils fled La Rochelle in the wake of the Revocation and scattered around the Anglo-Dutch world. For many families this dispersion was not accidental. By stationing members around the Atlantic, they ensured that trusted partners could help them move their goods around—and many families were not averse to encouraging some members to at least outwardly convert to Catholicism in order to stay in France and manage the family's trade there. At the time of the Revocation one of the three Faneuil brothers, Jean, was already established in Rotterdam, though he frequently visited La Rochelle well into the 1700s. His two younger brothers, Benjamin and André, relocated to British North America, the former to New Rochelle, the latter to Boston. Other members of the family created businesses in Ireland and London, while more distant relatives remained in France but continued to trade with their contacts around the Refuge.[78]

The relocation of merchant families like the Faneuils to the British empire seemed at first to be mostly a marriage of convenience. For André Faneuil, for instance, living in Boston allowed him to continue much of his previous trade to New France, Acadia, and Newfoundland—at least as much as global geopolitics would allow. Some merchants, like David Basset, maintained delicate balancing acts between empires. Basset resided in Plaisance, Newfoundland in 1689, where he maintained a low profile until officials there exposed him as a "religionnaire." They sent him in irons back to France, where he abjured his faith and, like other merchants, soon set out from La Rochelle to Newfoundland on a commercial expedition. He managed to convince Plaisance's French governor to allow him to visit Boston for purposes of trade, but once he was in the English port he promptly switched sides, helping with the English conquest of Acadia and then leading filibustering expeditions against his countrymen both in the St. Lawrence Seaway and off the coast of Africa. French officials were unaware of Basset's act until the early years of the eighteenth century, when they seized the merchant's goods in Plaisance. He had managed to play both sides, to great personal advantage, for the better part of a decade.[79]

The Faneuils and other Huguenot merchant families in the colonial Northeast followed similar trajectories as Basset, even if their stories were somewhat less dramatic. Benjamin and André Faneuil traded extensively with other French merchants, on both sides of the imperial border, in legal and extralegal ways. In some cases they dabbled in privateering—André, for instance, owned a share of the *Peter*, a French ship taken as a "lawful prize" off Newfoundland in 1702, and was the sole owner of the *St. James*, another French ship captured that same year.[80] His brother Benjamin briefly faced charges of trading with the enemy and espionage during the War of the Spanish Succession, demonstrating the degree to which the Huguenots' frequent border crossing made them objects of suspicion. In 1706 a Dutch New Yorker named Morris Newinghuysen saw letters addressed to La Rochelle in Faneuil's sloop and claimed "he believed there was roguery in them." One letter in particular claimed that the French would meet "less Resistance" if they targeted Nevis. Newinghuysen had no evidence—he claimed to have thrown the letters overboard—but the charges represented a significant challenge to Faneuil's reputation and livelihood.[81]

After the return of peace the brothers managed a robust trade with family members and contacts in La Rochelle, Ireland, and elsewhere. In the 1720s, when their surviving account books begin, the family traded extensively in French silks and other goods, which they transported throughout the English Atlantic. Being French, and able to manage trade with both France and its colonies, provided the key to success for eighteenth-century Huguenot merchant dynasties.[82] The Bayeux brothers, Thomas and Jean, provided a similar example. Thomas resided in New York and Jean in London, but they maintained contacts in their Norman hometown of Caen and brought in a number of French goods—most notably onions and wine—that they sold in various English and imperial ports.[83]

As the century progressed, however, most of these refugee merchants became decidedly more British. The transition appeared clearly in the correspondence of another heir to a La Rochelle family, Peter Jay, who worked in New York through much of the 1700s and left a remarkable letterbook detailing decades of his commercial activities. The son of Auguste Jay, Peter went to Europe during the 1720s in a kind of extended apprenticeship in global trade with his cousins David and John Peloquin in Bristol. He also made shorter visits to family members in La Rochelle and Paris, including another cousin who had converted and remained in France. On returning to New York he made the best of these connections, running a robust trade that brought manufactured goods from France and England to New York and sent back American raw materials, especially Caribbean sugar. Jay's early correspondence included letters back to France as well as extensive correspondence with the Peloquins, whose connections to West Country manufacturers allowed the whole trading web to work. In addition, Jay took advantage of the diaspora of Huguenot merchants— some of whom were relations by marriage—who had set up in English ports from Boston to Jamaica. Huguenots never worked exclusively with each other; they set up ties with English and Dutch merchants as well, and were not loath to working with French Catholics. Nonetheless, there is no question that they preferred their own coreligionists in business, whether due to family or community links or previous connections back in France.[84]

Jay's correspondence in the 1730s and beyond showed subtle but steady changes in his business network. He continued to work closely with the Peloquins, but the French correspondence dried up and his business contacts became more English in composition. Jay's main role, it seemed, was to use New York as a conduit for trade between Bristol and the Caribbean, including managing his cousins' attempts to sell Irish flax seed in the colonies.[85] In the meantime, the nature of Peter's letter writing showed more cultural affinity with the British world than the French one. During the 1720s and 1730s he often corresponded in French with his aunt Françoise Peloquin, and he included many details not only of his family but also New York's French church, which he related to be in a state of chaos and division—clearly a subject of interest to Françoise, who had herself fled from La Rochelle to Bristol in the 1680s.[86] After her death, however, nearly all of Peter's letters were in English—even those to his cousins—and he rarely mentioned happenings in the French community. In fact, the exception that proved the rule appeared in the 1750s, when Peter's son James Jay went to Europe for his medical education. After a stint in Edinburgh James considered going to Paris for further training, and his father set out to use his old contacts to help James make his way in that foreign capital. He wrote to his cousin and old business contact, one Monsieur Mouchard, but his letter indicated that they had not communicated in decades. "Though it has been many years since we saw each other at your father's house," Jay wrote to his cousin in French, "I hope that neither this nor the distance between use can be the least impediment to our reciprocal friendship" that came from their close family ties. In a letter to his son Peter took a more cautious tone, warning James to avoid talking about religion since "he is not of our persuasion." In the end, James did not meet with Mouchard and Peter Jay never wrote to him again, nor to any other relations in France. So long neglected, the commercial and cultural links to the homeland no longer held much power.[87]

Much like his counterpart in New York, Peter Faneuil became less recognizably French as time went by. He left his native New Rochelle as a young man to work for his bachelor uncle André, who by the 1730s was purportedly the richest man in Boston. On his uncle's death Peter inherited most of his fortune and used his own connections to expand his uncle's commercial empire—trading in Madeira wine, one of British America's most treasured commodities, as well as Caribbean sugar and on at least one occasion African slaves. A sample of his surviving correspondence does reveal some residual French connections. In 1737, for instance, Peter wrote in French to Jean Tigal, a business contact in Bordeaux, who was trading in American indigo.[88] Nonetheless, these contacts made up less and less of his business, and his cultural links suggested significant Anglicization as well. While his uncle had been instrumental in bringing Andrew Lemercier to Boston as pastor of the French church, André himself spent more time at King's Chapel, Boston's Anglican church, during his final years, and Peter did the same, where he joined other prominent Huguenots like Paul Mascarene. By the 1740s, on Lemercier's retirement, the French church no longer operated. Boston's Huguenots had integrated not just into the English world, but into the Anglican one. Merchants like Faneuil operated the imperial economy, while soldier-administrators like Mascarene saw to imperial political expansion and minister-missionaries like Le Jau attended to its spiritual needs.[89]

If merchants' correspondence indicated fewer direct connections to the homeland, this did not mean they had ceased to be Huguenots. Like their counterparts in the church and government, merchants also did their part to help the refugee cause. Indeed, they may have done the most, even if they rarely wrote about their place in the Huguenot diaspora. As they integrated into British imperial society, turning their backs on the distinctive refugee communities they came from, these merchants bankrolled the creation of new Huguenot colonies that would continue to preserve the French Protestant faith. No one was more central to this process than Peter Simond. Although he never resided in the colonies, Simond made his money off of colonial trade, especially through transporting American tobacco to France. He also maintained close links to the Huguenot community in London and beyond. Indeed, his wife Suzanne was Claude Grosteste de la Mothe's sister, and during the mid-1720s Simond managed trade for the deceased minister's widow Louise.[90] That same decade he partnered with Jean-Pierre Purry, an eccentric Swiss merchant who hoped to establish a silk and wine colony in South Carolina, worked by Swiss, Huguenot, and other various foreign Protestants. With Simond's help, Purry formed the town of Purrysburgh, the first new refugee settlement in North America since Manakintown.[91] Thus began a new age of prospective Huguenot colonization, in which the old dreams of the seventeenth century came back, refashioned for a new, enlightened age.

A New Age of Projects

Louis de Mesnil de Saint-Pierre had a simple vision: to turn the American south into a vast vineyard. In 1770 the French gentleman and Protestant refugee traveled from his adopted home of New Bordeaux, South Carolina, to sell his dream to possible English benefactors. One of the leaders of a settlement of Huguenots and Germans on the Savannah River, Saint-Pierre believed that planting vineyards would solve virtually all of the empire's looming problems. "The Vine is a native of America," wrote the Frenchman, "And this divine plant may be found throughout that vast continent, from the mouth of the Missisippi to that of the St. Lawrence, where it is as common as now, and much more so than formerly in France and Italy." With the help of foreign experts, Americans of all classes could turn their energies to the cultivation of this valuable commodity that would provide the entire empire with lucrative products and give employment to thousands—and put a stop to the political divisions that threatened to tear the empire apart. "Perhaps Government may find out, *when too late*," Saint-Pierre scolded, "that the number of *emigrants* daily resorting to *America*, as well as the *natives* of our colonies there, would have been much more usefully employed for the *benefit* of the *mother* country, by the cultivation of the lands, in producing *Silk*, and raising *Vines*, &c. than in the *rivaling* of the *mother* country in *arts* and *manufactures*."[1]

Saint-Pierre's revolutionary scheme revealed that the old dream of creating Huguenot colonies in the New World was very much alive in the latter decades of the eighteenth century. Indeed, his design was only the boldest of dozens that would have planted refugee colonies not just in South Carolina but also in Florida, Nova Scotia, Maine, and non-American locales like Ireland and Minorca. To be sure, most of these plans came to naught. Probably only a few hundred Huguenots crossed the ocean between the 1740s and the 1770s, and many of the proposed colonies either failed quickly or never got off the ground at all. Nonetheless, the persistence of the Huguenot overseas vision revealed the special place the refugees occupied in the eighteenth-century world. Still, even nearly a century after the Revocation of the Edict of Nantes, descendants of the

The Global Refuge. Owen Stanwood, Oxford University Press (2020). © Oxford University Press.
DOI: 10.1093/oso/9780190264741.001.0001

original refugees possessed enormous influence in the Protestant Atlantic—and especially in Britain and its empire, where they had insinuated themselves in many leading institutions. British in almost everything but name, these seemingly assimilated French people used their influence to attempt to build a new Huguenot empire.[2]

While it corresponded to many of the patterns of the late seventeenth-century colonial push, the new era of Huguenot colonization also drew from the spirit of the eighteenth century. This was an age of Enlightenment, when fresh ideological movements transformed European societies. Huguenots were at the center of the world of European letters; some of them, like Pierre Bayle, could be seen almost as founders of the Enlightenment.[3] Along with other thinkers, these French intellectuals succeeded in making religious toleration one of the key ideas of the new century. Advocates of toleration, whether Protestant or Catholic, tended to latch on to the earlier Revocation as a signal event that revealed both the cruelty and the shortsightedness of persecution. France, the story went, had inflicted great harm on itself when Louis XIV expelled the Huguenots. The removal of so many productive inhabitants had robbed the kingdom of revenue and permanently damaged the French economy. This proved a lesson both to France itself—which would be best advised to loosen its laws and let Protestants practice in peace—and to other European nations that might be tempted to implement similar programs of persecution. Even if the French economy was not as weak as it appeared, and those weaknesses had little to do with the Huguenots, the important thing was that many in the eighteenth century believed it to be true—and this belief extended from refugees and their descendants to Catholic commentators like Voltaire and even ministers in Louis XV's court.[4]

The Enlightenment influenced this new colonial age in a second, related way. The middle of the century saw a renewal of what Daniel Defoe had earlier coined as the "Projecting Age." Defoe dated the beginning of the age of projects to the late 1600s, when people all over England "rack[ed] their Wits for New Contrivances, New Inventions, New Trades, Stocks, Projects, and any thing to retrieve the desperate Credit of their Fortunes." If they began as private schemes, these projects were "doubtless in general of publick Advantage, as they tend[ed] to Improvement of Trade, and Employment of the Poor, and the Circulation and Increase of the publick Stock of the Kingdom."[5] In some ways the projecting age never stopped, but by any measure the British taste for projects boomed in the middle years of the eighteenth century. New schemes appeared everywhere, conceived by ambitious men but often with the support of corporations or states. The symbol of this new age was the "Honourable Society for the Encouragement of Arts, Manufactures, and Commerce," later known as the Royal Society of Arts, which sponsored plans for improvement around Britain and its empire.[6]

Tolerationist arguments and a new appetite for projects combined to create opportunities for Huguenots. Back in France, Protestants began to come out of the shadows, attempting to rebuild their churches and petitioning the king for religious liberty. In order to make their demands more relevant, they threatened to leave France if they did not get their way, and in the new age of projects they would not lack good offers if they wanted to depart the kingdom. British projectors came up with new versions of the old Huguenot colonial visions, promoting Huguenots as good, Protestant subjects who would settle empty and vulnerable parts of the empire and produce valuable commodities, especially the never forgotten silk, wine, and olive oil. In addition, the Huguenot model of foreign colonization became an example for other groups of migrants, including Germans, Swiss, Irish, and others, who scattered around the Atlantic in unprecedented numbers.[7] Perhaps after years of tribulation, the refugees could finally find Eden in a new, enlightened age.

In 1762 the French philosopher François-Marie Arouet, better known by his pen name Voltaire, issued a clarion call for religious toleration. The occasion for his writing was the judicial murder of Jean Calas, a Protestant shopkeeper in the southern city of Toulouse. In October 1761 Calas's son Marc-Antoine hanged himself in the family's house—a fact that the family predictably hid from authorities, given the stigma usually attached to suicide in the early modern era. In the days after Marc-Antoine's death, rumors circulated that it had been not a suicide but a diabolical plot. Marc-Antoine had been set to convert to Catholicism, leading his zealous parents to kill their son before allowing him to embrace another faith. Despite a decided lack of evidence, authorities in Toulouse put the parents on trial for the murder, and in March 1762, after rounds of torture that could not convince the father to falsely confess, the judges sentenced Jean Calas to be executed in an especially brutal fashion, by being broken on the wheel.[8]

To Voltaire and his fellow philosophes, Calas's judicial murder was a grave injustice that exemplified an intolerant age. The actions of the Toulousains— from the judges in the parlement to the Catholic masses who believed the worst rumors about their Protestant neighbors—reeked of fanaticism and unreason. Religious violence, Voltaire proclaimed, was an unfortunate holdover from the distant dark ages, whether it was committed in the name of pope who "approved, celebrated, and consecrated" the Saint Bartholomew massacre, or by "the fanatics of the Cévennes" who believed they would gain heavenly rewards "in proportion to the number of priests, religious, and Catholic women whose throats they had cut." Voltaire called for an end to such misguided bloodshed and a move toward what he called a "universal tolerance."[9]

Voltaire may have been the most famous French voice calling for toleration in the eighteenth century, but he was just one participant in a conversation that stretched back to the time of the Revocation. Protestants themselves pioneered many of the arguments that the philosophes later popularized. Voltaire drew on some of them, but Protestant polemicists tended to stress different things. For Pierre Jurieu in 1681, for instance, there was no need to decry "fanaticism" or call up enlightenment values to defend the rights of Protestants. They deserved religious liberty because their religion was the true one. Jurieu also drew on an argument that would inspire his eighteenth-century Protestant successors as well as enlightened Catholics like Voltaire. Persecution, Jurieu noted, was bad for the state. "There is no body but knows," he wrote, "that the force of States depends on the multitude of Inhabitants." By persecuting the Protestants, Louis XIV had already cost his state dearly in inspiring thousands to flee. Frontier towns languished while England, the Netherlands, and Switzerland gained new productive subjects, who filled foreign armies and contributed to "Commerce and Arts."[10]

Jurieu's entreaties fell on deaf ears. Louis XIV continued his program of persecution, and the expected exodus of Protestants accelerated after the Revocation. In official statements, the Revocation had ended the problem of religious difference that had plagued the kingdom for decades. The former Huguenots had become "new converts," and the military victory of the king's forces over the Camisard rebels in 1708 had put out the last flickers of armed resistance. Nonetheless, officials understood that Protestantism had not ceased to exist; it had just gone underground. Protestants were still there, even if no one dared to refer to them as such. As a result, Jurieu's argument continued to have power. The kings' ministers periodically renewed and strengthened their edicts against Protestants—most notably in 1698, 1715, and 1724—but the enforcement of these laws was inconsistent. Royal officials believed Protestants to be naturally disloyal, but they also agreed with Jurieu's statement about population and revenue loss. The most noteworthy statement of this position came from Louis XIV's famous military mastermind the Maréchal de Vauban, who in 1689 called for relaxing strictures against the Protestants. Vauban noted that Louis had acted for "piety and the good of the state" when he revoked the Edict of Nantes, but argued that his action had failed to really produce conversions and instead had led to economic ruin and the loss of thousands of soldiers and sailors. The only way to stop the hemorrhage of people was to enact a new policy that allowed a degree of freedom of conscience. Vauban knew that the mass exodus of the 1680s had cost France dearly, and he did not want to risk a repeat of that event.[11]

Vauban was unable to influence the Sun King to relax his approach, but similar ideas continued to circulate in the next century. At the end of the War of the Spanish Succession and following Louis XIV's death, an anonymous royal official demonstrated the "Protestant problem" in revealing detail. He began by claiming that Protestants constituted a potential fifth column in the heart of the kingdom, a seditious minority who could not be trusted. The "newly converted" were better called the "poorly converted," he claimed, since they maintained only a veneer of Catholic faith or loyalty to the king. The existence of these hidden Protestants had caused numerous problems during the last two wars, since many of them maintained correspondence with friends and relatives who now lived in enemy countries like Britain or the Netherlands. The author wavered in describing these links. He originally referred to "the treasons that the French Huguenots have had with enemies of the state," and on second thought replaced the word "treasons" [*trahisons*] with "liaisons" —but the implication was the same. By passing intelligence to their exiled brethren overseas and thus to the enemy, the Huguenots undermined the national interest. The only solution was the "entire conversion" of France's Protestants.[12]

Nonetheless, there was a problem with this program. The very existence of friends and family members living with liberty of conscience in the Refuge presented a temptation to those new converts who languished under a persecutory state. Freedom waited just beyond France's borders for those who could get there, risking a second exodus as bad or worse than the original one. This fear of losing people made it difficult for officials to treat "the poorly converted" with the harshness they seemed to deserve. Even this report's author admitted as much, noting that attempts to bring about mass conversions by force had rarely succeeded, in France or elsewhere. They were more likely to push people away. The loss of so many Protestants after the Revocation, he admitted, had been "such a considerable injury to the Kingdom."[13]

The crown thus found itself in an awkward position regarding the *religionnaires*. Officials continued to decry toleration and believe that religious unity would buttress national strength. At the same time they accepted the political economic argument that emigration was bad for the state, and that persecution would lead to even worse evils than toleration. Prominent early Enlightenment theorists drew unfavorable comparisons between France and other, more tolerant nations. Pierre-Daniel Huet, for example, ascribed the success of the Dutch to their embrace of religious refugees from around Europe—a line of interpretation that dated back to the seventeenth century. The baron de Montesquieu, in his famous *Persian Letters*, raised the example of the Persian empire, where the Shah tolerated Armenian Christians largely because "by banishing the Armenians" they would "destroy, in a single day, all the merchants and almost all the craftsmen of the kingdom." The parallel to Louis XIV and the Protestants would have been immediately apparent to any French reader.[14]

Protestants within France were well aware of these debates and used them to their own advantage, silently beginning a campaign to rebuild their church.

Beginning in 1715 minister Antoine Court began to create what became known as the churches of the Desert in an allusion to the Jewish people's tribulations during their exodus. A native of Languedoc, the minister determined to build a French Protestant church that could peacefully exist within Bourbon France; he rejected the millennial violence that had animated past generations of southern Protestant rebels. At the same time, he drew on a trans-European network to aid his efforts. By 1730 Court had retreated to Lausanne, where he established an academy dedicated to training ministers for the churches of the Desert. Soon the school was sending new ministers to various corners of southern and western France, and in 1744 Huguenot leaders gathered in secret for the first national synod in nearly ninety years.[15] While they silently built churches and continued to present petitions to the king, Protestants also put forth justifications of toleration. In 1748 Laurent Angliviel de la Beaumelle anonymously published his work *L'Asiatique tolérant*, which in a paraphrase of Montesquieu used a fictional Asian kingdom to argue for the natural rightness of toleration. Antoine Court published his masterwork on the subject, *Le patriote français et impartial*, five years later, in which he underscored the argument that religious dissenters could remain faithful subjects.[16]

The efforts of Court and his compatriots tied the French state in knots. On the one hand, the ministers' efforts were clearly illegal. Synods were "still more dangerous than assemblies," claimed one official, since "it is from there that all the most dangerous designs against the state originate." Court himself was the mastermind, who from his perch in Lausanne acted as a conduit between the French Protestants and "powerful enemies of France" abroad, a bridge between Desert and Refuge.[17] At the same time, the Huguenots rejected militancy and presented themselves as loyal subjects. In frequent appeals to the king against persecution the pastors protested that they wanted only the right to be good subjects while remaining clear in their consciences. Although they discussed, briefly, the theological basis of their synods and assemblies, they learned to argue their cause in a tongue the ministers in Versailles spoke fluently—the language of political economy. In one missive, the Protestants noted that for two hundred years the French state had used every imaginable method to stamp out Protestantism, with the only result being "that France is considerably weakened by the loss of more than four million of its subjects" while "its neighbors have been enriched by these spoils."[18]

What was more, these appeals contained both a history lesson and an implicit threat. The loss of hundreds of thousands of refugees in the late 1600s had weakened France and strengthened its rivals, but the losses would be even worse if the remaining Reformed subjects still in France—those who decided, out of love for their homeland, to stay in a realm that persecuted them—decided finally to leave. In 1758, for instance, facing a new upsurge in "cruel persecution,"

petitioning Protestants foresaw the impending "depopulation of the most beautiful provinces of your Kingdom, the abandonment of the countryside, and the
languor of agriculture, the loss of manufactures, and the decline of commerce."
Because of this "emigration that persecution causes every day . . . Germany,
Russia, England, Holland, [and] the English colonies of America are peopled
with your subjects." The Huguenots had no desire to strengthen the king's rivals;
they were forced to do so by circumstance. Only a change in religious policy
would keep them at home.[19]

In essence, the Huguenots attempted to blackmail the French state into
tolerating them. Though the king and his allies continued to distrust Protestants,
this strategy was surprisingly successful for much of the eighteenth century.
Treatment of Huguenots waxed and waned across the century as monarchs
rose and fell and peace followed war. Often with the blessing of ecclesiastical
officials, the king's ministers sporadically enforced strictures forcing Protestants
to attend church and present their children for Catholic baptism, but especially
during wartime they relaxed these regulations. For example, when in 1745 a
local intendant cracked down on a clandestine assembly and took a number of
prisoners, the official in charge of Protestant affairs, the comte de St. Florentin,
cautioned him to change his approach, making reference to the the king's "plan
of moderation."[20] Royal representatives feared that their subjects would desert
them and give their labor and intelligence to foreign enemies if treatment got
too bad. From a Protestant point of view, however, there was one problem: this
strategy could only work if the Huguenots were willing to leave, but since 1700
there had been no significant movement of refugees out of France. As one of
Court's lieutenants in Languedoc testified, those who possessed property or estates usually showed an "extreme repugnance to abandoning them."[21] More than
that, most of the leaders of the new church had devoted themselves to rebuilding
Protestantism within France itself. The threat of emigration was a strategy to extract concessions from the king, but if they actually followed through, the loss
of people would damage the attempts to rebuild the French Protestant church
more than it would the French economy.

Nonetheless, during the 1750s more French people started to consider
leaving France to be a viable option. Antoine Court changed his mind about
emigration after French religious policy showed no signs of substantial liberali-
zation.[22] Even as early as the mid-1740s he received word from contacts around
France about new possible migrants. From Poitou, for instance, André Migault
told Court of numerous people who hoped it was "a favorable occasion for those
who wanted to leave France." The potential Poitevin refugees were "makers of
cloth and of handkerchiefs, all good workers, and I don't believe they will be
any charge to those who employ them."[23] Many French Protestants, like those
discontented Poitevins, seemed ready to abandon their attempts to rebuild the

church in France and embrace the uncertain life of a refugee. No one embodied the transformation more than Jean-Louis Gibert, one of Court's fellow ministers and loyal foot soldiers in the Huguenot cause.[24]

Gibert was one of the more remarkable of Court's allies in the design to rebuild the church. According to a German Moravian who worked with the minister, Gibert first gained zeal for the cause after hearing heroic tales of his Cévenol forbears who had killed and died for the church. He attended Court's academy in Lausanne, where he formed the design "to deliver his Protestant compatriots from the yoke of persecution." An "enthusiast in his projects," Gibert traveled the kingdom in an effort to improve the condition of his fellow Huguenots. He ministered first in the Cévennes, where he found the villagers less zealous in the cause than he preferred. He moved from there to Paris, where he unsuccessfully lobbied the French court to tolerate Protestants.[25] Finally, he ended up in the western provinces of Poitou and Saintonge, where he encountered a more receptive audience. For over a decade he worked to build churches there, convincing leading new converts to finance the building of illegal chapels, the famous *maisons d'oraison* or "houses of prayer." These efforts attracted notice from the local intendant, who eventually condemned Gibert to death in absentia. Still, official efforts to destroy the churches and silence the renegade minister proved haphazard at best. By 1755, in the midst of the Seven Years' War, hundreds of Protestants flocked to services, Jean-Louis told his brother Étienne, and met no resistance at all from authorities. During the war officials feared that any demonstration of force would push the Protestants into the arms of the enemy across the Channel. Perhaps deliverance from Babylon was near at hand.[26]

In fact, Gibert's flocks experienced not a gradual move toward freedom, but a roller coaster of toleration and repression that followed their home country's fortunes in the war. Early in the conflict officials worried that the Huguenots could leave and aid the enemy, and treated them well, but matters got worse during times when the French army was ascendant. In the meantime, popular opinion proved fickle. Prejudice against the Huguenots increased as the conflict wore on, most dramatically in the case of Jean Calas. While it would eventually lead Voltaire and others to advocate for toleration, in 1763 the Calas affair highlighted the persistence of anti-Protestantism and the dangers for Protestants who stayed in France.[27]

One possible solution to this problem appeared in Voltaire's own correspondence. As the war moved toward a conclusion, and France dealt with the humiliating loss of most of its North American empire, the king's chief minister the duc de Choiseul spearheaded a new initiative: the settlement of the nearly empty colony of Guiana, on the South American coast east of Dutch Suriname. The French had maintained a post there in the town of Cayenne since the seventeenth century, but had never been able to attract many settlers or make the colony productive.[28] Choiseul hoped to change all that and raved about the design to Voltaire. The new colony would more than make up for the loss of Canada with its revenues from sugar, indigo, and other commodities, and the duke had a clear "plan of government," endeavoring to find German and French settlers (not African slaves) to serve as free laborers in the colony. Voltaire lauded this idea, calling the colony "Eldorado," but he had a different suggestion for peopling Guiana. He had recently received appeals for aid from Protestant galley slaves in Marseille—Huguenots who had chosen imprisonment over conversion, but who hoped that with the aid of their philosophe ally they might again find freedom.[29]

Echoing English policies in the seventeenth century, as well as aborted efforts by the French in the 1680s, Voltaire recommended the galley slaves begin new lives in Guiana. The climate, he claimed, was not much different from southern France, and the newcomers would prove a great boon to the governor as they would "augment his colony with many active and industrious people who will cost the state nothing." In order to get them to willingly go, Voltaire suggested that officials offer them a kind of unofficial religious liberty. Certainly, they would cross the seas to be productive economic subjects, not "to go and sing the Psalms of Marot." Nonetheless, they might be allowed to bring over ministers in secret, and once they reached Guiana, Voltaire predicted that the governor would offer them full religious liberty, knowing well "the value of Tolerance." The use of economic language suggested that Voltaire understood the deleterious effects of losing productive people. By sending Protestants to the colonies rather than the galleys, the king could preserve uniformity at home while making more productive colonies abroad. The plan represented a tactical compromise between earlier attempts, by both Louis XIV and the Protestants themselves, to turn the Indies into a home for Protestant settlers. This time, they would be allowed to migrate and keep their faith.[30]

For whatever reason, Voltaire's Protestant Guiana was not to be. At least one piece of evidence, from a physician practicing in Cayenne, suggests that the philosopher was not the only one to consider the plan. The doctor stated that Louis XV "sought to attract foreigners of any country and any religion" to Guiana, and in that interest had forbade the intendant "from interfering in the conscience and the worship" of any settler. Still, there were plenty of other candidates, from Maltese islanders to French convicts and displaced Acadians, and in the end mostly Germans settled the colony. The French Protestants evaded disaster by avoiding Guiana, since Choiseul's colony became one of the eighteenth century's worst death traps.[31]

In the end, it is not surprising that the Huguenots failed to enlist in the design. Choiseul drew openly and enthusiastically from the strategies the British had used to people their own colonies. If Huguenots wanted to go to America, therefore, why not go to an established British colony? British North America welcomed increasing numbers of European migrants in the eighteenth century, and they already had freedom of worship for Protestants. For Jean-Louis Gibert,

the British empire seemed more appealing than the French, so in 1761 he traveled to London. His initial aim seems to have been to influence the British to
put pressure on the French to relax strictures against Protestants in negotiations
for peace. This had been a favorite goal of Huguenot lobbyists dating back to
the negotiations surrounding the Treaty of Ryswick in 1697. But it had never
worked, and proved no more successful for Gibert. Instead, Jean-Louis decided
on a different strategy: the threatened departure from France with the thousands
of Protestants stretching from Poitou to Bordeaux. If the king and his ministers
would not relax their strictures against the Huguenots, it was time at last to go.[32]

Gibert's plans to migrate represented the culmination of the Huguenots' many
missives to Louis XV. The minister loudly proclaimed that he would follow through
on the threat to leave that had animated so many Protestant petitions over the previous
decades. As the war moved toward its conclusion Gibert wandered the country, from
Saintonge to Languedoc, searching for willing migrants. According to one French official, the pastor bragged that he had been appointed "Vice Roy" of an "island in America"
where "the land is very fertile," and new migrants would not need to pay any taxes and
would receive provisions up until their first harvest. Gibert had little success attracting
migrants from the Cévennes, where most Protestants were peasants rooted to their
farms and villages. Nonetheless, in the town of Valleraugue he found "several peasants
all heads of family" who joined his cause, headed for England and eventually North
America. Gibert went from there to greener pastures—his old stomping grounds in
Atlantic France, places where Protestants had always looked to the sea and migrated out
of the kingdom in much greater numbers than their southern counterparts.[33]

Worried French officials did all they could to stop Gibert's scheme. They even
issued a detailed description of the fugitive, who they described as a tall man
with skinny legs and a "naturally seditious" nature.[34] Nonetheless, agents of the
crown viewed the design as more than the work of one man. They believed it
to be a British plot to "quietly debauch the French Protestants" and win over
the Huguenots' skills, labor, and capital, perhaps even bringing along disloyal
Catholics as well. Spies and contacts in London reported that Gibert received
£4000 from the funds of the old Royal Bounty to aid his effort to steal France's
subjects.[35] While the French grossly overestimated the amount of money the
British were willing to spend on any scheme involving Huguenots or colonization, they were not altogether wrong. In fact, Gibert's arrival in London did
arouse great interest among British officials, who saw the opportunity to profit
from France's religious problems.

Gibert was far from the first French projector to find a receptive British audience for somewhat quixotic colonial designs. He followed on a trail blazed in

some ways by Jean-Pierre Purry. Over several decades in the early eighteenth century Purry told everyone he met about his theory. A failed wine merchant from the Swiss city of Neuchâtel, Purry dreamed of settling colonies on what he deemed to be the best climate in the world: anyplace at thirty-three degrees north or south latitude. Those spots, between the "torrid zones" and the frozen poles, could best support life and labor. They were lands "of milk and honey," new Canaans awaiting Europe's miserable masses. He first conceived the idea as he traveled to take up a posting in Batavia, where he served for a time as a reader in the town's Reformed church. He tried to sell his plan to the Dutch East India Company, calling for a colony in present-day South Australia, known as the "Land of Nuyts" after a Dutch explorer who had charted its coast. Purry thought a new colony there, peopled with persecuted Europeans of all nations, could become the "Repository of the Wine and Corn" for all of the East Indies. The climate, after all, was ideal, even better than the Mediterranean places that produced most wine already, but it was much closer to Asian markets. If the Dutch considered the Land of Nuyts to be too far away, Purry also suggested the "pays de Cafres," on the coast of southern Africa just to the east of the Cape Colony in lands inhabited by the Xhosa. "Either of these Countries is able to produce better Wines than any of those which are imported hither," Purry wrote, and they could make the East India Company a great deal of money. The promise went beyond any one commodity; countries on thirty-three degrees were also perfect for many products, and "the Article of Silk alone would be abundantly sufficient to repay all the Expence, provided this Affair was well regulated."[36]

The Dutch did not care for Purry's plans. Perhaps remembering the marginal returns in their previous attempt to do much the same thing in the Cape Colony, they rejected his entreaties and, in his telling at least, did so with so much prejudice that Purry was forced to leave the Netherlands altogether. After being run out of the Dutch empire, Purry turned his attention to the French. They had interests in the East Indies, but their colony of Louisiana also lay at the magic latitude, and as it happened the newly founded Mississippi Company, led by the Scottish banker John Law, was in the process of making plans for developing the colony. Purry was warmly received in Versailles and Paris, even earning praise from the *Journal des Sçavans* and gaining appointment as a director general of Law's Company of the Indies. Soon the Mississippi bubble burst, leading to John Law's abrupt departure from Paris and the end of any plans that could have benefited Purry.[37] At this point he turned to a final option, contacting the British ambassador to France, Sir Horace Walpole. Intrigued, the ambassador forwarded Purry's proposal to the Board of Trade in 1724, who decided that Purry's talents could be best put to use in South Carolina, which also lay near thirty-three degrees. Purry claimed that he believed Carolina to be "not just one of the best countries in America, but even in all the universe," and he specifically asked for land and aid to settle a Swiss colony there. Soon he published a French-language tract claiming Carolina as the place "best adapted to evoke abundantly from the earth,—and that without much labor or expense,—everything essential to life."[38]

Thus emerged the new colony of Purrysburgh. It took nearly a decade for Purry to actually find settlers and transport them to the colony, where they took up land on the Savannah River that had been inhabited by the now defeated Yamasee Indians. The design has usually appeared as a Swiss colony, but Purry's effort drew from the same traditions as the earlier Huguenot plantations. He promoted his town as a center for the wine and especially the silk trades, and while Huguenots were certainly not the majority in the town, they were present. The Swiss, Purry noted, faced population pressures and lack of resources, particularly the refugees and their children who still abounded in Neuchâtel and neighboring towns. Swiss officials, meanwhile, were just as eager to be rid of poor refugees in the 1720s as they had been in the 1690s, while they placed various restrictions on the emigration of their own subjects. Purry also made note of the Huguenots who had stayed or returned to their homeland, noting that "many Protestants remain in France, enduring tyranny and persecution, influenced much less by a just horror of the idolatry which they there behold and frequently have the misfortune to commit." Purrysburgh offered them "a sure and honest retreat where they may, by cultivating their own lands, guard themselves against poverty, and dispense with the charity of their brethren." The Swiss projector wrote in the same tradition of Protestant utopian literature as Duquesne and Rochefort in an earlier century. His writing was replete with biblical analogies and he weaved a plan that combined dreams of profit with the desire for *salut*. Some French, like the native of Orange Hector Bérenger de Beaufain, answered the call, while others, like Pierre Simond the younger, invested heavily in Purrysburgh, clearly believing that Purry's theories had some merit. By the mid-1730s, the town had become the first new substantial settlement of French Protestant refugees since the turn of the century. Although Purrysburgh never lived up to its founder's great vision, it did become the center of the region's modest silk industry.[39]

It was no accident that Purry found success in Britain rather than the Netherlands or France. The British empire in the eighteenth century was fertile ground for such projects—even those, like Purry's, based on questionable theories of climate and environment. Moreover, these designs only multiplied in the years after Purry settled in South Carolina. New projectors appeared everywhere, from the English countryside to the farthest reaches of the American and Asian empire, legions of ambitious gentlemen (and a few women) who hoped that their schemes would bring riches to themselves and prosperity to Britain. These plans tended to be driven by the same political economic logic that had inspired the earlier vision of the 1680s and 1690s. Political economic writers worried about Britain's place in the world: that its balance of trade was skewed and that British consumers endangered the realm with their dependence on foreign superfluities. More than anything they advocated for foreign trade, defining Britain as the "trading nation" par excellence whose connections to the larger world, including its colonies, could ensure its wealth and power. One writer, perhaps Daniel Defoe, laid out an expansive vision of an integrated imperial system, in which metropolitan manufacturers sold their goods to colonial consumers, who improved new lands and sent new raw materials into the world. "Manufacture for Employment at Home, and Navigation for Employment Abroad, both together, seem to set all the busy World at Work," he wrote. "They seem to joyn Hands to encourage the industrious Nations, and if well managed, infallibly make the World rich."[40]

The British obsession with projects sometimes dovetailed nicely with the French Protestant quest for toleration. Advocates of both noted the importance of a large population, and like the contemporary French design in Guiana, many of these British schemes involved population engineering on a substantial scale. As political economist Joshua Gee noted, "Multitudes of People . . . are uneasy under their present Circumstances in the several Parts of *Europe*, and would be glad to be under the free Government of *Great-Britain*."[41] While these multitudes came from lots of places, from Germany to the fringes of the British Isles, Huguenots still tended to be favorites. Their reputation as good, productive Protestants survived intact, even though many of the earlier Huguenots overseas colonies had ended in disappointment. Not surprisingly, during times of persecution in France, British projectors often tried to capitalize, offering retreats to the beleaguered French Protestants. While this rarely resulted in large movements of people, there were times when it seemed that it would, as happened during an era of crisis in France during the first years of the 1750s.

The controversy began with a dispute over baptism. Priests in the south of France claimed that Protestants were altering the ceremony, substituting the words "in the name of the Holy Trinity" for the prescribed "in the name of the Father, the Son, and the Holy Ghost." From this small beginning matters escalated, and soon priests and authorities were forcibly rebaptizing children, as well as cracking down on clandestine church services. This led to a small but significant exodus toward Switzerland, encouraged by Antoine Court. In the summer of 1752 he welcomed 114 newcomers to Lausanne, and in the spirit of earlier leaders like Henri de Mirmand in the previous century, he began negotiating to find a place for them. Several German states made offers, as did Denmark, but Court favored another longstanding retreat—the kingdom of Ireland.[42]

At this point the religious visions of Court and his fellow refugee ministers dovetailed with imperial projects managed from London and Dublin. Though Ireland had rebounded to some degree from the turmoil of the 1690s, it still lacked settlers and especially manufacturers, and leaders in Dublin wanted productive newcomers who could "Counterballance the great Number of Papists and to strengthen the Protestant interest."[43] Silk proved an especially attractive option; even back in 1693 Charles de Sailly had identified "the manufacturing of silk" as something that could be undertaken in Ireland, and Antoine Court seemed to push the same scheme in the 1740s. Writing to his fellow minister Jacques Serces in London, Court bragged of a number of people in the silk business who were nearly ready to move. One prospective emigrant was a silk dyer, while another was a merchant who could instruct locals in the culture of mulberry trees and the raising of silkworms. Court suggested that the refugees could manage nearly all aspects of an Irish silk industry, from making raw silk to manufacturing it and marketing it on the European continent through their networks. All they needed was the push of persecution to get them to leave, which the baptism crisis of 1752 conveniently provided. By that time, many in Languedoc had come around to considering "expatriation," including "skillful merchants and craftsmen" with special insights into the silk industry that were "known to only a few people."[44]

Over the summer and fall of 1752 over a hundred refugees migrated to Dublin. Court arranged their transportation, generally over the well-worn path of the refugees through Basel and the Rhine River Valley to Rotterdam, where they found relief from the minister and flock of the venerable Église Wallonne before continuing on to Dublin on merchant ships. There they collected modest assistance from the French church, which welcomed anyone who could "augment the number of Protestants in the kingdom," even as officials lobbied against the transportation of too many newcomers who would need shelter, food, and support. Despite challenges, Serces thought the project would benefit both the refugees and Irish authorities, since the absolute lack of manufacturing made Ireland a blank slate for schemes of all sorts. "There is room there for those who make wool covers or blankets, hats, socks, or silk," Serces wrote, "flowerly fabrics, velvet, paper or lace, those who spin flax, or hemp, who cultivate the earth, who raise mulberry trees and silkworms, etc." The minister added that while the refugees would naturally settle in places that already had French churches, they would soon expand to new places, essentially making Ireland French—and Protestant to boot.[45]

Antoine Court's design to use refugees to jumpstart Ireland's silk industry went nowhere, but it fit with other contemporary designs to promote key industries in various parts of the empire using refugee labor. One design that never got very far was that of Minorca, the Mediterranean island conquered by Britain in the War of the Spanish Succession where Jean Louis Ligonier had previously served. As in Ireland, Catholics dominated Minorca, and authorities desired more Protestant settlers to provide balance and give the island an economic purpose to augment its strategic one. Its state, one report noted, was "totally miserable." The island had few exports and in fact depended on French ports like Marseille for many of its goods. Nonetheless, it had great promise. One report claimed the island was "very proper for mulberry trees, olives, figs" and that silk in particular could be "superior to much of that from Spain, the Levant, and Italy."[46]

Huguenot refugees constituted a perfect prospective labor force for the island. Many of them lived only a few hundred miles away in southern France, and of course they could claim expertise in the very industries that central planners believed could prosper on the island. One anonymous projector complained that the island's Catalan inhabitants were "averse to us our Religion and Industry" and could never make good subjects. Instead, he advocated that "foreign Protestants" come to the island and devote themselves to wine, silk, and olive oil—pursuits that would succeed better than in America since the Mediterranean climate was perfect for these crops. The projector called for oppressed Protestants from all over Europe to come to Minorca, but geography meant that most of them would be French. Indeed, he credited the original idea to his French father-in-law who had served in the Dutch armed forces during the War of the Spanish Succession. The projector believed the king would be "graciously pleased to make it a place of Safety" for the refugees, "where they [could] peaceably enjoy the fruits of their labour, the full Exercise of their Religion and all the sweets of British Liberty."[47] While few or no Huguenots seem to have ever settled there, word of the plan did get out. In 1752, for instance, a Genevan minister mentioned that the Minorca scheme had circulated among Swiss refugees.[48]

As tempting as European retreats like Ireland and Minorca could be, America retained its pride of place in Huguenot colonization schemes. Political economic writers lauded the value of the colonies to the mother country and believed they could be even more productive with some extra attention. Daniel Defoe waxed poetic about "what a glorious Trade to *England* it would be to have those Colonies encreased with a Million of People, to be cloth'd, funrish'd, and supply'd with all their needful Things, Food excepted, only from us." But they would be more than just consumers. Presenting a list of commodities usually brought in from the Mediterranean and the East Indies, Defoe noted that "*Every one of them*" could come "from our own Colonies, the Product of the *British* proper Dominions, the Labour of the *British* People, and which is equal to it, all brought by our own Ships, to the vast Encrease of the *British* Navigation."[49]

One particular focus of attention was Paul Mascarene's stomping ground of Nova Scotia. Despite the half-hearted efforts to encourage Protestant migration after the conquest in 1710, it was not until 1749 that imperial planners began turning to the task in earnest. Nova Scotia was difficult to develop. It lay on the border with Britain's French rivals, was filled with undependable Catholic subjects, and most of it was rocky and cold, giving lie to the promotional tract that claimed "There is no part of *North America* where they can boast of a more fertile soil." Another tract more honestly admitted that that climate was "*rather unfavourable to* European *constitutions*," but also laid out the benefits of the fishing and naval stores industries. Its key value, however, was strategic. "It is however certain," one tract's author continued, "that while this settlement remains in our hands, no enemy will have in their power to annoy, from thence, our other colonies on the continent, which has principally engaged the Brittish ministry to expend such sums, and to take such pains in supporting it." Another writer concurred, adding simply that if the French took back Nova Scotia "it would be not only the ruin of *New England*, but of almost all our colonies on the continent."[50]

In 1749 the new governor, Edward Cornwallis, spearheaded a plan to settle the colony with Protestants. His instructions from the Board of Trade identified "the better Peopling our said province" as a key priority, and Cornwallis set out to fulfill the order. Many of the newcomers would be British subjects, whether from the North American colonies or the home islands, who he placed mostly in the new capital of Halifax, which grew quickly. Foreign Protestants, whether Germans or French, also figured in the Board's plans. Many Germans and a few French settled in the new town of Lunenberg, just to the west of Halifax, while several Huguenot schemes percolated in Whitehall. In 1749 the Board suggested "French Protestants from Martinico" as possible settlers, but there is little indication either that there were significant numbers of Protestants in Martinique or that any of them wanted to move to the frozen, windswept north.[51]

A new captive population of Huguenots appeared in the early months of 1750. A group of four hundred French Protestants "retired from Persecution into His Majesty's Island of Jersey," and officials in the Channel Islands and London began figuring out to do with them, since the island did not have enough resources for the new arrivals. The Duke of Bedford brought the situation to the Board of Trade, asking for proposals to settle the refugees that would be "most consistent with Oeconomy." The Board responded by suggesting they settle in Nova Scotia, since "their Knowledge of the Language and other Circumstances, which will facilitate their Intercourse with His Majesty's French Roman Catholick Subjects, will make them more useful Settlers than they would be in any other Province."[52] The Board then got in touch with Huguenot leaders in London, especially the minister Jacques Serces, and tried to find merchants who would contract to take the refugees across the ocean.[53] The Archbishop of Canterbury also heartily supported the scheme, noting that if the Board of Trade could not find a place

for these "poor French Protestants . . . they will soon find themselves in the unhappy Dilemma, of resolving to dye thro want in the Island, or to return again to
the Country they have left; a thing probably worse than Death to them."[54]

The plan soon began to unravel. For one thing, the Board began to doubt its
own scheme. They worried that too many of the refugees might be manufacturers,
and would want to set up industries in Nova Scotia that would compete with
those in the home country—a violation of the tenets of mercantilism. In addition, they seemed to fall victim to some of the francophobia that often complicated Huguenot colonial designs. They originally intended the Huguenots
as missionaries of sorts to the Acadians—people who could finally turn
those recalcitrant Catholics into good subjects, and perhaps even make them
Protestants, just as Paul Mascarene had dreamed. Now they seemed to worry
that the opposite could occur. The Board instructed Cornwallis that "it would
not be adviseable to suffer these French Protestants at their first Arrival to mix
much with the french Papists in Your Province, the more distinct they are kept,
the more secure will be the good Affection and Principles of the Protestants, and
consequently the better will it be for the Colony."[55] In the end, none of this much
mattered anyway, as the Huguenots in Jersey "all declared that they are unwilling
to go to Nova Scotia."[56] Apparently the colony's reputation among refugees was
not a good one. Just one year after the collapse of the Jersey project, Antoine
Court reported that "the very name [of Nova Scotia] makes them tremble."[57]

If Nova Scotia largely failed as a refugee haven, the subtropical colonies of
the South seemed to provide more promising retreats. Since Jean-Pierre Purry
had ended up in the Savannah River Valley in the 1730s, the far reaches of South
Carolina and the new neighboring colony of Georgia had become critical to
imperial strategy. The Carolina Lowcountry was profitable for its rice and indigo exports, but projectors in the piedmont hoped for new cash crops—naval
stores, to be sure, but also the old standbys of wine, silk, and olive oil. Indeed,
the mania for these products seemed to match or go beyond the earlier craze of
the seventeenth century, as interested parties in both the colonies and England
sought ways to bring these industries into being.[58] The rationale appeared most
clearly in the introduction to John Locke's earlier speculations on vineyards, finally printed and released in 1766. The editor noted the dangers of allowing the
colonies to become "rivals in trade," but insisted instead that the mother country
encourage them in "the growth and produce of Vines and Olives, Silk and Fruits,
which cannot advantageously be raised in England," all of which would assure a
happy and lasting imperial union.[59]

No organization was more central to this push than the so-called Honourable
Society for the Encouragement of Arts, Manufactures, and Commerce, later
known as the Royal Society of Arts. The Society became something of a central institution for projectors in the mid-1700s. It served to identify projects

that would improve the realm in some important way, especially in terms of advancing the national economy. From the beginning the RSA championed colonial projects, especially those that would help Britain's balance of trade. Their manifesto claimed that "the increase of trade with our colonies" was a key goal, since that would lead "to their taking manufactures" while providing important commodities in return. The Society endeavored to give "bounties" that would encourage economic development, everything from sturgeon and potash to myrtle wax, but especially silk and wine. "The importance of producing silk in our own dominions has been before touched upon," noted the Society's report, "and, indeed, required little elucidation." The RSA offered bounties to people throughout the colonies, even as far north as Connecticut, to grow mulberry trees and raise silkworms.[60]

Colonial planters, governors, and even ordinary farmers sought to work with the Society to bring these plans to fruition. On silk, the South Carolina planter Charles Pinckney argued there was "no doubt" that colonial silkmakers "will succeed . . . if they are but properly encouraged by their Mother Country, as to be shure they will as all things of that sort must ultimately so greatly redound to her own Benefit and Advantage and the distressing her Rival Trade in so considerable a Branch of her Manufactures." Pinckney predicted that "your Children and mine will live to see all the Silk we now import from france, imported from these Colonies."[61] His Virginia counterpart Charles Carter made the same arguments about wine, turning his plantation into a giant experiment in viticulture that resembled earlier designs by William Berkeley and Robert Beverley. By 1763 Carter sent samples of two of his wines back to London, and "they were both approved as good wines: and the Society gave their gold medal to Mr. Carter, as the first, who had made a spirited attempt towards the accomplishment of their views, respecting wine in America."[62]

As in earlier decades, Huguenots and other foreign Protestants attempted to capitalize on this silk and wine mania. The hamlet of Purrysburgh in particular became a center of activity. Purry had hoped that the project would center on silk and wine production; indeed, much of his eccentric enthusiasm for places on South Carolina's latitude stemmed from his belief that they were suited to such commodities.[63] Wine proved impossible to produce in that humid country, but residents of Purrysburgh had more luck with silk, especially after the foundation of the new colony of Georgia right across the Savannah River. At least in its early years, James Oglethorpe's colony was a projector's paradise; the Georgia Proprietors even put a silkworm on the colony's seal and publicly supported a silk filature in the province—a warehouse in which an expert would oversee the difficult task of turning raw silk into something that could be shipped out to market.[64] According to one petition, more than half of that raw silk came from Purrysburgh. The inhabitants asked the Royal Society of Arts to give them similar bounties to those offered to Georgia silk experimenters. Huguenots, along with Germans, Swiss, and other outsiders, continued to promote themselves as valuable experts who could bring these industries to perfection.[65]

This enthusiasm for silk, wine, and projects in general colored Jean-Louis Gibert's experience in Britain. When he arrived in London in 1761, as the Seven Years' War still raged between Britain and France, he did so as a religious emissary. A key soldier in the re-establishment of the Protestant churches in France, Gibert intended to make connections with fellow Protestants across the Channel. He also hoped to influence the coming peace negotiations in order to help his fellow Huguenots. He gained an audience with Thomas Secker, the Archbishop of Canterbury, who devoted much of his attention to helping oppressed Protestants around the continent. Perhaps more than any of his predecessors since Henry Compton, the archbishop made the relief of foreign Protestants a top priority and showed particular interest in the sufferings of the Huguenots. On his accession in 1758 Secker sent a letter to the administrators of Geneva's longstanding "Bourse Française," expressing his support for God's "afflicted servants, who suffer in France for the profession of the Truth, as it is in Jesus; & for whom you provide Consolation with so much Zeal & prudence."[66] Secker also maintained frequent correspondence with leaders in both the Desert and the Refuge, including exiled church leader Benjamin du Plan and Antoine Court de Gebelin, the son of the late founder of the churches of the Desert, who had taken over his father's duties. Court de Gebelin provided Secker a lengthy narrative of the state of church in France, of a people "spread out and dispersed over a vast kingdom, ceaselessly blown by the winds of persecution," but who had still managed to build churches. The Huguenot leader hoped that Secker would surpass even the examples of previous church leaders in helping the French Protestant cause, and the arrival of Gibert in England gave him just the avenue to do so. Secker first learned of the newcomer from his key Huguenot ally, Savoy Church minister John James Majendie, who related that "one of the Protestant Ministers of Xaintonge in France is just come over upon an Errand of a very delicate Nature."[67]

Once he came before the archbishop Gibert made a bold proposal. Back in 1758 the pastor had attended a synod in the Cévennes, and he reported that the Protestants agreed to "leave their Country, if they could not be relieved from the Hardships, which they now sufferd on account of their Religion." Gibert claimed that 60,000 Protestants were willing to finally depart France and take their chances in the Refuge, and Secker suggested that Britain find some means to relieve Gibert and his coreligionists. The archbishop eventually secured a meeting with George III himself, who said that "both Humanity & Religion disposed him to pity & relieve them," but he could only do so once they had fled France and arrived safely on British soil. The next step was to figure out what to do with the prospective new arrivals. The king's ministers suggested sending the refugees to "England, Ireland, or America, as it should be found most proper," but noted that they could not engage in manufacturing if they went to the colonies. Gibert himself preferred a North American retreat and noted that "his people should produce Silk," a suggestion that Secker endorsed.[68]

It took nearly two years for Gibert to return to Britain. Early in 1763, only a month after the Treaty of Paris ended the war, the minister arrived in London and began to make arrangements for his countrymen to join him. Things did not go smoothly. Officials in Whitehall were surprised to see the minister so soon after the peace, and warned him that he could expect little in the way of concrete assistance from the government. George Grenville chafed at the expected costs of caring for so many newly arriving French, claiming "that it may bring an immoderate Expence upon the Crown." Archbishop Secker, always the champion of persecuted Protestants, lobbied on their behalf to the famously cost-obsessed Chancellor of the Exchequer, claiming that "Some of them are expected in a few days & will probably come destitute of every thing." It was in the interest of "Humanity & publick Good" to care for the newcomers, and besides, the king himself had earlier pledged his support for the Huguenots. To reject them now would be to make a liar of the sovereign himself. When Grenville directed one of his officers to discourage Gibert from bringing his countrymen over, the Archbishop balked, claiming it was "unsuitable to the assurances I gave in the King's name" in 1761.[69]

Secker's efforts eventually succeeded in raising modest sums toward the relief of Gibert's expected hordes of Huguenots. Grenville relented and arranged some support for the refugees who arrived in Portsmouth and Plymouth—£1000 directly from the king's coffers—but he hoped that the numbers would not be as large as Gibert claimed, since it would be hard to support so many people, and besides a mass emigration could attract unwanted attention from French authorities.[70] In the meantime, Secker worked within the established networks that Huguenots had used for decades. He called on the Huguenot churches, the old Royal Bounty, and especially John James Majendie, whose father had been a refugee cleric. If "humanity" dictated some of this response, it was clear that the "publick Good" played just as central a role. The ambition to raise silk that Gibert cited in 1761 continued to motivate him two years later. In a letter to Secker near the end of the year, as his country folk arrived, the minister reiterated the value of silk and wine experiments, and he pledged that his people would "work in common in the cultivation of silk."[71]

The newcomers soon attracted attention from French observers in the British capital. Louis XV's emissary, the Chevalier d'Eon, learned of the arrival of "50 to 80 French families" who Gibert had lured to England with "circular letters" from "different provinces of France." Gibert had supposedly promised these migrants "good establishments in the Colonies with the option to return to France if these establishments no longer suited them." The purpose, d'Eon underscored, was more economic than religious. The ambassador described Gibert not just as a minister but as a "puller of silk," and claimed that the purpose of the colony would be "to establish manufactures and mulberry plantations there."[72]

The Frenchman must have had good information, as silk making was a central goal of imperial planners. These strategic concerns influenced the process by which imperial officials tried to locate lands for the newly arrived refugees. The Treaty of Paris had transformed the empire, giving Britain control over all of the former French territories in Canada and the cis-Mississippi West, along with a number of new Caribbean islands. Gibert's colonists looked to these new territories for possible retreats. The Board of Trade wanted to send the Huguenots to one of "the new established colonies in America," first considering the Ohio River Valley. The Royal Proclamation of October 1763 closed off official settlement there, however. At that point Gibert's and the Board's attention turned to the most fertile ground for projects in the 1760s, the newly acquired colony of Florida. The former Spanish colony consisted of two distinct provinces—one around the Atlantic port of Saint Augustine, the other on the Gulf Coast around Pensacola—both of which were "altogether unsettled & uncultivated," since most of the former Spanish settlers had decamped for Cuba. Peopling the two colonies became a key goal of the Board of Trade, both for strategic reasons and to develop the imperial economy.[73]

Speculation about Florida quickly came to focus on silk, wine, and other Mediterranean commodities. One imaginative projector, the Scot Archibald Menzies, claimed that "with proper culture," Florida and the other new colonies "would supply us with all the materials for our manufactures, that are produced in hot climates; and even with many of our most expensive luxuries." The problem, as ever, was finding proper laborers and artisans to bring the plans to completion, and Menzies suggested Greeks and Armenians, since they were "accustomed to a hot climate, and bred to the culture of the vine, olive, cotton, tobacco, madder, &c. &c. as also to the raising silk."[74] A few Greeks did eventually settle in the disastrous colony of New Smyrna, but at the same time Huguenot schemes proved popular as well. As Governor James Grant put it in a July 1763 missive, "French Protestants, who are not induced, to leave their Country out of Penury and Want, but from a desire to live under a free Government, and enjoy the Exercise of their Religion, would be the most valuable Colonists." He suggested working with that most well connected of Huguenots, Pierre Simond, to find settlers to bring to Florida.[75]

By October Gibert and his fellow refugees had determined to become the settlers who would fulfill Grant's vision. As Henry Laurens reported to

a correspondent, "he has happily engaged near two hundred french protestant families to come out with him. These are useful inhabitants & will
be some means of drawing forth other Emigrants to join them."[76] Gibert's
partner in the scheme, another minister named Pierre Boutiton, took the lead
in negotiating the terms of the new colonial venture with the Board of Trade.
A minister from the region of Perigord, Boutiton had arrived in London in
mid-1763 with a number of migrants from neighboring towns and villages,
dramatically increasing the population of the new colony. His proposals, set
out in a numbered list of eight particulars, mirrored many of the Huguenot
colonial appeals of the previous century. Boutiton requested the Board of
Trade give the refugees ample land on the St. John River, near the site where
in 1563 René de Laudonnière had first attempted to build a Huguenot colony
in North America, and that they receive money for supplies and temporary
relief from taxation. Since the colonists still intended to "make wine and raise
silkworms," they needed to be "placed in a spot proper for Commerce and
Navigation." Boutiton repeated Gibert's prediction that a "large number" of
French Protestants would flock to Florida, escaping the "yoke of servitude in
order to live according to their conscience" among their countrymen. Finally,
the minister repeated the calls for autonomy that had appeared in Huguenot
missives from Germany to America to the Cape of Good Hope in previous
decades. He asked that "the Colony be permitted to form its own council,
choose its magistrates, and make laws that it judges to be the most advantageous, on the condition that they do not contradict the laws of the Kingdom
and the crown's prerogatives." This was not quite a colony within a colony, but
close to it.[77]

The Board seemed to approve of most of Boutiton's terms, but still the
colonists never went to Florida. It is possible that the two ministers were simply
angling for the best deal, but for whatever reason by the end of 1763 their attention had turned from East Florida to the South Carolina backcountry. South
Carolina was of course an established and profitable colony, and one with
thousands of Huguenot descendants, but authorities had long wanted to expand the colony beyond the profitable lowcountry into the more remote piedmont. In 1755 Governor James Glen made an agreement with the Cherokee to
acquire land that became known as the Ninety-Six District, a large tract on the
upper reaches of the Savannah River nearly two hundred miles northwest of
Charleston. Six years later the Legislature passed a Bounty Act that provided financial assistance to any Protestant migrant willing to settle in this frontier area.
The land was appropriate for the Huguenots, so projectors thought, for the same
kind of Mediterranean commodities that would grow in Florida, and there was
plenty of land for the taking. So by 1763 the fate of the Huguenots was set: they
were headed to South Carolina.[78]

The story of all these prospective colonies in the 1750s and 1760s revealed deep continuities in the British imperial project. For one thing, the old dreams of silk and wine remained and motivated actors in Whitehall to support dubious projects that otherwise would have gone nowhere. More than that, the political economic logic of the time still combined with religious motivations to turn the Huguenots into the chosen people of empire. Thomas Secker played the role of Henry Compton in the era of the Revocation, advocating that Britons open the door to their persecuted French brethren, while networks of French Protestant merchants and ministers, stretching from Lausanne and Geneva to Languedoc and Saintonge and then to London and Dublin, sought to mobilize aid for the refugees. What was more, the political situation in France convinced many, both Huguenots and British, that the 1760s could be a golden age of migration that rivaled or even surpassed the 1680s.

Nonetheless, the British enthusiasm for Huguenots remained limited by the twin strands of confession and economy. This became clear in another failed scheme that the Board of Trade considered during the summer of 1763, along with Gibert and Boutiton's proposal. A French Protestant named Jacques Robins had received a grant for land in Miramichi, a remote part of Acadia in present-day New Brunswick. He proposed settling the colony in part with his own Huguenot coreligionists, but also with Catholic Acadians, who had been forcibly relocated around the British empire during the last war. Robins's colony would be wholly French and biconfessional, with freedom of conscience for all and a resident priest to give mass to the Catholics. As far as the economy went, he desired all men who wanted to "live honestly in whatever employment they preferred."[79] Even though he networked with many of the same London Huguenots as Gibert and Boutiton—including Pierre Simond—the Board of Trade quickly rejected Robins's proposal. Charity had its limits, and the Board saw no reason to give its blessing to a French colonial plan that neither furthered the Protestant cause nor the imperial economy.[80]

———

The tens of thousands of migrants Gibert envisioned heading to America in 1763 did not materialize. His visit to Languedoc only convinced a couple of people to leave France for South Carolina, so the minister continued on to his former home of Saintonge in western France, which had always provided more transatlantic migrants than the south. Here he found a few more recruits, but still not many, and in fact in his absence many of Gibert's fellow Protestants had turned against him. He found himself the subject of abuse from Louis XV's officials as well as from fellow Protestants, who accused him of abandoning his longtime efforts to rebuild the French Protestant church and leading his flock on a hopeless boondoggle. In an earlier letter Antoine Court had identified the problem. French policy had worked too well, and Huguenots within France heard too many bad stories from their brethren who, "not finding what they had been promised in their places of refuge," returned to France and actually found that the government repaid them with favors. Gibert left France in 1763, no longer a leader of the church, but a hapless exile with few followers.[81]

Nonetheless, there was a Huguenot migration to North America in the 1760s, and it led to the creation of several new and final refugee communities in the New World. The first one, New Bordeaux, consisted of Gibert's flock and a few other additions, French as well as German, who settled in the South Carolina upcountry. The other, smaller flow of refugees went to West Florida, where they founded Campbell's Town, while a few stragglers ended up in Nova Scotia and Maine.[82] These migrations were small, both compared to the movement of Huguenots in earlier decades and the massive movement of Germans, Scots, and others in the 1760s, but they demonstrated the lasting impact of the Huguenot colonial project. For one thing, despite the small number of migrants, these projects attracted a great deal of attention—local and imperial officials continued to favor Huguenots, even if they were far smaller in number than other migration streams, for their special skills or status as good subjects. Second, these new communities consciously followed in the footsteps of their seventeenth-century predecessors, whether in their emphasis on Mediterranean commodities or their location in strategic locations on colonial frontiers. Indeed, Campbell's Town and West Florida in general sought to make good on Daniel Coxe's Carolana scheme from so many years before.

By the middle of 1763 the first group of prospective colonists to New Bordeaux, around two hundred in number, gathered in Plymouth. They had arrived in that port town through a circuitous route; most came through Switzerland, by way of a complex network of Huguenot pastors who sought to spread the word of the new colony and find willing travelers. Others, like Pierre Moragne, who left a journal of his experiences, traveled by sea, through the Channel Islands and on to Plymouth. Moragne left his home in Dordogne in July 1763, traveling to the port town of Royan and from there, apparently without incident, to England where he arrived the following month.[83] Obviously, the colony found far fewer takers than they expected, and that was only the beginning of New Bordeaux's problems. Despite earlier promises of assistance, the British government did little to help. Over the course of 1763 ministers in England worked with the king and the Archbishop of Canterbury to raise funds to transport the first settlers to South Carolina, but as the project lagged many of the prospective colonists returned to France. By December only 113 remained, and according to one witness "a spirit of discord had risen up among the French refugees at Plymouth," who increasingly believed that Gibert had deceived them. The

French ambassador reported that the prospective migrants complained constantly of "persecution and misery."[84]

Aside from the natural anger at not receiving promised aid from the government, the refugees argued with Gibert about the proper mission of the colony. The minister had sold New Bordeaux to its backers as a community of French people who would "work in common in the production of silk." But even before they left England, many of the Huguenots had soured on that plan. Some hoped they would receive subsidies so they could go off on their own and dedicate themselves to "individual interests." Gibert worked hard to preserve New Bordeaux as a communal venture dedicated to preserving the church and furthering the imperial economy, but few agreed with him.[85] Nonetheless, funding for the voyage eventually materialized, and on Christmas Day 1763 the migrants departed Plymouth for Charleston. Word of the migration quickly reached the duc de Choiseul, who was in the midst of planning his own disastrous colonial venture in Guiana, and who sent circulars around France telling of the migrants who had been "debauched" by Gibert and Boutiton into leaving the kingdom.[86] The debauchees did not have an easy time. Storms and a near rebellion among the ranks of settlers initially forced the boat back to Plymouth, and it was not until April 10 that "We commenced seeing the shores of America," Pierre Moragne recalled, "which great rejoiced us."[87]

The dissensions that first appeared in Plymouth continued during the difficult months following the refugees' arrival. Huguenots in Charleston proved eager to help—the French church provided "hogshead of crackers (biscuits) and other liberalities," while the prominent merchant Gabriel Manigault offered his plantation, appropriately named Silk Hope, as the site of Gibert's first silk experiments.[88] The provincial government received strict instructions to local officials to do all they could for the poor French Protestants, whose "knowledge in the Culture of Silk and Vines" made them "particularly Usefull to the Colony and to the Publick." The Governor and Council gave the refugees some provisions and relief from taxation, but they had not yet surveyed the settlers' land on the Savannah River, so they had to spend an uncomfortable winter in an old military barracks in Port Royal. Governor William Bull lectured the settlers on staying together "with Peace and cordiality" and resisting divisions, which would lead them to "fall into States of Indigence and Misery."[89]

Bull's entreaties had little effect, and the French community soon fragmented. In May 1764 Gibert and Boutiton sent a cryptic appeal to the Council claiming that they could not live with certain of the refugees who were "the Occasion of Continual Troubles." Apparently the two men and thirty-one of their followers had decided to separate from the main group and requested temporary housing in a lowcountry plantation and cooper's tools "for the Cultivation of Silk which they intend to go upon in the Neighborhood of Charles Town." The petitioners understood the irony of their request. Gibert had always requested that the refugees "settle together" and had argued against those among his countryfolk who wanted to go off on their own, but "some had crept in among them with whom it was impossible to live," and Gibert had given up—not only on France, but now on the idea of building a coherent Huguenot community in South Carolina.[90]

New Bordeaux lived on, however—and did so, for the most part, without its founder and primary champion. Gibert received a 200-acre plot of land in the new settlement and occasionally spent time there, but did not occupy a leadership role as the first settlers carved the town out of the wilderness during 1764 and 1765. Even more surprisingly, he seems never to have officiated as a minister there. His business partner and now brother-in-law Pierre Boutiton did settle in the town and at least occasionally ministered to its inhabitants, and Gibert's nephew Pierre sometimes filled that role as well.[91] In the meantime a surveyor platted the land according to the Council's instructions, and several representatives of the new colony accompanied him to identify the best lands.[92] For the next few years little happened to attract attention to the settlers on the upper Savannah River, but the surviving letters depicted a stable if unexciting life. "The French Refugees are highly pleased with their New settlement," noted Henry Laurens in 1764, "I am in hopes of seeing in a few Years a fine Colony rising upon the Spots where they are fixed."[93] At least one New Bordeaux resident confirmed Laurens's portrait. "My situation is, God be thanked, very agreable," wrote Pierre Moragne to his father in France. "I live in peace with my family, and cultivate the earth with success. I have an abundance of what is necessary for me and mine."[94] Moragne presented the classic image of a New World utopia, a place not suited for riches but for peace and comfort.

New Bordeaux's often absent founder, on the other hand, dedicated himself to other pursuits. While his countrymen built a town, he made good on his earlier pledges to jumpstart South Carolina's silk industry, with the help of Gabriel Manigault and other prominent Carolinians. From his perch at Silk Hope Plantation, Gibert petitioned the Royal Society of Arts for help with his project. After many "ill conveniences" he succeeded in producing 620 pounds of cocoons, from which he extracted 35 pounds of raw silk that he presented to leading experts in London who confirmed "the goodness of the Silk." He requested the Society's bounty to continue his work, which he intended to do on a 100-acre tract of land where he had left his family, from which he hoped "to emmulate the whole Province in the said Culture."[95]

While no evidence confirms whether or not the Society granted any aid to Gibert's efforts, he soon found assistance from the provincial government. For decades administrators in the colony had granted assistance to those willing to work at producing valuable crops, and they also saw the example of Georgia, where a public silk filature operated at public expense. By 1766 a similar facility opened in Charleston, and word of the endeavor appeared in newspapers around colonial America. According to a Boston newspaper report, the South Carolina Assembly pledged £1000 to the building of a silk filature in Charleston and made Gibert its director.[96] A year later he had gathered "a considerable number of silkworms" in an old schoolhouse, where he endeavored to "teach the winding of silk" to local inhabitants. Numerous families answered the call, and Gibert had become the colony's agent "concerned on behalf of the public in the encouragement of this manufacture," even setting up detailed exhibits that included examples of silkworms in various stages of life.[97] The *Virginia Gazette* added that not only was Gibert teaching about silk making in Charleston, but French settlers in Purrysburgh and New Bordeaux (and their German neighbors) were also making it.[98] It was the end of a stunning transformation; the man who had dedicated much of his life to building churches had abandoned his flock in favor of silkworms.

Some hundred miles to the southwest, a similar settlement developed in West Florida. The colony on the Gulf of Mexico included the old French fort at Mobile as well as former Spanish Pensacola, which consisted of "an assemblage of poor despicable Huts."[99] Nonetheless, it was the theater of grand ambitions. Indeed, in 1763 the heirs of the old proprietor of Carolana, the Coxe family, began another bid to advocate for their old claim. In a tract claiming to show the justness for a British claim of the territories west as well as east of the Mississippi, the Coxes lauded their ancestor's efforts to settle the Gulf of Mexico and called for a renewal of his plan. "Perhaps there is not in the World a finer Country" than the southern part of the old Carolana patent, they claimed, and in particular it was a place that could fix Britain's balance of trade. Wild grapes grew everywhere, they noted, and "were they properly cultivated and pruned, they would yield as good Grapes, and consequently as good Wine, as any Part of *Europe* affords." The region also contained forests of mulberry trees, "and certainly, with proper Encouragement, a considerable Quantity of Silk might be produced here by the Labour of the Women and Children of even an Infant Colony." The Coxes' plans attracted the attention of Benjamin Franklin, but foundered when Franklin's chief contact in London failed to locate definitive proof of the family's claim to the land.[100]

The West Florida design went ahead, however, as a crown colony under the command of a naval veteran named George Johnstone. The new governor and his underlings had ambitious plans that hewed closely to the Coxes' vision, but they needed migrants to make the plan work. Like Daniel Coxe, Johnstone settled partially on French refugees as his new laborers, not surprisingly given the colony's ambitions to become a silk and wine mecca. In November 1763 the Board of Trade placed an advertisement in the *London Gazette* searching for

French emigrants, and in 1765 "several French Protestants" responded with a proposal, noting that they could "become usefull subjects . . . by applying themselves to the Culture of Vines, and bringing up Silkworms." Lieutenant Governor Montfort Browne supported the idea and offered to provide transportation for some of the migrants on his own ship. In addition, the Huguenots would receive some financial assistance for "some apparel and tools for carrying their plans into Execution."[101]

In the end only sixty French Protestants settled in West Florida. While smaller in scale, however, the settlement that became known as Campbell's Town fit many of the patterns of other Huguenot ventures, whether in the 1760s or earlier decades. For one thing, it duplicated some of the same power struggles that had raged in places like Manakintown and the Cape Colony during previous ventures. Even on the crossing, the group's de facto leader, a minister named Pierre Levrier, jockeyed for position, insisting on lodging in Browne's own stateroom, and then flying into a "Violent Passion" when Browne declined the request. In addition, the lieutenant governor engaged in some of the same francophobia that had often emerged in times of war, alleging that some of the names on Levrier's list of settlers were not Protestants at all but "Papists, pticularly one who I know was a French Officer and Partisan in Canada." Browne suggested requiring all the newcomers to take oaths of allegiance to the king before being allowed to settle in such a strategic, valuable territory. Despite these qualms, the Huguenots retained their value. According to Governor Johnstone, a French settler was worth twice that of an English one, since most of the latter were "always the Outcast[s] of some corrupted City." Johnstone retained his optimism that the "Vine, Olive, and Almond, will flourish here," but also expressed skepticism that "a Parcel of Spittlefield Weavers should come out here to cultivate those Things, and not a Plant of either imported." He realized what few officials cared to admit: that despite being French, few of the refugees had the kind of experience in cultivating Mediterranean commodities that would allow these designs to succeed.[102]

Once the newcomers reached Pensacola, the difficulties only increased. Apparently the land specified for the new community, on the Escambia River just miles away from the former Spanish settlement, was "a very Unhealthy spot for their settlement," and the small amount of aid pledged by the government proved insufficient for the task of establishing a new community. Many of the newcomers wanted to leave and find better land—perhaps in nearby Mobile or New Orleans where some of their fellow countrymen still resided. The Council tried to prevent this exodus by making the Huguenots promise not to abandon Campbell's Town.[103] In addition, their leader Levrier continued to cause trouble. Despite receiving a large advance on his salary from the West Florida agent John Ellis, he drew from it again from two different people in Pensacola, and

then promptly began plotting to leave the settlement. After considering relocation in Natchez on the Mississippi River, Levrier ended up in South Carolina,
where various reports suggest he either ministered to the congregation at New
Bordeaux or in Charleston's French Church.[104]

If Campbell's Town faded into obscurity, New Bordeaux lived on, and even
received a new lease on life when new colonists arrived in the late 1760s. Louis
de Mesnil de Saint-Pierre was a Huguenot gentleman and merchant from the
town of Honfleur in Normandy, and like Gibert, he chose to flee France in the
years immediately after the Seven Years' War. He also attracted the attention
of French authorities, who reported that as early as 1767 Saint-Pierre had
begun plotting with the English to form a settlement of French Protestants
"in one of their Colonies." In 1772 a French spy witnessed Saint-Pierre in
Portsmouth with "French workers of different Trades, who this gentleman
had succeeded in persuading to quit the country and to join him, with the
most lovely promises, to install them to form a new colony in New Carolina
[*la Nouvelle Caroline*]."[105] In fact, by this time Saint-Pierre had already established himself at New Bordeaux and was on a return mission to find more
settlers and aid. His original group had left England in 1768 intending to settle
in Nova Scotia, where he received a sizable grant of land near Cape Sable, but
contrary winds sent them to Charleston, where the leader decided to take
advantage of the bounties offered by the government to settle on the colony's
frontier, since his frightened and seasick passengers proved unwilling to risk
another sea voyage. They received grants of land in Hillsborough Township
on the Savannah River, alongside Gibert and Boutiton's colonists in New
Bordeaux.[106]

Like Gibert, Saint-Pierre attempted to lead an exodus of productive people
out of France, and he also learned to speak the language of political economy current in the British court. While he also occasionally mentioned the value of silk,
he turned most of his attention to wine. It is unclear whether or not Saint-Pierre
or his neighbors had any experience in vineyards. Most came from Normandy,
not a region known for its wine, and Saint-Pierre himself was a merchant and
gentleman rather than a farmer. Nonetheless, he knew that his English neighbors
considered all French people to be skilled vintners, and he was perfectly willing
to humor them in this belief. To be sure, there were some with experience in
vineyards among the settlers already living in New Bordeaux; the original list
identified 20 of the original 112 landholders as "*vignerons,*" and the original
instructions called for the laying out of "vineyard lots." Still, it is not clear that
many of these vineyards bore fruit before Saint-Pierre's initiative jumpstarted
the industry. Colonists seemed more interested in tobacco; in 1770 the *South-
Carolina Gazette* advertised "New Bordeaux rappee," a kind of coarse snuff made
by French Protestants which was "allowed, by Connoisseurs, to be very good."[107]

Saint-Pierre's sudden mania for wine may have come from the encouragement of Lieutenant Governor William Bull. The governor had dedicated himself
to diversifying the colonial economy, something he saw as especially important
in an era of rising tensions between colonists and Parliament. By finding employment in new fields of agricultural production South Carolinians would give
up any thoughts of establishing manufacturing and remain happy in the empire.
In 1767 he encouraged the efforts of one Christopher Sherb, who he called the
"poor German," to make wine in the upcountry, even recommending him to the
Royal Society of Arts for one of their medals. The German's death ended these
plans, but Saint-Pierre's arrival turned Bull's gaze toward New Bordeaux. The
two men shared the dream of turning this remote frontier town into the center
for a colonial wine industry.[108]

Over the next few years Saint-Pierre and Bull hatched their plans. In 1770 Bull
encouraged the Royal Society of Arts to send vine-cuttings to New Bordeaux,
and within several years French and German inhabitants had planted vineyards.
One of the most successful was John Lewis Gervais, who according to the surveyor William De Brahm perfected a new kind of vine raising in the town, "so
that New Bourdeaux is justly intitled to that Merit; which must be allowed a great
Acquisition in the Culture of Vine upon the extensive Continent of America,
when a sixty years experimental Inquiry has met with no more Discovery than
to condemn America as not possessed with the Faculty to produce Wine."[109]
Saint-Pierre went to London convinced that with a new infusion of cash he
could move beyond Gervais's efforts and finally realize the promise of North
American viticulture. Thanks to Bull's connections, Saint-Pierre gained the
support of the Secretary of State Lord Hillsborough, and he published several
detailed tracts that laid out best practices of maintaining vineyards and lauded
the particular benefits of his home community. Saint-Pierre's proposals laid
out a theory of empire that would have been familiar to Daniel Defoe and political economists going back to the seventeenth century. A turn to viticulture
would turn America into a thriving emporium, where happy settlers sold their
produce to the home country while consuming British products in return. He
specifically lauded the role of "foreigners of the protestant communion" in this
pursuit, who were "the fittest for this branch of agriculture, as that to which they
have been trained from their cradles." New Bordeaux's settlers were the perfect
imperial subjects. "They are all Vignerons to a man," Saint-Pierre claimed, "experienced and trained in this sort of husbandry from their infancy." The climate,
meanwhile, was "the Same as at Marseilles but with this difference, that the Soil
is here infinitely superior."[110]

Saint-Pierre's writings were almost entirely unoriginal. He drew on the
arguments of generations of Huguenot projectors before him, all of whom
argued that the special skills of their countrymen could help to solve the empire's

most longstanding problems. Saint-Pierre envisioned a harmonious, integrated empire—one in which metropolitans and colonials understood their proper roles in the imperial system. And it would all be made possible by vineyards. Indeed, the wholesome grape would literally guarantee the health of the body politic. Like many Huguenots, Saint-Pierre held up the example of France as both a model and a warning. The kingdom's large population, which allowed it to build a powerful army, came about because "the wholesomeness of this divine liquor" provided both employment and health to the population. The British empire stood in a position to inherit this wealth, because France's foolish perse-cutory policies pushed its Protestants away while Britain's guarantees of freedom of religion brought in refugees. People were the "only true riches of a nation," Saint-Pierre concluded, and by providing jobs and freedom the British empire stood poised to bring many of the world's peoples into its benevolent union. His argument represented a counterpoint to earlier appeals to the French crown. No longer welcome in France, the Huguenots were poised to take their people and talents to Britain.[111]

While the Frenchman found some support in London—including from the Royal Society of Arts, who awarded him its gold medal—he left the cap-ital with little money to help him build his wine empire. According to a later report, French interest groups lobbied the Secretary of State to make sure that Saint-Pierre's project failed, though given the failure of all previous colonial wine endeavors there were numerous reasons for potential investors to be wary of the scheme.[112] Others simply suggested that Saint-Pierre was a difficult character, and his repeated entreaties put off prospective patrons.[113] Grapes continued to grow in New Bordeaux, but they never provided the personal wealth or stra-tegic advantages that Saint-Pierre or Bull imagined. New Bordeaux lived on as a small agricultural settlement, not a boon for the empire, and by 1776 the empire was gone anyway, as were Jean-Louis Gibert and Louis de Saint-Pierre. The great merchant and wine speculator seems to have met his end as part of the 1776 expedition of the South Carolina militia against the British-allied Cherokee. Jean-Louis Gibert died in a far less glorious way. The man who had evaded royal authorities, a death sentence, and the galleys fell victim to a poisonous mush-room in August 1773.[114]

If Saint-Pierre really did die in action in the Revolutionary War, it would rep-resent a fitting conclusion to the Huguenot overseas experiment. Saint-Pierre believed that the Huguenots could save the empire in a moment of the crisis—that the turn to wine, or perhaps silk, could reorient the transatlantic relation-ship in a way that would sustain the imperial system. Such a vision lay behind this last concerted push for Huguenot colonies: the idea that legions of French expert producers could reorient the imperial economy and make the whole system work again. Even an assimilated Huguenot like Henry Laurens found the vision appealing. When his son James was in France in the 1774, Henry asked him to send vine cuttings, hoping to use them to make wine on his plantation. Combining a biblical reference with the language of no taxation without representation then current in the colonies, he hoped to "plant & Cultivate my Vine & my Fig Tree, from a well grounded assurance that I may Sit quietly under them & enjoy the fruit of my Labour, as my own property, not to be taken from me but my own Consent."[115] He was drawing from the longstanding dreams of silk and wine that had driven European expansion since the late 1500s, but repackaging them for an enlightened age. The coming political storms, however, would bring new challenges to the Huguenots' attempts to make new worlds.

Epilogue

The End of the Global Refuge

The story of the Beaufain family epitomized many of themes of Huguenot history in the eighteenth century. The family patriarch Frédéric de Bérenger de Beaufain left the family's hometown of Orange in southern France in 1703, fleeing alongside other Protestants who chose exile over conversion to Catholicism. Since 1685 Orange's substantial Protestant population had been protected by that city's unique political status. While geographically part of France, it remained the legal possession of the princes of Orange—Protestant quasi-monarchs whose recently deceased member, William, had been king of England and leader of the coalition against Louis XIV. Yet in 1703 the Sun King ended this beneficent arrangement and banned Protestantism in the city.[1] Alongside many neighbors, Frédéric went to Geneva and Berlin before eventually settling in the Swiss city of Neuchâtel. His son Hector moved even farther, first to the Dutch university town of Leiden and then to England, where he studied at Oxford and Cambridge and rubbed shoulders with projectors such as James Oglethorpe, the founder of Georgia. It may have been Oglethorpe who inspired Hector to set out for America, where he invested in a scheme by Jean-Pierre Purry, one of his father's neighbors in Neuchâtel, to form a new Swiss colony on the Savannah River. Hector spent the last thirty years of his life in the Carolina Lowcountry, where he became a leading landowner, experimented in silk production, and eventually won a post as George III's commissioner of customs before dying as an old man in 1766. Beaufain seems to have been a popular fellow. According to his nephew and heir Jean Henry de Bérenger, who set out to collect his inheritance during the late 1760s, Hector received "the good will and unanimous friendship of the whole province."[2]

Jean Henry's efforts to collect his uncle's fortune revealed much about the place of Huguenot refugees in a world that was held together by state power and patronage. The nephew had not traveled as far as the uncle, but had made a career in the Prussian military, eventually coming to live in the German city of

The Global Refuge. Owen Stanwood, Oxford University Press (2020). © Oxford University Press.
DOI: 10.1093/oso/9780190264741.001.0001

Bayreuth after his retirement in 1761. When he heard that his childless uncle had died, he set out on a long quest to collect his rightful inheritance, and he used all his connections to make it happen. One of his key conduits in this task was Peter Simond, who had worked with Hector in the Purrysburgh project and helped Jean Henry to gain some of his cash inheritance. Hector's large land holdings in South Carolina, however, were more problematic. As a foreigner Jean Henry could not legally own land in the colony, and Simond advised that he would need to obtain naturalization in order to inherit, leading Bérenger to contact a Carolina lawyer and start this process. Matters became even more complicated when Simond told Jean Henry about Patrick Mackey, Simond's brother-in-law, who had worked the lands while Hector lived in Charleston and wanted to continue using them after his benefactor Hector's death.[3]

The tale looked similar to dozens of other family dramas that unfolded when wealthy, childless people died, but it soon took a different turn. After the case had dragged on, Jean Henry began to pull strings. While not a wealthy man, his family connections and military service gave him influence, and he appealed to his local ruler, the Margrave of Ansbach and Bayreuth -- a distant kinsman of George III. From there word traveled to the Hanoverian minister in London and on to King George himself, who personally endorsed Bérenger's claim. With the approbation of the monarch, the secretary of state, Lord Dartmouth, sent word to South Carolina Governor William Bull to move matters along. Not surprisingly, the involvement of some of the world's most powerful people inspired cooperation, and in 1774 Bérenger had overcome the resistance of his uncle's friends and executors and was on the verge of receiving his inheritance.[4] The whole episode demonstrated the special place that Huguenots and their descendants occupied in the European world. Their families stretched between states and empires, but they knew how to tap into networks of patronage and power. It was Jean Henry's military service, which connected him to the Prussian royal family and from there to many of the royal courts of Europe, that allowed him to successfully call in a debt from halfway across the world.

But another drama was brewing in the Atlantic world that complicated matters significantly. In the summer of 1775, just as Bérenger expected to receive his inheritance, Britain went to war against its North American colonies. A year later, thirteen of those colonies declared independence as the United States, including South Carolina. In July 1776 Bérenger wrote to William Bull asking why he had not received his inheritance, but did not receive an answer for nearly two years. When the governor finally responded, he did so from England. The "disruption of the king's power in this, and other English provinces" meant that Bull was no longer in a position to help. To make matters worse, the executor of Hector de Beaufain's estate had fled South Carolina as a loyalist and then perished in a shipwreck, probably with all of Jean Henry's estate documents.[5]

In the wake of this disappointment, Jean Henry de Bérenger did what had worked so well in earlier years: he appealed to authority. Yet many of the authorities he contacted no longer had any control over the situation. If George III's influence made all the difference in 1774, it proved worthless in 1778, and petitions to the new Hanoverian ambassador and to the prime minister Lord North were similarly unsuccessful.[6] Thwarted on the British front, he turned to Americans he believed could satisfy his claims. One was John Rutledge, the lawyer who helped Bérenger with his property acquisition, who had become prominent in revolutionary South Carolina. Another was Henry Laurens, perhaps the most important Huguenot descendent in the province, and one with longstanding ties to London's merchant community, including Peter Simond. In these letters Bérenger frequently attempted to use his refugee roots to elicit sympathy. In correspondence to Rutledge he noted his descent from people who lost everything for faith, who "preferring Religion to the Opulence which they where then enjoying, renounced their riches, goods, Estates, [and] Titles."[7] Laurens expressed sympathy with Bérenger's request. He had known and respected Hector de Beaufain and wanted to help. There was a serious difficulty, however, in that the guardian of the land at the time of the war, David Montaigut, had been a loyalist and the state had accordingly confiscated Bérenger's land. Laurens pledged to try and do something about it, but two years later Jean Henry still had not received a response.[8]

During the mid-1780s the War for Independence ended, and Bérenger tried a different tack. He decided to find assistance not in America, where his stories seemed to fall on deaf ears, but in Versailles. After all, France had provided the assistance that won the war, and Bérenger hoped that his former homeland, the same one that had persecuted his kinfolk into leaving, might help him claim his estate. After yet another unsuccessful attempt to lobby the US ambassador to France, Benjamin Franklin, Bérenger took the extraordinary step of writing in April 1786 to the King of France himself, Louis XVI. The baron recounted his family history and mentioned his mother's family's roots in Dauphiné, hoping that as a Frenchman by descent he could count on the king's help. Since the American states were "indebted to your Majesty, for their Salvation [*Salut*], and for the happy conclusion of this War," they would listen to the king's counsel on the matter.[9] It is hard to know what Louis XVI, already facing the beginnings of popular unrest that would culminate in revolution, thought about receiving a letter from a German officer of French Protestant descent trying to get restitution for property in an independent republic halfway across the world. He probably did not think much of it, because he did not answer. Neither did George Washington, who received letters from Bérenger in both French and German in 1788, just before his inauguration as the first US president.[10]

Jean Henry had one final act. In 1788 he saw a notice in a newspaper from Erlangen, stating that Loyalists who had lost property in the recent war could petition for redress from the British government. This revelation "made me determined," wrote Bérenger, "although in the sixty-first year of my age, and in a state of health much impaired by many years Military service, to come to London, and solicit, as it became a Parent anxious for his Children, to obtain a suitable indemnity for my losses." Of course, such a claim was not entirely honest. Bérenger had not been a Loyalist; he had not even lived in America, and the British noted this fact in quickly rejecting his petition, since he never "bore Arms for the Service of Great Britain." They offered him a mere £50, which he used to pay for the printing costs of a long letter to Prime Minister William Pitt relating his sad story once again. He noted that while he had not actually resided in South Carolina, "the Congress of America looked upon me, and treated me during the War, as other Loyalists; seized all that belonged to me, and never returned an Answer to any of the many Letters." He was, Bérenger concluded, "quite rejected by the United States of America."[11] He never received any satisfaction from Great Britain either. The political connections that proved so valuable in an ancien régime world of kings, dukes, and ministers proved useless in one of republics and unitary nation-states. Cut off from the political networks that had given them power, Huguenots like Bérenger became mere curiosities.[12]

———

Jean Henry de Bérenger's failure to collect his inheritance serves as a fitting denouement to the story of the global Refuge. More than anything else, the Age of Revolution brought an end to the conditions that had allowed the Huguenots to prosper in a world of states and empires. Their mastery had rested on several foundations. One, as Jean Henry knew well, was the Huguenots' status as Protestant heroes, who had supposedly given up everything for their faith. Another was the strength of their family and community ties, which even in the late 1700s bound together Huguenot descendants living around Europe and beyond, and meant that even someone living in Germany could find a receptive correspondent in London, Charleston, or Amsterdam. Finally, the refugees and their children had managed to infiltrate other nations' institutions. For Jean Henry the Prussian military was the avenue to influence. For others it could be the Church of England, or the Dutch East India Company. Once they mastered these institutions, former refugees had become some of the most influential people in the European world. This influence, however, depended on patronage networks that did not survive the turmoil that started in the mid-1770s. Empires made the global Huguenot Refuge; the age of Revolution left it in tatters.

Most Huguenots attempted to ride out the Revolution as they had previous conflicts in their various adopted homelands. They tried to blend in. A majority of the North American refugees and their descendants, like Louis de Saint Pierre, joined the patriot side in the American Revolution, and a few, like Henry Laurens and John Jay, became important leaders in the new republic.[13] As in past conflicts, however, the Huguenots were not unanimous in their inclinations. The Faneuil family, for instance, divided between patriots and loyalists, with some members fleeing Massachusetts, even as the hall that bore the family's name became a center for the patriot cause in Boston.[14] Naturally, those members of the diaspora who lived in England chose the opposite side. Peter Simond, for instance, lost a great deal of property in South Carolina after the Revolution, though he retained his important ties to the British West Indies, which had remained loyal to Britain.[15] In previous decades, people like Simond had linked the disparate parts of the empire together, joining with Huguenot and non-Huguenot partners and family members around the British world and beyond. As everyone was forced to choose sides, the networks that had sustained the Refuge for so long weakened under the strain. Mercantile partnerships remained in place, and reconstituted themselves somewhat after the Revolutionary War ended, but their close ties to political power never fully returned.

The beginning of a second revolution in the 1780s had an even greater impact on the world's Huguenots. The campaign for toleration in France itself, led over the years by Protestants like Antoine Court and philosophers like Voltaire, finally made progress. In 1787, just after receiving and probably ignoring a letter from Jean Henry de Bérenger, Louis XVI issued a new Edict of Toleration. Despite its name, the act did not allow Protestants freedom of worship, but it did grant civil status to Protestants, especially by recognizing their marriages, which had been a major bone of contention for decades. Little did the king know that soon afterward his own realm would be embroiled in turmoil. By 1789 revolution had come to France, and the following year the country's new authorities went far beyond the earlier edict, offering full religious liberty and, in the more dramatic gesture, French citizenship to "any person who, born in a foreign country, who descends in any way whatever, from a French man or woman expatriated for the cause of religion."[16]

The recovery of religious liberty in France did not lead to a reverse exodus of Huguenots and their descendants back to the land of their birth. Nonetheless, the fall of the Bourbon persecutors, along with the decline of the British Atlantic empire, removed much of the Huguenot Refuge's raison d'être. Even if Pierre Jurieu's dreams of returning and transforming France had long since faded, the specter of French tyranny had been central to the refugees' appeal. As late as the 1770s, in the wake of decades of warfare between France and Britain, the refugees could gain sympathy from their status as targets of Bourbon aggression, even as their brethren back in France used the existence of a foreign diaspora to win concessions from rulers at home. With the heir of their longstanding enemy about to face the guillotine, and with the states that granted them refuge rent in pieces by the turmoil of revolution, the refugees had lost their place. Like Jean Henry de Bérenger in his fruitless search for an inheritance, they found themselves pushed to the margins of a new revolutionary world.[17]

In time, the Huguenots' kinfolk remade their history in national molds. Rather than an international elite, the refugees became key actors in a number of distinct histories. In France itself, the coming of a republic allowed for a reconsideration of the Protestants' place in national history. Rather than aberrant heretics trying to undermine national unity, the Huguenots looked instead like distant ancestors of the Revolution.[18] For the nineteenth-century historian Jules Michelet, notably, the Revocation of the Edict of Nantes was the most important event in seventeenth-century French history, a tragedy that impacted not just the Protestants, but all of France, when the foolish king, driven by lust for power and religious zeal, inspired the exodus of many of his most productive subjects. At the same time, Michelet saw the Protestants' search for religious liberty as predictive of the later push for liberties of all kinds. He even adopted Pierre Jurieu as a proto-revolutionary, contending that his writings called not only for the return of freedom of worship, but for the liberation of the whole country, "to restore to the nation control of its destiny." Rejected by France, Huguenots leaders like Jurieu instead liberated the rest of Europe, especially by inspiring England's Glorious Revolution.[19] In a France strongly influenced by anticlericalism, even a millennialist like Jurieu became an advocate for a decidedly secular brand of liberation, one that would finally return to the homeland in 1789 and again in 1830 and 1848.

Across the Channel the Huguenots attained a very different, but also important, place in British history. Much like Michelet, British commentators bought in to the idea that the migration of thousands of Huguenots had provided one of the keys to Britain's economic success, even as France lost so many of its productive people. More than that, the Huguenots became the quintessential "good immigrants" in a society that struggled with how to welcome newcomers over the subsequent two centuries. In the eyes of Samuel Smiles, the first British writer to fully consider the Huguenots' impact, the arrival of those "industrious, intelligent, and high-minded Frenchmen" was one of the key factors in Britain's rise to global prominence. They made whole industries, especially as skilled artisans, and contributed greatly to British commerce. After doing that they quickly assimilated, which proved the superiority of British culture. Through their economic impact and cultural disappearance, the Huguenots set the pattern for what future immigrant groups should do. Of course, Smiles and others conveniently forgot the vast resistance French migrants faced from native English who feared outsiders would take their jobs, and they downplayed the role of radicals like the French Prophets.[20]

In the new United States, meanwhile, descendants of the refugees stressed religion rather than economy. Certainly, the Huguenots had been productive people. John Jay recollected, quite wrongly, that none of the French Protestants in New York had ever so much as collected poor relief.[21] Above all, they were people who had sacrificed everything for faith. The Kentuckian Daniel Trabue, for instance, left a lengthy memoir describing his grandfather Anthony's escape from France, proud that his progenitors had left "their estates and native country, their relations and every other thing for the sake of Jesus who Died for them."[22] Some decades later Virginian Richard Maury lauded his Huguenot forbears as "staunch and inflexible, courageous to brave all perils and make all sacrifices, save one, in their determination to worship God according to the dictates of their own conscience, to keep the faith at every cost, and rather than abandon the church of their fathers, to abandon all else."[23]

Such narratives flattened the motives of the actual refugees who scattered around the world in the seventeenth and eighteenth centuries. They did, on the other hand, serve as one of the inspirations of the developing myth of American religious liberty. Like the mythical Pilgrim Fathers who had founded Plymouth Colony, the Huguenots provided a suitably innocent origin story for an embattled republic that would soon split in two. The French migrant appeared as a perfect stock character of the religious martyr, and throughout the nineteenth century Americans eagerly sought and bragged about their Huguenot roots. One of them, New Yorker John Pintard, wrote a newspaper article singing the praises of his ancestors, noting that they were not just "eminent for their piety," but also "an industrious, prudent, and frugal people."[24] In the most interesting case, James Louis Pettigrew, a grandson of Jean Louis Gibert whose father and surname were English, changed the spelling of his name to Petigru to accentuate his refugee roots. The Huguenots may have disappeared, but everyone wanted to be one.[25]

———

Of course, the refugees had not completely vanished. They left traces across the landscape from one side of the world to the other, traces that sometimes gestured to a history far richer and more complex than the simplistic morality tales favored by nineteenth-century historians. One such remnant appeared in the Massachusetts town of Oxford, where Abiel Holmes and his young son Oliver took walks in the 1810s and 1820s. The French settlers had long since gone, but they left behind the remnants of their fortification on a high hill overlooking what had become a pleasant New England town. "Grape vines . . . were growing luxuriously along the line of the fort," Abiel related, "and these, together with currant bushes, roses, and other shrubbery, nearly formed a hedge around it."[26] In subsequent years these vines became something of an obsession for local historians and writers. In 1856, for example, Mary DeWitt Freeland tried to make wine out of the "Huguenot grapes," assuming perhaps that since French people had planted them they would have to produce a good vintage. Even later Oliver Wendell Holmes, now one of Boston's leading writers and thinkers, remembered walking with his father around the fort and was happy to hear from a correspondent that the vine "still flourishes in luxuriance." Reflecting on the people who planted the vine in the wilderness, Holmes noted their strangeness. "The French exiles rested there," Holmes recalled, "as a flight of tropical birds might alight on one of our New England pines, and one can hardly visit the places that knew them without looking for some relics of their sojourn as he would for an empty nest or a painted feather after the bird has flown."[27] The fact that they left a ruined fort and a grapevine, of course, was highly poetic. The Huguenots had ended up in Oxford not because of religious freedom—they could have found that in any number of less exotic locales. They came there as subjects of an empire that wanted them to defend a distant frontier and make it productive at the same time.

In some places the vines had taken deeper root. Such was the case in southern Africa, where a group of French Protestant missionaries landed in 1828. The newcomers were representatives of the Société des Missions Évangéliques de Paris, the international missionary society of the newly reconstituted French Reformed Churches. Beginning in the 1820s they established a robust network of global missions, partly in the hope of providing a path to Christianity for Africans and Asians that was not connected to European imperialism.[28] On the way to their mission ground in Lesotho, the missionaries first landed at Cape Town, which several decades earlier had passed from Dutch to British rule. As they journeyed from the port city into the interior, through the vineyards, farms, and plantations of the Paarl and Drakenstein Valleys, they came across "many little villages that had been built by the French refugees" nearly 150 years before, from the principal town of Paarl to the newer one called Franschhoek (or "French corner"), in direct reference to its Huguenot origins. The missionaries were excited to find descendants of their coreligionists even there, at what seemed to them like the end of the earth. The reunion, they noted, was like that of the brothers Jacob and Esau in the book of Genesis, brought back together after so many years of separation. The original church was long since gone, but the missionaries did see a house that had been built by one of the original refugees in 1694, and wherever they went they found family bibles tracing back the generations. "Genealogy was always the subject that served as the introduction of our interviews," wrote one missionary. "Degree by degree, they recounted their ancestors, until they were French again."[29]

The descendants of the Cape Huguenots had been in a reflective mood. Four years earlier a Reformed minister of French heritage, Abraham Faure, had written a paean to the "virtuous and pious" refugees who had settled the Cape, calling for the construction of a memorial to the good people who had "sought refuge in this colony, to exercise their religion undisturbed amongst the then wild and rough inhabitants of Africa."[30] Not surprisingly, the burghers in Paarl and Franschhoek were just as excited to see the French missionaries as the missionaries were to meet them. They could not easily communicate with each other—the missionaries spoke in English and one of them served as an interpreter—but the French clerics found a rapt audience as they described the coming of religious liberty to France and the state of the Protestant churches there. "As they listened to us," one missionary said, "the elderly people shed tears, and it seemed impossible to them that their brethren could enjoy such privileges in a country where their ancestors had been so cruelly persecuted." The locals also thronged the church when the missionaries performed a French-language service—the first, they said, since 1739, when the Dutch East India Company had banned services in that language in the colony, an event that many of the refugees' descendants recounted and lamented.[31]

The French missionaries and the Dutch-speaking farmers on the Cape were no longer the same people. They belonged to different national stories. Just a little more than a decade later a South African of French descent, Piet Retief, would lead the "Great Trek" into the interior, an event that paved the way for the reconsideration of the refugees as forbears of the white Afrikaner nation.[32] But in the meeting between these strangers, memories of lost connections reappeared, showing how this small band of settlers in southern Africa had once been part of a vast community that stretched to France, the Netherlands, and the far reaches of the British empire. The dispersion of the Huguenots started as a tragedy, and many had ended up in remote parts of the world, like Oxford, Massachusetts or the Drakenstein Valley, where they faced great obstacles as they worked to develop other people's empires. Nonetheless, becoming global opened up possibilities for the Huguenots, and in their connections—both with each other and with powerful Protestants of other nationalities—they managed to forge an important place for themselves in an interconnected, expanding European world. They promoted themselves as the chosen people of empire, Protestants who combined a status as self-proclaimed religious heroes with one as skilled producers, bringing bibles and grapevines to the ends of the earth. By the nineteenth century, the system that gave the Huguenots such power had ceased to exist, and the refugees' children became little more than historical curiosities. In the end, the global saga of the Huguenots is not a parable about religious freedom as much as a tale of how individuals often get swept up in the current of history and taken to unusual places. In our own era of unprecedented movement and diversity, but also of resurgent nationalism and closing borders, the story of these boundary crossers resonates more than ever.

NOTES

Abbreviations

AN	Archives Nationales de France, Paris
ANOM	Archives Nationales d'Outre Mer, Aix-en-Provence, France
BGE	Bibliothèque de Genève, Switzerland
BL	British Library, London
BSHPF	*Bulletin de la société de l'histoire du protestantisme français*
HSP	*Proceedings of the Huguenot Society of London/Proceedings of the Huguenot Society of Great Britain and Ireland*
LPL	Lambeth Palace Library, London
MAE	Archives Diplomatiques, Ministère des Affaires Étrangères, La Courneuve, France
Mass. Arch.	Massachusetts Archives Collection, Massachusetts Archives, Boston
NYCD	E. B. O'Callaghan and John Romeyn Brodhead, eds., *Documents Relative to the Colonial History of the State of New York* (Albany, 1853–1887).
TNA	The National Archives, Kew, U.K.
VMHB	*Virginia Magazine of History and Biography*
WCA	Western Cape Archives and Record Centre, Cape Town, South Africa
WMQ	*William and Mary Quarterly*, 3d. ser.

Introduction

1. Didier Poton and Bertrand Van Ruymbeke, eds., *Histoire des souffrances du sieur Élie Neau, sur les galères, et dans les cachots de Marseille* (Paris: Les Indes Savantes, 2014), 54, 58, 65. The book first appeared from Abraham Ascher in Rotterdam in 1701.
2. Cotton Mather, *A Present from a Farr Countrey, to the People of New England* (Boston: B. Green and J. Allen, 1698). See also Elias Neau, *An Account of the Sufferings of the French Protestants, Slaves on board the French King's Galleys* (London: Richard Parker, 1699). Mather's masterwork

of New England history was *Magnalia Christi Americana: or, the Ecclesiastical History of New-England* (London: Thomas Parkhurst, 1702).

3. W. C. Moragne, *An Address Delivered at New Bordeaux, Abbeville District, S.C., November 15, 1854 on the 90th Anniversary of the Arrival of the French Protestants at that Place* (Charleston, SC: James Phynney, 1857), 6.

4. On the general contours of Neau's story see Jon Butler, *The Huguenots in America: A Refugee People in New World Society* (Cambridge, MA: Harvard University Press, 1983), 161–69; and Sheldon Cohen, "Elias Neau, Instructor to New York Slaves," *New-York Historical Society Quarterly* 55:1 (1971), 7–27.

5. The idea of a Protestant International comes from Herbert Lüthy, *La Banque protestante en France de la révocation de l'édit de Nantes à la Révolution* (Paris: S.E.V.P.E.N., 1959–1961); see also J. F. Bosher, "Huguenot Merchants and the Protestant International in the Seventeenth Century," *WMQ* 52:1 (1995), 77–102; and Robin Gwynn, "The Huguenots in Britain, the 'Protestant International' and the Defeat of Louis XIV," in *From Strangers to Citizens: The Integration of Immigrant Communities in Britain, Ireland, and Colonial America, 1550–1750*, ed. Randolph Vigne and Charles Littleton (Brighton: Sussex Academic Press, 2001), 412–24. On population dynamics and political economy more generally see Steve Pincus, "From Holy Cause to Economic Interest: The Study of Population and the Invention of the State," in *A Nation Transformed: England after the Restoration*, ed. Steve Pincus and Alan Houston (Cambridge: Cambridge University Press, 2001), 272–98; Daniel Statt, *Foreigners and Englishmen: The Controversy over Immigration and Population, 1660–1760* (Newark: University of Delaware Press, 1995); Jacob Soll, "Accounting for Government: Holland and the Rise of Political Economy in Seventeenth-Century Europe," *Journal of Interdisciplinary History* 40:2 (2009), 215–38; and on consumption, Linda Levy Peck, *Consuming Splendor: Society and Culture in Seventeenth-Century England* (Cambridge: Cambridge University Press, 2005).

6. The concept of mercantilism, which undergirds the study of imperial political economy, has been controversial of late. For summaries see especially Philip J. Stern and Carl Wennerlind, eds., *Mercantilism Reimagined: Political Economy in Early Modern Britain and its Empire* (New York: Oxford University Press, 2013); Steve Pincus, "Rethinking Mercantilism: Political Economy, the British Empire, and the Atlantic World in the Seventeenth and Eighteenth Centuries," *WMQ* 69:1 (2012), 3–34. On silk and wine see Ben Marsh, "Silk Hopes in Colonial South Carolina," *Journal of Southern History* 78:4 (2012), 807–54; Owen Stanwood, "Imperial Vineyards: Wine and Politics in the Early American South," in *Experiencing Empire: Power, People, and Revolution in Early America*, ed. Patrick Griffin (Charlottesville: University of Virginia Press, 2017), 50–70.

7. On the crisis in France itself and the making of the diaspora see especially Carolyn Chappell Lougee, *Facing the Revocation: Huguenot Families, Faith, and the King's Will* (New York: Oxford University Press, 2016); Philippe Joutard, *La révocation de l'édit de Nantes ou les faiblesses d'un état* (Paris: Gallimard, 2018); Joutard, "The Revocation of the Edict of Nantes: End or Renewal of French Protestantism?," in *International Calvinism, 1541–1715*, ed. Menna Prestwich (Oxford: Clarendon Press, 1985), 339–68; Patrick Cabanel, *Histoire des protestants en France, XVIe-XXIe siècles* (Paris: Fayard, 2012). On the origins of the colonial program see François David, "Les colonies des réfugiés protestants français en Brandebourg-Prusse, 1685–1809: Institutions, géographie, et évolution de leur peuplement," *BSHPF* 140:1 (1994), 111–42.

8. The usual accepted population estimate for North America is around 1500–2000 people, from Butler, *Huguenots in America*, 49. This explicitly did not include Manakintown or eighteenth-century migrants, and was based only on counting the passenger lists for a few of the better known ships. For a reconsideration for America as a whole that includes eighteenth-century migrants, see Bertrand Van Ruymbeke, "Le Refuge dans les marches atlantiques," *Diasporas: Histoire et sociétés* 18 (2011), 18. For numbers beyond North America see Hans Buddingh', *Geschiedenis van Suriname* (Utrecht: Nieuw Amsterdam, 1995), 52–53; Marilyn Garcia-Chapleau, *Le Refuge huguenot du cap de Bonne-Espérance: Genèse, assimilation, héritage* (Paris: Honoré Champion, 2016), 201–202. Of course, all of these totals are only of known travelers and stress those who traveled in large groups. Many more Huguenots must have traveled as single migrants or families beyond the radar of any official recorder. Thus, the number will have to remain a subject of speculation.

9. Henri Duquesne, *Recueil de quelques mémoires servant d'instruction pour l'établissement de l'Ile d'Eden* (Amsterdam: Henry Desbordes, 1689); Émile Rainer, *L'utopie d'une république huguenote du marquis du Quesne et la voyage du François Leguat* (Paris: Ecrivains Associés, 1959); Paolo Carile, *Huguenots sans frontières: Voyage et écriture à la Renaissance et à l'Âge classique* (Paris: Honoré Champion, 2001), 97–136.

10. Butler, *Huguenots in America*, 199. The paradigm of assimilation has been central to studies of Huguenot refugees for decades; see especially Myriam Yardeni, *Le Refuge huguenot: Assimilation et culture* (Paris: Honoré Champion, 2002), 83–92, 137–50; Susanne Lachenicht, "Intégration ou coexistence? Les huguenots dans les îles britanniques et le Brandebourg," *Diasporas: Histoire et sociétés* 18 (2011), 108–22. More recent works have pushed back gently against the thesis; see Paula Wheeler Carlo, *Huguenot Refugees in Colonial New York: Becoming American in the Hudson Valley* (Brighton: Sussex Academic Press, 2005); and Neil Kamil, *Fortress of the Soul: Violence, Metaphysics, and Material Life in the Huguenots' New World, 1517–1751* (Baltimore: Johns Hopkins University Press, 2005), esp. 755–57; Bertrand Van Ruymbeke, *From New Babylon to Eden: The Huguenots and their Migration to Colonial South Carolina* (Columbia: University of South Carolina Press, 2006); and Bosher, "Huguenot Merchants and the Protestant International in the Seventeenth Century."

11. These later Huguenot colonies have not received nearly enough attention from historians, but see Arlin C. Migliazzo, *To Make this Land Our Own: Community Identity and Social Adaptation in Purrysburg Township, South Carolina, 1732–1865* (Columbia: University of South Carolina Press, 2007); Owen Stanwood, "From the Desert to the Refuge: The Saga of New Bordeaux," *French Historical Studies* 40:1 (2017), 1–28; J. Barton Starr, "French Huguenots in British West Florida," *Florida Historical Quarterly* 54:4 (1976), 532–47.

12. Nineteenth-century historians created the concept of the "Huguenot Refuge" and highlighted the religious character of their migration. See especially Charles Weiss, *Histoire des réfugiés huguenots* (Paris: Ampelos Editions, 2007 [1853]); and for the American migrants, Charles Baird, *History of the Huguenot Emigration to America* (New York: Dodd Mead and Co., 1885). In South Africa the heroic interpretation has lasted even longer; see Pieter Coertzen, *The Huguenots in South Africa, 1688–1988* (Cape Town: Tafelberg, 1988). For an astute analysis of how the refugees' stories inspired historical interpretations see David van der Linden, *Experiencing Exile: Huguenot Refugees in the Dutch Republic, 1680–1700* (Farnham: Ashgate, 2015), 163–223.

13. The biggest exceptions to this trend have been Susanne Lachenicht and Bertrand Van Ruymbeke, who have written important comparative studies; see among others Lachenicht, *Hugenotten in Europa und Nordamerika: Migration und Integration in der Frühen Neuzeit* (Frankfurt: Campus Verlag, 2010); Lachenicht, "Huguenot Immigrants and the Formation of National Identities, 1548–1787," *Historical Journal* 50:2 (2007), 309–31; Bertrand Van Ruymbeke, "Un refuge atlantique: Les réfugiés huguenots et l'Atlantique anglo-américain," in *D'un Rivage à l'Autre: Villes et Protestantisme dans l'Aire Atlantique (XVIe-XVIIe siècles)*, ed. Guy Martinière, Didier Poton, and François Souty (Paris: Imprimérie Nationale, 1999), 195–204. In addition, a number of edited volumes allow a global look at the diaspora: Eckart Birnstiel and Chrystel Bernat, eds., *La Diaspora des Huguenots: Les réfugiés protestants de France et leur dispersion dans le monde (XVIe-XVIIIe siècles)* (Paris: Honoré Champion, 2001); Mickaël Augeron, Didier Poton, and Bertrand Van Ruymbeke, eds., *Les Huguenots et l'Atlantique: Pour Dieu, la Cause, ou les Affaires* (Paris: Presses Université Paris Sorbonne, 2009); and Augeron, Poton, and Van Ruymbeke, eds., *Les Huguenots et l'Atlantique: Fidélités, racines, et mémoires* (Paris: Presses Université Paris Sorbonne, 2012); Bertrand Van Ruymbeke and Randy J. Sparks, eds., *Memory and Identity: The Huguenots in France and the Atlantic Diaspora* (Columbia: University of South Carolina Press, 2003).

14. For an analysis of refugee politics in general see Susanne Lachenicht, "Refugees and Refugee Protection in the Early Modern Period," *Journal of Refugee Studies* 30:2 (2017), 261–81. The two most interesting groups, for comparative purposes, are Sephardic Jews and Germans. See for example Francesca Trivellato, *The Familiarity of Strangers: The Sephardic Diaspora, Livorno, and Cross-Cultural Trade in the Early Modern Period* (New Haven, CT: Yale University Press, 2009); Richard L. Kagan and Philip D. Morgan, eds., *Atlantic Diasporas: Jews, Conversos, and Crypto-Jews in the Age of Mercantilism, 1500–1800* (Baltimore: Johns Hopkins University Press,

2008); Philip Otterness, *Becoming German: The 1709 Palatine Migration to New York* (Ithaca, NY: Cornell University Press, 2006); Katherine Carte Engel, *Religion and Profit: Moravians in Colonial America* (Philadelphia: University of Pennsylvania Press, 2009).

Chapter 1

1. The fullest biography of Jurieu is Frederick Reinier Jacob Knetsch, *Pierre Jurieu: Theoloog en politikus der Refuge* (Kampen: J. H. Kok, 1967). For an English synopsis see Knetsch, "Pierre Jurieu: Theologian and Politician of the Dispersion," *Acta Historiae Neerlandica* 10 (1971), 213–41. See also Elisabeth Labrousse, "Note sur Pierre Jurieu," in *Conscience et conviction: Etudes sur le XVIIe siècle* (Oxford: Voltaire Society, 1996), 209–29; Hubert Bost, *Ces Messieurs de la R.P.R.: Histoires et écritures de huguenots, XVIIe-XVIIIe siècles* (Paris: Honoré Champion, 2001), 175–213; and Guy Howard Dodge, *The Political Theory of the Huguenots of the Dispersion, with Special Reference to the Thought and Influence of Pierre Jurieu* (New York: Columbia University Press, 1947).

2. Pierre Jurieu, *L'Accomplissement des Prophéties*, ed. Jean Delumeau (Paris: Imprimerie Nationale, 1994), 142–43. The modern edition includes only part two of the original work, which appeared in French in Rotterdam: Abraham Acher, 1686. The English edition is *The Accomplishment of the Scripture Prophecies, or the Approaching Deliverance of the Church* (London, 1687).

3. Robert Middlekauff, *The Mathers: Three Generations of Puritan Intellectuals, 1596–1728* (Berkeley: University of California Press, 1999 [1971]), 338; William Byrd to Perry and Lane, August 8, 1690, in *The Correspondence of the Three William Byrds of Westover, 1684–1776*, ed. Marion Tinling (Charlottesville: University of Virginia Press, 1977), 1:135.

4. On the idea of martyrdom see especially Brad S. Gregory, *Salvation at Stake: Christian Martyrdom in Early Modern Europe* (Cambridge, MA: Harvard University Press, 1999), 139–96.

5. The idea of a "Protestant International" dominated by Huguenots started with Herbert Lüthy, *La Banque Protestante en France de la Révocation de l'Édit de Nantes à la Révolution* (Paris: S.E.V.P.E.N., 1959); see also J. F. Bosher, "Huguenot Merchants and the Protestant International in the Seventeenth Century," *WMQ* 52:1 (1995), 77–102; and Robin Gwynn, "The Huguenots in Britain, the 'Protestant International' and the Defeat of Louis XIV," in *From Strangers to Citizens: The Integration of Immigrant Communities in Britain, Ireland, and Colonial America, 1550–1750*, ed. Randolph Vigne and Charles Littleton (Brighton: Sussex Academic Press, 2001), 412–24.

6. Jurieu, *Accomplissement des Prophéties*, 150.

7. Jean Valat, *Mémoires d'un protestant du Vigan: Des dragonnades au Refuge (1683–1686)*, ed. Eckart Birnstiel and Véronique Chanson (Paris: Les Éditions de Paris, 2011), 27.

8. There is a massive amount of scholarship on the religious wars of the sixteenth century; for good introductions see Mark Greengrass, *The French Reformation* (New York: Wiley-Blackwell, 1991); and Mack P. Holt, *The French Wars of Religion, 1562–1629* (Cambridge: Cambridge University Press, 2005).

9. This portrait of seventeenth-century French Protestantism depends heavily on Élisabeth Labrousse, "Calvinism in France, 1598–1685," in *International Calvinism, 1541–1715*, ed. Menna Prestwich (Oxford: Clarendon Press, 1985), 285–314 (see esp. 293). On the geography of seventeenth-century French Protestantism see Philip Benedict, "The Huguenot Population of France, 1600–85," in *Faiths and Fortunes of France's Huguenots* (Aldershot: Ashgate, 2001), 34–120. For a study of this period that stresses coexistence at the level of communities see Keith P. Luria, *Sacred Boundaries: Religious Coexistence and Conflict in Early Modern France* (Washington, DC: Catholic University of America Press, 2005).

10. Janine Garrisson, *L'Édit de Nantes et sa révocation: L'histoire d'une intolérance* (Paris: Le Seuil, 1985), 119–83; Elisabeth Labrousse, *La révocation de l'Edit de Nantes: Une foi, une loi, un roi?* (Geneva: Labor et Fides, 1985), 153–81. The most recent work to examine the coming of religious persecution, focusing on Normandy, is Luc Daireaux, *Réduire les huguenots: Protestants et pouvoirs en Normandie au XVIIe siècle* (Paris: Honoré Champion, 2010).

11. Jean Migault, *Journal de Jean Migault, ou malheurs d'une famille protestante du Poitou (1682–1689)*, ed. Yves Krumenacker (Paris: Les Éditions de Paris, 1995), 32.

12. Samuel de Pechels, *Mémoires de Samuel de Pechels*, ed. Raoul Cazenove (Toulouse: Société des livres réligieux, 1878), 27–36. For another example of how the Revocation became a family drama see Carolyn Chappell Lougee, *Facing the Revocation: Huguenot Families, Faith, and the King's Will* (New York: Oxford University Press, 2016).

13. "Lettre de Consul de Bie de Nantes," December 11, 1685, Correspondance Politique, Hollande, vol. 144, f. 149, MAE.

14. Migault, *Journal*, 27.

15. Dianne W. Ressinger, ed., *Memoirs of Isaac Dumont de Bostaquet, a Gentleman of Normandy, Before and After the Revocation of the Edict of Nantes* (London: Huguenot Society of Great Britain and Ireland, 2005), 102.

16. *Memoirs of Isaac Dumont de Bostaquet*, 103; Migault, *Journal*, 75.

17. The complete text of the Edict of Fontainebleau is in *Édits, Déclarations et Arrests concernans la Réligion P. Réformée, 1662–1751* (Paris: Fischbacher, 1885), 239–45.

18. [Pierre Jurieu,] *Lettres pastorales addressees aux fideles de France, qui gemissent sous la captivité de Babylon, Où sont dissipées les illusions que Monsieur de Meaux dans sa Lettre Pastorale, & les autres Convertisseurs emploient pour seduire* (Rotterdam: Abraham Ascher, 1686), 6. On Brousson's "revolt" see Valat, *Mémoires*, 32–37, and Walter C. Utt and Brian E. Strayer, *The Bellicose Dove: Claude Brousson and Protestant Resistance to Louis XIV, 1647–1698* (Brighton: Sussex Academic Press, 2003), 20–33.

19. Migault, *Journal*, 37.

20. Nonetheless, women did leave as well. For one example see Caroline Lougee Chappell, "'The Pains I Took to Save My/His Family': Escape Accounts by a Huguenot Mother and Daughter after the Revocation of the Edict of Nantes," *French Historical Studies* 22:1 (1999), 1–64.

21. "Declaration du Roy, du 14 juillet 1682," in *Édits, Déclarations et Arrests*, 119–20.

22. "Ordonnance du Roy, du 20 Novembre 1685," in *Édits, Déclarations et Arrests*, 254.

23. My readings of these "escape memoirs" depend heavily on analysis by Caroline Chappell Lougee; see especially "Writing the Diaspora: Escape Memoirs and the Construction of Huguenot Memory," in *L'Identité huguenote: faire mémoire et écrire l'histoire (XVIe–XXIe siècle)*, ed. Philip Benedict, Hugues Daussy, and Pierre-Olivier Léchot (Geneva: Droz, 2014), 261–78.

24. "Isaac Minet's Narrative," *HSP* 2 (1887–88), 443–44.

25. Migault, *Journal*, 81, 90.

26. Durand of Dauphiné, *A Huguenot Exile in Virginia; or Voyages of a Frenchman exiled for his Religion with a description of Virginia and Maryland*, ed. Gilbert Chinard (New York: Press of the Pioneers, 1934), 66–70.

27. Valat. *Mémoires*, 102–17 (quotations on 111, 117).

28. Dianne W. Ressinger, ed., *Memoirs of the Reverend Jaques Fontaine, 1658–1728* (London: Huguenot Society of Great Britain and Ireland, 1992), 122.

29. "Lettre d'un amy a son amy sur lestat ou la violence des dragons a reduit les protestans en France," MSS Fr. 21619, f. 265, Bibliothèque Nationale de France.

30. Jurieu, *Lettres Pastorales* (1686), 5.

31. *Imperial Protestant Mercury*, no. 48, October 4–7, 1681.

32. Newdigate Newsletters, September 8, 1683, L. C. 1431, Folger Library, Washington, DC.

33. The fullest study of the Popish Plot is John Kenyon, *The Popish Plot* (New York: St. Martin's Press, 1972). See also Tim Harris, *Restoration: Charles II and his Kingdoms, 1660–1685* (London: Allen Lane, 2005), 136–202.

34. See Jonathan Israel, *The Dutch Republic: Its Rise, Greatness, and Fall, 1477–1806* (Oxford: Oxford University Press, 1995), 825–41.

35. Saint-Didier to Croissy, October 25, 1685, Correspondance Politique, Hollande, vol. 143, ff. 126–7, MAE.

36. Jacques Flournoy, *Journal, 1675–1692*, ed. Olivier Fatio (Geneva: Droz, 1994), 110, 125. On the political background see Jérôme Sautier, "Politique et Refuge: Genève face a la révocation de l'édit de Nantes," in *Genève au temps de la Révocation de l'Edit de Nantes, 1680–1705*, ed. Olivier Fatio (Geneva: Droz, 1985), 1–42.

37. Increase Mather, *A Sermon Wherein is shewed that the Church of God is sometimes a Subject of Great Persecution; Preached on a Publick Fast At Boston in New England: Occassioned by the Tidings of a Great Persecution Raised against the Protestants in France* (Boston: Samuel Sewall, 1682), 5, 17, 23.

38. *Impartial Protestant Mercury*, numb. 41, September 9–13, 1681.

39. Rawlinson Mss. C 984, fol. 43, Bodleian Library, Oxford, reprinted in *HSP*, 7 (1901–04), 164–66. On Compton's status as a champion of the Huguenots see Edward Carpenter, *The Protestant Bishop: Being the Life of Henry Compton, 1632–1713, Bishop of London* (London: Longmans, Green, 1956), 322–43. For the latest perspective on Huguenots in Stuart Britain more generally see Robin Gwynn, *The Huguenots in Later Stuart Britain: Crisis, Renewal, and the Ministers' Dilemma* (Brighton: Sussex Academic Press, 2015); and *The Huguenots in Later Stuart Britain: Settlement, Churches, and the Role of London* (Brighton: Sussex Academic Press, 2018).

40. David Primerose, *Remerciement fait un Roi de la part de l'Eglise Francoise et de l'Eglise Flamande de la Ville de Londres, pour Les graces que sa Majesté a accordées aux Etrangers Protestans qui se retirent sand son Roiaume* (London: George Wells, 1681), 2.

41. Flournoy, *Journal*, 125; Registres de Conseil, R.C. 185, fol. 152, Archives d'Etat de Genève. On the history of the bourse française see Cécile Holtz, "La Bourse française de Genève et le refuge de 1684 à 1686," in *Genève au temps de la Révocation de l'Édit de Nantes*, ed. Fatio, 439–500.

42. "Estat des familles et personnes qui se trouvant presentement a Vevey et a Aigle," September 17, 1685, E 1 25.11: Franz. Angelegenheiten, amtliche Akten, 1685–86, Staatsarchiv Zürich.

43. Rémy Scheurer, "Passage, accueil, et intégration des réfugiés huguenots en Suisse," in *Le Refuge huguenot*, ed. Michelle Magdelaine and Rudolf von Thadden (Paris: A. Colin, 1985), 49.

44. Jürgen Wilke, "Statut et pratiques judiciaires des huguenots en Brandebourg-Prusse (1685–1809), in *Le Refuge huguenot*, ed. Magdelaine and Thadden, 124–25. See also Susanne Lachenicht, "Intégration ou coexistence? Les huguenots dans les îles britanniques et le Brandebourg," *Diasporas: Histoire et sociétés* 18 (2011), 108–22; and François David, "Refuge protestant et assimilation: le cas de la Colonie française de Berlin," in *La diaspora des huguenots: Les réfugiés protestants de France et leur dispersion dans le monde (XVIe–XVIIIe siècles)*, ed. Eckart Birnstiel and Chrystel Bernat (Paris: Honoré Champion, 2001), 75–97.

45. Croissy to Dupré, February 11, 1687, in *Correspondance de Roland Dupré, second résident de France a Genève, 1680–1688*, ed. Frédéric Barbey (Geneva: A. Jullien, 1906), 295.

46. *Livre synodal contenant les articles résolus dans les synodes des églises wallonnes des Pays-Bas* (The Hague: M. Nijhoff, 1896), 1:804. On the larger context of Dutch refugee policies see Geert H. Janssen, "The Republic of the Refugees: Early Modern Migrations and the Dutch Experience," *Historical Journal* 60:2 (2017), 233–52.

47. Saint-Disdier to Croissy, November 15, 1685, Correspondance Politique, Hollande, vol. 143, f. 167, MAE. Hans Bots has estimated the number as 5200 in Amsterdam and 35,000 in all the Netherlands between 1681 and 1705; see Bots, "Le Refuge dans les Provinces-Unies," in *La diaspora des huguenots*, ed. Birnstiel and Bernat, 69.

48. *Memoirs of Isaac Dumont de Bostaquet*, 143. For background on Bostaquet's statement see David van der Linden, *Experiencing Exile: Huguenot Refugees in the Dutch Republic, 1680–1700* (Farnham: Ashgate, 2015), 15–38.

49. Hubert Bost, ed., *Le consistoire de l'Église wallonne de Rotterdam, 1681–1706* (Paris: Honoré Champion, 2007), 69–70.

50. *Memoirs of Isaac Dumont de Bostaquet*, 149.

51. *Memoirs of Isaac Dumont de Bostaquet*, 150, 169; Saint-Disdier to Croissy, November 24, 1685, Correspondance Politique, Hollande, vol. 143, ff. 182–83, MAE. For Orange and the Huguenots see also Jacques Solé, "L'exploitation de la Révocation par le prince d'Orange," in *Tricentenaire de la Revocation de l'Edit de Nantes: La Revocation et l'exterieur du royaume*, ed. Michel Perronet (Montpellier: Presses Universitaires de la Méditeranée, 1985), 147–56.

52. Newdigate Newsletters, March 2, 1686[/7], L. C. 1787, Folger Library.

53. Flournoy, *Journal*, 209, 214. On the situation in Savoy see Geoffrey Symcox, *Victor Amadeus II: Absolutism in the Savoyard State, 1675–1730* (Berkeley: University of California Press, 1983), 93–99.

54. Louis XIV to Roland Dupré, October 17, 1685, in *Correspondance de Roland Dupré*, 254.

55. Dupré to Louis XIV, October 30, 1685, in *Correspondance de Roland Dupré*, 257–59.

56. Dupré to Louis XIV, November 6, 1685, in *Correspondance de Roland Dupré*, 260–61; Registres du conseil, R.C. 185, fol. 166v, Archives d'Etat de Genève. The tract was *Tableau naïf de la persecution qu'on fait en france contre ceux de la Religion Reformée* published in Rotterdam (although like many similar tracts it falsely claimed to be published in Cologne), which may have been written by Claude Brousson.

57. Registres du conseil, R.C. 185, fol. 142v, 144, Archives d'Etat de Genève.

58. Dupré to Croissy, June 28, 1685, in *Correspondance de Roland Dupré*, 284–85.

59. Claude Brousson, *La sortie de France pour cause de religion de Daniel Brousson & de sa famille*, ed. Nathaniel Weiss (Paris: Fischbacher, 1885), 32. Claude's tract was originally published as *Des plaintes des protestants cruellement opprimez dans le Royaume de France* (Cologne [Rotterdam], 1686), and appeared in four London editions (and another in Dublin) in 1686. For the order to burn the book see Roger Morrice, *The Entering Book of Roger Morrice*, ed. Mark Goldie (Woodbridge: Boydell and Brewer, 2007), 3:117. James II's attitude toward the Huguenots, and his toleration program more generally, has inspired great debate from the 1680s through the present between those who view James as a genuine advocate of toleration and those who believe he only meant to reintroduce Catholicism. Compare Robin Gwynn, "James II in Light of his Treatment of Huguenot Refugees in England, 1685–86," *HSP* 23:4 (1980), 212–24, with John Miller, "The Immediate Impact of the Revocation in England," in *The Huguenots and Ireland: Anatomy of a Migration*, ed. C. E. J. Caldicott, H. Gough, and J.-P. Pittion (Dublin: Glendale Press, 1987), 161–74.

60. Newdigate Newsletters, October 11, 1681, L. C. 1135, Folger Library.

61. Fontaine, *Memoirs*, 138–39. On anti-Huguenot sentiment more generally see Malcolm Thorp, "The Anti-Huguenot Undercurrent in Late-Seventeenth-Century England," *HSP* 23:6 (1976), 569–80.

62. Jean Robert Chouët to Bouhéreau, February 13, 1685, in Newport J. D. White, ed., "Gleanings from the Correspondence of a great Huguenot: Elie Bouhéreau of La Rochelle," *HSP* 9 (1909–1911), 226.

63. *Nouvelles extraordinaires de divers endroits*, August 18, 1681, quoted in Bots, "Le Refuge dans les Provinces-Unies," 66. The best analysis of the refugees' economic impact in the Netherlands is Van der Linden, *Experiencing Exile*, esp. 39–78. See also Willem Frijhoff, "Uncertain Brotherhood: The Huguenots in the Dutch Republic," in *Memory and Identity: The Huguenots in France and the Atlantic Diaspora*, ed. Bertrand Van Ruymbeke and Randy J. Sparks (Columbia: University of South Carolina Press, 2003), 143–51.

64. On the Ipswich project see "Declaration in Favor of the French Linen Manufacture in Ipswich," June 8, 1685, Rawlinson Mss. C 984, fol. 59, Bodleian Library; Newsletter to Roger Garstell, September 3, 1681, in *Calendar of State Papers, Domestic Series, Charles II* (London: Longman, Brown, Green, 1856–1924), 22:437; and Proposals, April 23, 1683, ibid., 24:199–200. On silk workers see Natalie Rothstein, "Huguenots in the English Silk Industry in the Eighteenth Century," in *Huguenots in Britain and their French Background, 1550–1800*, ed. Irene Scouloudi (London: Macmillan, 1987), 125–40.

65. William Lloyd, bishop of St. Asaph, to Thomas Mostyn, April 14, 1685, Mostyn Mss., 9069, no. 28, Bangor University Library, Bangor, Wales; Lloyd to Mostyn, September 6, 1686, ibid., no. 58.

66. Migault, *Journal*, 112.

67. My ideas about refugee political networks are influenced by Marie de Chambrier, *Henri de Mirmand et les réfugiés de la révocation de l'édit de Nantes, 1650–1721* (Neuchâtel: Attinger Frères, 1910).

68. "Edit du Roy, du mois d'Octobre 1685," in *Édits, declarations et arrests*, 242–43.

69. Hans Bots, "Les pasteurs français au Refuge des Provinces-Unies: Un groupe socio-professionnel tout particulier, 1680–1710," in *La vie intellectuelle aux Refuges protestants*, ed. Jens Häseler and Antony McKenna (Paris: Honoré Champion, 1999), 9–18.

70. Bishop of St. Asaph to the Archbishop of Canterbury, July 30, 1686, Tanner Mss. 30, fol. 71, Bodleian Library, Oxford. On the conception of the plan see Archbishop of Canterbury to Compton, September 28, 1683, Rawlinson Mss. C 984, fol. 46, Bodleian Library.

71. These links are clearly visible in Robin Gwynn, ed., *Minutes of the Consistory of the French Church of London, Threadneedle Street, 1679–1692* (London: Huguenot Society of Great Britain and Ireland, 1994). See also Bertrand Van Ruymbeke, "Le Refuge atlantique: la diaspora huguenote et l'Atlantique anglo-américain," in *D'un rivage à l'autre: Villes et protestantisme dans l'aire atlantique, XVIe–XVIIIe siècles*, ed. Guy Martinière, Didier Poton, and François Souty (Paris: Imprimerie Nationale, 1999), 195–204.

72. Saint-Disdier to Croissy, November 15, 1685, Correspondance Politique, Hollande, vol. 143, fol. 167v, MAE. On Claude's role in the Netherlands see Van der Linden, *Experiencing Exile*, 87–90.

73. The *Lettres pastorales* appeared almost monthly from April 1686 through 1689, with another few issues in 1694. They appeared in many French editions (published in Rotterdam) as well as English translations. Much of the scholarship on Jurieu has analyzed the *Lettres*; see for instance Knetsch, *Pierre Jurieu*, 219–43; Elisabeth Labrousse, "Les *Pastorales* de Pierre Jurieu," in *Conscience et conviction*, 230–37.

74. Mede's masterwork was *The Key of the Revelation, searched and demonstrated out of the naturall and proper characters of the visions* (London: R. B. for Phil Stephens, 1643).

75. Jurieu, *Accomplissement des prophéties*, 141–73. The relevant passages are in Rev. 11:3–13 (all English quotations from the King James version).

76. Jurieu, *Accomplissement des prophéties*, 151–52, 154–55. Jurieu wrote another work that laid out the rationale for this union, shorn of much of its apocalyptic rhetoric; see *Avis aux Protestants de l'Europe, tant de la Confession d'Augsbourg que de celle de Suisses* (1685), translated as *Seasonable Advice to all Protestants of Europe of what Persuasion soever, for defending themselves against Popish Tyranny* (London: R. Baldwin, 1689).

77. On the larger intellectual climate see Elisabeth Labrousse, *Pierre Bayle: Du pays de Foix a la cite d'Erasme* (Dordrecht: Martinus Nijhoff, 1985), esp. 201–10; and Gerald Cerny, *Theology, Politics, and Letters at the Crossroads of European Civilization: Jacques Basnage and the Baylean Huguenot Refugees in the Dutch Republic* (Dordrecht: Martinus Nijhoff, 1987), 54–121.

78. Chambrier, *Henri de Mirmand*; Marie Léoutre, "*Député Général* in France and in Exile: Henri de Massue de Ruvigny, Earl of Galway," in *The Huguenots: France, Exile, and Diaspora*, ed. Jane McKee and Randolph Vigne (Brighton: Sussex Academic Press, 2013), 145–54; Solange Deyon, *Du loyalisme au refus: Les protestants français et leur député générale entre la Fronde et la Révocation* (Lille: Publications de l'Université de Lille, 1976).

79. "Les pasteurs, anciens et autres chrétiens protestants de France réfugiés en Suisse pour le cause de l'Evangile, aux rois, princes, magistrats et tous autres chrétiens protestants évangeliques," *BSHPF* 9:4/6 (1860), 151–52.

80. These sources, which Antoine Court collected to serve as sources for a history of French Protestantism, reside in the Collection Court, BGE. In addition, nineteenth-century transcripts of most of the collection are housed at the Bibliothèque de la Société de l'Histoire du Protestantisme Français, Paris.

81. Wilke, "Statut et pratique judiciaires des huguenots en Brandebourg-Prusse," 111–13; François David, "Les colonies françaises en Brandebourg-Prusse: Une étude statistique de leur population," in *Hugenotten zwischen Migration und Integration: Neue Forschungen zum Refuge in Berlin und Brandenburg*, ed. Manuela Böhm, Jens Häseler, and Robert Violet (Berlin: Metropol-Verlag, 2005), 74–77. On the national characteristics of the refugees see Susanne Lachenicht, "Huguenot Immigrants and the Formation of National Identities, 1548–1787," *Historical Journal* 50:2 (2007), 309–31.

82. David, "Les colonies françaises," 70–71; David, "Les colonies des réfugiés protestants français en Brandebourg-Prusse: Institutions, géographie, et évolution de leur peuplement," *BSHPF* 140:1 (1994), 111–42.

83. "Mémoire pour le dessein des colonies," Collection Court, vol. 17L, ff. 105–107, BGE.

84. "Substanßliche Verzeichnis Wieviel Franze Exulanten," E 1 25.13: Franz. Angelegenheiten, amtliche Akten, 1688–1693 Juni, Staatsarchiv Zürich.

85. "Mémoires de Henri de Mirmand," in *Henri de Mirmand et les réfugiés de la révocation de l'édit de Nantes, 1650–1721*, ed. Marie de Chambrier, appendice, 9; Mirmand au comité de Lausanne, 30/20 Septembre 1688, Collection Court, vol. 15, ff. 15–22, BGE.

86. Flournoy, *Journal*, 234–35.

87. Scheurer, "Passage, accueil et intégration des réfugiés huguenots en Suisse," 52; Marie-Jeanne Ducommun and Dominique Quadroni, *Le Refuge protestant dans le pays de Vaud (fin XVIIe–début XVIIIe s.): Aspects d'une migration* (Geneva: Droz, 1991), 189.

88. "Petition de Consistoire français de Berne," E 1 25.14: Franz. Angelegenheiten, amtliche Akten, 1693 Juli–1694, Staatsarchiv Zürich.

89. Charles-François d'Iberville to Croissy, in Iberville, *Correspondance, 1688–1690*, ed. Laurence Vial-Bergon (Geneva: Droz, 2003), 1:11.

90. La Direction de Lausanne to de Jossaud and Mesnard, March 12, 1689, Collection Court, vol. 15, ff. 42, 45; Flournoy, *Journal*, 258. The role of these Huguenot soldiers is covered in detail in Matthew Glozier, *The Huguenot Soldiers of William of Orange and the "Glorious Revolution" of 1688: The Lions of Judah* (Brighton: Sussex Academic Press, 2002).

91. "Declaration by William and Mary, 1689," *HSP* 7 (1901–04), 162; *Calendar of State Papers, Domestic Series, of the Reign of William and Mary* (London: Longman, Green, 1895–1906), 1:78, 90.

92. "Memoire touchant les françois Refugiez en Suisse pour la Religion," [1690?], Blathwayt Papers, OSB MSS 2, Box 4, folder 78, Beinecke Library, Yale University

93. Earl of Nottingham to Bishop of London, August 23, 1689, *Calendar of State Papers, Domestic Series, William and Mary*, 1:227. Susanne Lachenicht has explicitly compared the Huguenot policies in Brandenburg and the British Isles; see for example "Integration ou coexistence?;" and *Hugenotten in Europa und Nordamerika: Migration und Integration in der Frühen Neuzeit* (Frankfurt: Campus Verlag, 2010), esp. 193–215.

94. Ruvigny to Mirmand (extrait), December 1691, Collection Court, vol. 15, ff. 78–79, BGE. The "milk and honey" line comes from "Memoire pour encourager les Protestans de venir habiter en Irelande," MSS Fr. 21623, f. 74, Bibliothèque Nationale de France. On previous promotional literature on Ireland see Ruth Whelan, "Promised Land: Selling Ireland to French Protestants," *HSP* 29:1 (2008), 37–50.

95. "Considerations concerning Ireland," 1691, *Calendar of State Papers, Domestic Series, William and Mary*, 2:67.

96. "Copie of the Remonstrance of the Protestants in France to remove into Ireland," Rawlinson Mss. A 478, f. 30, Bodleian Library.

97. "Mémoires de Henri de Mirmand," 15–16. Reboulet wrote a letter to Mirmand on December 25, 1691 sharing the news.

98. Thomas Coxe to the earl of Nottingham, January 6, 1692, SP 96/9 (unpaginated), TNA. On Coxe's mission see Christopher Storrs, "British Diplomacy in Switzerland (1689–1789) and Eighteenth-Century Diplomatic Culture," *Études de lettres* 3 (2010), 181–216.

99. Coxe to Nottingham, January 13, 1692, SP 96/9 (unpaginated), TNA.

100. For a characteristic plan see "Mémoire Sur l'établissement des François Réfugiez en Irlande," 1697, Portland Papers, PwA2375, Nottingham University Library.

101. "Propositions de Monsr le Comte de Bellomont por lestablissemt d'une Colonie Francoise en Irelande," Collection Court, vol. 175, fols. 135–36, BGE.

102. "Memoires," E 1 25.14: Franz. Angelegenheiten, amtliche Akten, 1693 Juli–1694, Staatsarchiv Zürich.

103. For background on the mission see Michelle Magdelaine, "Conditions et préparation de l'intégration: le voyage de Charles de Sailly en Irlande (1693) et le projet d'Edit d'accueil," in *From Strangers to Citizens*, ed. Vigne and Littleton, 435–41.

104. Sailly's original journal is in the Collection Court; it is reproduced in "L'émigration en Irlande: Journal de voyage d'un réfugié français, 1693," *BSHPF* 17:12 (1868), 591–602. For the specific references see pp. 594, 596, 597–98.

105. The fullest study of these Huguenot settlements is Raymond Hylton, *Ireland's Huguenots and their Refuge, 1662–1745: An Uncertain Refuge* (Brighton: Sussex Academic Press, 2005); see also the collected essays in Caldicott, Gough, and Pittion, eds., *The Huguenots and Ireland*. On the larger history of Irish settlement schemes see Nicholas Canny, *Making Ireland British, 1580–1640* (Oxford: Oxford University Press, 2001).

106. On Jurieu's spy ring see the collected documents in Add. Mss. 57943, BL, and Lucien Bely, *Espions et ambassadeurs au temps de Louis XIV* (Paris: Fayard, 1990), 193–95. On Jurieu and the Glorious Revolution see F. R. J. Knetsch, "Pierre Jurieu and the Glorious Revolution

according to his 'Lettres Pastorales,'" in *Church, Change, and Revolution*, ed. Johannes van den Berg and Paul Gerardus Hoftijzer (Leiden: Brill, 1991).

107. Nyon to Mirmand, August 8, 1689, Collection Court, vol. 17O, f. 142, BGE; Chambrier, *Henri de Mirmand*, 100.

108. *Memoirs of Jacques Fontaine*, 155–83 and passim. For background on Fontaine's endeavors see John de Courcy Ireland, "Maritime Aspects of the Huguenot Immigration into Ireland," in *The Huguenots and Ireland*, ed. Caldicott, Gough, and Pittion, 357–58.

Chapter 2

1. Reboulet to Jacques Tronchin, October 4, 1687, Archives Tronchin, vol. 50, f. 80–81, BGE. For background on Reboulet see Eugène and Émile Haag, *La France Protestante*, 10 vols. (Paris: Joël Cherbuliez, 1846–59), 8:396. Part of this paragraph, and some of the general ideas in this chapter, appeared in another form in Owen Stanwood, "Between Eden and Empire: Huguenot Refugees and the Promise of New Worlds," *American Historical Review* 118:5 (2013), 1319–44.

2. Miriam Yardeni, "Refuge et integration: le cas d'Erlangen," in *Le Refuge Huguenot*, ed. Michelle Magdelaine and Rudolf van Thadden (Paris: A. Colin, 1985), 161–76.

3. Henri Duquesne, *Recueil de quelques mémoires servant d'instruction pour l'établissement de l'Ile d'Eden* (Amsterdam: Henry Desbordes, 1689), avertissement. The tract is most easily accessible as an appendix in François Leguat, *Voyage et aventures de François Leguat et de ses compagnons en deux îles désertes des Indes orientales (1690–1698)*, ed. Jean-Michel Racault and Paolo Carile (Paris: Éditions de Paris, 1995), 241–64 (quotation on 241).

4. Pierre Jurieu, *Lettres pastorales: addressees aux fideles persecutés de France, Seconde Année* (Rotterdam: Abraham Acher, 1688), 136. The best study of these New England missions is Richard W. Cogley, *John Eliot's Mission to the Indians Before King Philip's War* (Cambridge, MA: Harvard University Press, 1998).

5. Jurieu, *The Accomplishment of the Scripture Prophecies, or the Approaching Deliverance of the Church* (London, 1687), preface, 8–9.

6. Denis Veiras, *The History of the Sevarambians: A Utopian Novel*, ed. John Christian Laursen and Cyrus Masroori (Albany: State University of New York Press, 2006). On French Protestant utopian literature see Myriam Yardeni, *Utopie et révolte sous Louis XIV* (Paris: Nizet, 1980); Yardeni, "Protestantisme et utopie en France aux XVIe et XVIIe siècles," *Diasporas: Histoire et sociétés* 1 (2002), 51–58; Jean-Michel Racault, *L'utopie narrative en France et en Angleterre, 1675–1761* (Oxford: Voltaire Foundation, 1991). On the relation between religion and utopia see Miriam Eliav-Feldon, *Realistic Utopias: The Ideal Imaginary Societies of the Renaissance, 1516–1630* (Oxford: Oxford University Press, 1982), 5.

7. The most famous of these narratives was Jean de Léry, *History of a Voyage to the Land of Brazil*, trans. Janet Whatley (Berkeley: University of California Press, 1990). See also René de Laudonnière, *Three Voyages*, ed. Charles Bennett and Jerald T. Milanich (Tuscaloosa: University of Alabama Press, 2001). For a thorough analysis see Frank Lestringant, *Le huguenot et le sauvage: L'Amérique et la controverse coloniale, en France, au temps des guerres de religion* (Geneva: Droz, 2004). On links between exploration accounts and utopian literature see Raymond Trousson, "Le mirage américain dans les utopies et les voyages imaginaires depuis la renaissance," in *D'utopie et d'utopistes* (Paris: L'Harmattan, 1998), 81–102. He drew on earlier work by the literary critic Gilbert Chinard, especially his essay on "le mirage américain" in *Les réfugiés huguenots en Amérique, avec une Introduction sur Le Mirage Américain* (Paris: E. Aubin, 1925).

8. On Colbert's imperial policies see James Pritchard, *In Search of Empire: The French in the Americas, 1670–1730* (Cambridge: Cambridge University Press, 2007), 230–63; Kenneth J. Banks, *Chasing Empire Across the Sea: Communications and the State in the French Atlantic, 1713–1763* (Montreal: McGill-Queen's University Press, 2002), 22–27; Jacob Soll, *The Information Master: Jean-Baptiste Colbert's Secret State Intelligence System* (Ann Arbor: University of Michigan Press, 2009). Tavernier and Chardin's writings about the Indies proved popular in France and elsewhere in Europe. See Michèle Longino, *French Travel Writing in the Ottoman Empire: Marseille to Constantinople* (New York: Routledge,

2015), 23–38, 129–44; and S. Amanda Eurich, "Huguenot Self-Fashioning: Sir John Chardin and the Rhetoric of Travel and Travel Writing," in *From Strangers to Citizens: The Integration of Immigrant Communities in Britain, Ireland and Colonial America, 1550–1750*, ed. Randolph Vigne and Charles Littleton (Brighton: Sussex Academic Press, 2001), 214–22. For Barbot see P. E. H. Hair, ed., *Barbot on Guinea: The Writings of Jean Barbot on West Africa, 1678–1712* (London: Hakluyt Society, 1992).

9. Duquesne, *Recueil de quelques mémoires*, 242.

10. The three French editions have been collected into a wonderful modern edition; see Charles de Rochefort, *Histoire naturelle et morale des îles Antilles de l'Amérique*, ed. Bernard Grunberg, Benoît Roux, and Josiane Grunberg (Paris: L'Harmattan, 2012). For the English version (from the 1658 edition) see Rochefort, *The History of the Caribby-islands, viz, Barbados, St Vincents, Martinico, Dominico, Barbouthos, Mevis, Antego, &c* (London, 1666).

11. Rochefort, *Histoire naturelle et morale*, 1:92. While there is little reliable information on Rochefort, see Everett C. Wilkie, "The Authorship and Purpose of the *Histoire naturelle et morale des îles Antilles*, an Early Huguenot Emigration Guide," *Harvard University Library Bulletin* 38:1 (1991), 27–82; and Benoît Roux, "Le pasteur Charles de Rochefort et l'*Histoire naturelle et morale des îles Antilles de l'Amérique*," in *Les Indiens des Petites Antilles: Des premiers peuplements aux débuts de la colonization européenne*, ed. Bernard Grunberg (Paris: L'Harmattan, 2011), 175–216. Another interesting analysis is in Susanne Lachenicht, "Histoires naturelles, récits de voyage et géopolitique religieuse dans l'Atlantique français XVIe et XVIIe siècles," *Revue d'histoire de l'Amérique française* 69:1 (2016), 27–45.

12. Rochefort, *Histoire naturelle et morale*, 1:53.

13. Hyacinthe de Caen, *Relation des îles de Saint Christofle, Gardelouppe et la Martinique, gisantes par les 15 degrés au deçà de l'Équateur*, ed. Yvon Le Bras and Réal Ouellet (Quebec City: Presses de l'Université Laval, 2012), 130.

14. Gérard Lafleur, *Les Protestants aux Antilles françaises du Vent sous l'Ancien Régime* (Basse-Terre: Société d'Histoire de la Guadeloupe, 1988), 154. Lafleur's work provides the best description of the role of Protestants on the islands; see also Lafleur, "Huguenots et Hollandais aux Îles d'Amérique," in *Les Huguenots et l'Atlantique: Pour Dieu, la Cause, ou les Affaires*, ed. Mickaël Augeron, Didier Poton, and Bertrand Van Ruymbeke (Paris: Les Indes Savantes, 2009), 257–70; Lafleur and Lucien Abénon, "The Protestants and the Colonization of the French West Indies," in *Memory and Identity: The Huguenots in France and the Atlantic Diaspora*, ed. Bertrand Van Ruymbeke and Randy J. Sparks (Columbia: University of South Carolina Press, 2003), 267–84. For a general survey of the French Antilles during these years see Philip P. Boucher, *France and the American Tropics to 1700: Tropics of Discontent?* (Baltimore: Johns Hopkins University Press, 2008).

15. Jean-Baptiste du Tertre, *Histoire generale des Antilles, Habitées par les François* (Fort-de-France, Martinique: Éditions des Horizons Caraïbes, 1973), 1:173–78.

16. Du Tertre is quoted in Lafleur, *Les protestants aux Antilles françaises*, 35.

17. Rochefort, *Histoire naturelle et morale*, 1:92.

18. Rochefort, *Histoire naturelle et morale*, 1:62–73 (quotation on 71).

19. "Lettre de François Chaillou," November 1, 1660, in *Livres des Actes des Eglises Wallonnes aux Pays-Bas, 1601–1697*, ed. Guillaume H. H. Posthumus Meyjes and Hans Bots (The Hague: Instituut voor Nederlandse Geschiedenis, 2005), 607–608.

20. Charles de Rochefort, *Relation de l'isle de Tabago, ou de la Nouvelle Oüalcre, l'une des isles Antilles de l'Amerique* (Paris: Chez Louys Billaine, 1666), 72–73, 108–109, 116–17. The entire tract is included as an appendix in the modern edition of Rochefort, *Histoire naturelle et morale*, 2:282–353.

21. Rochefort, *Histoire naturelle et morale*, 2:73–134. Scholars have rarely known what to do with this part of Rochefort's work, since so much of it was clearly fanciful. Most scholars have concluded that the minister created the Apalachites out of his own imagination, though they have not given much thought as to why he would create such an elaborate lie. For the latest appraisal see Rodney M. Baine, "Another Lost Colony? Charles de Rochefort's Account of English Refugees and the Apalachites," *Georgia Historical Quarterly* 83:3 (1999), 558–64.

22. Rochefort, *Histoire naturelle et morale*, 2:128–29.

23. "Memoire sur les huguenots de l'Amerique" [1685?], Archives des Colonies, C⁸ᴮ 1, no. 93, ANOM.

24. For a printed version see *Code Noir. Ou recueil d'edits, declarations et arrets concernant Les Esclaves Nègres de l'Amérique, avec Un recueil de Réglemens, concernant la polices des Isles Françoises de l'Amérique et les Engagés* (Paris, 1743). There has been a great deal of scholarship on the Code Noir, though most has logically focused on the parts of the Code that concerned slavery. For the most recent work see Malick W. Ghachem, *The Old Regime and the Haitian Revolution* (Cambridge: Cambridge University Press, 2012).

25. "Memoire du Roy au Sr Comte de Blenac et Dumaitz de Goimpy," September 30, 1686, Archives des Colonies, B¹², f. 74, ANOM.

26. Mickaël Augeron, "Les Huguenots dans la marine du roi (1572–1688)," in *Les Huguenots et l'Atlantique*, ed. Augeron, Poton, and Van Ruymbeke (2009), 329–46.

27. "Memoire pour le Roy," July 8, 1686, Archives des Colonies, C⁸ᴬ 4, fol. 100, ANOM.

28. Johnson to the Lords of Trade and Plantations, June 2, 1688, CO 1/64, no. 71, TNA.

29. The Irish in particular have attracted a great deal of scholarship, though not specifically on convict labor. See Hilary McD. Beckles, "A 'Rioutous and Unruly Lot': Irish Indentured Servants and Freemen in the English West Indies," *WMQ* 47:4 (1990), 503–22; Kristen Block and Jenny Shaw, "Subjects without an Empire: The Irish in the Early Modern Caribbean," *Past and Present* no. 210 (2011), 33–60. Studies of convict labor include Abbot Emerson Smith, *Colonists in Bondage: White Servitude and Convict Labor in America, 1607–1776* (Chapel Hill: University of North Carolina Press, 1947); Cynthia Herrup, "The Punishing Pardon: Some Thoughts on the Origins of Penal Transportation," in *Penal Practice and Culture, 1500–1900: Punishing the English*, ed. Simon Devereux and Paul Griffiths (Cambridge: Cambridge University Press, 2002), 124–40; Lauren Benton, *A Search for Sovereignty: Law and Geography in European Empire, 1400–1900* (Cambridge: Cambridge University Press, 2010), 162–221.

30. Yvonne Bezard, *Fonctionnaires maritimes et coloniaux sous Louis XIV: Les Bégon* (Paris: Albin Michel, 1932), 72–77. On the galleys more generally see Paul W. Bamford, *Fighting Ships and Prisons: The Mediterranean Galleys of France in the Age of Louis XIV* (Minneapolis: University of Minnesota Press, 1973). The most thorough accounting of the experiment is in Lafleur, *Les protestants aux Antilles françaises*, 180–201.

31. The number comes from counting the totals related in Seignelay to Blenac, November 25, 1686, Archives des Colonies, B¹², f. 130, ANOM; Seignelay to Blenac, March 16, 1687, Archives des Colonies, B¹³, fol. 8; Seignelay to Blenac, April 16, 1687, Archives des Colonies, B¹³, f. 16; and in Raoul de Cazenove, ed., *Mémoires de Samuel de Pechels* (Toulouse: Société des Livres Religieux, 1878), 48.

32. Seignelay to Blenac, November 25, 1686, Archives des Colonies, B¹², fol. 130, ANOM.

33. *Brief, Van seeker Frans Heer, Geschreeven uyt Cadix Den 17 April 1687, Behelsende, hoe dat die van de Geformeerde Religie uyt Vrankrijk na de Eylanden van America werden toegevoert, en aldaar tot slaven verkogt* (Rotterdam, 1687), 3. A French version of the letter appeared in Jurieu, *Lettres Pastorales, addressées aux fideles de France, qui gemissent sous la captivité de Babylon* (Rotterdam: Abraham Acher, [1686–1687]), 177–78. While the author did not mention the name of the ship it is clear that it was the *Nôtre-Dame*, since Etienne Serres mentioned the encounter in his memoir; see Serres, *Un déporté pour la foi: quatre lettres du sieur Serres de Montpellier*, ed. Matthiew Lelière (Paris: Librairie évangelique, 1881), 56–57.

34. Newdigate Newsletters, January 27, 1686[/7], L.C. 1766, Folger Library.

35. Serres's memoir first appeared as *Quatre relations veritables du sieur Serres de Montpellier* (Amsterdam, 1688). Pechels's manuscript passed down through his family and did not seem to circulate before its initial publication in the 1880s. Neither work has received much attention from scholars.

36. Jurieu, *Lettres pastorales: addressees aux fideles persecutés de France, Seconde Année* (Rotterdam: Abraham Acher, 1688), 31–32, 38–40, 46–48.

37. Cazenove, ed., *Mémoires de Samuel de Pechels*, 52–53.

38. Serres, *Un déporté pour la foi*, 60.

39. Jurieu, *Lettres pastorales* (1688), 32. For more on the Caribs see Philip P. Boucher, *Cannibal Encounters: Europeans and Island Caribs, 1492–1763* (Baltimore: Johns Hopkins University Press, 1992).

40. Cazenove, ed., *Mémoires de Samuel de Pechels*, 56.

41. Serres, *Un déporté pour la foi*, 97, 100–101.

42. Jurieu, *Lettres pastorales* (1688), 32.

43. Cazenove, ed., *Mémoires de Samuel de Pechels*, 60.

44. Serres, *Un déporté pour la foi*, 141.

45. Jacques Flournoy, *Journal, 1675–1692*, ed. Olivier Fatio (Geneva: Droz, 1994), 234–35.

46. Serres, *Un déporté pour la foi*, 94–95. On the long genealogy of these sorts of images for Huguenots see Lestringant, *Le huguenot et le sauvage*, 21.

47. The complete "Récit" is in Rochefort, *Histoire naturelle et morale*, 2:253–84 (quotation on 254).

48. Rochefort, *Histoire naturelle et morale*, 2:257.

49. Rochefort, *Histoire naturelle et morale*, 2:259–60.

50. Rochefort, *Histoire naturelle et morale*, 2:263.

51. Rochefort, *Histoire naturelle et morale*, 2:261, 263.

52. Rochefort, *Histoire naturelle et morale*, 2:269.

53. Rochefort, *Histoire naturelle et morale*, 1:28.

54. For a great exposition of this lack of understanding see Elisabeth Labrousse, "Great Britain as Envisaged by the Huguenots of the Seventeenth Century," in *Huguenots in Britain and their French Background, 1550–1800*, ed. Irene Scouloudi (London: Macmillan, 1987), 143–57.

55. Rochefort, *Histoire naturelle et morale*, 2:277, 280–81.

56. Henry Mouche to François Cupif, March 20, 1669, in Posthumus Meyjes and Bots, eds. *Livres des Actes des Eglises Wallonnes aux Pays-Bas*, 819–20.

57. "Lettre de Charles de Rochefort," September 12, 1677; and Charles de Rochefort to Mr. Drelincourt, March 12, 1668, both in *Livre des Actes des Eglises Wallonnes aux Pays-Bas*, ed. Posthumus Meyjes and Bots, 804–805, 818. The money never went to New England, as Mouche preferred it be used in Dutch colonies, and it became a subject of substantial dispute for Dutch Huguenots for decades, though some did go to missionary efforts in Suriname and Tobago. Incredibly, Mouche's bequest continued to be used until 1890; see "Livre des deniers de Mons. Mouche, Anno 1680–1753," Collectie Bibliothèque Wallonne 445–47, Special Collections, University of Leiden Library.

58. The fullest account of this propaganda is in Bertrand Van Ruymbeke, *From New Babylon to Eden: The Huguenots and their Migration to Colonial South Carolina* (Columbia: University of South Carolina Press, 2006), 25–50. See also Van Ruymbeke, "Vivre au paradis? Représentations de l'Amérique dans les imprimés de propagande et des lettres de réfugiés," *BSHPF* 153:3 (2007), 343–56; and Chinard, *Les Réfugiés Huguenots en Amérique*, 58–76.

59. *Description du Pays nommé Carolina* (London, 1679), 1.

60. *Nouvelle Relation de la Caroline par Un Gentil-homme François arrivé, depuis deux mois, de ce nouveau pais* (The Hague, 1686), 14.

61. *Plan pour former en Establissement en Caroline* (The Hague, 1686), 1.

62. *Description du Pays nommé Carolina*, 3.

63. *Plan pour former un Establissement en Caroline*, 2, 5–7.

64. *Recueil de Diverses Pieces Concernant la Pensylvanie* (The Hague, 1684), 19, 27–28, 32. Another Pennsylvania tract, *Instruction Très-Exacte pour ceux qui ont dessein de se transporter en Amerique, Et Principalement Pour Ceux qui sont déjà intéressés dans la Province de Pennsylvanie* (Amsterdam, 1686), is no longer extant.

65. *Report of a French Protestant Refugee, in Boston, 1687*, trans. E. T. Fisher (Brooklyn, NY: J. Munsell, 1868), 19, 24–26, 36. The original is in the Collection Court, vol. 17L, no. 71, BGE, with a printed French version in the *BSHPF* (1867).

66. "Questions et Responces faites au sujet de la Caroline," MS 1909, Mediathèque Michel Crepeau, La Rochelle. (Quotation on f. 54v.)

67. Duquesne, *Recueil de quelques mémoires*, 242. Duquesne's only biographer was distinctly un-sympathetic: Émile Rainer, *L'utopie d'une république huguenote du marquis du Quesne et la voyage du François Leguat* (Paris: Ecrivains Associés, 1959). For more recent shorter treatments of the episode see Philippe Haudrère, "À la recherche de l'île d'Éden, aventures de protestants français sur la route des Indes orientales," in *Les Huguenots et l'Atlantique*, ed. Augeron, Poton, and Van Ruymbeke (2009), 389–95; and Randolph Vigne, "Huguenots to the Southern

Oceans: Archival Fact and Voltairean Myth," in *The Huguenots: France, Exile, and Diaspora*, ed. Jane McKee and Randolph Vigne (Brighton: Sussex Academic Press, 2013), 113–24.

68. For a thorough modern biography see Michel Vergé-Franceschi, *Abraham Duquesne: Huguenot et marin du Roi-Soleil* (Paris: France-Empire, 1992). The best place to find details of Henri's early biography is in Émile Rainer, *L'utopie d'une republique huguenote*, 12–16; Vergé-Francesci, *Abraham Duquesne*, 317–18.

69. Tavernier published a number of books chronicling his travels. See for example *Les six voyages de Jean Baptiste Tavernier, euyer Baron d'Aubonne, en Turquie, en Perse, et aux Inde* (Amsterdam, 1679). On the experiences of Huguenot mariners during this period see Mickaël Augeron, "Se convertir, partir, ou résister? Les marins huguenots face à la révocation de l'édit de Nantes," in *Les Huguenots et l'Atlantique*, ed. Augeron, Poton, and Van Ruymbeke (2009), 349–68.

70. Rainer, *L'utopie d'une republique huguenote*, 13–15. For an analysis of the book in the context of French utopian literature see Yardeni, *Utopie et revolte*, 24–25, 39; Paolo Carile, *Huguenots sans frontières: Voyage et écriture à la Renaissance et à l'Âge classique* (Paris: Honoré Champion, 2001), 97–136. Only one copy of the final book has survived, in the Bibliothèque Nationale de France, while one of the preliminary tracts is in the Collection Court, vol. 17D, no. 62, BGE.

71. Duquesne, *Recueil de quelques mémoires*, 242.

72. Duquesne, *Recueil de quelques mémoires*, 243. On his troubles in Aubonne see Rainer, *L'utopie d'une republique huguenote*, 16.

73. For a good brief survey see Myriam Yardeni, "French Calvinist Political Thought, 1534–1715," in *International Calvinism, 1541–1715*, ed. Menna Prestwich (Oxford: Clarendon Press, 1985), 315–37. See also Guy Howard Dodge, *The Political Theory of the Huguenots of the Dispersion, with Special Reference to the Thought and Influence of Pierre Jurieu* (New York: Columbia University Press, 1947).

74. Duquesne, *Recueil de quelques mémoires*, 243–45.

75. Duquesne, *Recueil de quelques mémoires*, 255.

76. Duquesne, *Recueil de quelques mémoires*, 227; "Projet de M. le Marquis du Quesne touchant une nouvelle colonie en l'Isle Eden," Collection Court, vol. 17D, no. 62, BGE.

77. Duquesne, *Recueil de quelques mémoires*, 247–48, 250.

78. Duquesne, *Recueil de quelques mémoires*, 258–64.

79. Étienne de Flacourt, *Histoire de la Grande Isle Madagascar*, ed. Claude Allibert (Paris, 1995), 306–308. Interestingly, one of the early governors of Madagascar, Jacques Pronis, was himself a Huguenot, and religious strife was one of the factors that doomed the French colony there. For background see Pier Martin Larson, "Colonies Lost: God, Hunger, and Conflict in Anosy (Madagascar) to 1674," *Comparative Studies of South Asia, Africa and the Middle East* 27:2 (2007), 345–66.

80. Ricous to Ponant, September 8, 1681, Archives des Colonies, C^3 1, f. 39, ANOM; "Memoire du Ch. de Ricous sur l'Isle de Bourbon," Archives des Colonies, C^3 1, f. 25.

81. "Memoire de toutes les choses necessaires pour L'establissement de L'isle de Bourbon," August 23, 1681, Archives des Colonies, $C^3$1, f. 34, ANOM.

82. Duquesne, *Recueil de quelques mémoires*, 264.

83. Duquesne, *Recueil de quelques mémoires*, 247.

84. Duquesne, *Recueil de quelques mémoires*, 250. See *Dictionnaire de l'Académie Française*, first ed. (1694), available at https://artfl-project.uchicago.edu/content/dictionnaires-dautrefois

85. Duquesne, *Recueil de quelques mémoires*, 249.

86. Charles-François de La Bonde d'Iberville to Charles Colbert, marquis de Croissy, March 8, 1689, in Charles-François d'Iberville, *Correspondance, 1688–1690*, ed. Laurence Vial-Bergon (Geneva: Droz, 2003), 1:41; d'Iberville to Croissy, March 17, 1689, ibid., 1:45.

87. Duquesne to Mirmand, February 19, 1689, Collection Court, vol. 17O, ff. 79–80, BGE.

88. Durand de Dauphiné, *A Huguenot Exile in Virginia; or Voyages of a Frenchman exiled for his Religion with a description of Virginia and Maryland*, ed. Gilbert Chinard (New York: Press of the Pioneers, 1934), 87, 162–63.

89. François Leguat published his story in English and French in 1708. All quotations are from the most recent English edition, Leguat, *The Voyage of François Leguat of Bresse to Rodriguez, Mauritius, Java, and the Cape of Good Hope* (London: Hakluyt Society, 1891), 1: lxxxvi.

90. Leguat, *Voyage of François Leguat,* 1:3–4.
91. Site de la Base de données du refuge Huguenot, Laboratoire de recherches historiques Rhône-Alpes (LARHRA), www.refuge-huguenot.fr, Notice no. 72738.
92. The records of these travelers are in Royal Bounty Papers, MS 2/1-2/7, Huguenot Library, University College London. For specific references see MS 2/3, f. 13; Base de données, No. 84497.
93. D'Avaux to Croissy, June 11 and 17, 1686, Correspondance Politique, Hollande, v. 146, ff. 231–32, 293–92, MAE. On the spy who revealed the news see Caroline Lougee Chappell, "Through the Eyes of a Spy: Venom and Value in an Enemy's Report on the Huguenot Emigration," in *The Huguenots,* ed. McKee and Vigne, 77–88.
94. "Questions et Responces faites au sujet de la Caroline," MS 1909, f. 51v, Mediathèque Michel Crepeau, La Rochelle.
95. "Proposition en general pour la Caroline," Rawlinson Mss. C 982, f. 217, Bodleian Library.
96. Royal Bounty Papers, MSS 2/5, f. 6; Base de données, Nos. 83417, 84217-19, 85724, 88384-5, 89045; Stafford County, Record Book, 1686–1694, f. 95, Library of Virginia, Richmond.
97. Durand, *A Huguenot Exile in Virginia,* 159, 180.
98. Fitzhugh to Hayward, May 20, 1686, in Richard Beale Davis, ed., *William Fitzhugh and his Chesapeake World, 1676–1701: The Fitzhugh Letters and Other Documents* (Chapel Hill: University of North Carolina Press, 1963), 189. For more on the settlement see Fairfax Harrison, "Brent Town, Ravensworth, and the Huguenots," in *Landmarks of Old Prince William* (Richmond: Old Dominion Press, 1924), 1:177–96.
99. The Bishop of St. Asaph to the Archbishop of Canterbury, February 6, 1686/7, Tanner Mss. 30, f. 137, Bodleian Library.
100. "Copie d'une lettre ou fragment de lettre de Sr Varis," December 1685, Correspondance Politique, Hollande, v. 144, f. 155, MAE. For background see Matthew Glozier, "Huguenots and the Dutch East India Company (VOC)," *HSP* 29:3 (2010), 385–96.
101. Court of Committees, May 11, 1688, June 1, 1688, December 9, 1689, IOR B/39, fol. 128, 130, 236, BL; "Commission to Lieutt De La Serre & Ensign Dubrois," June 1, 1688, IOR E/3/91, f. 268v, BL; *Records of Fort St George: Letters from Fort St George for 1689* (Madras: Government Press, 1916), 63, 65. On Chardin's Armenian scheme see Philip J. Stern, *The Company-State: Corporate Sovereignty and the Early Modern Foundations of the British Empire in India* (New York: Oxford University Press, 2011), 39.
102. [William Petyt], *Britannia Languens, or a Discourse of Trade: Shewing The Grounds and Reasons of the Increase and Decay of Land-Rents, National Wealth and Strength* (London, 1680), 154. On the politics of population during this period see especially Ted McCormick, "Modes of Seventeenth-Century Demographic Thought," in *Mercantilism Reimagined: Political Economy in Early Modern Britain and its Empire,* ed. Philip J. Stern and Carl Wennerlind (New York: Oxford University Press, 2013); Mildred Campbell, "'Of People Either Too Few or Too Many': The Conflict of Opinion on Population and its Relation to Emigration," in *Conflict in Stuart England: Essays in Honour of Wallace Notestein,* ed. William A. Aiken and Basil D. Henning (London: Jonathan Cape, 1960), 170–201.
103. Sir Josiah Child, *A New Discourse of Trade* (London, 1693).
104. Sir Francis Brewster, *Essays on Trade and Navigation* (London, 1695), 18.
105. For the context of Dutch settlements in the Caribbean at this time see especially Wim Klooster, *The Dutch Moment: War, Trade, and Settlement in the Seventeenth-Century Atlantic World* (Ithaca, NY: Cornell University Press, 2016).
106. "Reflexions sur le Règlement de la Compagnie des Indes Orientales du 20 Oct. 1687," in *Bouwstoffen voor de geschiedenis der Nederduitsch-Gereformeerde Kerken in Zuid-Afrika, deel II, Brieven van de Classis Amsterdam E.A. aan de Kaapsche kerken enz., 1651–1804,* ed. Spoelstra (Amsterdam: Hollandsch-Africaansche Uitgevers-Maatschappij, 1907), 645.
107. *Reglement, De l'assemblée des Dix-sept, qui representent la Compagnie des Indes Orientales des Païs-Bas, suivant lequel les Chambres de le ditte Compagnie auront pouvoir de transporter au Cap de Bonne Esperance des Personnes de tout sexe de la Religion reformée, entre autres les refugies de France, & des Vallees de Piedmont* (The Hague, 1687), in Collection Court, vol. 17U, ff. 207–208, BGE. The publication was simply a translation of the resolution by the VOC. It is reprinted, in Dutch and French, in *Brieven van de Classis Amsterdam E.A. aan de Kaapsche kerken,* ed. Spoelstra, 641–45.

Chapter 3

1. Durand of Dauphiné, *A Huguenot Exile in Virginia; or Voyages of a Frenchman exiled for his Religion with a description of Virginia and Maryland,* ed. Gilbert Chinard (New York: Press of the Pioneers, 1934), 86–87. Silk production in America has never received adequate attention until the recent work of Ben Marsh; see his "Silk Hopes in Colonial South Carolina," *Journal of Southern History* 78:4 (2012), 807–54. See also Charles E. Hatch Jr., "Mulberry Trees and Silkworms: Sericulture in Early Virginia," *VMHB* 65:1 (1957), 3–61.

2. Durand, *A Huguenot Exile in Virginia,* 127, 154. Early American wine production has been studied even less than silk. See Thomas Pinney, *A History of Wine in America: From the Beginnings to Prohibition* (Berkeley: University of California Press, 1989); Owen Stanwood, "Imperial Vineyards: Wine and Politics in the Early American South," in *Experiencing Empire: Power, People, and Revolution in Early America,* ed. Patrick Griffin (Charlottesville: University of Virginia Press, 2017), 50–70. Wine consumption, on the other hand, has received more attention; see David Hancock, *Oceans of Wine: Madeira and the Emergence of American Trade and Taste* (New Haven, CT: Yale University Press, 2009); and for Britain itself, Charles Ludington, *The Politics of Wine in Britain: A Cultural History* (London: Palgrave, 2013).

3. Samuel Fortrey, *Englands Interest and Improvement, Consisting in the Increase of the Store, and Trade of this Kingdom* (Cambridge, 1663), 2. For a portrait of a Huguenot family in the silk industry see Jean-Paul Chabrol, *Les Seigneurs de la soie: Trois siècles de la vie d'une famille cévenole* (Montpellier: Presses du Languedoc, 1994). Many more Huguenots worked in silk manufacturing than production, and vineyard labor tended to be heavily Catholic, though especially in western France Huguenots were often active in the wine trade. On their influence on silk manufacturing in the British world see Zara Anashanslin, *Portrait of a Woman in Silk: Hidden Histories of the British Atlantic World* (New Haven, CT: Yale University Press, 2016).

4. Mercantilism has inspired great debate lately, with some historians questioning its utility as a concept. See Steve Pincus, "Rethinking Mercantilism: Political Economy, the British Empire, and the Atlantic World in the Seventeenth and Eighteenth Centuries," *WMQ* 69:1 (2012), 3–34, with the responses by other historians; and Jonathan Barth, "Reconstructing Mercantilism: Consensus and Conflict in the British Imperial Economy in the Seventeenth and Eighteenth Centuries," *WMQ* 73:2 (2016), 257–90. See also Jacob Soll, "Accounting for Government: Holland and the Rise of Political Economy in Seventeenth-Century Europe," *Journal of Interdisciplinary History* 40:2 (2009), 215–38; and Philip J. Stern and Carl Wennerlind, eds., *Mercantilism Reimagined: Political Economy in Early Modern Britain and its Empire* (New York: Oxford University Press, 2013).

5. [William Petyt], *Britannia Languens, or a Discourse of Trade: Shewing The Grounds and Reasons of the Increase and Decay of Land-Rents, National Wealth and Strength* (London, 1680), 184.

6. On consumption during this period see especially Linda Levy Peck, *Consuming Splendor: Society and Culture in Seventeenth-Century England* (Cambridge: Cambridge University Press, 2005).

7. Rochefort, *Histoire naturelle et morale des îles Antilles de l'Amérique,* ed. Bernard Grunberg, Benoît Roux, and Josiane Grunberg (Paris: L'Harmattan, 2012), 2:257; Reboulet to Jacques Tronchin, October 4, 1687, Archives Tronchin, vol. 50, ff. 80–81, BGE.

8. Rene de Laudonnière, *Three Voyages,* ed. Charles Bennett and Jerald T. Melanich (Tuscaloosa: University of Alabama Press, 2001), 65.

9. John Smith, "The Generall History of Virginia, the Somer Iles, and New England, with the Names of the Adventurers, and Their Adventures" [1623], in *The Complete Works of Captain John Smith (1580–1631),* ed. Philip L. Barbour (Chapel Hill: University of North Carolina Press, 1986), 2:89.

10. Thomas Harriott, *A Brief and True Report of the New Found Land of Virginia* (New York: J. Sabin & Sons, 1871), 9. (Electronic edition at http://docsouth.unc.edu/nc/hariot/hariot. html.) .

11. "The Description of Virginia by John Smith," in *The Complete Works of Captain John Smith,* ed. Barbour, 1:152; William Strachey, *The Historie of Travell into Virginia Britania,* ed. Louis B. Wright and Virginia Freund (London: Hakluyt Society, 1951), 121.

12. Council of Virginia to the Virginia Company, July 7, 1610, in *The Genesis of the United States,* ed. Alexander Brown (New York: Houghton, Mifflin, & Co., 1890), 409–10.

13. Laudonnière, *Three Voyages*, 21.
14. Smith, "Generall Historie," in *The Complete Works of John Smith*, ed, Barbour, 2:108.
15. Mary Anne Everett Green, ed., *Calendar of State Papers, Domestic Series, James I, 1603–1610* (London: Longman Green, 1857), 344, 562.
16. Smith, "Generall Historie," in *Complete Works of Captain John Smith*, ed. Barbour, 2:108.
17. Declaration of the King, September 5, 1622, in *The Records of the Virginia Company of London*, ed. Susan Myra Kingsbury (Washington, DC: Government Printing Office, 1906–35), 2:102.
18. [John Bonoiel], *Observations to be followed, for the making of fit roomes, to keep Silk-wormes in: As also, for the best manner of planting of Mulbery trees, to feed them* (London, 1620), 4, 16, and passim.
19. John Pory to Sir Edwin Sandys, January 14, 1619/20, *Records of the Virginia Company*, 3:256.
20. "A Note of the Shipping, Men, and Provisions, sent and provided for Virginia," 1620, *Records of the Virginia Company*, 3:240.
21. Instructions to Francis Wyatt, July 24, 1621, in *The Statutes at Large: Being a Collection of all the Laws of Virginia, from the First Session of the Legislature, in the Year 1619*, ed. William Waller Hening (Richmond: Samuel Pleasants, 1819–23), 1:115.
22. Treasurer, Council, and Company of Virginia to the Governor and Council, July 9, 1622, *Records of the Virginia Company*, 3:663.
23. "An Answere to a Petition delivered to his Matie by Alderman Johnson in the names of sundry Adventurers and Planters of Virginia and Sumer Ilands Plantacons," May 23, 1623, *Records of the Virginia Company*, 2:396.
24. General Assembly to the King, March 26, 1628, and "Act XVI," February 1631/2, in Hening, *Statutes at Large*, 1:136, 161.
25. Antoine de Ridouet, baron de Sancé, to [Sec. Dorchester], 14 [June?] 1629, CO 1/5, no. 14, TNA.
26. Paul E. Kopperman, "Profile of Failure: The Carolana Project, 1629–1640," *North Carolina Historical Review* 59:1 (1982), 1–23.
27. The King to the Governor and Council of Virginia, November 1627, CO 1/4, no. 32, TNA.
28. [Edward Williams], *Virginia: More especially the South part thereof, Richly and truly valued* (London: T. H. for John Stevenson, 1650), 16.
29. Williams, *Virginia Richly Valued*, 16–18.
30. [Samuel Hartlib], *The Reformed Virginian Silk-Worm, Or, a Rare and New Discovery of A speedy way, and easie means, found out by a young Lady in England, she having made a full proof thereof in May, Anno 1652* (London, 1655), 11 and passim. A German emigrant, Hartlib was one of the most fascinating figures in mid-seventeenth-century England. For some sense of his circle see Charles Webster, *The Great Instauration: Science, Medicine, and Reform, 1626–1660* (Oxford: Peter Lang, 2002). Interestingly, his circle was involved with a different Huguenot colonization scheme in the 1640s, though it never got off the ground. See Thomas Leng, "'A Potent Plantation well armed and Policeed': Huguenots, the Hartlib Circle, and British Colonization in the 1640s," 66:1 (2009), 173–94.
31. Carew Reynall, *The True English Interest* (London: Giles Widdows, 1674), 34.
32. Berkeley to Edward Hyde, earl of Clarendon, April 18, 1663, in *The Papers of Sir William Berkeley, 1605–1677*, ed. Warren M. Billings (Richmond: Library of Virginia, 2007), 193. For a thorough biography see Billings, *Sir William Berkeley and the Forging of Colonial Virginia* (Baton Rouge: Louisiana State University Press, 2010).
33. Charles II to Berkeley, February 20, 1662/3, *Berkeley Papers*, 185.
34. "An Account concerning Silk-wormes sent by Mr Edward Diggs to Mr Palmer for the Society," MS/215/45, Royal Society, London.
35. Berkeley to Charles II, July 22, 1668, *Berkeley Papers*, 343.
36. Berkeley to the Council for Foreign Plantations, June 20, 1671, *Berkeley Papers*, 393.
37. For the latest scholarly perspective on the proprietors see L. H. Roper, *Conceiving Carolina: Proprietors, Planters, and Plots, 1662–1729* (New York: Routledge, 2004).
38. William Hilton, *A Relation of a Discovery lately made on the Coast of Florida* (1664), in *Narratives of Early Carolina, 1650–1708*, ed. Alexander S. Salley Jr. (New York: C. Scribner's Sons, 1911), 44, 47.

39. Robert Horne, *A Brief Description of the Province of Carolina* (1666), in *Narratives*, ed. Salley, 68.

40. Jos. Dalton to Lord Ashley, January 20, 1672, PRO 30/24/48, no. 87, TNA.

41. These terms appeared as an appendix to Horne, *Brief Description*, in *Narratives*, ed. Salley, 71.

42. [Samuel Wilson], *An Account of the Province of Carolina in America* (London, 1682), 10 [mislabeled page 9].

43. *Carolina; or a Description Of the present State of that Country, and The natural Excellencies thereof* (London, 1682), i.

44. John Locke, *Observations upon the Growth and Culture of Vines and Olives: The Production of Silk: The Preservation of Fruits* (London: W. Sandby, 1766), 2, 18–22, 71. On the tract's larger context see David Armitage, "John Locke, Carolina, and the *Two Treatises of Government*," *Political Theory* 32:5 (2004), 611–12.

45. John Locke, *Locke's Travels in France, 1675–1679*, ed. John Lough (New York: Facsimiles-Garl, 1984), 28–29.

46. Sir William Temple, *Observations upon the United Provinces of the Netherlands*, ed. George Clark (Oxford: Clarendon Press, 1972), 111, 113.

47. One version of "The Fundamental Constitutions of Carolina" is available online at http:// avalon.law.yale.edu/17th_century/nc05.asp. See Vicki Hsueh, "Giving Orders: Theory and Practice in the Fundamental Constitutions of Carolina," *Journal of the History of Ideas* 63:3 (2002), 425–47.

48. Reynall, *The True English Interest*, 70–71.

49. Bethel, *The Interest of the Princes and States of Europe*, 2d ed. (London, 1680), 55.

50. For a comparative analysis of Huguenots and Covenanters see Kurt Gingrich, "'That Will Make Carolina Powerful and Flourishing': Scots and Huguenots in Carolina in the 1680s," *South Carolina Historical Magazine* 110:1 (2009), 6–34. On the covenanting diaspora in general, which has interesting parallels to the Huguenot story, see Craig Gallagher, "Covenants and Commerce: Scottish Networks and the Making of the British Atlantic World" (PhD diss., Boston College, 2017).

51. "Humble Proposition faite au Roy et à Son Parlement pour donner retraite aux Etrangers protestans et au proselites dans ses Colonies de L'amerique et sur tout en la Carolina," March 1679, in *Records in the British Public Record Office Relating to South Carolina, 1663–1684*, ed. Alexander S. Salley (Columbia: Historical Commission of South Carolina, 1928), 62–68; Rene Petit and J. Guerard to the Committee on Trade and Plantations, March 1679, ibid., 73–74.

52. "Humble Proposition," March 1679, in *Records in the British Public Record Office Relating to South Carolina, 1663–1684*, ed. Salley, 68; "Humble Proposalls for Carolina," March 1679, ibid., 75.

53. Opinion of the Proprietors, March 6, 1679, in *Records in the British Public Record Office Relating to South Carolina, 1663–1684*, ed. Salley, 71.

54. On Shaftesbury and the Popish Plot see see J. P. Kenyon, *The Popish Plot* (London: Heinemann, 1973); Tim Harris, *Restoration: Charles II and his Kingdoms, 1660–1685* (London: Allen Lane, 2005), 136–202.

55. Thomas Dolman and Lords Commr of Treasury to Commissioners of the Customs, March 14, 1678/9, in Salley, *Records in the British Public Record Office Relating to South Carolina, 1663–1684*, 76.

56. "At ye Court at Whitehall," May 28, 1679, in Salley, *Records in the British Public Record Office Relating to South Carolina, 1663–1684*, 79–80.

57. St. Julien R. Childs, "The Petit-Guérard Colony," *South Carolina Historical and Genealogical Magazine* 43:1 (1942), 9–10.

58. Order of the King in Council, November 29, 1682, CO 1/51, no. 115, TNA.

59. Journal of Lords of Trade and Plantations, CO 391/4, p. 347–48. TNA.

60. Charles W. Baird, *History of the Huguenot Emigration to America* (New York: Dodd Mead and Co., 1885), 1:308; Pinney, *History of Wine in America*, 32.

61. "Memoire touchant la maniere de recevoir & employer les Proselites & Protestans qui se refugient en Ang[leter]re," Rawlinson Mss. C 984, f. 228, Bodleian Library.

62. "Memoire," Rawlinson Mss. C 984, f. 228.

63. William Penn to James Harrison, August 25, 1681; and Moses Charas to William Penn, August 25, 1682, both in Richard S. Dunn and Mary Maples Dunn, eds., *The Papers of William Penn* (Philadelphia: University of Pennsylvania Press, 1982), 2:108, 285–86.

64. *Recüeil de Diverses Pieces, Concernant la Pensylvanie* (The Hague, 1684), 19, 27.

65. *Recüeil de Diverses Pieces, Concernant la Pensylvanie,* 58–60, 97–98.

66. Temple, *United Provinces,* 109. On the Dutch silk industry see Jan de Vries and Ad van der Woude, *The First Modern Economy: Success, Failure, and Perseverance of the Dutch Economy, 1500–1815* (Cambridge: Cambridge University Press, 1997), 293–94; on wine see Henriette de Bruyn Kops, *A Spirited Commerce: The Wine and Brandy Trade between France and the Dutch Republic in its Atlantic Framework, 1600–1650* (Leiden: Brill, 2007).

67. The classic English-language work on the Dutch empire in the east is C. R. Boxer, *The Dutch Seaborne Empire, 1600–1800* (London: Hutchinson, 1965). On the founding of the Cape Colony in its larger context see Hermann Giliomee, *The Afrikaners: Biography of a People* (Charlottesville: University of Virginia Press, 2003), 1–21; Kerry Ward, *Networks of Empire: Forced Migration in the Dutch East India Company* (Cambridge: Cambridge University Press, 2009); and for the role of Huguenots, especially Marilyn Garcia-Chapleau, *Le Refuge huguenot du cap de Bonne-Espérance: Genèse, assimilation, héritage* (Paris: Honoré Champion, 2016), 73–110.

68. "A Short Exposition of the Advantages to be Derived by the Company from a Fort and Garden at the Cape of Good Hope," July 26, 1649, in *Precis of the Archives of the Cape of Good Hope: Riebeeck's Journal, &c.,* ed. H. C. V. Leibbrandt (Cape Town: W. A. Richard and Sons, 1897), 1:6.

69. "Report of Van Riebeeck on the above 'Remonstrance,' Addressed to the Directors of the General Company," June 1651, *Riebeeck's Journal,* 1:8.

70. "Journal of Commander Johan van Riebeeck," *Riebeeck's Journal,* 1:20.

71. Gerald Groenewald, "Entrepreneurs and the Making of a Free Burgher Society," in *Cape Town Between East and West: Social Identities in a Dutch Colonial Town,* ed. Nigel Worden (Johannesburg: Verloren, 2012), 45–64. For the population numbers see "'t Getal der vrye luyden en derselver vee, etc. aan 't fort de Goede Hoop, bestont in 't jaar 1685 in," in *Beschryvinge van de Oostindische Compagnie,* tweede boek, deel III, ed. Pieter van Dam (The Hague: Martinus Nijhoff, 1939), 544–45.

72. Robert Ross, "Khoesan and Immigrants: The Emergence of Colonial Society in the Cape, 1500–1800," in *The Cambridge History of South Africa,* vol. 1, *From Early Times to 1885,* ed. Carolyn Hamilton, Bernard K. Mbenga, and Robert Ross (Cambridge: Cambridge University Press, 2009), 181 and passim.

73. *Riebeeck's Journal,* 3:5; George McCall Theal, *Chronicles of the Cape Commanders* (Cape Town: W. A. Richards and Sons, 1882), 63, 87; Jeanne Viall, Wilmot James, and James Gerwel, *Grape: Stories of the Vineyards in South Africa* (Cape Town: NB Publishers, 2011), 36–40.

74. Abbé de Choisy, *Journal du voyage de Siam fait en 1685, & 1686,* 2nd ed. (Paris, 1687), 123, 125.

75. "Extract from the Resolutions of the Assembly of the Seventeen," October 3, 1685, in C. Graham Botha, *The French Refugees at the Cape* (Cape Town: C. Struik, 1970), 126.

76. "Extract from the Resolutions of the Assembly of the Seventeen," in Botha, *French Refugees,* 126.

77. "Reglement, ter vergaderinge van de Seventiene, de Generale Geoctroyeerde Oostindische Compagnie representerde, gearresteert, waarop de Cameren sullen vermogen eenige luyden en familiën, haar voorkomende, te transporteren en over te brenge na de Cabo de Bonne Esperance," October 3, 1685, in Van Dam, *Beschryvinge van de Oostindische Compagnie,* tweede boek, deel III, 540–41.

78. Simon van der Stel to the Heren XVII, April 26, 1688, in H. C. V. Leibbrandt, *Rambles through the Archives of the Colony of the Cape of Good Hope, 1688–1700* (Cape Town: J. C. Juta and Co., 1887), 37.

79. This document appears in a number of places; the Dutch version is in Van Dam, *Beschryvinge van de Oostindische Compagnie,* tweede boek, deel III, 542–44; Dutch and French versions appear in *Bouwstoffen voor de geschiedenis der Nederduitsch-Gereformeerde Kerken in Zuid-Afrika,* deel II, *Brieven van de Classis Amsterdam E.A. aan de Kaapsche kerken enz., 1651–1804,* ed.

Spoelstra (Amsterdam: Hollandsch-Africaansche Uitgevers-Maatschappij, 1907), 641–45. The printed version ended up in the Collection Court, vol. 17U, ff. 207–208, BGE. For the Polish ambassador see Antony Moreau to the King of Poland, May 18, 1688, Add. Mss. 38494, f. 68v, BL.

80. "Reflexions sur le Règlement de la Compagnie des Indes Orientales du 20 Oct. 1687," in *Brieven van de Classis Amsterdam E.A. aan de Kaapsche kerken*, ed. Spoelstra, 645–60.

81. "Reflexions," 645–46.

82. "Reflexions," 647, 651.

83. "Reflexions," 648–49, 656.

84. The Seventeen to the Cape, November 16, 1687, extract, Botha, *French Refugees*, 134. The complete, original version is in C340: Inkomende Briewe, Feb. 28-Des. 18, 1687, ff. 78–81, WCA.

85. From Chamber of Amsterdam, December 23, 1687, extract, Botha, *French Refugees*, 142.

86. See the letters from the Heren XVII to the Cape, October 21, 1688 and July 21, 1688, C343: Inkomende Briewe, Apr. 1–Okt. 6, 1688, ff. 22, 31, WCA; Pieter Coertzen, *The Huguenots of South Africa, 1688–1988* (Cape Town: Tafelberg, 1988), 71; Botha, *French Refugees*, 10. On the "Glorieuse Rentrée" see Albert de Lange, ed., *Dall'Europa alle valli valdesi: atti del XXIX convegno storico internazionale: il glorioso rimpatrio, 1689–1989* (Turin: Claudiana, 1990).

87. Hans Bots, "Les pasteurs français au Refuge des Provinces-Unies: un groupe socio-professionnel tout particulier, 1680–1710," in *La Vie intellectuelle aux Refuges protestants*, ed. Jens Häseler and Anthony McKenna (Paris: Honoré Champion, 1999), 64; Coertzen, *The Huguenots of South Africa*, 70; Maurice Boucher, *French Speakers at the Cape: The European Background* (Pretoria: University of South Africa, 1981), 174–78. His publication was *La Discipline de Jésus-Christ* (Leiden, 1687), whose dedication suggested that Simond had family links to the Prince of Orange. See Randolph Vigne, "South Africa's First Published Work of Literature and its Author, Pierre Simond," *South African Historical Journal* 39:1 (1998), 4.

88. London to St. Helena, August 1, 1683, in *Extracts from the St. Helena Records*, ed. Hudson Ralph Janisch (Jamestown, St. Helena: B. Grant, 1885), 20. On the early history of St. Helena see Philip J. Stern, "Politics and Ideology in the Early East India Company-State: The Case of St. Helena, 1673–1709," *Journal of Imperial and Commonwealth History* 35:1 (2007), 1–23; Trevor W. Hearl, *St. Helena Britannica: Studies in South Atlantic Island History*, ed. A. H. Schulenburg (London: Society of Friends of St. Helena, 2013).

89. London to Surat, February 3, 1686/7, IOR E/3/91, f. 132v, BL.

90. London to St. Helena, April 5, 1689, IOR E/3/92, f. 17v, BL.

91. London to St. Helena, April 5, 1689, IOR E/3/92, f. 17v, BL. Several Poiriers lived in the small town of Is-sur-Tille, just north of Dijon. See Site de la Base de données du refuge Huguenot, Laboratoire de recherches historiques Rhône-Alpes (LARHRA), www.refuge-huguenot.fr, Notice no. 7701, 15708, 41320, 41410-12.

92. "Instructions for Mr Poirier Supervisor of all the Companyes Plantations Vineyards and Cattle in the Island of St. Helena," IOR E/3/92, fol. 18v-19, BL; London to St. Helena, April 5, 1689, IOR E/3/92, f. 17v.

93. Judith Giton Manigault to Her Brother, in Slann Simmons, ed., "Early Manigault Records," *Transactions of the Huguenot Society of South Carolina* 59 (1954), 25–27, also printed in Baird, *History of the Huguenot Emigration to America*, 2:396–97. See Bertrand Van Ruymbeke, "Judith Giton: From Southern France to the Carolina Lowcountry," in *South Carolina Women: Their Lives and Times*, ed. Marjorie Julian Spruill, Valinda W. Littlefield, and Joan Marie Johnson (Athens: University of Georgia Press, 2009), 1:26–39.

94. Molly McClain and Alessa Ellefson, "A Letter from Carolina, 1688: French Huguenots in the New World," *WMQ* 64:2 (2007), 390–91.

95. Childs, "The Petit-Guérard Colony," 7; A. S. Salley, ed., *Warrants for Land in South Carolina, 1672–1711* (Columbia: Historical Commission of South Carolina, 1910), 2:106.

96. Childs, "The Petit-Guérard Colony," 16–17.

97. Letter of Louis Thibou, September 20, 1683, South Caroliniana Library, University of South Carolina, Columbia (available online at http://teachingushistory.org/lessons/Thibou.htm); Jean Boyd to his sister, 1691, in Harriot Cheves Leland and Diane W. Ressinger, "'Ce Païs Tant Desiré': This Much Longed for Country," *Transactions of the Huguenot Society of South Carolina* 110 (2005), 31.

98. Boyd to Matrine, 1686, RB/3/1/42J, fol. 93, Royal Society, London. On the Boyd family see Dianne W. Ressinger, Harriott Cheves Leland, and Vivien Costello, "The Boyd Family: Global Huguenot Merchants," *HSP* 29 (2009), 168–79. For a translation of most of the letter see Susan Baldwin Bates and Harriott Cheves Leland, *French Santee: A Huguenot Settlement in Colonial South Carolina* (Baltimore: Otter Bay Books, 2015), 360–69.

99. Lords Proprietors to Archdale, December 17, 1694, in A.S. Salley, ed., *Records in the British Public Record Office Relating to South Carolina, 1691–1697* (Columbia: Historical Commission of South Carolina, 1931), 150; Jon Butler, *The Huguenots in America: A Refugee People in New World Society* (Cambridge, MA: Harvard University Press, 1983), 97. On their trade in wine see L. M. Cullen, "The Boyds in Bordeaux and Dublin," in *Ireland, France, and the Atlantic in a Time of War: Reflections on the Bordeaux-Dublin Letters, 1757*, ed. Thomas M. Truxes (London: Routledge, 2017), 51–69.

100. Robert Cohen and Myriam Yardeni, eds., "Un Suisse en Caroline du Sud à la fin du XVII siècle." *BSHPF* 134:1 (1988), 68.

101. "Extrait d'une lettre de Mr Lescot ministre de l'Eglise françoise de Charlestown en Caroline du Sud," April 6, 1701, Archives Tronchin, vol. 81, f. 194, BGE.

102. William Salmon, *Botanologia: The English Herbal, or History of Plants* (London, 1710), ch. 95.

103. *Carolina; or a Description Of the present State of that Country, and The natural Excellencies thereof* (London, 1682), 9.

104. McClain and Ellefson, "A Letter from Carolina," 392–93.

105. Proprietors to Nathaniel Johnson, October 19, 1699, in A. S. Salley, ed., *Records in the British Public Record Office Relating to South Carolina, 1698–1700* (Columbia: Historical Commission of South Carolina, 1946), 117.

106. John Archdale, *A New Description of that Fertile and Pleasant Province of Carolina* (London: John Wyat, 1707), 30.

107. Samuel Gaillard Stoney, ed., "Nicholas de Longuemare: Huguenot Goldsmith and Silk Dealer in Colonial South Carolina," *Transactions of the Huguenot Society of South Carolina* 55 (1950), 63–69.

108. John Ovington, *A Voyage to Suratt* (London: Jacob Tonsen, 1696), 97.

109. "Consultation booke and St. Helena Memorandum," June 18, 1695, IOR G/32/2, p. 3, BL; London to St Helena, December 15, 1698, IOR E/3/93, f. 75.

110. Ovington, *A Voyage to Suratt*, 487, 502–503.

111. From the Chamber of Amsterdam, July 21, 1688, in Botha, *French Refugees*, 144.

112. Pierre Simond to the Council of the Seventeen, 15 juin 1689, VOC 4026, ff. 1298–1304, Nationaal Archief, The Hague. For a transcription of the letter, based on the copy in the Western Cape Archives, see Garcia-Chapleau, *Le Refuge huguenot du cap de Bonne-Espérance*, 644–52.

113. Boucher, *French Speakers at the Cape*, 232–33; Delft Chamber to the Cape, December 16, 1688, C344: Inkomende Briewe, 1688 Okt 6–Des 16, WCA.

114. Boucher, *French Speakers at the Cape*, 223–24; François Leguat, *The Voyage of François Leguat of Bresse to Rodriguez, Mauritius, Java, and the Cape of Good Hope* (London: Hakluyt Society, 1891), 2:287. For more on Taillefert see J. G. Le Roux, *Hugenotebloed in ons are* (Pretoria: HSRC Press, 1988), 63–64; and Garcia-Chapleau, *Le Refuge huguenot du cap de Bonne-Espérance*, 598–602.

115. Leguat, *Voyage of François Leguat*, 2:277; Peter Kolb, *The Present State of the Cape of Good Hope* (London: W. Innys, 1731), 2:76–77, 80; François Valentyn, *Description of the Cape of Good Hope with the Matters Concerning It*, ed. P. Serton, R. Raven-Hart, and W. J. de Kock (Cape Town: Van Riebeeck Society, 1971), 1:189. On the making of a kind of wine aristocracy in the eighteenth-century Cape Colony see Robert Ross, "The Rise of the Cape Gentry," *Journal of Southern African Studies* 9:2 (1983), 193–217.

116. Leguat, *Voyage of François Leguat*, 2:287; Kolb, *Present State of the Cape of Good Hope*, 2:48–49. The Huguenot influence on the origins of South Africa's wine industry is a matter of debate; compare Viall, James, and Gerwel, *Grape*, which labels the Huguenot origin story little more than a myth, with Charles D. Hérisson, "La contribution des huguenots français et de leurs descendants à la vie nationale sud-africaine," *BSHPF* 98:1 (1953), 57–93;

Garcia-Chapleau, *Le Refuge huguenot du cap de Bonne-Espérance*, 355–56; and Johan Fourie and Dieter von Fintel, "Settler Skills and Colonial Development: The Huguenot Wine-Makers in Eighteenth-Century Dutch South Africa," *Economic History Review*, 67:4 (2014), 932–963.
117. "Table alphabetique des noms de toutes les personnes qui ont esté assistées de la collecte, continus dans les trois registres, des deliberations faites aux assemblées du Committé, a commencer le 4 Juin 1686 Jusqu'au 28 août 1687 inclusivement," Royal Bounty Papers, MS 1, Huguenot Library, University College London.
118. John Oldmixon, *The British Empire in America, Containing The History of the Discovery, Settlement, Progress and present State of all the British Colonies, on the Continent and Islands of America* (London: John Nicholson, 1708), 1:306.
119. Robert Beverley, *The History and Present State of Virginia*, ed. Louis B. Wright (Chapel Hill: University of North Carolina Press, 1947), 134, 282.

Chapter 4

1. This portrait of La Case's life comes from François Leguat, *The Voyage of François Leguat of Bresse, To Rodriguez, Mauritius, Java, and the Cape of Good Hope*, ed. Samuel Pasfield Oliver (London: Hakluyt Society, 1891), 1:6, 53; 2:156, 194, 217–18; Émile Rainer, *L'utopie d'une république huguenote du marquis Henri Du Quesne et la voyage de François Leguat* (Paris: Ecrivains Associés, 1959), 52–53, 111–12, 115; R. A. Brock, ed., *Documents, Chiefly Unpublished, Relating to the Huguenot Emigration to Virginia and to the Settlement at Manakin-Town* (Richmond: Virginia Historical Society, 1886), 30, 37–69–70. For his will, see Henrico County, Wills and Administrations (1662–1800), 92–93, Library of Virginia, Richmond.
2. There has been a great deal of work on Huguenot soldiers; see especially Matthew Glozier, *The Huguenot Soldiers of William of Orange and the Glorious Revolution of 1688: The Lions of Judah* (Brighton: Sussex Academic Press, 2008); Matthew Glozier and David Onnekink, eds., *War, Religion, and Service: Huguenot Soldiering, 1685–1713* (Aldershot: Ashgate, 2007).
3. On Jurieu's espionage network see Lucien Bely, *Espions et ambassadeurs au temps de Louis XIV* (Paris: Fayard, 1990), 193–95; and the correspondence in Add. Mss. 61548, BL. On the role of Huguenots in the French Navy in particular see Michel Vergé-Franceschi, "Les huguenots dans la marine du roi (1572–1688)," in *Les Huguenots et l'Atlantique: Pour Dieu, la Cause ou les Affaires*, ed. Mickaël Augeron, Didier Poton, and Bertrand Van Ruymbeke (Paris: Les Indes Savantes, 2009), 329–46.
4. The most noteworthy spy was the so-called sieur de Tillieres, who infiltrated refugee circles in the Netherlands and reported back to Versailles; see Caroline Lougee Chappell, "Through the Eyes of a Spy: Venom and Value in an Enemy's Report on the Huguenot Migration," in *The Huguenots: France, Exile, and Diaspora*, ed. Jane McKee and Randolph Vigne (Brighton: Sussex Academic Press, 2013), 77–88.
5. Henry Morgan to the Lords of Trade and Plantations, March 8, 1682, CO 1/48, no. 37, TNA. The only background I have found on Pain comes from the brief outline in Jacques de Cauna, *L'Eldorado des Aquitains: Gascons, Basques, et Béarnais aux Iles d'Amériques (XVIIe–XVIIIe siècles)* (Biarritz: Atlantica, 1998), 61.
6. See Mickaël Augeron, "Se convertir, partir ou résister? Les marins huguenots face à la révocation de l'édit de Nantes," in *Les huguenots et l'Atlantique*, ed. Augeron, Poton, and Van Ruymbeke (2009), 349–68.
7. For overviews of the French and English Caribbean at this time see, respectively, Philip P. Boucher, *France and the American Tropics to 1700: Tropics of Discontent?* (Baltimore: Johns Hopkins University Press, 2008); and Richard S. Dunn, *Sugar and Slaves: The Rise of the Planter Class in the English West Indies, 1624–1713* (Chapel Hill: University of North Carolina Press, 1972).
8. Thomas Lynch to Leoline Jenkins, November 6, 1682, CO 1/50, no. 91, TNA; Alphonse Martin, *Histoire de la marine militaire au Havre (XVIe & XVIIe siecles)* (Fécamp: Imprimerie de M.-L. Durand, 1899), 181. On piracy in Jamaica during this era see Mark G. Hanna, *Pirate Nests and the Rise of the British Empire, 1570–1740* (Chapel Hill: University of North Carolina Press, 2015), ch. 3.

9. There has been some interesting work on boundary crossers and religious minorities in the Caribbean; see especially Kristen Block, *Ordinary Lives in the Early Caribbean: Religion, Colonial Competition, and the Politics of Profit* (Athens: University of Georgia Press, 2012); and Jenny Shaw, *Everyday Life in the Early English Caribbean: Irish, Africans, and the Construction of Difference* (Athens: University of Georgia Press, 2013).

10. See for example "The past and present state of the Leeward Charribbee Islands," March 15, 1678, CO 1/42, no. 36, TNA. On the Scots see Council of Saint Christopher to the Lords of Trade and Plantations, July 12, 1680, CO 1/45, no. 46.

11. Johnson to the Lords of Trade and Plantations, February 20, 1688, CO 1/64, no. 25, TNA. On the political background see Natalie A. Zacek, *Settler Society in the English Leeward Islands, 1670–1776* (Cambridge: Cambridge University Press, 2011).

12. On James II's toleration campaign more generally see Scott Sowerby, *Making Toleration: The Repealers and the Glorious Revolution* (Cambridge, MA: Harvard University Press, 2013); and on its implications in the West Indies Jenny Shaw, *Everyday Life*, 101–28.

13. Johnson to the Lords of Trade and Plantations, June 2, 1688, CO 1/64, no. 71, TNA. On denization see Daniel Statt, *Foreigners and Englishmen: The Controversy over Immigration and Population, 1660–1760* (Newark: University of Delaware Press, 1995).

14. Charles W. Baird, *History of the Huguenot Emigration to America* (New York: Dodd, Mead and Co., 1885), 1:231–34; Gérard Lafleur, *Les Protestants aux Antilles françaises du Vent sous l'Ancien Régime* (Basse-Terre: Société d'Histoire de la Guadeloupe, 1988).

15. On Suriname's history during this period see Karwan Fatah-Black, *White Lies and Black Markets: Evading Metropolitan Authority in Colonial Suriname, 1650–1800* (Leiden: Brill, 2015); Charles Ch. Goslinga, *The Dutch in the Caribbean and in the Guianas, 1680–1791* (Assen: Van Gorcum, 1985), 267–311; Johannes Postma, "Suriname and Its Atlantic Connections, 1667–1795," in *Riches from Atlantic Commerce: Dutch Transatlantic Trade and Shipping, 1585–1817*, ed. Postma and Victor Enthoven (Leiden: Brill, 2003), 287–322; and Alison Games, "Cohabitation, Suriname Style: English Inhabitants in Dutch Suriname after 1667," *WMQ* 72:2 (2015), 195–242. On the larger Dutch Atlantic context see Wim Klooster, *The Dutch Moment: War, Trade, and Settlement in the Seventeenth-Century Atlantic World* (Ithaca, NY: Cornell University Press, 2016).

16. "Résolution des Etats de Zélande," October 13, 1671; "Lettre de François Chaillou," December 28, 1673, both in *Livres des Actes des Eglises Wallonnes aux Pays-Bas, 1601–1697*, ed. Guillame H. W. Posthumus Meyjes and Hans Bots (The Hague: Instituut voor Nederlandse Geschiedenis, 2005) 751, 772.

17. David Nassy, *Historical Essay on the Colony of Surinam, 1788*, trans. Simon Cohen (Cincinnati: American Jewish Archives, 1974), 38–39.

18. "Lettre de Pierre Albus," August 23, 1683, in Posthumus Meyjes and Bots, eds., *Livres des Actes des Eglises Wallonnes aux Pays-Bas*, 891–92; Hans Bots, "Les pasteurs français au Refuge des Provinces-Unies: Un groupe socio-professionnal tout particulier, 1680–1710," in *La vie intellectuelle aux Refuges protestants*, ed. Jens Häseler and Antony McKenna (Paris: Honoré Champion, 1999), 20.

19. Flournois was the author of one of the more interesting works of religious literature during the period, *Entretiens des voyageurs sur la mer* (Cologne [Rotterdam]: Pierre Marteau, 1683), which recounted the religious discussions on an imaginary voyage from Amsterdam to Hamburg. Little is known of his career in Suriname.

20. Site de la Base de données du refuge Huguenot, Laboratoire de recherches historiques Rhône-Alpes (LARHRA), www.refuge-huguenot.fr, Notice no. 72738. Of all the places in the global Refuge none has attracted as little scholarship as Suriname. One of the best brief portraits is still in Charles Weiss, *Histoire des réfugiés huguenots* (Paris: Ampelos Editions, 2008 [1853]), 2:143–45. See also S. Kalff, "Franschen in Suriname," *West-Indische Gids* 11:3 (1930), 316–34; and Jean-Louis Poulalion, "Les français dans l'histoire du Surinam," *Mondes et cultures* 46:4 (1986), 775–89. The population numbers come from Hans Buddingh', *Geschiedenis van Suriname* (Utrecht: Nieuw Amsterdam, 1995), 52–53.

21. J. D. Herlein, *Beschryvinge van de volk-plantinge Zuriname* (Leeuwarden, 1718), 48; Kalff, "Franschen in Suriname," 324.

22. Jean Briffault to the Societeit van Suriname, May 26, 1684 [misdated, probably 1687], in J. M. van der Linde, *Surinaamse Suikerheren en hun kerk: Plantagekolonie en heldelskerk ten tijde van Johannes Baselliers, predikant en planter in Suriname, 1667–1689* (Wageningen: H. Veenman, 1966), 229–30.
23. For details on these ministers see van der Linde, *Surinaamse Suikerheren*, 137–38, 150–51; Bots, "Les pasteurs français," 26, 63. Population numbers come from van der Linde, 58.
24. "Contre le droit des Gens," Sainte-Marthe to Sommelsdijk, May 28, 1685, Societëit van Suriname 214, f. 15, Nationaal Archief, The Hague.
25. "Relation du Voyage de Cayenne à Surinam fait par Isaac Maret Maitre du Navire le Marin de Bourdeaux, à la poursuite de cinq hommes de Son Equipage qui ont deserté de Son Bord," 1687, Archives des Colonies, C^{14} 2, f. 177–82, ANOM. There is some evidence of a substantial, though largely underground Huguenot community in French Guiana; see Marie Polderman, *La Guyane française, 1676–1763: Mise en place et évolution de la société coloniale, tensions et métissages* (Cayenne: Ibis Rouge Ed., 2004), 61–63.
26. On the battle see Kalff, "Franschen in Suriname," 325.
27. On this military rivalry see James Pritchard, *In Search of Empire: The French in the Americas, 1670–1730* (Cambridge: Cambridge University Press, 2004), 303–13; and Owen Stanwood, *The Empire Reformed: English America in the Age of the Glorious Revolution* (Philadelphia: University of Pennsylvania Press, 2011), 143–76.
28. Nathaniel Johnson to the Committee on Trade and Plantations, July 15, 1689, CO 153/4, p. 138, TNA.
29. Christopher Codrington to the Committee on Trade and Plantations, March 17, 1690, CO 153/4, p. 209, TNA.
30. "Mr Steph: Deport's Meml in behalf of the French Protestant Refugies," recd. August 3, 1698, CO 152/2, no. 107, TNA.
31. *The Case of the French Protestants Refugees, settled in and about London, and in the English Plantations in America* ([London], [1697]).
32. The place of Huguenots and Walloons in New Netherland is covered in Baird, *Huguenot Emigration to America*, 1:148–200. On the English period see Jon Butler, *The Huguenots in America: A Refugee People in New World Society* (Cambridge, MA: Harvard University Press, 1983), 144–98; Joyce Goodfriend, *Before the Melting Pot: Society and Culture in Colonial New York City, 1664–1730* (Princeton, NJ: Princeton University Press, 1992); Goodfriend, "The Huguenots of Colonial New York City: A Demographic Profile," in *Memory and Identity: The Huguenots in France and the Atlantic Diaspora*, ed. Bertrand Van Ruymbeke and Randy J. Sparks (Columbia: University of South Carolina Press, 2003), 241–54; Neil Kamil, *Fortress of the Soul: Violence, Metaphysics, and Material Life in the Huguenots' New World* (Baltimore: Johns Hopkins University Press, 2005); and Paula Wheeler Carlo, *Huguenot Refugees in Colonial New York: Becoming American in the Hudson Valley* (Brighton: Sussex Academic Press, 2005).
33. "Declaration regarding French Protestants," June 15, 1682, Mass. Arch. 11:22a. On New England's Huguenots see Baird, *Huguenot Emigration to America*, 2:188–340; Butler, *Huguenots in America*, 71–143; Lauric Henneton, "L'autre refuge: huguenots et puritains en Nouvelle-Angleterre," in *Les Huguenots et l'Atlantique: Fidelités, Racines, et Mémoires*, ed. Augeron, Poton, and Van Ruymbeke (Paris: Les Indes Savantes, 2012), 103–12; Adrian Chastain Weimer, "Huguenot Refugees and the Meaning of Charity in Early New England," *Church History* 86:2 (2017), 365–97.
34. Emerson Baker and John Reid, "Amerindian Power in the Early Modern Northeast: A Reappraisal," *WMQ* 61:1 (2004), 77–106.
35. See Marc-André Bédard, *Les protestants en Nouvelle-France* (Quebec City: Société historique de Québec, 1978); Leslie Choquette, *Frenchmen into Peasants: Modernity and Tradition in the Peopling of French Canada* (Cambridge, MA: Harvard University Press, 1997), 129–36; Choquette, "A Colony of 'Native French Catholics'? The Protestants of New France in the Seventeenth and Eighteenth Centuries," in *Memory and Identity*, ed. Van Ruymbeke and Sparks, 255–66.
36. Mgr de Laval to the marquis de Seignelay, November 12, 1682, sme 2.1/n/068a, Archives de Séminaire de Québec.

37. Sir John Werden to Dongan, March 10, 1684, *NYCD*, 3:341.
38. "Extrait des réponses du ministre aux lettres reçues du Canada pendant la présente année 1686," Archives des Colonies, C¹¹ᴬ 8, f. 42, ANOM; "Abstract of M. de Denonville's Letters and of the Ministers Answers thereto," *NYCD*, 9:312.
39. Denonville to the minister, June 8, 1687, Archives des Colonies, C¹¹ᴬ 9, ff. 24–25, ANOM. A translation of the document appears in *NYCD*, 9:326. See also Mickaël Augeron and Didier Poton, "La Rochelle, port canadien: le négoce protestant et la Nouvelle-France," in *Mémoires de Nouvelle-France: De France en Nouvelle-France*, ed. Philippe Joutard and Thomas Wien (Rennes: Presses universitaires de Rennes, 2005), 114; Bédard, *Les Protestants en Nouvelle-France*, 82–83.
40. Denonville to Seignelay, November 10, 1686, *NYCD*, 9:309.
41. "Pierre Baudouin's Petition," in *The Andros Tracts: Being a Collection of Pamphlets and Official Papers of the Andros Government and the Establishment of the Second Charter of Massachusetts*, ed. W. H. Whitmore (New York: Prince Society, 1868–74), 3:79–80; "Petition of the French Protestants to be pmitted to settle there," [1687], CO 1/61, no. 69.iv, TNA. A translation appears in *NYCD*, 3:419–20.
42. Petition of Peter Reverdy, October 13, 1686, CO 391/6, p. 17, TNA; "A Memoriall Concerning forainge Plantations," Fulham Papers 6, ff. 179–80, LPL.
43. Denonville to the minister, November 13, 1685, Archives des Colonies, C¹¹ᴬ 7, f. 100v–101, ANOM.
44. "An Abridgement of the Afflictions of the French Protestants, and also their Petition, extracted from a Letter written from Rochele the 1st of October 1684," Thomas Prince Papers, Massachusetts Historical Society, Boston.
45. "Statement of the Concerns of the Oxford Purchase," Gabriel Bernon Papers, Rhode Island Historical Society, Providence.
46. Sir Francis Brewster, *Essays on Trade and Navigation* (London: Tho. Cockerill, 1695), 88–89.
47. "Agreement with Jacques Hipaud to work two years in Oxford Farm," April 28, 1687, and "Contract between Gabriel Bernon and Pierre Cornilly," April 26, 1688, both in Bernon Papers, RIHS.
48. *Report of a French Protestant Refugee, in Boston, 1687*, trans. E. T. Fisher (Brooklyn, NY: J. Munsell, 1868), 19, 25–26.
49. Robert Thompson to William Stoughton, November 2, 1692, and Thompson to Phips and Stoughton, May 14, 1694, Company for the Propagation of the Gospel in New England, Letter Book, 1688–1761, p. 15, Alderman Library, University of Virginia.
50. The tract was Ezechiel Carré, *Echantillon de la Doctrine que les Jésuites ensegnent aus Sauvages du Nouveau Monde* (Boston, 1690), based on the manuscript "Inventaire des certains papiers trouvé dans une maison particulière vers Albanie depuis ces derniers troubles," Livingston Family Papers, misc. mss., New-York Historical Society. For a complete exposition and translation see Evan Haefeli and Owen Stanwood, "Jesuits, Huguenots, and the Apocalypse: The Origins of America's First French Book," *Proceedings of the American Antiquarian Society* 116, part 1 (2006), 59–119 (quotation on 109).
51. "Declaration regarding French Protestants," Mass. Arch. 11:45; John Russell Bartlett, ed., *Records of the Colony of Rhode Island and Providence Plantations in New England* (Providence: Knowles, Anthony, & Co., 1858), 3:227–28. On Philip English and the Jerseymen see David Thomas Konig, "A New Look at the Essex 'French': Ethnic Frictions and Community Tensions in Seventeenth-Century Essex County, Massachusetts," *Essex Institute Historical Collections* 110:2 (1974), 167–80.
52. "Note of Representatives relative to French people, pretending to be Protestants, but suspected of being Papists," October 1692, Mass. Arch. 11:65; Robert Earle Moody and Richard Clive Simmons, eds., *The Glorious Revolution in Massachusetts: Selected Documents, 1689–1692* (Boston: Colonial Society of Massachusetts, 1988), 343–44; *The Acts and Resolves, Public and Private, of the Province of the Massachusetts Bay* (Boston: Wright & Potter, 1869), 1:90.
53. Ezechiel Carré, *The Charitable Samaritan* (Boston: Samuel Green, 1689), Advertisement and Dedication, 1.
54. Fletcher to the Committee on Trade and Plantations, October 10, 1693, *NYCD*, 4:68. On his acquittal see "Minutes of the Council of New York," CO 5/1184, p. 52–54, TNA.

55. "Benjamin Faneuil's Deposition," September 4, 1694, Mass. Arch. 61:497A.
56. St. Aubin to the Governor and Magistrates of Boston, Mass. Arch. 2:538.
57. Villebon to Pontchartrain, August 20, 1694, Archives des Colonies, C¹¹ᴬ 13, f. 135, ANOM; Villebon to Pontchartrain, Journal of Acadia from November 11, 1692 to August 7, 1693, in John C. Webster, ed., *Acadia at the End of the Seventeenth Century: Letters, Journals, and Memoirs of Joseph Robineau de Villebon, Commandant in Acadia, 1690–1700, and Other Documents* (Saint John: New Brunswick Museum, 1934), 44–45.
58. Bellomont to the Board of Trade, September 21, 1698, *NYCD*, 4:379.
59. Robin Gwynn, ed., *Minutes of the Consistory of the French Church of London, Threadneedle Street, 1679–1692* (London: Huguenot Society of Great Britain and Ireland, 1994), 335. Carré published one more tract during his time in the Channel Islands and left two extant letters which, sadly, made no reference to his transatlantic journeys; see Carré to Lord Hatton, June 27, 1697, Add. Mss. 29566, f. 458, BL; and Carré to Hatton, June 23, 1698, Add. Mss. 29567, ff. 82–84.
60. Petition of Gabriel Bernon of Boston, December 18, 1696, CO 5/859, no. 49, TNA.
61. Petition of Gabriel Bernon, 1696, CO 5/859, no. 52, TNA.
62. Petition of James Labourie, 1699, Mass. Arch. 11:140; Mary de Witt Freeland, *The Records of Oxford, Mass.: Including Chapters of Nipmuck, Huguenot, and English History from the Earliest Date, 1630* (Albany: J. Munsell's Sons, 1894), 157–58; Jacques Laborie to the earl of Bellomont, June 17, 1700, in *Documentary History of the State of Maine*, ed. James Phinney Baxter (Portland, ME: Fred L. Tower Co., 1889–1916), 10:59–60.
63. See the petitions in Bernon Papers, RIHS.
64. Duquesne declared his innocent intentions in "Projet de M. le Marquis du Quesne touchant une nouvelle colonie en l'Isle Eden," Collection Court, vol. 17D, fol. 62, BGE.
65. Vachet to Directeurs des Missions etrangeres, n.d., VOC 4026, f. 570, Nationaal Archief; H. C. V. Leibbrandt, ed., *Rambles through the Archives of the Colony of the Cape of Good Hope, 1688–1700* (Cape Town: J. C. Juta and Co., 1887), 22.
66. See for example "Coppie de la Req[ue]te des Habittans De L'Isle de Bourbon," November 28, 1686, VOC 4026, f. 1194, Nationaal Archief, which asked for a priest, surgeon, and a number of goods for the colony.
67. "Requesten van den Marquis du Quesne en geassocieerden, om permissie tot het doen van sen equipagie om het eylant Bourbon ofte Mascarenhas op de franschon te ucuperen, met een advis van de Oostinde compe. daer op, overgegeven in den jaere 1689," Staaten Generaal 12851.40, Nationaal Archief. For copies of the agreement between Duquesne and the VOC, see Pieter Van Dam, *Beschryvinge van de Oostindische Compagnie*, ed. F. W. Stapel (The Hague: Martinus Nijhoff, 1927), tweede boek, deel III, 574–79.
68. Secret Committee to Cape, January 28, 1690, in Leibbrandt, *Rambles*, 112.
69. Leguat, *The Voyage of François Leguat*, 1:39. Valleau's feud with the other Huguenots appears in "Requête des huguenots au commandant du Cap"; and "Projet du capitaine Valleau," both reprinted in Émile Rainer, *L'utopie d'une république huguenote du marquis du Quesne et la voyage du François Leguat* (Paris: Ecrivains Associés, 1959), 112–15. See also Commander and Council to the Heren XVII, June 29, 1691, in Leibbrandt, *Rambles*, 126–27.
70. "Interrogatoire du nommé Valleau de l'Isle de Rhé," May 20, 1692, Archives des Colonies, C³ 1, ff. 185–86, ANOM. For the captive's interrogation by the Dutch in Cape Town (who referred to him as Athenas Garrel) see Leibbrandt, *Rambles*, 127–30. For the most recent analyses of the mission see Randolph Vigne, "Huguenots to the Southern Oceans: Archival Fact and Voltairean Myth," in *The Huguenots*, ed. McKee and Vigne, 113–24; Alfred North-Coombes, *The Vindication of François Leguat* (Rose Hill, Mauritius: Editions de l'Ocean Indien, 1991 [1979]), esp. 21–22.
71. The note appears after the title page of the copy of Duquesne, *Recueil de quelques memoires servans d'instruction pour l'etablissement de l'isle d'Eden* (Amsterdam, 1689), in the Bibliothèque Nationale de France, Paris.
72. Leguat, *Voyage of François Leguat*, 1:48–49, 52, 120.
73. Leguat, *Voyage of François Leguat*, 2:152–56. From Diodati's perspective, the ambergris belonged to the Company, since they claimed all of the substance that appeared on the island. La Haye, naturally, argued that since it came from Rodrigues the governor had no just claim.

74. Leguat, *Voyage of François Leguat*, 2:159–60, 216, 272. The records of the men's trial is in "Diverse papieren de 3 Fransche persoonen van den Marquies du Quesne wegens de mishandelindgh haer aen 't eijlant mauritiun aengedaen volgens apart register," 1697, VOC 1588, ff. 909–1042, Nationaal Archief.

75. On de Seine's case see CJ780, f. 1152, WCA; the Cape to Batavia, July 11, 1696, in H. C. V. Leibbrandt, ed. *Precis of the Archives of the Cape of Good Hope: Letters Dispatched, 1696–1708* (Cape Town: W. A. Richard and Sons, 1896), 15; C. Graham Botha, *The French Refugees at the Cape* (Cape Town: C. Struik, 1970), 57–58; Marilyn Garcia-Chapleau, *Le Refuge huguenot du cap de Bonne-Espérance: Genèse, assimilation, héritage* (Paris: Honoré Champion, 2016), 453.

76. Simon van der Stel's instructions to his son, March 10, 1699, in Leibbrandt, *Rambles*, 10. He repeated the same sentiments in van der Stel to Middleburg, July 2, 1699, C1417: Uitgaande Briewe, Jul. 1–Nov. 17, 1699, f. 26, WCA.

77. The most complete portrait of the colony's origins is in David E. Lambert, *The Protestant International and the Huguenot Migration to Virginia* (New York: Peter Lang, 2010). On the earlier history of the grant see Paul E. Kopperman, "Profile of Failure: The Carolana Project, 1629–1640," *North Carolina Historical Review* 59:1 (1982), 1–23.

78. "Requête des réfugiés français au roi d'Angleterre avant la paix de Ryswick," Collection Court, 17M, fol. 134, BGE. The refugees appealed directly to Louis XIV as well; see TT 430, fol. 124, AN. For a scholarly consideration see David van der Linden, *Experiencing Exile: Huguenot Refugees in the Dutch Republic, 1680–1700* (Farnham: Ashgate, 2015), 131–41.

79. Thomas Coxe to the earl of Nottingham, February 23/13, 1692, SP 96/9, TNA.

80. M. Sondreville to Zurich comité, n.d., E 1 25.18: Franz. Angelegenheiten, 1699 Dez.–1703, Staatsarchiv Zürich.

81. "Memorial from Capt John Pointz giving an account of the Isld of Tobago from the first set-tling thereof by the Spaniards till the late Warr," recd. November 17, 1699, CO 28/4, no. 27, TNA. On moral reform movements see especially Brent S. Sirota, *The Christian Monitors: The Church of England and the Age of Benevolence, 1680–1730* (New Haven, CT: Yale University Press, 2014).

82. On this scheme see Albright G. Zimmerman, ed., "Daniel Coxe and the New Mediterranean Sea Company," *Pennsylvania Magazine of History and Biography* 76:1 (1952), 86–96 (quota-tion on 92); "Coxe's Account of the Activities of the English in the Mississippi Valley in the Seventeenth Century," in Clarence Alvord and Lee Bidgood, eds., *The First Explorations of the Trans-Allegheny Region by the Virginians, 1650–1674*, ed. Clarence Alvord and Lee Bidgood (Cleveland: A. H. Clark Co., 1912), 245; "A Description of ye Great Western Lake," [1687] CO 1/66, no. 58, TNA. For background on Le Tort see Evelyn A. Benson, "The Huguenot Letorts: First Christian Family on the Conestoga," *Journal of the Lancaster County Historical Society* 65:1 (1961), 92–105.

83. Daniel Coxe, *A Description Of the English Province of Carolana, By the Spaniards call'd Florida, And by the French La Louisiane* (London: B. Cowse, 1722), 62, 74, 90; "A Demonstration of the Just Pretensions of his Majesty The King of England unto the Province of Carolana alias Florida and of the present Proprietary under his Majesty," CO 5/1259, no. 23, TNA.

84. "An Account of the Commodities of the growth and Production of the Province of Carolana alias Florida," CO 5/1259, no. 24, TNA.

85. "Draught of the Scheme I drew for Dr Daniel Cox many years since for the settlemt of New which wee called the New Empire written by Mr Spooner," Rawlinson Mss. A 305, ff. 2–6, Bodleian Library; [Daniel Coxe], *Proposals for Settling a Colony in Florida* ([London, 1698]), 1–2; "A Summary of the Title of the English to the Country of fflorida," Fulham Papers 2, ff. 16–17, LPL.

86. Michelle Magdelaine, "Conditions et préparation de l'intégration: le voyage de Charles de Sailly en Irlande (1693) et le projet d'Edit d'accueil," in *From Strangers to Citizens: The Integration of Immigrant Communities in Britain, Ireland, and Colonial America, 1550–1750*, ed. Randolph Vigne and Charles Littleton (Brighton: Sussex Academic Press, 2001), 435–41.

87. Nathaniel Weiss, "Le Mirage de la Floride (1698–1699)," *BSHPF* 39 (1890), 142–45, 329; *Gazette d'Amsterdam*, November 27, 1698.

88. "Coxe's Account of the Activities of the English in the Mississippi Valley in the Seventeenth Century," 246–47.

89. D'Iberville to the Ministre de la Marine, June 18, 1698, in Pierre Margry, ed., *Découvertes et établissements des français dans l'ouest et dans le sud de l'Amérique Septentrionale (1614–1754): Mémoires et documents originaux* (Paris: Impr. D. Jouaust, 1880), 4:58.

90. "Extrait d'une lettre de M. de Callières au Ministre de la Marine," June 2, 1699, in *Découvertes et établissements*, ed. Margry, 4:304–305; Callière to the minister, 7 novembre 1700, Archives des Colonies, C^{11A} 17, ff. 48–49, ANOM.

91. "Lettre de Sauvole, commandant au Biloxi, sur ce qui passé dans l'intervalle du 1er et 2e voyage de d'Iberville, et instructions qui lui sont laissées par ce dernier en mai 1700," in *Découvertes et établissements*, ed. Margry, 4:456; d'Iberville to the minister, February 26, 1700, ibid., 4:361; "Memoir of the Services of Sieur de Bienville, Commandant General of Louisiana, 1725," in *Mississippi Provincial Archives, 1701–1729: French Dominion*, ed. Dunbar Rowland and Albert Godfrey Sanders (Jackson: Press of the Mississippi Department of Archives and History, 1929), 3:489.

92. Richebourg Gaillard McWilliams, ed., *Iberville's Gulf Journals* (Tuscaloosa: University of Alabama Press, 1981), 107–109. The most thorough analysis of the encounter, which concludes that it was probably apocryphal, is Bertrand Van Ruymbeke, "'A Dominion of True Believers' Not a Republic for Heretics': French Colonial Religious Policy and the Settlement of Early Louisiana, 1699–1730," in *French Colonial Louisiana and the Atlantic World*, ed. Bradley G. Bond (Baton Rouge: Louisiana State University Press, 2005), 83–94.

93. "Opinion of the Board of Trade," December 21, 1699, CO 5/1288, pp. 139–43, TNA.

94. "Original Papers Relating to the Vaudois & French Refugiès From May 12 1699 to April 1. 1703," MS. 1028, LPL.

95. See Warrants (COL/CHD/PR/006/004), nos. 17, 20, 35, 37, 38, 41, 42, London Metropolitan Archives.

96. "List of all ye Passingers from London to James River, in Virginia, being French Refugees imbarqued in the ship ye Peter and Anthony, Galley of London, Daniel Perreau Commander," in *Documents, Chiefly Unpublished, Relating to the Huguenot Emigration to Virginia and to the Settlement at Manakin-Town*, ed. R. A. Brock (Richmond: Virginia Historical Society, 1886), 14–16.

97. "Proposalls humbly submitted to the L'ds of ye Councill of Trade and Plantations for sending ye French Protestants to Virginia," 1698, in Brock, *Documents*, 6–7; William Byrd Notebook, ff. 34–36, Robert Alonzo Brock Collection, Huntington Library, San Marino, Calif. [copy in the Library of Virginia, Richmond].

98. Nicholson to the Board of Trade, August 1, 1700, CO 5/1312, no. 1, TNA.

99. William Byrd to Perry and Lane, August 8, 1690, in Marion Tinling, ed., *The Correspondence of the Three William Byrds of Westover, 1684–1776* (Charlottesville: University of Virginia Press, 1977), 1:135. On Nicholson's attempts to strengthen the frontiers see Stanwood, *The Empire Reformed*, 207–20; Stephen Saunders Webb, "The Strange Career of Francis Nicholson," *WMQ* 23:4 (1966), 513–48.

100. "The state of the ffrench refugees," May 10–11, 1701, in Brock, *Documents*, 43–44.

101. Original copies of the map are in both the National Archives and the Bodleian Library. For a reproduction see Brock, *Documents*, between pp. xii–xiii.

Chapter 5

1. The issue of assimilation or integration is perhaps the central theme of Huguenot refugee historiography. The most strident and well-argued version of the thesis is in Jon Butler, *The Huguenots in America: Refugee People in New World Society* (Cambridge, MA: Harvard University Press, 1983). For other statements see Myriam Yardeni, "Assimilation et sécularisation dans le Refuge huguenot," and "Refuge et intégration: le cas d'Erlangen," both in *Le Refuge huguenot: Assimilation et culture*, ed. Yardeni (Paris: Honoré Champion, 2002), 83–92, 137–50; Susanne Lachenicht, *Hugenotten in Europa und Nordamerika: Migration und Integration in der Frühen Neuzeit* (Frankfurt: Campus Verlag, 2010); Susanne Lachenicht, "Intégration ou coexistence? Les huguenots dans les îles britanniques et le Brandebourg," *Diasporas: Histoire et sociétés* 18 (2011), 108–22; François David, "Refuge protestant et assimilation: le cas de la Colonie française de Berlin," in *La diaspora des huguenots: Les réfugiés*

protestants de France et leur dispersion dans le monde (XVIe–XVIIIe siècles), ed. Eckart Birnstiel and Chrystel Bernat (Paris: Honoré Champion, 2001), 75–97; Robin Gwynn, *Huguenot Heritage: The History and Contributions of the Huguenots in Britain* (London: Routledge & Kegan Paul, 1985), 160–75; Thera Wijsenbeek, "Identity Lost: Huguenot Refugees in the Dutch Republic and its Former Colonies in North America and South Africa, 1650 to 1750, a Comparison," *South African Historical Journal* 59:1 (2007), 79–102.

2. Henry Laurens to Messieurs and Madame Laurence, February 25, 1774, in *The Papers of Henry Laurens*, ed. George C. Rogers Jr. and David R. Chestnutt (Columbia: University of South Carolina Press, 1974), 9:309–11. For background on Laurens see Daniel J. McDonough, *Christopher Gadsden and Henry Laurens: The Parallel Lives of Two American Patriots* (Cranbury, NJ: Susquehanna University Press, 2000).

3. Several historians, particularly those of the North American refugees, have recently argued for persistence of cultural values beyond the first generation; see especially Bertrand Van Ruymbeke, *From New Babylon to Eden: The Huguenots and their Migration to Colonial South Carolina* (Columbia: University of South Carolina Press, 2006); Paula Wheeler Carlo, *Huguenot Refugees in Colonial New York: Becoming American in the Hudson Valley* (Brighton: Sussex Academic Press, 2005); and Neil Kamil, *Fortress of the Soul: Violence, Metaphysics, and Material Life in the Huguenots' New World, 1517–1751* (Baltimore: Johns Hopkins University Press, 2005), esp. 755–57. On the survival of merchant and family networks see especially J. F. Bosher, "Huguenot Merchants and the Protestant International in the Seventeenth Century," *WMQ* 52:1 (1995), 77–102.

4. Jean Tirel, *Lettres fraternelles d'un prisonnier*, ed. Eva Avigdor and Elisabeth Labrousse (Paris: Nizet, 1984), 53–57, 64, 83.

5. Testimony of Joshua Gee, March 11, 1701[/02], Mass. Arch. 87:20.

6. The tract in question was *The Lawfulness, Glory and Advantage of Giving Immediate and Effectual Relief to the Protestants in the Cevennes* (London, 1703), quotation on 4; Add. Mss. 61648, f. 98, BL. On the war see Philippe Joutard, *Les Camisards* (Paris: Gallimard, 1976); W. Gregory Monahan, *Let God Arise: The War and Rebellion of the Camisards* (New York: Oxford University Press, 2014). Catharine Randall has attempted to extend the effects of the war to North America; see her *From a Far Country: Camisards and Huguenots in the Atlantic World* (Athens: University of Georgia Press, 2009).

7. Add. Mss. 61648, ff. 98–99, BL. The manuscript is unsigned but attributed to Boyer in Lionel Laborie, "Huguenot Propaganda and the Millenarian Legacy of the *Désert* in the Refuge," *HSP* 29:5 (2012), 643.

8. London to St Helena, December 15, 1698, IOR E/3/93, ff. 74–76, BL. For a brief biographical sketch of Poirier see Michael Courage, "St Helena in the Time of the Huguenot Governor Stephen Poirier," *HSP* 29:3 (2010), 316–20.

9. Hudson Ralph Janisch, ed., *Extracts from the St. Helena Records* (Jamestown, St. Helena: B. Grant, 1885), 65.

10. Janisch, *Extracts from the St. Helena Records*, 68, 75.

11. Janisch, *Extracts from the St. Helena Records*, 73–74.

12. Janisch, *Extracts from the St. Helena Records*, 83. The charges of entertaining passing French ships went back to 1702; see London to St. Helena, February 26, 1702, IOR E/3/93, f. 314, BL. The original version of Poirier's will is in PROB 11/517/405, TNA.

13. The most important recent work on the prophets' place in England is Lionel Laborie, *Enlightening Enthusiasm: Prophecy and Religious Experience in Early Eighteenth-Century England* (Manchester: University of Manchester Press, 2015). See also Hillel Schwartz, *The French Prophets: The History of a Millenarian Group in Eighteenth-Century England* (Berkeley: University of California Press, 1980); and Schwartz, *Knaves, Fools, Madmen, and that Subtile Effluvium: A Study of the Opposition to the French Prophets in England, 1706–1710* (Gainesville: University Press of Florida, 1978).

14. "Declaration of the French church about the Prophets," October 2, 1706, Rawlinson Mss. C 984, f. 152, Bodleian Library.

15. "Memoire sur l'Etablissement d'une Eglise françoise conformiste differente de l'Eglise de la Savoye," Rawlinson Mss. B 376, f. 383, Bodleian Library. For more on the rivalry between the Threadneedle and Savoy churches, which stretched back into the seventeenth century,

see Robin Gwynn, *Huguenot Heritage,* 91-109; Gwynn, "Conformity, Non-conformity, and Huguenot Settlement in England in the Later Seventeenth Century," in *The Religious Culture of the Huguenots, 1660-1750,* ed. Anne Dunan-Paige (Aldershot: Ashgate, 2006), 23-42.

16. On this program of imperial consolidation see for example Owen Stanwood, *The Empire Reformed: English America in the Age of the Glorious Revolution* (Philadelphia: University of Pennsylvania Press, 2011); Stephen Saunders Webb, *Marlborough's America* (New Haven, CT: Yale University Press, 2012); Ian K. Steele, *The Politics of Colonial Policy: The Board of Trade in Colonial Administration, 1696-1720* (New York: Oxford University Press, 1968); and for the French, James Pritchard, *In Search of Empire: The French in the Americas, 1670-1730* (Cambridge: Cambridge University Press, 2004).

17. For one attempt to put the Cape in imperial context see Kerry Ward, *Networks of Empire: Forced Migration in the Dutch East India Company* (Cambridge: Cambridge University Press, 2012).

18. Van der Stel to the Heren XVII, April 26, 1688; and van der Stel to the Amsterdam Chamber, June 12, 1690, both in H. C. V. Leibbrandt, ed., *Rambles through the Archives of the Colony of the Cape of Good Hope, 1688-1700* (Cape Town: J. C. Juta and Co., 1887), 37, 41.

19. Simond to the Heren XVII, 15 juin 1689, VOC 4026, ff. 1298-1304, Nationaal Archief, The Hague. The letter is reprinted in Marilyn Garcia-Chapleau, *Le Refuge huguenot du cap de Bonne-Espérance: Genèse, assimilation, héritage* (Paris: Honoré Champion, 2016), 644-52.

20. For comparisons with Germany see Susanne Lachenicht, "Intégration ou coexistence?" and Lachenicht, "Huguenot Immigrants and the Formation of National Identities, 1548-1787," *Historical Journal* 50:2 (2007), 309-31.

21. Resolution of November 28, 1689, in "Journal, 1689-1692 [LM11]," pp. 823-24, Leibbrandt Mss., WCA, reprinted in C. Graham Botha, *The French Refugees at the Cape* (Cape Town: C. Struik, 1970), 151-52. It's possible that Simond opposed the plan for an independent church council as being impractical, or that he worried that a council of laypeople could reduce his own influence and authority as minister.

22. "Simon van der Stel's letter of 24 June 1691," in *Rambles,* ed. Leibbrandt, 67-68.

23. "Reflexions sur le Règlement de la Compagnie des Indes Orientales du 20 Oct. 1687," in *Bouwstoffen voor de geschiedenis der Nederduitsch-Gereformeerde Kerken in Zuid-Afrika,* deel II, *Brieven van de Classis Amsterdam E.A. aan de Kaapsche kerken enz., 1651-1804,* ed. Spoelstra (Amsterdam: Hollandsch-Africaansche Uitgevers-Maatschappij, 1907), 651.

24. Garcia-Chapleau, *Le Refuge huguenot du cap de Bonne-Espérance,* 255; Randolph Vigne, "The Rev. Pierre Simond: 'lost leader' of the Huguenots at the Cape," *Journal of Theology for Southern Africa* 65:1 (1988), 21.

25. Chamber of Amsterdam to van der Stel, December 17, 1690, in Botha, *French Refugees,* 153; "Dispatch of the Seventeen," in *Rambles,* ed. Leibbrandt, 50-51. The full letter in Dutch is in C349: Inkomende Briewe, Jul. 12, 1690-Oct. 1691, 1, ff. 347-49, WCA.

26. For summaries of the affair see Garcia-Chapleau, *Le Refuge huguenot du cap de Bonne-Espérance,* 252-54; J. L. M. Franken, *Die Hugenote aan die Kaap* (Pretoria: Die Staatsdrukker, 1978), 34-51. For "calomnies scandaleuses" see Petition to Simon van der Stel, VOC 4028, ff. 618-21, Nationaal Archief.

27. Huguenot petition to Simon van der Stel, VOC 4028, f. 574, Nationaal Archief.

28. "Lettre du pasteur François Simon," March 19, 1692; "Lettre de recommandation de Martin de la Court," March 7, 1692; "Lettre de recommandation de Christian Crayener et Jaq des Obry," March 1, 1692, in C353, ff. 22, 29, 33, WCA, reprinted in Garcia-Chapleau, *Le Refuge huguenot du cap de Bonne-Espérance,* 662-64.

29. Governor and Council to Holland, June 29, 1691, in Leibbrandt, *Rambles,* 52-53.

30. Maurice Boucher, *French Speakers at the Cape of Good Hope in the First Hundred Years of Dutch East India Company Rule* (Pretoria: University of South Africa, 1981), 355-61; Randolph Vigne, "South Africa's First Work of Literature and its Author, Pierre Simond," *South African Historical Journal* 39:1 (1988), 3-16; see also Philippe Denis, "A Late Seventeenth Century Translation of the Psalms at the Cape," in *The Bible in Africa: Transactions, Trajectories and Trends,* ed. Gerald O. West and Musa W. Dube (Leiden: Brill, 2000), 197-222.

31. Letter from Chamber of Amsterdam, September 20, 1701, in Botha, *French Refugees,* 156.

32. The Classis of Amsterdam to the Kerkenraad te Drakensteyn [December 17, 1713], in *Bouwstoffen voor de geschiedenis der Nederduitsch-Gereformeerde Kerken in Zuid-Afrika,* deel II,

Brieven van de Classis Amsterdam E.A. aan de Kaapsche kerken enz., 1651–1804, ed. Spoelstra (Amsterdam, 1907), 34.

33. Nicolas de la Caille, *Journal historique du voyage fait au Cap de Bonne-Espérance* (Paris, 1763), 166–67, quoted in Garcia-Chapleau, *Le Refuge huguenot du cap de Bonne-Espérance,* 266.

34. Adam Tas to Francois du Toit, February 24, 1706, reprinted in Franken, *Die Hugenote aan die Kaap,* 110. The best source on the controversy is Leo Fouché, ed., *The Diary of Adam Tas (1705–1706)* (London: Longmans, Green & Co., 1914).

35. On New York's ethnic and religious composition during this period see Joyce Goodfriend, *Before the Melting Pot: Society and Culture in Colonial New York City, 1664–1730* (Princeton, NJ: Princeton University Press, 1994) and Randall Balmer, *A Perfect Babel of Confusion: Dutch Religion and English Culture in the Middle Colonies* (New York: Oxford University Press, 1989). On the Huguenot population see, in addition to Carlo, *Huguenot Refugees in Colonial New York;* Eric J. Roth, "'Where Ye Walloens Dwell': Rethinking the Ethnic Identity of the Huguenots of New Paltz and Ulster County, New York," *New York History* 89:4 (2008), 346–73; and Anne-Claire Faucquez, "Les réfugiés huguenots au coeur de la mosaïque ethno-religieuse de la colonie de New York: Une assimilation partielle ou complète? (1670–1730)," *BSHPF* 155:4 (2009), 795–808.

36. The best historian of Leisler's rebellion and life is David William Voorhees. See especially "The 'Fervant Zeale' of Jacob Leisler," *WMQ* 51:3 (1994), 447–72; "All Authority turned up-side downe': The Ideological Origins of Leislerian Political Thought," in *Jacob Leisler's Atlantic World in the Later Seventeenth Century: Essays on Religion, Militia, Trade, and Networks,* ed. Hermann Wellenreuther (Berlin: Lit Verlag), 89–118; and, on his connections to Huguenots, "'Hearing . . . What Great Success the Dragonnades in France Had': Jacob Leisler's Huguenot Connections," *de Haelve Maen* 67:1 (1994), 15–20.

37. "John Pell's Grant of New Rochelle," September 20, 1689, in *Records of the Town of New Rochelle, 1699–1828,* ed. Jeanne A. Forbes (New Rochelle: Paragraph Press, 1916), xiii–xvi.

38. Peter Reverdy to the Bishop of London, December 30, 1689, *NYCD,* 3:650.

39. The plan is detailed in Marcel Trudel, "Louis XIV et son projet de déportation—1689," *Revue d'histoire de l'Amérique française* 42:2 (1950), 157–71.

40. Dutch Church of New York to the Classis of Amsterdam, October 21, 1698, in Edward T. Corwin, ed., *Ecclesiastical Records of the State of New York* (Albany: J. B. Lyon, 1901), 2:1256. On Daillé see Charles Baird, *History of the Huguenot Emigration to America* (New York: Dodd, Mead and Co., 1885), 2:226–28.

41. Petition of Abraham Tourneau, Alexander Morisset, and Peter Fillon [May 1691], New York Colonial Mss., 37:81, New York State Archives, Albany. On Leisler's fall and its political af-termath see especially Patricia U. Bonomi, *A Factious People: Politics and Society in Colonial New York* (New York: Columbia University Press, 1971).

42. Bellomont to the Board of Trade, September 21, 1698, *NYCD,* 4:379; Petition of Daniel Bondet to Lord Cornbury, in E. B. O'Callaghan, ed., *Documentary History of the State of New York* (Albany: C. Van Benthuysen, 1850), 3:562.

43. "Copie d'une Lettre écrite a Messrs de l'Eglise francoise de la Nouvelle York," March 27, 1699, Gabriel Bernon Papers, RIHS. This letter, along with the consistory's response, is reprinted in *Collections of the Huguenot Society of America,* vol. 1 (New York: Huguenot Society of America, 1886), 338–39.

44. For scholarly perspectives on Manakintown's development, see David E. Lambert, *The Protestant International and the Huguenot Migration to Virginia* (New York: Peter Lang, 2010); and James L. Bugg. Jr., "The French Huguenot Frontier Settlement of Manakin Town." *VMHB* 61:4 (1953), 359–94. Myriam Yardeni deals with the issue of assimilation in Manakintown in "Assimilation et sécularisation dans le refuge huguenot," in *Le Refuge huguenot,* 83–92.

45. On Nicholson's politics see esp. Stanwood, *The Empire Reformed,* 207–20; Stephen Saunders Webb, "The Strange Career of Francis Nicholson," *WMQ* 23:4 (1966), 513–43; and Kevin Hardwick, "Narratives of Villainy and Vice: Governor Francis Nicholson and the Character of the Good Ruler in Seventeenth-Century Virginia," *Journal of Southern History* 72:1 (2006), 39–74.

46. General Assembly minutes, December 5, 1700, CO 5/1312, no. 20v, TNA.

47. "A Collection of several matters relating to the French Refugees from the 12th of March 1701/2," CO 5/1312, no. 40.xli, TNA.

48. "Mémoire pour le dessein des colonies," Collection Court, vol. 17L, ff. 105–107, BGE.

49. David Bonrepos to Jacob Leisler, October 20, 1690, in O'Callaghan, *Documentary History*, 2:305.

50. "A Catalogue of the Parochial Library at Manicantown on James River in Her Majesties Colony of Virginia," Fulham Papers 11, f. 184, LPL.

51. Olivier de la Muce to Francis Nicholson, February 15, 1700/1, in R. A. Brock, ed., *Documents, Chiefly Unpublished, Relating to the Huguenot Emigration to Virginia and to the Settlement at Manakin-Town* (Richmond: Virginia Historical Society, 1886), 25.

52. "A Collection of all Matters Relating to the ffrench Protestant Refugees—1700," in Brock, *Documents*, 51.

53. "French Refugees's Supplication to Nicholson," in Brock, *Documents*, 55–57.

54. "A Collection of several matters relating to the French Refugees from the 12th of March 1701/2," CO 5/1312, no. 40.xli, TNA; Bugg, "The French Huguenot Frontier Settlement of Manakin Town," 367.

55. "The Vestry Book of King William Parish, Va., 1707–1750," *VMHB* 11:4 (1904), 427; Abraham Salle to the President and Council, September 2, 1707, Colonial Papers, Library of Virginia, Richmond.

56. Richebourg's petition, April 22, 1707, in H. R. McIlwaine, ed., *Executive Journals of Colonial Virginia* (Richmond, 1927), 3:143; Claude Philippe de Richebourg to Pres. Edmund Jenings, MS 1932.4: Miscellaneous Manuscripts, Rockefeller Library, Williamsburg, Va.; Salle to the President and Council, Colonial Papers, Library of Virginia.

57. R. H. Fife, ed., "The Vestry Book of King William Parish, Va., 1707–1750," *VMHB* 13:2 (1905), 181–82.

58. "Report of the Journey of Francis Louis Michel from Berne, Switzerland, to Virginia, October 2, 1701–December 1, 1702," ed. and trans. William J. Hinke, *VMHB* 24:2 (1916), 122.

59. R. H. Fife, ed., "The Vestry Book of King William Parish, Va.," *VMHB* 12:1 (1904), 30, and 12:4 (1905), 380.

60. R. H. Fife, ed., "The Vestry Book of King William Parish, Va.," *VMHB* 13:2 (1905), 183.

61. A. S. Salley, ed., *Journals of the Commons House of Assembly of South Carolina for 1703* (Columbia: Historical Commission of South Carolina, 1934), 123–24.

62. For the most recent statement on North Carolina's political climate see Noeleen McIlvenna, *A Very Mutinous People: The Struggle for North Carolina, 1660–1713* (Chapel Hill: University of North Carolina Press, 2009).

63. John Lawson, *A New Voyage to Carolina*, ed. Hugh Talmage Lefler (Chapel Hill: University of North Carolina Press, 1967), 90, 119–20. See also William Gordon to the Secretary, May 13, 1709, in William L. Saunders, ed., *The Colonial Records of North Carolina* (Raleigh: P. M. Hale, 1886), 1:714. Lawson placed the community on the Trent River and Gordon on the Neuse, some miles away. It is not clear if the men referred to two different communities or if Gordon was simply mistaken as to the refugee town's location.

64. On Carolina politics during this period L. H. Roper, *Conceiving Carolina: Proprietors, Planters, and Plots, 1662–1729* (New York: Routledge, 2004); and M. Eugene Sirmans, *Colonial South Carolina: A Political History, 1663–1763* (Chapel Hill: University of North Carolina Press, 1966). My interpretation is particularly indebted to Van Ruymbeke, *From New Babylon to Eden*, 161–90. On the census see Daniel Ravenel, ed., *Liste des François et Suisses: From an Old Manuscript List of French and Swiss Protestants Settled in Charleston, Santee, and at the Orange Quarter in Carolina Who Desired Naturalization Prepared Probably about 1695–6* (Baltimore: Genealogical Publishing Company, 1990 [1868]), analyzed in Van Ruymbeke, *From New Babylon to Eden*, 87–90. He also listed all 395 documented arrivals in the colony, 225–41.

65. On the Boyd family's role in the community see Dianne W. Ressinger, Harriott Cheves Leland, and Vivien Costello, "The Boyd Family: Global Huguenot Merchants," *HSP* 29:2 (2009), 168–79; and Susan Baldwin Bates and Harriott Cheves Leland, *French Santee: A Huguenot Settlement in Colonial South Carolina* (Baltimore: Otter Bay Books, 2015), 56–62.

66. Jacques Boyd to John Archdale, September 2, 1695, John Archdale Record Book, ff. 136–38, Library of Congress.
67. Council to the Proprietors, August 20, 1695, in A. S. Salley, ed., *Commissions and Instructions from the Lords Proprietors of Carolina to Public Officials of South Carolina, 1685–1715* (Columbia: Historical Commission of South Carolina, 1916), 81.
68. Deposition of Isaac Caillabaeuf, May 25, 1696, in "Hostility of the English Settlers to the French," *Transactions of the Huguenot Society of South Carolina* 5 (1897), 20.
69. Lords Proprietors to the House of Assembly, April 10, 1693, in A. S. Salley, ed., *Journal of the Commons House of Assembly of South Carolina For the Four Sessions of 1693* (Columbia: Historical Commission of South Carolina, 1907), 31.
70. Boyd to Archdale, September 2, 1695, Archdale Record Book, ff. 136–38; Boyd to Lord Ashley, n.d., Archdale Record Book, f. 73.
71. Boyd to Lord Ashley, n.d., Archdale Record Book, ff. 72–73.
72. Proprietors to Trouillard et al., April 12, 1693, in A. S. Salley, ed., *Records in the British Public Record Office Relating to South Carolina, 1691–1697* (Columbia: Historical Commission of South Carolina, 1931), 103–104.
73. Council to the Proprietors, December 6, 1696, in Salley, ed., Commissions and *Instructions*, 100. On the naturalization debate in Britain and the colonies see especially Daniel Statt, *Foreigners and Englishmen: The Controversy over Immigration and Population, 1660–1760* (Newark: University of Delaware Press, 1995); and James H. Kettner, *The Development of American Citizenship, 1608–1870* (Chapel Hill: University of North Carolina Press, 1975).
74. Randolph to the Board of Trade, March 16, 1698/9, CO 5/1258, no. 22, with Girard's notes added as no. 22.1, TNA. For more on Randolph's mission see Michael Garibaldi Hall, *Edward Randolph and the American Colonies, 1676–1703* (Chapel Hill: University of North Carolina Press, 1960).
75. *The Case of the Church of England in Carolina* (London, 1705), 2. The dispute over establishment in Carolina inspired something of a pamphlet war that even brought in such luminaries as Daniel Defoe. See for instance Defoe, *The case of the Protestant dissenters in Carolina* (London, 1706).
76. A. S. Salley, ed., *Journal of the Commons House of Assembly of South Carolina, June 5, 1707–July 19, 1707* (Columbia: Historical Commission of South Carolina, 1940), 23–25.
77. On the Church Acts and their implications for Huguenots see Van Ruymbeke, *From New Babylon to Eden*, 125–31.
78. The classic statement on this move toward the established church is Robert Kingdon, "Why Did the Huguenot Refugees in the American Colonies Become Episcopalians?" *Historical Magazine of the Protestant Episcopal Church* 49:4 (1980), 317–35. See also Butler, *Huguenots in America*, 84–85, 112–20, 169–73.
79. The most important qualifications to Kingdon's thesis come from Paula Wheeler Carlo, who has argued from sermon notes that New York's Huguenots continued to be doctrinally Calvinist even after joining the Church of England; see *Huguenot Refugees in Colonial New York*, esp. 44–73; and "Huguenot Congregations in Colonial New York and Massachusetts: Reassessing the Paradigm of Anglican Conformity," in *A Companion to the Huguenots*, ed. Raymond A. Mentzer and Bertrand Van Ruymbeke (Leiden: Brill, 2016), 371–93.
80. For details on Richebourg see Van Ruymbeke, *From New Babylon to Eden*, 134–39; Bates and Leland, *French Santee*, 290–97.
81. Francis Le Jau to Gideon Johnston, December 20, 1712, in *The Carolina Chronicle of Dr. Francis Le Jau, 1706–1717*, ed. Frank J. Klingberg (Berkeley: University of California Press, 1956), 126; "The Present State of the Clergy of South Carolina" [c. 1713], Rawlinson Mss. C 943, f. 28–31, Bodleian Library. An incomplete version of the report appears in Amy Friedlander, ed., "Commissary Johnston's Report, 1713," *South Carolina Historical Magazine* 83:4 (1982), 259–71.
82. "The Present State of the Clergy in South Carolina," f. 35. For background on L'Escot see Bertrand Van Ruymbeke, "Paul L'Escot: Un pasteur genevois à Charles Town (1700–1719)," *Nouvelles études francophones* 14:1 (1999), 147–62.
83. L'Escot to Friedrich Bonet, March 24, 1709, SPG 16, f. 244, LPL.

84. These two lengthy letters, dated April 6, 1701 and March 1, 1703, are contemporary copies, suggesting that they were meant to be circulated in manuscript or print. They are located in Archives Tronchin, v. 81, ff. 194–202, BGE.

85. L'Escot to Turrettini, August 10, 1719, Collection Turrettini, MS. fr. 488, f. 19, BGE.

86. Lawson, *A New Voyage to Carolina*, 20.

87. Thomas Bayeux to [Gabriel Bayeux], March 10, 1715/16; Bayeux to Jeanne Bonnel, May 16, 1715, Thomas Bayeux Lettres, 2 E 38, Archives Départementales du Calvados, Caen, France. For a valuable analysis of this and the other Bayeux letters see Luc Daireaux, "Un Normand à New York: Le Refuge huguenot vu à travers la correspondance de Thomas Bayeux (1708– 1719)," in *Les Huguenots et l'Atlantique: Fidélités, racines et mémoires*, ed. Mickaël Augeron, Didier Poton, and Bertrand Van Ruymbeke (Paris: Les Indes Savantes, 2012), 135–46; Daireaux, "Au miroir des lettres: destins contrastés de réfugiés pour la foi, fin XVIIe–début XVIIIe siècle," *Diasporas: Histoire et sociétés* 18 (2012), 49–61.

88. In addition to Butler, *The Huguenots in America*, see also the demographic analysis in Joyce D. Goodfriend, "The Huguenots of Colonial New York City: A Demographic Profile," in *Memory and Identity: The Huguenots in France and the Atlantic Diaspora*, ed. Bertrand Van Ruymbeke and Randy J. Sparks (Columbia: University of South Carolina Press, 2003), 241–54.

89. The only scholar to consider these petitions is Natalie A. Zacek, *Settler Society in the English Leeward Islands, 1670–1776* (Cambridge: Cambridge University Press, 2010), 159–66, whose book provides essential background on the islands during that period. On West Indian Huguenots during this period see Gérard Lafleur, *Les Protestants aux Antilles françaises du Vent sous l'Ancien Régime* (Basse-Terre: Société d'Histoire de la Guadeloupe, 1988).

90. "The Humble Petition of Alletta De La Coussage of St Christophers," CO 152/10, #19. iv, TNA.

91. "The Humble Petition of Mary & Margaret De Nampon french Refugee's," CO 152/10, #19.x, TNA.

92. "The Humble Petition of Martha Assailly daughter of Peter Assailly late of St Christophers planter," CO 152/10, #19.xvi, TNA.

93. "The Humble Petition of Stephen Duport of the Island of St Christopher Planter," CO 152/ 10, #19.i, TNA.

94. "The Humble Petition of Paul Minvielle De Bonnemere," CO 152/10, #19.vii, TNA.

95. "Petition of Elizabeth Renoult, April 30, 1715, CO 152/11," #22, TNA.

96. Order of Council, April 30, 1715, CO 153/12, p. 451, TNA. For Madame Maigne see Wm Popple to Edwd Northey, October 25, 1715, CO 153/12, p. 354–56.

97. Laurens to Messieurs and Madame Laurence, February 25, 1774, *Laurens Papers*, 9:311

98. Robert Janssen to Peter Manigault, July 29, 1755, in Slann Simmons, ed., "Early Manigault Records," *Transactions of the Huguenot Society of South Carolina* 59 (1954), 31.

Chapter 6

1. The only biographical study of the younger Simond is Norma Perry, "Voltaire's London Agents for the *Henriade*: Simond and Bénézet, Huguenot Merchants," *Studies in Voltaire and the Eighteenth Century* 102 (1973), 265–99 (the section on Simond is on 283–98); see also Maurice Boucher, *French Speakers at the Cape of Good Hope in the First Hundred Years* (Pretoria: University of South Africa, 1981), 363–69.

2. On these merchant networks see J. F. Bosher, "Huguenot Merchants and the Protestant International in the Seventeenth Century," *WMQ* 52:1 (1995), 77–102; R. C. Nash, "Huguenot Merchants and the Development of South Carolina's Slave-Plantation and Atlantic Trading Economy, 1680–1775," in *Memory and Identity: The Huguenots in France and the Atlantic Diaspora*, ed. Bertrand VanRuymbeke and Randy J. Sparks (Columbia: University of South Carolina Press, 2003), 208–40.

3. There is little current scholarship on the Huguenot mastery of foreign institutions; it is best pieced together by reading through the nineteenth-century histories, which often included lengthy biographical sketches; see especially Charles Weiss, *Histoire des réfugiés huguenots* (Paris: Ampelos Editions, 2008 [1853]); Samuel Smiles, *The Huguenots: Their Settlements, Churches, & Industries in England and Ireland* (London: John Murray, 1867); Charles W. Baird,

History of the Huguenot Emigration to America (New York: Dodd, Mead and Co., 1885). See also Robin Gwynn, *Huguenot Heritage: The History and Contributions of the Huguenots in Britain* (London: Routledge & Kegan Paul, 1985), 79–90.

4. A number of scholars have stressed the key role of *nouveaux convertis* in the eighteenth-century French empire, and many of these families retained connections to family members and business partners in the Refuge; see J. F. Bosher, *The Canada Merchants, 1713–1763* (Oxford: Oxford University Press, 1987); Bosher, *Business and Religion in the Age of New France, 1600–1760* (Toronto: Canadian Scholars Press, 1994); Dale Miquelon, *Dugard of Rouen: French Trade to Canada and the West Indies, 1729–1770* (Montreal: McGill-Queen's University Press, 1978); and Herbert Lüthy, *La Banque Protestante en France de la Révocation de l'Edit de Nantes à la Révolution* (Paris: S.E.V.P.E.N., 1959–61).

5. For the rise of Britain as a global power at this time see especially Linda Colley, *Britons: Forging the Nation, 1707–1837* (New Haven, CT: Yale University Press, 1992); John Brewer, *The Sinews of Power: War, Money, and the English State, 1688–1783* (Cambridge, MA: Harvard University Press, 1988); David Armitage, *The Ideological Origins of the British Empire* (Cambridge: Cambridge University Press, 2000). On the Act of Union and the Hanoverian succession, respectively, see Ned Landsman, "The Episcopate, the British Union, and the Failure of Religious Settlement in Colonial British North America," in *The First Prejudice: Religious Tolerance and Intolerance in Early America*, ed. Chris Beneke and Christopher Grenda (Philadelphia: University of Pennsylvania Press, 2011), 75–97; and Andrew Thompson, *Britain, Hanover, and the Protestant Interest, 1688–1756* (Woodbridge: Boydell and Brewer, 2006).

6. On the Church of England in this period see especially Brent S. Sirota, *The Christian Monitors: The Church of England and the Age of Benevolence, 1680–1730* (New Haven, CT: Yale University Press, 2014); William J. Bulman, *Anglican Enlightenment: Orientalism, Religion, and Politics in England and its Empire, 1648–1715* (Cambridge: Cambridge University Press, 2015). On the role of the British empire and America in the Protestant world see recent and forthcoming work by Katherine Carte Engel, especially "Connecting Protestants in Britain's Eighteenth-Century Atlantic Empire," *WMQ* 75:1 (2018), 37–70; and Jeremy Gregory, "Establishment and Dissent in North America: Organising Religion in the New World," in *Oxford History of the British Empire, Companion Series: British North America in the Seventeenth and Eighteenth Centuries*, ed. Stephen Foster (Oxford: Oxford University Press, 2013), 136–69.

7. Claude Grosteste de la Mothe, *Relation de la Societe etablie pour la Propagation de l'Evangile dans les Pays Etrangers, par les Lettres Patentes du Roi Guillaume III* (Rotterdam: Abraham Acher, 1708), iv–vii, xii–xiii. For background see Smiles, *The Huguenots*, 310–11.

8. La Mothe, *Relation*, xviii, 251.

9. La Mothe, *Relation*, xix–xx. He also wrote several other French-language tracts lauding the Church of England; see *Correspondance fraternelle de l'église anglicane avec les autres églises réformées et étrangères, prouvée par une dissertation et par plusieurs sermons* (The Hague, 1705).

10. Historians have long puzzled over the refugees' move toward Anglicanism. The most critical work on this subject is Robert M. Kingdon, "Why Did the Huguenot Refugees in the American Colonies Become Episcopalians?" *Historical Magazine of the Protestant Episcopal Church* 49:4 (1980), 317–35. For a survey of Huguenots in the SPG see William A. Bultmann, "The SPG and the French Huguenots in Colonial America," *Historical Magazine of the Protestant Episcopal Church* 20:2 (1951), 156–72.

11. Reboulet to Jacques Tronchin, October 4, 1687, Archives Tronchin, vol. 50, f. 81, BGE.

12. Thomas Bray, *A Memorial Representing the Present State of Religion, on the Continent of North-America* (London, 1700), 7.

13. On this moral reform push see especially Sirota, *The Christian Monitors*.

14. "Lettre de M. Pictet Pasteur & Professeur en Theologie dans Geneve, à la Societé de la Propagation de l'Evangile," in La Mothe, *Relation*, after 255. On the Huguenots as religious controversialists see Carolyn Chappell Lougee, *Facing the Revocation: Huguenot Families, Faith, and the King's Will* (New York: Oxford University Press, 2016), 54–60. For a good example of a printed work that captures this style see Gédéon Flournois, *Entretiens des voyageurs sur le mer* (Cologne [Rotterdam]: Pierre Marteau, 1683).

15. Godfrey Dellius to the Secretary, August 20, 1703, SPG 9, f. 32–33, LPL.

16. Elie Neau, *Histoire des souffrances du sieur Élie Neau, sur les galères, et dans les cachots de Marseille* [1701], ed. Didier Poton and Bertrand Van Ruymbeke (Paris: Les Indes Savantes, 2014).

17. Minutes for March 22, 1703, SPG 1, f. 9, LPL. For Neau's English-language publications see Elias Neau, *An Account of the Sufferings of the French Protestants, Slaves on board the French King's Galleys* (London: Richard Parker, 1699); and Cotton Mather, *A Present from a Farr Countrey* (Boston, 1697). For more background see Sheldon Cohen, "Elias Neau, Instructor to New York Slaves." *New-York Historical Society Quarterly* 55:1 (1971), 7–27; and Jon Butler, *The Huguenots in America: Refugee People in New World Society* (Cambridge, MA: Harvard University Press, 1983), 161–69; and Catherine Randall, *From a Far Country: Camisards and Huguenots in the Atlantic World* (Athens: University of Georgia Press, 2009), 101–10.

18. Neau to the Secretary, November 6, 1704, SPG 13, fol. 97, LPL.

19. Elie Neau to Gabriel Bernon, June 25, 1701, Gabriel Bernon Papers, Rhode Island Historical Society.

20. Vesey to Secretary, October 26, 1704, SPG 13, f. 91, LPL.

21. Vesey to Secretary, November 21, 1705, SPG 13, f. 154, LPL. Neau reported on his conversion in Neau to Secretary, November 6, 1704, SPG 13, f. 97, and Neau to Treasurer, December 20, 1704, SPG 13, f. 102.

22. Kennett, *The Lets and Impediments in Planting and Propagating the Gospel* (London, 1712).

23. Neau to Secretary, November 15, 1705, SPG 13, f. 169, LPL.

24. Neau to the Bishop of London, February 28, 1718/9, Fulham Papers 6, f. 187, LPL. The best work on slavery and the SPG more generally is Travis Glasson, *Mastering Christianity: Missionary Anglicanism and Slavery in the Atlantic World* (New York: Oxford University Press, 2012). On Neau see 75–86. See also Katharine Gerbner, *Christian Slavery: Conversion and Race in the Protestant Atlantic World* (Philadelphia: University of Pennsylvania Press, 2018).

25. Minutes for May 18, 1711, SPG 2, f. 265, LPL; Testimonial to Bondet, May 24, 1696, SPG 14, f. 145; Secretary to Bondet, June 6, 1709, SPG 14, f. 157; Neau to Secretary, July 5, 1709, SPG 14, f. 186. For background see Paula Wheeler Carlo, *Huguenot Refugees in Colonial New York: Becoming American in the Hudson Valley* (Brighton: Sussex Academic Press, 2005), 54–71.

26. On Le Jau see Edgar L. Pennington, "The Reverend Francis Le Jau's Work among Indians and Negro Slaves," *Journal of Southern History* 1:4 (1935), 442–58; Charles Bolton, "South Carolina and the Reverend Doctor Francis Le Jau: Southern Society and the Conscience of an Anglican Missionary," *Historical Magazine of the Protestant Episcopal Church* 40:1 (1971), 63–79. On his time in the Leeward Islands see Minutes for November 12 and 19, 1705, SPG 1, ff. 71, 74, LPL. His report on the Leewards is in SPG 17, ff. 286–92.

27. Compton to Secretary, December 23, 1708, SPG 8, f. 72, LPL.

28. Le Jau to Secretary, April 22, 1708, in Frank J. Klingberg, ed., *The Carolina Chronicle of Dr. Francis Le Jau, 1706–1717* (Berkeley: University of California Press, 1956), 39.

29. Le Jau to Secretary, September 15, 1708, in Klingberg, *The Carolina Chronicle of Dr. Francis Le Jau,* 41.

30. Le Jau to Secretary, May 10, 1715, in Klingberg, *The Carolina Chronicle of Dr. Francis Le Jau,* 153; Le Jau to Secretary, May 21, 1715, ibid., 159. On Indian slavery and the Yamasee War see especially Alan Gallay, *The Indian Slave Trade: The Rise of the English Empire in the American South, 1670–1717* (New Haven, CT: Yale University Press, 2002); William L. Ramsey, *The Yamasee War: A Study of Culture, Economy, and Conflict in the Colonial South* (Lincoln: University of Nebraska Press, 2010).

31. Le Jau to Stubs, July 3, 1707, in Klingberg, *The Carolina Chronicle of Dr. Francis Le Jau,* 30; Le Jau to Secretary, September 9, 1706, ibid., 16.

32. Le Jau to Secretary, February 23, 1713, in Klingberg, *The Carolina Chronicle of Dr. Francis Le Jau,* 129.

33. Le Jau to Secretary, March 19, 1715/16, in Klingberg, *The Carolina Chronicle of Dr. Francis Le Jau,* 174.

34. Le Jau to Secretary, September 18, 1711, in Klingberg, *The Carolina Chronicle of Dr. Francis Le Jau,* 102.

35. Le Jau to Secretary, August 10, 1713, in Klingberg, *The Carolina Chronicle of Dr. Francis Le Jau,* 133.

36. Le Jau to Secretary, July 10, 1711, in Klingberg, *The Carolina Chronicle of Dr. Francis Le Jau*, 93; Le Jau to Secretary, January 10, 1712, ibid., 106.

37. "Queries to Albert Pouderous," April 25, 1724, and Pouderous to the Bishop of London, April 25, 1724; Fulham Papers 9, ff. 136, 169, LPL. For more details on his life see Susan Baldwin Bates and Harriott Cheves Leland, *French Santee: A Huguenot Settlement in Colonial South Carolina* (Baltimore: Otter Bay Books, 2015), 277–80.

38. For biographical details see Lillian Fordham Wood, "The Reverend John LaPierre," *Historical Magazine of the Protestant Episcopal Church* 40:4 (1971), 407–30.

39. Josia Dupré to John Dupré, August 27, 1708, SPG 16, ff. 218–19, LPL.

40. Jean Lapierre to C. G. de la Mothe, August 13, 1714, in Winifred Turner, ed. *The Aufrère Papers: Calendar and Selections* (Frome: Huguenot Society of London, 1940), 211.

41. Peter Stouppe to the Bishop of London, May 12, 1725, Fulham Papers 6, f. 183, LPL.

42. See John La Pierre to the Bishop of London, November 29, 1732, Fulham Papers 6, f. 240, LPL. Gideon Johnston believed that La Pierre, like Claude Philippe de Richebourg, was a troublesome character who did not do enough for the church. See Amy Friedlander, ed., "Commissary Johnston's Report," *South Carolina Historical Magazine* 83:4 (1982), 259–71.

43. Thomas Hill to Dr. Bearcroft, CO 218/3, pp. 200–201, TNA; General Meeting Minutes, April 17, 1761, MS. 1124/II, f. 156r, LPL. There is little known about Moreau's life and career, but see the biographical sketch in Judith Fingard, "Moreau, Jean-Baptiste," *Dictionary of Canadian Biography*, http://www.biographi.ca/en/bio/moreau_jean_baptiste_3E.html. On the larger history of Lunenberg and efforts to settle Nova Scotia see Winthrop Packer Bell, *The "Foreign Protestants" and the Settlement of Nova Scotia: The History of a Piece of Arrested British Colonial Policy in the Eighteenth Century* (Toronto: University of Toronto Press, 1961).

44. General Meeting Minutes, December 20, 1765, MS. 1124/III, f. 127v, LPL; General Meeting Minutes, December 19, 1766, MS. 1124/III, f. 265. On the role of Catholic missionaries in the imperial contest for Nova Scotia see Geoffrey Plank, *An Unsettled Conquest: The British Campaign against the Peoples of Acadia* (Philadelphia: University of Pennsylvania Press, 2001), esp. 68–86.

45. General Meeting Minutes, November 16, 1764, MS 1124/II, f. 298v, LPL. Stephen identified Samuel as his son in his will; see PROB 11/517/405, TNA.

46. On Guiscard see Peter Jones, "Antoine de Guiscard, 'Abbé de la Bourlie,' 'Marquis de Guiscard,'" *The British Library Journal* 8:1 (1982), 94–113 (Monsegur on 106).

47. There has been a fair amount of scholarship on Huguenots in the military during this period. See especially Matthew Glozier and David Onnekink, eds., *War, Religion, and Service: Huguenot Soldiering, 1685–1713* (Aldershot: Ashgate, 2007).

48. Monsegur to Sunderland, received December 19, 1706, Add. Mss. 61648, f. 7, BL.

49. "Le Projet de L'entreprise du port de Plaisance," Add. Mss. 61648, f. 4, BL. Some of Monsegur's intuitions were not so far-fetched. Subercase was a Protestant, and indeed a copy that he owned of the Geneva bible still resides at the Bibliothèque Nationale du Québec. See Isabelle Crevier Denomée, "Régards sur une bible hébraïque, une bible polyglotte et une bible de Genève conservées par Bibliothèque et Archives nationales du Québec," in *Ouvrages phares de la Réforme et de la Contre-réforme dans les collections montréalaises*, ed. Brenda Dunn-Lardeau (Quebec City: Presses de l'Université du Québec, 2014).

50. "Le Projet de L'entreprise du port de Plaisance," ff. 5–6.

51. Monsegur to Sunderland, n.d., Add. Mss. 61648, f. 9; "Memoire du Michel de Monsegur a Sa Grandeur Mylord Sunderland sur l'entreprise du port de Plaisance," February 14, 1707, f. 11. On Subercase see James Pritchard, *In Search of Empire: The French in the Americas, 1670–1730* (Cambridge: Cambridge University Press, 2004), 394–98; René Baudry, "Auger de Subercase, Daniel d'," *Dictionary of Canadian Biography*, http://www.biographi.ca/en/bio/auger_de_subercase_daniel_d_2E.html

52. Monsegur to Sunderland, endorsed December 19, f. 7.

53. The role of the Army in the colonies has been studied most extensively by Stephen Saunders Webb. See especially his "Army and Empire: English Garrison Government in England and America, 1569 to 1763," *WMQ* 34:1 (1977), 1–31; and *Marlborough's America* (New Haven, CT: Yale University Press, 2012).

54. Grandpré's correspondence with M. de Candos in Île de France (Mauritius) is in MOOC 14/ 29, WCA. For basic biographical details see Marilyn Garcia-Chapleau, *Le Refuge huguenot du cap de Bonne-Espérance: Genèse, assimilation, héritage* (Paris: Honoré Champion, 2016), 196, 442.

55. On Ligonier's early life see Rex Whitworth, *Field Marshal Lord Ligonier: A Story of the British Army, 1702–1770* (Oxford: Oxford University Press, 1958), 1–12. On Mascarene see his letter "to my dear children" in Mascarene Family Papers, Massachusetts Historical Society, Boston; and Barry Morris Moody, "'A Just and Disinterested Man': The Nova Scotia Career of Paul Mascarene, 1710–1752," (PhD diss., Queen's University, 1976), 8–21. On the complicated politics of conversion in noble families see Lougee, *Facing the Revocation*; and Raymond A. Mentzer, *Blood and Belief: Family Survival and Confessional Identity among the Provincial Huguenot Nobility* (West Lafayette, IN: Purdue University Press, 1994).

56. Whitworth, *Field Marshal Lord Ligonier*, 4; Mascarene "to my dear children," Mascarene Family Papers, MHS; Moody, "'A Just and Disinterested Man'," 21–23.

57. Ligonier to his mother, September 11, 1698, reprinted in Whitworth, *Field Marshal Lord Ligonier*, 9.

58. Paul Mascarene to John Mascarene, October 23, 1752, Mascarene Family Papers, MHS; Moody, "'A Just and Disinterested Man.'" On the most famous Rapin, who distinguished himself as a historian of England, see Hugh Trevor-Roper, "Our First Whig Historian: Paul de Rapin-Thoyras," in *Huguenots in Britain and their French Background, 1550–1800*, ed. Irene Scouloudi (London: Macmillan, 1987), 3–19; Owen Stanwood, "Liberty and Prophecy: The Huguenot Diaspora and the Whig Interpretation of History," in *L'Identité huguenote: Faire mémoire et écrire l'histoire (XVIe–XXIe siècle)*, ed. Philip Benedict, Hugues Daussy, and Pierre-Olivier Léchot (Geneva: Droz, 2014), 295–309; and David Onnekink, *The Anglo-Dutch Favorite: Willem Bentinck, 1st Earl of Portland (1649–1709)* (New York: Routledge, 2007).

59. On British ambitions in Minorca and the conquest see Desmond Gregory, *Minorca, the Illusory Prize: A History of the British Occupations of Minorca between 1708 and 1802* (Rutherford, NJ: Fairleigh Dickinson University Press, 1990), esp. 15–34. On how the conquerors dealt with the question of religion see Jessica Harland Jacobs, "Incorporating the King's New Subjects: Accommodation and Anti-Catholicism in the British Empire, 1763–1815," *Journal of Religious History* 39:2 (2015), 203–23.

60. Whitworth, *Field Marshal Lord Ligonier*, 31–37.

61. On the conquest of Nova Scotia see John G. Reid, Maurice Basque, Elizabeth Mancke, Barry Moody, Geoffrey Plank, and William Wicken, *The Conquest of Acadia, 1710: Imperial, Colonial, and Aboriginal Constructions* (Toronto: University of Toronto Press, 2016); Plank, *An Unsettled Conquest*, 40–67; John Mack Faragher, *A Great and Noble Scheme: The Tragic Story of the Expulsion of the French Acadians from their American Homeland* (New York: Norton, 2005), 99–124.

62. Paul Mascarene, "Description of Nova Scotia," in *Selections from the Public Documents of the Province of Nova Scotia*, ed. Thomas B. Akins (Halifax: C. Annand, 1869), 39–41.

63. Mascarene, "Description of Nova Scotia," 41–43.

64. "Proposals for settling a colony of French Protestants in the Province of Nova Scotia," September 28, 1729, CO 217/38, no. 227, TNA. On Lemercier see Paula Wheeler Carlo, "Huguenot Identity and Protestant Unity in Colonial Massachusetts: The Reverend André Le Mercier and the 'Sociable Spirit'," *Historical Journal of Massachusetts* 40 (2012), 123–47. On the larger Protestant orientation of New England see Mark Peterson, "*Theopolis Americana*: The City-State of Boston, the Republic of Letters, and the Protestant International, 1689–1739," in *Soundings in Atlantic History: Latent Structures and Intellectual Currents, 1500–1825*, ed. Bernard Bailyn and Patricia Denault (Cambridge, MA: Harvard University Press, 2009), 329–70; Thomas Kidd, *The Protestant Interest: New England after Puritanism* (New Haven, CT: Yale University Press, 2004). Peterson deals explicitly with Mascarene's Boston links in *The City-State of Boston: The Rise and Fall of an Atlantic Power, 1630–1865* (Princeton, NJ: Princeton University Press, 2019), 257-65.

65. This interpretation is shared by most scholars of the period: Moody, "'A Just and Disinterested Man;'" Plank, *An Unsettled Conquest*, 102–103; Faragher, *A Great and Noble Scheme*,

209–43. See also Christopher Hodson, *The Acadian Diaspora: An Eighteenth-Century History* (New York: Oxford University Press, 2012), 34–40.

66. Mascarene to Desenclaves, July 20, 1741; and Mascarene to Desenclaves, September 5, 1741, in Akins, *Public Documents*, 112–13.

67. Mascarene to St. Poncy, February 20, 1733/4, Paul Mascarene Papers, ff. 6–15, Houghton Library, Harvard University. The book in question was probably Bossuet's *Histoire des variations des Églises Protestantes* (Paris, 1688).

68. Mascarene to St. Poncy, 22 Avril 1739, Paul Mascarene Papers, f. 35, Houghton Library. Mascarene retained some of his father's letters about his experience in prison, which are now in the Mascarene Family Papers, MHS. Some have been reprinted in Baird, *History of the Huguenot Emigration to America*, 2:340–78.

69. People of Mines to M. de Ganne, October 10, 1744, in Akins, *Public Documents*, 135.

70. Mascarene to ------, Dec 1744, in Akins, *Public Documents*, 148.

71. Paul Mascarene to John Mascarene, October 21, 1752 and October 25, 1752, Mascarene Family Papers, MHS.

72. On this phase of Ligonier's career see Whitworth, *Field Marshal Lord Ligonier*, 89–198.

73. Whitworth, *Field Marshal Lord Ligonier*, 209–10.

74. *An Act for Naturalizing such Foreign Protestants as have served, or shall serve for the Time therein mentioned, as Officers or Soldiers in His Majesty's Royal American Regiment, or as Engineers in America* (London, 1762); "Capitulation d'un Regiment Suisse & Allemand pour le Service de la Grand Bretagne levé parmy les Gens de Cette Nation Sujets de Sa Majesté," Add. Mss. 73648, no. 912A, BL. See Alexander V. Campbell, *The Royal American Regiment: An Atlantic Microcosm, 1755–1772* (Norman: University of Oklahoma Press, 2010), esp. 15–48. On Prevost's ancestry see Weiss, *Réfugiés huguenots*, 1:288.

75. James Prevost, "Mémoire sur la Guerre d'Amérique," in *Military Affairs in North America, 1748–1765: Selected Documents from the Cumberland Papers in Windsor Castle*, ed. Stanley Pargellis (New York: Archon Books, 1969 [1936]), 339. On Portarlington see Raymond Hylton, "The Huguenot Settlement at Portarlington, 1691–1771," in *The Huguenots and Ireland: Anatomy of an Emigration*, ed. C. E. J. Caldicott, H. Gough, and J.-P. Pittion (Dublin: Glendale Press, 1987), 297–320.

76. John Lovell, *A Funeral Oration Deliver'd At the Opening of the Annual Meeting of the Town, March 14th 1742, in Faneuil-Hall in Boston: Occasion'd by the Death of the Founder, Peter Faneuil, Esq* (Boston: Green, Bushell, and Allen, 1743), 7, 12–13. On Faneuil Hall see Jonathan Beagle, "Remembering Peter Faneuil: Yankees, Huguenots, and Ethnicity in Boston, 1743–1900," *New England Quarterly* 75:3 (2002), 388–414.

77. Arnoul to Seignelay, May 6, 1687, MS. NAF 21334, f. 91, Bibliothèque Nationale de France. See Mickaël Augeron and Didier Poton, "La Rochelle, port canadien: le négoce protestant et la Nouvelle-France," in *Mémoires de Nouvelle-France: De France en Nouvelle-France*, ed. Philippe Joutard and Thomas Wien (Rennes: Presses universitaires de Rennes, 2005).

78. For biographical details on the Faneuils see Abram English Brown, *Faneuil Hall and Faneuil Hall Market: or, Peter Faneuil and his Gift* (Boston: Lee and Shepard, 1900), 8–13; Bosher, "Huguenot Merchants and the Protestant International."

79. "Memoire à Monseigneur de Pontchartrain sur le nommé David Basset de Mareine, Religionnaire refugié a Baston," Archives des Colonies, C^{11D} 4, ff. 165–66, ANOM; "The Examination of David Bassett of Boston Marriner," June 30, 1694, Mass. Arch., 61:446; "Extrait de la lettre du ministre à M. Brouillan," March 15, 1702, Archives des Colonies, C^{11D} 4, f. 158, ANOM.

80. Mass. Arch. 7:117, 214.

81. The depositions are collected in *NYCD*, 3:259–62. New York's Council exonerated Faneuil, though the Huguenots noted that the rumors had spread far and damaged the reputation of the refugees in general. See also Gilbert Chinard, *Les réfugiés huguenots en Amérique* (Paris: E. Aubin, 1925), 138–42.

82. Brown, *Faneuil Hall and Faneuil Hall Market*, 12. His account books are in Peter Faneuil Papers, Hancock Family Papers, Baker Library, Harvard Business School.

83. Thomas and Jean's letters are in Thomas Bayeux Lettres, 2 E 38, Archives Départementales du Calvados, Caen. See especially Jean Bayeux to Thomas Bayeux, November 28, 1712 and

February 16, 1714. For an analysis see Luc Daireaux, "Un Normand à New York: Le Refuge huguenot vu à travers la correspondance de Thomas Bayeux (1708–1719)," in *Les Huguenots et l'Atlantique: Fidélités, racines et mémoires*, ed. Mickaël Augeron, Didier Poton, and Bertrand Van Ruymbeke (Paris: Les Indes Savantes, 2012), 135–46.

84. Peter Jay Letterbooks, John Jay Papers, Columbia University Library. Jay has generally been of interest to scholars mostly due to the fact that his son, John Jay, became a prominent politician in the early United States. For a sketch of Jay and the family see Walter Stahr, *John Jay: Founding Father* (New York: Diversion Books, 2005), 1–16. For more on Jay's commercial networks see also Peter Jay, Account book and Daybook, New-York Historical Society. On the New York merchant community more generally see Cathy D. Matson, *Merchants and Empire: Trading in Colonial New York* (Ithaca, NY: Cornell University Press, 1998).

85. See for example Peter Jay to James Harding, July 23, 1733 and October 15, 1733, Jay Letterbooks, Box 16.

86. See for example Peter Jay to Françoise Peloquin, January 8, 1724/5, June 28, 1726, June 26, 1727, May 10, 1728, March 25, 1729, December 30, 1729 all in Jay Letterbooks, Box 16. The divisions occurred in the aftermath of a dispute involving the minister Louis Rou. See Paula Wheeler Carlo, "The Huguenot Soul: The Calvinism of Reverend Louis Rou," in *The Religious Culture of the Huguenots, 1660–1750*, ed. Anne Dunan-Page (Aldershot: Ashgate, 2006), 109–20.

87. Peter Jay to M. Mouchard, June 26, 1753; Peter Jay to James Jay, July 2, 1753, both in Peter Jay Letterbooks, Box 18.

88. Peter Faneuil to Jean Tigal, June 27, 1737, Letterbook, 7–8, Peter Faneuil Papers.

89. This interpretation dovetails with that in Phyllis Whitman Hunter, *Purchasing Identity in the Atlantic World: Massachusetts Merchants, 1670–1780* (Ithaca, NY: Cornell University Press, 2001), 119–24, who contends that the Faneuils cemented their British identity through consuming British goods. On the decline of the Boston Huguenot church see Butler, *The Huguenots in America*, 88–90.

90. See the correspondence between Simond and Groteste in the Aufrère Papers, F/Af/3, #52, 63, 76, Huguenot Library, University College London. On his tobacco links, see Jacob M. Price, *France and the Chesapeake: A History of the French Tobacco Monopoly, 1674–1791, and of its Relationship to the British and American Tobacco Trades* (Ann Arbor: University of Michigan Press, 1973) 1:540–41.

91. On Purry see Arlin C. Migliazzo, *To Make this Land Our Own: Community, Identity, and Cultural Adaptation in Purrysburg Township, South Carolina, 1732–1865* (Columbia: University of South Carolina Press, 2007).

Chapter 7

1. Louis de Saint-Pierre, *The Art of Planting and Cultivating the Vine; as also, of Making, Fining, and Preserving Wines &c. According to the Most Approved Methods in the Most Celebrated Wine-Countries in France* (London: J. Wilkie, 1772), xx–xxi; [Saint-Pierre], *The great Utility of establishing the Culture of Vines, Silk, Indigo, and Fruit Trees, in such parts of North America, where the Climate is particularly favourable to those Productions* ([London], 1772), 3. Parts of this chapter appear in two other places: Owen Stanwood, "Imperial Vineyards: Wine and Politics in the Early American South," in *Experiencing Empire Power, People, and Revolution in Early America*, ed. Patrick Griffin (Charlottesville: University of Virginia Press, 2017), 50–70; and Stanwood, "From the Desert to the Refuge: The Saga of New Bordeaux," *French Historical Studies* 40:1 (2017), 1–28.

2. These eighteenth-century colonies have been almost entirely neglected by historians of the Refuge. For Ireland see Susanne Lachenicht, "New Colonies in Ireland? Antoine Court and the Settlement of French Refugees in the Eighteenth Century," *HSP* 29:2 (2009), 29 (2009), 227–37; for the small colony in Maine, Elizabeth Gardner Hayward, Jane Hawkes Liddell, and Corinne Ingraham Pigott, "Hardships, Privation, and Massacres in Maine," in *Huguenot Refugees in the Settlement of Colonial America*, ed. Peter Steven Gannon (New York: Huguenot Society of America, 1985), 282–93; and on South Carolina, Arthur H. Hirsch, *The Huguenots of Colonial South Carolina* (Columbia: University of South Carolina Press, 1999), 81–89.

3. Pierre Bayle has attracted a great deal of scholarship, especially from French scholars; see Elisabeth Labrousse, *Pierre Bayle* (The Hague: Martinus Nijhoff, 1963–64); Hubert Bost, *Pierre Bayle* (Paris: Fayard, 1996); and for the larger context, Jonathan Israel, *Enlightenment Contested: Philosophy, Modernity, and the Emancipation of Man, 1670–1752* (New York: Oxford University Press, 2006), esp. 63–93, 135–63.
4. Most modern scholars have concluded that the Huguenot emigration was not the primary cause of France's economic decline; see Warren C. Scoville, *The Persecution of Huguenots and French Economic Development, 1680–1720* (Berkeley: University of California Press, 1960); Myriam Yardeni, "Naissance et essor d'un mythe: La révocation de l'édit de Nantes et le déclin économique de la France," *BSHPF*, 142:1 (1993), 79–96. On the movement toward toleration more generally, see John Marshall, *John Locke, Toleration and Early Enlightenment Culture* (Cambridge: Cambridge University Press, 2006); Perez Zagorin, *How the Idea of Religious Toleration Came to the West* (Princeton, NJ: Princeton University Press, 2005); and specifically on the role of Huguenots, Geoffrey Adams, *The Huguenots and French Opinion, 1685–1787: The Enlightenment Debate on Toleration* (Waterloo, ON: Wilfrid Laurier University Press, 1991); and David Garrioch, *The Huguenots of Paris and the Coming of Religious Freedom, 1685–1789* (Cambridge: Cambridge University Press, 2014).
5. Daniel Defoe, *An Essay Upon Projects* (London: R. R. for Tho. Cockerill, 1697), 1, 6, 10–11. See Maximillian E. Novak, ed., *The Age of Projects* (Toronto: University of Toronto Press, 2008).
6. The RSA still awaits a comprehensive, scholarly history; but see Derek Hudson and Kenneth W. Luckhurst, *The Royal Society of Arts, 1754–1954* (London: Murray, 1954).
7. On German and Irish migration during this period see Philip Otterness, *Becoming German: The 1709 Palatine Migration to New York* (Ithaca, NY: Cornell University Press, 2004); Patrick Griffin, *The People With No Name: Ireland's Ulster Scots, America's Scots Irish, and the Creation of a British Atlantic World, 1689–1764* (Princeton, NJ: Princeton University Press, 2001); Aaron Spencer Fogleman, *Hopeful Journeys: German Immigration, Settlement, and Political Culture in Colonial America, 1717–1775* (Philadelphia: University of Pennsylvania Press, 1996); Katherine Carte Engel, *Religion and Profit: Moravians in Colonial America* (Philadelphia: University of Pennsylvania Press, 2009); James Van Horn Melton, *Religion, Community, and Slavery on the Southern Colonial Frontier* (Cambridge: Cambridge University Press, 2015).
8. The best English-language account of the affair is David Bien, *The Calas Affair: Persecution, Toleration, and Heresy in Eighteenth-Century Toulouse* (Princeton, NJ: Princeton University Press, 1960); see also Janine Garrisson, *L'Affaire Calas: Miroir des passion françaises* (Paris: Fayard, 2004).
9. Voltaire, *Traité sur la Tolérance à l'occasion de la mort de Jean Calas*, ed. Jacques van den Heuvel (Paris: Fayard, 1975), 69. For background on the publication see John Renwick, "Voltaire and the Politics of Toleration," in *The Cambridge Companion to Voltaire*, ed. Nicholas Cronk (Cambridge: Cambridge University Press, 2009), 179–91.
10. Pierre Jurieu, *The Policy of the Clergy of France* (London: R. Bentley and M. Magnes, 1681), 164, 168. Jurieu is of course better known as an advocate of intolerance; see Marshall, *John Locke, Toleration, and Early Enlightenment Culture*, 419–32.
11. Maréchal de Vauban, *Mémoire Pour le Rappel des Huguenots* (La Bégude-de-Mazenc: Textes d'histoire protestante, 2011), esp. 14–15, 22; Patrick Cabanel, *Histoire des protestants en France, XVIe–XXIe siècles* (Paris: Fayard, 2012), esp. 881.
12. "Personne n'ignore les ~~trahisons~~ <liaisons> que les huguenots de france ont eües avec les ennemis de l'Etat durant les deux dernieres guerres." "Memoire pour L'entier Conversion des nouveaux convertis de France," 1715, TT 435, dossier 8, AN.
13. "Memoire pour L'entier Conversion des nouveaux convertis de France," TT 435, dossier 8, AN.
14. Charles de Secondat, baron de Montesquieu, *Persian Letters*, trans. Margaret Mauldon (New York: Penguin, 2008), 115; Adams, *The Huguenots and French Opinion*, 85–87; Paul Cheney, *Revolutionary Commerce: Globalization and the French Monarchy* (Cambridge, MA: Harvard University Press, 2010), 31. On Huet see April G. Shelford, *Transforming the Republic of Letters: Pierre-Daniel Huet and European Intellectual Life, 1650–1720* (Woodbridge: Boydell and Brewer, 2007).
15. There has been a lot of writing on Court's career; see especially his autobiography, *Mémoires pour servir à l'histoire et à la vie d'Antoine Court*, ed. Pauline Dulay-Haour and Patrick Cabanel

(Paris: Éditions de Paris, 1995); and Hubert Bost and Claude Loriel, eds., *Entre désert et Europe: Le pasteur Antoine Court (1695-1760)* (Paris: Honoré Champion, 1998).

16. For modern editions of these books see La Beaumelle, *Deux traités sur la tolerance*, ed. Hubert Bost (Paris: Honoré Champion, 2012); and Antoine Court, *Le patriote français et impartial*, ed. Otto H. Selles (Paris: Honoré Champion, 2002).

17. "Memoire sur les Religionnaires" [1750], TT 440, fol. 8, AN. On links between France and the Refuge see especially Myriam Yardeni, "La France protestante et le Refuge," in *Le Refuge huguenot: Assimilation et culture* (Paris: Honoré Champion, 2002), 163-76.

18. "Supplique des religionnaires," August 30, 1751, TT 440, fol. 79, AN. The writer heavily exaggerated the number of refugees in this petition, as was common.

19. "Memoire des protestans," September 9, 1758, TT 442, dossier 10, fol. 100, AN.

20. The case is described in Bien, *The Calas Affair,* 54.

21. Viala to Court, September 10, 1746, Collection Court, vol. 1, f. 29, BGE.

22. See Pauline Haour, "Antoine Court and Refugee Political Thought (1719-1752)," in *New Essays on the Political Thought of the Huguenots of the Refuge*, ed. John Christian Laursen (Leiden: Brill, 1995), 131-54.

23. Migault to Court, January 3, 1747, Collection Court, vol. 1, f. 411, BGE.

24. Gibert's life, along with that of his brother Étienne who ministered in Bordeaux before eventually settling in England, is the subject of the thorough but hagiographic Daniel Benoît, *Les frères Gibert: Pasteurs du "Désert" puis du "Refuge,"* (Paris: Le Croît Vif, 2005 [1889]). See also Robert Martel, "L'Atlantique, route vers l'Amérique: Les frères Gibert, 'pasteurs au Refuge," in *Les Huguenots et l'Atlantique: Pour Dieu, la Cause, ou les Affaires*, ed. Mickaël Augeron, Didier Poton, and Bertrand Van Ruymbeke(Paris: Les Indes Savantes, 2009), 375-82.

25. Dieter Gembicki and Heidi Gembicki-Achtnich, eds., *Le Réveil des coeurs: Journal de voyage du frère morave Fries (1761-1762)* (Saintes: Le Croît Vif, 2013), 235-45 (quotations on 236).

26. The letter is quoted at length in Benoît, *Les frères Gibert*, 11-12. On Gibert's role in Poitou see Yves Krumenacker, *Les Protestants du Poitou au XVIIIe siècle (1681-1789)* (Paris: Honoré Champion, 1998), 339.

27. Bien, *The Calas Affair*, esp. 43-76; Adams, *The Huguenots and French Opinion*, 211-28.

28. The most thorough recent history of the colony is Marie Polderman, *La Guyane française, 1676-1763: Mise en place et évolution de la société coloniale, tensions et métissages* (Cayenne: Ibis Rouge Ed., 2004).

29. Etienne François de Choiseul-Stainville, duc de Choiseul, to Voltaire, November 27, 1763, in Theodore Besterman, ed., *Voltaire's Correspondence* (Geneva: Institut et Musée Voltaire, 1960), 53:132-33; Voltaire to Charles Augustin Feriol, comte d'Argental, and Jeanne Grâce Bosc du Bouchet, comtesse d'Argental, December 15, 1763, ibid., 177.

30. Voltaire to Louis Necker, March 19, 1764, and Voltaire to Anne Robert Jacques Turgot, March 19, 1764, both in Besterman, ed., *Correspondence*, 54:204-207.

31. Dr. Artur is quoted in Marion F. Godfroy, *Kourou and the Struggle for a French America* (Basingstoke: Palgrave, 2015), 68. On the tragic denouement of the plan see Godfroy, 125-40, and Emma Rothschild, "A Horrible Tragedy in the French Atlantic," *Past and Present* no. 192 (2006), 67-108. On Acadians in Guiana see Christopher Hodson, *The Acadian Diaspora: An Eighteenth Century History* (New York: Oxford University Press, 2012), 92-105.

32. Gibert to the Archbishop of Canterbury, in Francis Waddington, "Projet d'émigration de la Saintonge et des provinces voisines d'après des documents inédits, 1761-1764," BSHPF 6:9/10 (1858), 371. Waddington only reprinted some of the Archbishop's correspondence regarding Gibert. For the originals see MS. 1122/III, ff. 170-213, LPL.

33. "Description de Gibert," TT 447, fol. 173, AN.

34. "Signalement du nommé Gibert," TT 447, no. 174, AN.

35. Fitzjames to Preslin, September 26, 1763, TT 447, fol. 171, AN; Chevalier d'Eon to the Minister, August 11, 1763, Correspondance Politique, Angleterre, v. 451, ff. 51-52, MAE.

36. John Peter Purry, *A Method For Determining the Best Climate of the Earth, On a Principle to which All Geographers and Historians have been hitherto Strangers* (London, 1744), 1-4, 46. For a good summary of Purry's life see Arlin C. Migliazzo, "Introduction: Jean Pierre Purry—A Life Lived Beyond the Horizon," in *Lands of True and Certain Bounty: The Geographical Theories and Colonization Strategies of Jean Pierre Purry* (Selinsgrove, Penn.: Susquehanna University

Press, 2002), 13–44; and Carlo Ginzburg, "Latitude, Slaves, and the Bible: An Experiment in Microhistory," *Critical Inquiry* 31:3 (2005), 665–83. Purry wrote several French-language tracts selling his colony to the Dutch, all of which are reprinted, in translation, in Migliazzo, ed., *Lands of True and Certain Bounty.*

37. Purry, *Method*, Advertisement, 3–4. On Law's Mississippi scheme and its context see Christopher Hodson, "Rethinking Failure: The French Empire in the Age of John Law," in *Experiencing Empire*, ed. Griffin, 127–46.

38. Walpole to Newcastle, June 7, 1724; Purry to Walpole, June 6, 1724, Add. Mss. 32739, ff. 39–41, BL; Purry to the King, May 27/June 7, 1724, CO 5/359, f. 18, TNA; Jean Pierre Purry, *Memorial presented to His Grace My Lord the Duke of Newcastle, Chamberlain of his Majesty King George, &c., and Secretary of State: upon the present condition of Carolina, and the Means of its Amelioration* (Augusta, GA, 1880), 10.

39. Purry, *Memorial presented to His Grace My Lord the Duke of Newcastle*, 19–20. The most thorough study of the development of the colony is Arlin C. Migliazzo, *To Make This Land Our Own: Community, Identity, and Cultural Adaptation in Purrysburg Township, South Carolina, 1732–1865* (Columbia: University of South Carolina Press, 2007). Carlo Ginzburg noted the Protestant orientation of Purry's work in "Latitude, Slaves, and the Bible."

40. [Daniel Defoe], *A Plan of the English Commerce. Being a Compleat Prospect of The Trade of this Nation, as well the Home Trade and the Foreign* (London: Charles Rivington, 1728). See also [Defoe], *A General History of Trade, and Especially Consider'd as it Respects the British Commerce, As well at Home, as to all Parts of the World* (London: J. Baker, 1713); [Charles Davenant], *Discourses on the Publick Revenues, and on the Trade of England* (London: James Knapton, 1698).

41. Joshua Gee, *The Trade and Navigation of Great-Britain Considered.* 3d ed. (London: Sam Buckley, 1731), preface.

42. Many of the relevant documents appear in A. Picheral-Dardier, "L'émigration en 1752 (Documents inédits)," *BSHPF* 35 (1886), 241–51, 289–306, 337–61, 385–405. For a good summary see Lachenicht, "New Colonies in Ireland?" On the controversy over baptism see Benjamin du Plan to Thomas Herring, July 23, 1752, MS. 1122/I, ff. 188–91, LPL.

43. James Simon to Thomas Herring, September 29, 1752, MS. 1122/I, f. 222, LPL.

44. "L'émigration en Irlande: Journal de voyage d'un réfugié français, 1693," *BSHPF*, 17 (1868), 596; Court to Serces, April 7, 1747, in Frédéric Gardy, ed., *Correspondance de Jaques Serces* (Frome: Huguenot Society of London, 1952), 1:179; Court to Serces, May 24, 1752, ibid., 138.

45. Jacques Pelletreau to Court, April 10, 1752, in Picheral-Dardier, "L'émigration," 249; Serces to Court, May 5, 1752, in *Correspondance de Serces*, ed. Gardy, 1:132.

46. "A Brief Account of the Government and State of the Island of Minorca," CO 174/1, no. 3, TNA; "Memoire sur l'Amélioration de L'Isle de Minorque et augmentation de ses production," CO 174/4, no. 46.

47. "A Plan for settling the Island of Menorca with a Sett of Substantial and industrious Inhab[itants]," n.d., CO 174/1, no. 65, TNA.

48. Ami Lullin to Jacques Serces, July 7, 1752, *Correspondance de Serces*, 1:150. While no Huguenots settled there authorities did encourage Jewish and Greek migration that was more successful; see Desmond Gregory, *Minorca, the Illusory Prize: A History of the British Occupations of Minorca between 1708 and 1802* (Rutherford, NJ: Fairleigh Dickinson University Press, 1990), 131–35.

49. [Defoe], *A Plan of the English Commerce*, 223, 360–61.

50. *The Importance of Settling and Fortifying Nova Scotia: With a Particular Account of the Climate, Soil, and Native Inhabitants of the Country, By a Gentleman lately arrived from that Colony* (London: J. Scott, 1751), 10, 27; *A True Account Of the Colonies of Nova-Scotia, and Georgia, Containing An Account of the Bounds, Rivers, Climate, Soil, Produce, Face of the Country; Chief Towns, and Exports &c.* (Newcastle, 1774), 7–8.

51. Board of Trade to Cornwallis, October 16, 1749, CO 218/3, p. 167, TNA.

52. Board of Trade to the Duke of Bedford, March 8, 1750, CO 218/3, p. 204, TNA.

53. Board of Trade to Bedford, March 29, 1750, CO 218/3, p. 215–16; Serces to Antoine Court, 10 avril 1750, *Correspondance de Serces*, 2:42.

54. Thomas Herring to [?], May 1750, MS. 1122/I, ff. 126–27, LPL.
55. Board of Trade to Cornwallis, April 2, 1750, CO 217/3, p. 227, TNA.
56. Board of Trade to Bedford, May 24, 1750, CO 217/3, p. 247, TNA.
57. Antoine Court to Jacques Serces, September 29–30, 1752, *Correspondance de Serces*, 2:228. On the larger context of these settlements see Winthrop Pickard Bell, *The 'Foreign Protestants' and the Settlement of Nova Scotia: The History of a Piece of Arrested British Colonial Policy in the Eighteenth Century* (Toronto: University of Toronto Press, 1961), 41–42, 212–14.
58. The best work on these projects is Joyce Chaplin, *An Anxious Pursuit: Agricultural Innovation and Modernity in the Lower South, 1730–1815* (Chapel Hill: University of North Carolina Press, 1993). See also S. Max Edelson, *Plantation Enterprise in Colonial South Carolina* (Cambridge, MA: Harvard University Press, 2006), and Robert L. Meriwether, *The Expansion of South Carolina, 1729–1765* (Kingsport, TN: Southern Publishers, 1940).
59. John Locke, *Observations upon the Growth and Culture of Vines and Olives* (London: W. Sandby, 1766), ix–x.
60. Robert Dossie, *Memoirs of Agriculture, and other Oeconomical Arts* (London, 1768–82), 1:231. For particular attention to the colonial program of the RSA see Chaplin, *An Anxious Pursuit*, 137–64.
61. Charles Pinckney to Mr Baker, April 1, 1755, PR/GE/110/1/19, Royal Society of Arts Archives. For a thorough exploration of South Carolina's silk industry see Ben Marsh, "Silk Hopes in Colonial South Carolina," *Journal of Southern History* 78:4 (2012), 807–54.
62. Dossie, *Memoirs of Agriculture*, 1:242.
63. Purry, *A Method For Determining the Best Climate of the Earth*, esp. 45–47.
64. On Georgia's silk industry see Marguerite B. Hamer, "The Foundations and Failure of the Silk Industry in Provincial Georgia," *North Carolina Historical Review* 12:1 (1935), 125–48; W. Calvin Smith, "Utopia's Last Chance? The Georgia Silk Boomlet of 1751," *Georgia Historical Quarterly* 59:1 (1975), 25-37.
65. "The Humble Petition of The Church Wardens Vestry and Inhabitants of the Parish of Saint Peters Purisburgh in the Province of South Carolina in America," n.d., PR/MC/104/10/42, RSA Archives.
66. Secker to the Gentlemen of the Committee at Geneva for the Relief of the distressed French Protestants, September 20, 1658, MS. 1122/II, f. 82, LPL. On Secker see especially Robert G. Ingram, *Religion, Reform, and Modernity in the Eighteenth Century: Thomas Secker and the Church of England* (Woodbridge: Boydell and Brewer, 2007); on his efforts to help foreign Protestant churches see 260–82.
67. Court de Gebelin to Secker, February 18, 1761, MS. 1122/III, ff. 9–10, LPL; Majendie to Secker, April 24, 1761, MS. 1122/III, f. 21. Du Plan's letter, which requested an increase in the amount of the Royal Bounty, is in MS. 1122/II, ff. 191–94.
68. "Message from the Protestants in France by M. Gibert," April 1761, MS. 1122/III, f. 170, LPL; Waddington, "Projet d'émigration," 371–72.
69. Secker to John James Majendie, n.d., MS. 1122/III, f. 193, LPL; Secker to George Grenville, April 21, 1763, MS. 1122/III, f. 194.
70. "Directions abt the Fr. Protestants with M. Gibert," April 29, 1763, MS. 1122/III, f. 198, LPL.
71. Waddington, "Projet d'émigration," 378.
72. Chevalier d'Eon to Minister, August 30, 1763 and September 6, 1763, Correspondance Politique, Angleterre, v. 451, ff. 162–63, 196, MAE.
73. *Journal of the Commissioners for Trade and Plantations* (London: His Majesty's Stationery Office, 1920), 11:284; "Representation to His Majesty upon the most reasonable and frugal method for peopling and settling the New Govts in America," CO 5/563, p. 122, TNA.
74. [Archibald Menzies], *Proposal for Peopling his Majesty's Southern Colonies on the Continent of America* ([Edinburgh?, 1763]), 1–2.
75. James Grant to John Pownall, July 30, 1763, CO 5/540, p. 2, TNA. On the New Smyrna project see Bernard Bailyn, *Voyagers to the West: A Passage in the Peopling of America on the Eve of the American Revolution* (New York: Knopf, 1986), 451–61.
76. Henry Laurens to John Augustus Schubart, December 31, 1763, in George C. Rogers Jr. and David R. Chestnutt, eds., *The Papers of Henry Laurens* (Columbia: University of South Carolina Press, 1974), 118.

77. Boutiton to the Board of Trade, October 21, 1763, CO 5/540, pp. 19-21, TNA. Boutiton's arrival is noted in d'Eon to Minister, September 6, 1763, Correspondance Politique, Angleterre, v. 451, f. 196, MAE.

78. On the switch from Florida to South Carolina see John Pownall to Charles Jenkinson, October 21, 1763, CO 5/563, no. 31, TNA. For some of the attempts to settle this area see Meriwether, *The Expansion of South Carolina*; A. S. Salley, "The Settlement of New Bordeaux," *Transactions of the Huguenot Society of South Carolina* 42 (1937), 38.

79. Jacques Robin to Mr Guigenon, May 21, 1763, Add. Mss. 19070, f. 198, BL. The collected papers regarding the plan are on ff. 196-200.

80. *Journals of the Board of Trade and Plantations* (London: His Majesty's Stationery Office, 1936), 12:202-204.

81. Antoine Court to Jacques Serces, September 1, 1750, *Serces Correspondance*, 2:51; Benoît, *Les Frères Gibert*, 13-15.

82. New Bordeaux has attracted relatively little attention from historians; see Salley, "The Settlement of New Bordeaux"; Nora Marshall Davis, "The French Settlement at New Bordeaux," *Transactions of the Huguenot Society of South Carolina* 56 (1951), 28-57; Bertrand Van Ruymbeke, *From New Babylon to Eden: The Huguenots and their Migration to Colonial South Carolina* (Columbia: University of South Carolina Press, 2006), 223. On Campbell's Town see J. Barton Starr, "French Huguenots in British West Florida," *Florida Historical Quarterly* 54:4 (1976), 532-47.

83. "Translation from the French of the Journal of Pierre Moragne, of New Bordeaux," in W. C. Moragne, *An Address Delivered at New Bordeaux, Abbeville District, S.C., November 15, 1854 on the 90th Anniversary of the Arrival of the French Protestants at that Place* (Charleston: James Phynney, 1857), 44-46.

84. Waddington, "Projet d'emigration," 373-77; d'Eon to Minister, September 6, 1763, Correspondance Politique, Angleterre, v. 451, f. 196, MAE.

85. Gibert to Archbishop Secker, November 29, 1763, in Waddington, "Projet d'emigration," 378.

86. Choiseul to M. de la Michodière, Intendant de Rouen, January 31, 1764, in Waddington, "Projet d'emigration," 381. The original is in the Archives Départementales de Seine-Maritime, Rouen.

87. "Journal of Pierre Moragne," 45.

88. "Journal of Pierre Moragne," 45. On Manigault see, Maurice A. Crouse, "Gabriel Manigault: Charleston Merchant," *South Carolina Historical Magazine* 68:4 (1967), 220-31.

89. "Journal of His Majesty's Council, 1763-1767," pp. 120, 152-53, South Carolina Department of Archives and History, Columbia.

90. "Journey of His Majesty's Council, 1763-1767," pp. 180-82, SCDAH; Salley, "The Settlement at New Bordeaux," 42-43.

91. On Pierre see Anne C. Gibert, *Pierre Gibert, the Devoted Huguenot: A History of the French Settlement of New Bordeaux, South Carolina* (Charleston: self-published, 1976).

92. The details of laying out the land are in the "Journal of His Majesty's Council, 1763-1767," pp. 194-95, SCDAH, reprinted in Janie Revill, ed., *A Compilation of the Original Lists of Protestant Immigrants to South Carolina* (Columbia, SC: The State Company, 1939), 16-18.

93. Laurens to Oswald, October 10, 1764, *Laurens Papers*, 4:464.

94. "Translation of a Copy of a Letter written by Pierre Moragne to his Father in France, Jan. 17, 1771," in Moragne, *An Address Delivered at New Bordeaux*, 46-47.

95. "The Humble Petition of John Lewis Gibert from Silk Hope in South Carolina," PR/GE/110/16/153, RSA Archives.

96. *Boston News-Letter*, issue 3280, August 14, 1766, p. 2.

97. *Boston News-Letter*, issue 3324, June 18, 1767, p. 1; *South Carolina Gazette*, May 11, 1767; Hirsch, *Huguenots of Colonial South Carolina*, 202.

98. *Virginia Gazette*, July 2, 1767, p. 2.

99. George Johnstone to the Board of Trade, February 19, 1765, CO 5/574, p. 233, TNA.

100. *An Impartial Enquiry into the Right of the French King to the Territory West of the Great River Mississippi, in North America, not ceded by the Preliminaries* (London: W. Nicoll, [1763]), 8, 40-41, 44-45. On the larger context of British West Florida see David Narrett, *Adventurism and Empire: The Struggle for Mastery in the Louisiana-Florida Borderlands, 1762-1803*

(Chapel Hill: University of North Carolina Press, 2015), 11–68 (the Coxes' claim is discussed on 30–31); Clinton N. Howard, *The British Development of West Florida, 1763–1769* (Berkeley: University of California Press, 1947).

101. "Memorial of Several French Protestants, praying to be settled in the Province of West Florida," received June 26, 1765, CO 5/574, pp. 217–18, TNA; *Journal of the Commissioners for Trade and Plantations from January 1764 to December 1767* (London: His Majesty's Stationery Office, 1936), 187–89. The *London Gazette* advertisement appeared in the Nov. 21, 1763 issue; see Starr, "French Huguenots in British West Florida," 534.

102. Johnstone to Pownall, April 2, 1766, CO 5/574, p. 968, TNA.

103. "Report of a Committee of the Council Appointed to draw up Certain Rules and Regulations to be entred into and Signed by the French Emigrants Established in the Township of Campbelltown," CO 5/575, pp. 261–62, TNA.

104. Browne to Pownall, February 27, 1768, CO 5/575, p. 335, TNA; "Case of Rev. Peter Levrier," October 24, 1766, in *Mississippi Provincial Archives, 1763–1766: English Dominion*, ed. Dunbar Rowland (Nashville: Brandon Printing Co., 1911), 533–34; Hirsch, *Huguenots of Colonial South Carolina*, 85; Ramsey, *History of South Carolina*, 2:39. By 1783 Levrier was advertising for students in a French school in Charleston; see *South Carolina Gazette and General Advertiser*, October 21–25, 1783.

105. Mestral to "Monseigneur," October 9, 1772, COL E 154 (Personnel Colonial Ancien), ANOM.

106. "Journal of His Majesty's Council, 1768–1772," pp. 101–102, SCDAH, reprinted in Revill, *A Compilation of the Original Lists of Protestant Immigrants*, 111–14; on Nova Scotia see Saint-Pierre to the Bishop of London, July 1, 1767, Fulham Papers 1, f. 88, LPL; "Representation to His Majesty recommending Monsieur St Pierre for a Grant of 5000 Acres of Land," December 18, 1771, CO 5/404, pp. 457–60, TNA.

107. Davis, "The French Settlement at New Bordeaux," 29–33; Revill, *A Compilation of the Original Lists of Protestant Immigrants*, 30; *South Carolina Gazette*, numb. 1800, April 5, 1770, p. 3.

108. On the German see Bull to Hillsborough, December 6, 1769, CO 5/393, f. 9, TNA; Bull to Hillsborough, June 6, 1770, CO 5/393, f. 130–31; Dossie, *Memoirs of Agriculture*, 3:460.

109. Bull to Hillsborough, March 6, 1770, CO 5/393, f. 45, TNA; Louis De Vorsey, ed., *De Brahm's Report of the General Survey in the Southern District of North America* (Columbia: University of South Carolina Press, 1971), 70.

110. Saint-Pierre, *The Art of Planting and Cultivating the Vine*, xvii–xviii, xxvii; Saint-Pierre, "Plan for the Culture of the Vine &c at New Bourdeaux," f. 6v, Library of Congress [photocopy at the SCDAH, Columbia].

111. Saint-Pierre, *The Art of Planting and Cultivating the Vine*, xvi–xviii.

112. Dossie, *Memoirs of Agriculture*, 3:460. The theory of French interference, which must be taken with a grain of salt, originated in *Memorial on Practicability of growing Vineyards in South Carolina* (Charleston: W. P. Young, 1798); see Hirsch, *Huguenots of Colonial South Carolina*, 208–10.

113. See for instance Henry Laurens to John Lewis Gervais, December 28, 1771, *Laurens Papers*, 8: 139–40.

114. Saint-Pierre wrote his will before heading out on the expedition and then disappeared from the record, though there is no definitive account of his death; see Davis, "The Huguenots of New Bordeaux," 51. The story of Gibert's poisoning came from a family story shared by his granddaughter; see Benoît, *Les Frères Gibert*, 289.

115. Henry Laurens to James Laurens, April 15, 1774, *Laurens Papers*, 9:409.

Epilogue

1. On the dispersion of the Orangeois see Françoise Moreil, "Une arrivée retardée: les Orangeois à Berlin en 1704," in *Hugenotten und deutsche Territorialstaaten: Immigrationspolitik und Integrationsprozesse*, ed. Guido Braun and Susanne Lachenicht (Munich: De Gruyter, 2007), 85–106; Letters in relation to ye Refugies of Orange, Add. Mss. 31133, BL.

2. Jean Henry de Bérenger to the Baron de Marconnay, May 27, 1785, F Br 5, de Bérenger Papers, Huguenot Library, University College London. On Beaufain's silk experimentation see Hector Berenger de Beaufain and William Bull to William Shipley, September 27, 1755, PR/GE/110/5/25, Royal Society of Arts Archives, London.

3. "Memoire Pour servir d'information dans les affaires et d'intérêts à regler dans l'hoirie de feu Hector de Berenger Baron de Beaufain"; Pierre Simond to Jean Henry de Bérenger, June 19, 1767; Simond to Bérenger, May 20, 1768; all in de Bérenger Family Papers, F Br 4.

4. Earl of Dartmouth to William Bull, May 4, 1774; Baron Alvensleben to Dartmouth, March 30, 1774, CO 5/390, pp. 43–48, TNA; Bull to Dartmouth, August 1, 1774, CO 5/390, p. 93; "Copy of a Letter from the Earl of Dartmouth to Gouvern. Bull, dated Whitehall 4th May 1774," de Bérenger Family Papers, F Br 4.

5. Bull to Bérenger, March 18, 1778, de Bérenger Family Papers, F Br 4. Interestingly, the Loyalist diaspora resembled that of the Huguenots in many respects, not least in their global ambitions; see Maya Jasanoff, *Liberty's Exiles: American Loyalists in the Revolutionary World* (New York: Knopf, 2011).

6. Bérenger to Lord North, July 1783; and Bérenger to Baron de Knebel, December 30, 1780, both in de Bérenger Family Papers, F Br 5.

7. Jean Henry de Bérenger to John Rutledge, April 19, 1785, de Bérenger Family Papers, F Br 5.

8. Henry Laurens to Jean Henry de Bérenger, June 3, 1783, de Bérenger Family Papers, F Br 5.

9. Bérenger to Franklin, March 23, 1784; Bérenger to Louis XVI, April 3, 1786, both in de Bérenger Family Papers, F Br 5.

10. Bérenger to Washington, 1788, de Bérenger Family Papers, F Br 5.

11. *Translation of a Letter, Sent on the 13th of February, 1792, to the Rt. Hon. William Pitt. With An Additional Supplement, by John Henry de Berenger, de Beaufain, Formerly Aid-de-Camp in the King of Prussia's Service, and at present Privy Councellor to His Most Serene Highness the Reigning Duke of Saxe, Coburg, and Saarfeld* (London, 1792), in de Bérenger Family Papers, F Br 5.

12. For a sense of the diplomatic system created by the Revolution see Eliga H. Gould, *Among the Powers of the Earth: The American Revolution and the Making of a New World Empire* (Cambridge, MA: Harvard University Press, 2012).

13. Walter Stahr, *John Jay: Founding Father* (New York: Diversion Books, 2005); Daniel J. McDonough, *Christopher Gadsden and Henry Laurens: The Parallel Lives of Two American Patriots* (Cranbury, NJ: Susquehanna University Press, 2000). The other famous Huguenot descendant in the Revolution was Paul Revere; on his family history see Donald Douglas, *The Huguenot* (New York: E. P. Dutton, 1954). On Huguenots in the Revolution more generally see Charles Weiss, *Histoire des réfugiés huguenots* (Paris: Ampelos Editions, 2007 [1853]), 1:327–51.

14. Abram English Brown, *Faneuil Hall and Faneuil Hall Market: or, Peter Faneuil and his Gift* (Boston: Lee and Shepard, 1900), 118–21; Jonathan Beagle, "Remembering Peter Faneuil: Yankees, Huguenots, and Ethnicity in Boston, 1743–1900," *New England Quarterly* 75:4 (2002), 388–414.

15. On Simond's losses, see Jacob M. Price, *France and the Chesapeake: A History of the French Tobacco Monopoly, 1674–1791, and of its Relationship to the British and American Tobacco Trades* (Ann Arbor: University of Michigan Press, 1973), 1:541, quoting Mabel L. Webber, ed., "Josiah Smith's Diary, 1780–1781," *South Carolina Historical and Genealogical Magazine* 34 (1933), 194–95.

16. On the Edict of Toleration and the revolutionary edicts see especially Patrick Cabanel, *Histoire des protestants en France, XVIe–XXIe siècle* (Paris, 2012), 900–24 (quotation from 919); Didier Boisson, "The Revocation of the Edict of Nantes and the *Désert*," in *A Companion to the Huguenots*, ed. Raymond A. Mentzer and Bertrand Van Ruymbeke (Leiden: Brill, 2016), 239–45; Hubert Bost, *Ces messieurs de la R.P.R.: Histoires et écritures de huguenots, XVIIe–XVIIIe siècles* (Paris: Honoré Champion, 2001), 365–76.

17. No one has done a thorough accounting of how many people took up the offer to return to France, though there were a few high profile people who did; see Eckert Birnstiel, "Le retour des huguenots du Refuge en France, de la Révocation à la Révolution," *BSHPF* 135:4 (1989), 763–90; Birnstiel, "La France en quête de ses enfants perdus: Mythe et réalité du retour au 'pays des ancêtres' des huguenots du Refuge de la Réforme à la Révolution," *Diasporas: Histoire et Sociétés*

8 (2006), 22–44. See also Bryan A. Banks, "The Huguenot Diaspora and the Politics of Religion in Revolutionary France," in *The French Revolution and Religion in Global Perspective: Freedom and Faith*, ed. Banks and Erica Johnson (Basingstoke: Palgrave, 2017), 3–24.

18. At the same time, some monarchists blamed Protestants for the Revolution; see Jacques Poujol, "Le changement d'image des protestants pendant la Revolution," *BSHPF* 135:4 (1989), 501–44.

19. Jules Michelet, *Louis XIV et la Révocation de l'Édit de Nantes* (Paris, 1985), 15.

20. Samuel Smiles, *The Huguenots, their Settlements, Churches, and Industries in England and Ireland* (London: John Murray, 1867), quotation on 448. See also Andrew Spicer, "1885: French Protestantism and Huguenot Identity in Victorian Britain," in *L'Identité huguenote: Faire mémoire et écrire l'histoire (XVIe–XXIe siècle)*, ed. Philip Benedict, Hugues Daussy, and Pierre-Olivier Léchot (Geneva: Droz, 2014), 391–422.

21. William Jay, *The Life of John Jay: With Selections from his Correspondence and Miscellaneous Papers* (New York: J. and J. Harper, 1833), 1:8.

22. Chester Raymond Young, ed., *Westward into Kentucky: The Narrative of Daniel Trabue* (Lexington: University of Kentucky Press, 1981), 37. For an analysis see Marco Sioli, "Huguenot Traditions in the Mountains of Kentucky: Daniel Trabue's Memories," *Journal of American History* 84 (1998), 1313–33.

23. R. H. Fife, ed., "The Vestry Book of King William Parish, Va., 1707–1750," *Virginia Magazine of History and Biography* 11:3 (1904), 292.

24. Quoted in Joyce D. Goodfriend, "The Last of the Huguenots: John Pintard and the Memory of the Diaspora in the Early American Republic," *Journal of Presbyterian History* 78:3 (2000), 187.

25. James Petigru Carson, ed., *Life, Letters, and Speeches of James Louis Petigru, the Union Man of South Carolina* (Washington, DC: W. H. Lowdermilk & Co., 1920), 35. These descendants then founded a number of influential Huguenot societies around the continent which shaped historical interpretations of the refugees into the twentieth century; see Bertrand Van Ruymbeke, "*Le Refuge*: History and Memory from the 1770s to the Present," in *A Companion to the Huguenots*, ed. Mentzer and Van Ruymbeke, 422–42.

26. Abiel Holmes, "Memoir of the French Protestants, who Settled at Oxford, Massachusetts, A.D. 1686; with a Sketch of the Entire History of the Protestants of France," *Collections of the Massachusetts Historical Society* 3d. ser., 2 (1830), 34.

27. Mary de Witt Freeland, ed., *The Records of Oxford, Mass., Including Chapters of Nipmuck, Huguenot and English History from the Earliest Date, 1630* (Albany: J. Munsell Sons, 1894), 200, 207.

28. On the Society's history see Jean-François Zorn, *Le siècle d'une mission protestante: la Mission de Paris, 1822–1914* (Paris: Karthala, 1993); Zorn, "When French Protestants Replaced British Missionaries in the Pacific and Indian Oceans; Or, How to Avoid the Colonial Trap," in *In God's Empire: French Missionaries and the Modern World*, ed. Owen White and J. P. Daughton (New York: Oxford University Press, 2012); and Mickaël Augeron, "L'Afrique, terre de mission au XIXe siècle," in *Les Huguenots et l'Atlantique: Fidélités, Racines, et mémoires*, ed. Mickaël Augeron, Didier Poton, and Bertrand Van Ruymbeke (Paris: Les Indes Savantes, 2012), 279–83.

29. "Rapports à la Société protestante des Missions par les missionaires chargé de prêcher l'Évangile en Afrique," reprinted in Weiss, *Histoire des réfugiés huguenots*, 2:335.

30. "Gedenkteeken Ter Eere der Fransche Vlugtelingen," *Het Nederduitsch Zuid-Afrikaansch Tijdschrift*, Jan–Apr 1824, pp. 69–71, quoted in Pieter Coertzen, "The Huguenots of South Africa in History and Memory," in *L'Identité huguenote*, ed. Benedict, Daussy, and Léchot, 430.

31. "Rapports à la Société protestante," in Weiss, *Histoire des réfugiés huguenots*, 335, 337.

32. On the links between Huguenots and Afrikaners, a controversial topic, see Philippe Denis, "The Cape Huguenots and their Legacy in Apartheid South Africa," in *Memory and Identity: The Huguenots in France and the Atlantic Diaspora*, ed. Bertrand Van Ruymbeke and Randy J. Sparks (Columbia: University of South Carolina Press, 2003), 285–311; Pieter Coertzen, "The Huguenots of South Africa in Documents and Commemoration," *Nederduitse Gereformeerde Teologiese Tydscrif* 52:3 (2011), 301–24. On the Great Trek see Hermann Giliomee, *The Afrikaners: Biography of a People* (Charlottesville: University of Virginia Press, 2003), 161–93.

INDEX

For the benefit of digital users, indexed terms that span two pages (e.g., 52–53) may, on occasion, appear on only one of those pages.